# Women Directors
## The Emergence of a New Cinema

**Barbara Koenig Quart**

PRAEGER

New York
Westport, Connecticut
London

## Copyright Acknowledgments

The author thanks the following magazines and book editors for permission to reprint parts of this book published in earlier, sometimes very different form, elsewhere.

The discussion of Márta Mészáros' *Diary for My Children*, *Film Quarterly* (Spring 1985); material on *Vagabond*, "A Conversation with Varda," *Film Quarterly* (Winter 1986); part of the *Vagabond* discussion, "Street Kid in the Wine Country," *Ms*, (July 1986).

The discussion of Margarethe von Trotta's *Sheer Madness*, *Cineaste* (Fall 1984); *Entre Nous* and *A Question of Silence*, *Cineaste* (Summer 1984).

A small part of the Mészáros discussion in the Márta Mészáros entry, *The Political Companion to Film*, edited by Gary Crowdus, from Pantheon.

The discussion of *Girlfriends*, "Friendship in Some Recent American Films," *Film Criticism* (Winter 1982).

## Library of Congress Cataloging-in-Publication Data

Quart, Barbara.
    Women directors.

    Bibliography: p.
    Includes index.
    1. Women motion picture producers and directors—
History.   2. Feminism and motion pictures.   I. Title.
PN1995.9.W6Q37   1988    791.43'0233'088042      88–1141
ISBN 0–275–92962–0 (alk. paper)

Library of Congress Catalog Card Number: 88-1141

ISBN: 0–275–92962–0

First published in 1988

Praeger Publishers, One Madison Avenue, New York, NY 10010
A division of Greenwood Press, Inc.

Printed in the United States of America

∞

The paper used in this book complies with the
Permanent Paper Standard issued by the National
Information Standards Organization (Z39.48–1984).

10  9  8  7  6  5  4  3  2  1

*For Lenny and Alissa*

# Contents

Illustrations                                                    ix

Preface                                                          xiii

1.    General Introduction                                        1

2.    Antecedents                                                 17

          *Alice Guy-Blache, Germaine Dulac, Lois Weber,*
          *Dorothy Arzner, Ida Lupino, Lina Wertmuller*

3.    American Women Directors                                   37

          *Elaine May, Joan Micklin Silver, Claudia Weill,*
          *Susan Seidelman, Joyce Chopra, Martha Coolidge,*
          *Donna Deitch, Barbra Streisand, Goldie Hawn, and*
          *others*

4.    Western European Women Directors                           93

          *Margarethe von Trotta, Doris Dörrie, Agnes Varda,*
          *Diane Kurys, Gunnel Lindblom, Marleen Gorris,*
          *and others*

5.    Eastern European Women Directors                    191

        *Márta Mészáros, Larisa Shepitko, Věra Chytilová,*
        *Agnieszka Holland*

6.    Notes on Third World Women Directors                241

        *Euzhan Palcy, Lu Xiaoya, Zhang Nuanxin, Ann*
        *Hui, Sachiko Hidari, Aparna Sen, Prema Karanth,*
        *Maria Luisa Bemberg, Susana Amaral, and others*

Selected Bibliography                                    259

Index                                                    263

# Illustrations

1. Elaine May in wedding dress, acting in and directing, *A New Leaf*. Courtesy of Paramount and the Museum of Modern Art/Film Stills Archive.　xv

2. Claudia Weill's *Girlfriends* (Susan photographing Ann). Courtesy of Warner Bros.　xvi

3. Germaine Dulac's *The Smiling Mme. Beudet*. Courtesy of the Museum of Modern Art/Film Stills Archive.　162

4. *Christopher Strong*. Courtesy of the Museum of Modern Art/Film Stills Archive.　163

5. Dorothy Arzner, with leading lady Joan Crawford, on the set of *The Bride Wore Red*. (1937) Courtesy of the Museum of Modern Art/Film Stills Archive.　164

6. Ida Lupino with Sally Forrest, *Never Fear*. Courtesy of the Museum of Modern Art/Film Stills Archive.　165

7. Elaine May as the heroine of *A New Leaf*. Courtesy of Paramount and the Museum of Modern Art/Film Stills Archive.　166

8.    Elaine May directing *A New Leaf.* Courtesy of
      Paramount and the Museum of Modern Art/Film
      Stills Archive.                                              167

9.    Joan Micklin Silver's *Between the Lines.* Courtesy of
      Midwest Film Productions, Inc.                               168

10.   Claudia Weill's *Girlfriends.* Courtesy of Warner
      Bros.                                                        169

11.   Susan Seidelman's *Smithereens.* Courtesy of New
      Line Films and Susan Seidelman.                             170

12.   Joyce Chopra's *Smooth Talk.* Courtesy of Spectra
      Films Inc. and the Museum of Modern Art/Film
      Stills Archive.                                              171

13.   Barbra Streisand on both sides of the camera, *Yentl.*
      Courtesy of MGM, UA Entertainment Co., and the
      Museum of Modern Art/Film Stills Archive.                    172

14.   Margarethe von Trotta's *The Second Awakening of
      Christa Klages.* Courtesy of New Line Films and the
      Museum of Modern Art/Film Stills Archive.                    173

15.   Von Trotta's *Marianne and Juliane.* Courtesy of New
      Yorker Films.                                                174

16.   Von Trotta and her two actresses: *Marianne and
      Juliane.* Courtesy of New Yorker Films and the
      Museum of Modern Art/Film Stills Archive.                    175

17.   Doris Dörrie's *In the Belly of the Whale.* Courtesy of
      the Film Society of Lincoln Center.                          176

18.   Agnes Varda's *Cleo from 5 to 7.* Courtesy of Zenith
      Films.                                                       177

19.   Agnes Varda with the leading actress of *Vagabond.*
      Courtesy of the International Film Exchange.                 178

20.   Diane Kurys' *Peppermint Soda.* Courtesy of New
      Yorker Films and the Museum of Modern Art/Film
      Stills Archive.                                              179

21.   Gunnel Lindblom's *Summer Paradise*. Courtesy of
      Almi Pictures, Inc.                                      180

22.   Marleen Gorris' *A Question of Silence*. Courtesy of
      Quartet and Castle Hill Films.                           181

23.   Márta Mészáros' *Adoption*. Courtesy of Kino
      International.                                            182

24.   Márta Mészáros' *Nine Months*. Courtesy of New
      Yorker Films.                                            183

25.   Márta Mészáros' *The Two of Them*. Courtesy of
      New Yorker Films.                                        184

26.   Larisa Shepitko's *Wings*. Courtesy of the Film
      Center, Art Institute of Chicago.                        185

27.   Shepitko on location. Courtesy of the Film Center,
      Art Institute of Chicago.                                186

28.   Věra Chytilová's *Daisies*. Courtesy of Films, Inc.
      and the Museum of Modern Art/Film Stills Archive.        187

29.   Agneiszka Holland's *Angry Harvest*. Courtesy of the
      Film Society of Lincoln Center and the Museum of
      Modern Art.                                              188

30.   Euzhan Palcy's *Sugarcane Alley*. Courtesy of New
      Yorker Films and Orion Classics.                         189

31.   Lu Xiaoya's *The Girl in Red*. Courtesy of the Asia
      Society.                                                 190

# Preface

I *do* think it's a feminist film because I give space to things which were never, almost never, shown in that way, like the daily gestures of a woman. They are the lowest in the hierarchy of film images. . . . But more than the content, it's because of the style. If you choose to show a woman's gestures so precisely, it's because you love them. In some way you recognize those gestures that have always been denied and ignored.
—Chantal Akerman, interviewed about *Jeanne Dielman*.

I vividly remember with what eagerness I went to each new film by Agnes Varda or Mai Zetterling in the 1960s. It was exactly the same emotion I brought to Doris Lessing's novels, after the initial shock of discovering them. I never thought of myself as a feminist then, but when I remember that hunger for a woman's vision in novels or films, in those years before feminism, I know now that I knew even then that a woman's voice has different things to express, in a different way, even if the differences cannot always be defined. That voice continues to have special things to say to me.

It is another world since then, feminism having utterly changed how we think about ourselves and also about art. Events have moved so quickly that Claudia Weill and Joan Micklin Silver, talking recently on different platforms about their struggles to produce their famous respective first films, spoke as though they were the very early pioneers of some unbelievably far away primitive time, which it turns out was only a decade ago. But it is true that enormities have occurred for women filmmakers in this one decade, changes that they indeed fought hard for and have earned many times over. One of the most exciting parts of writing this book was speaking with those remarkable women, the directors themselves—a striking lot of strong, energetic, remarkably open, earthy, and eloquent women. They are shrewd wheelers and dealers too, even seductresses, who perform the near miracle, often essentially on their own, of pushing these massive enterprises through to completion.

For encouraging me to see my own enterprise through to completion, I would like to express my gratitude for a PSC–CUNY Research Foundation grant and an NEH Summer Stipend. Warm thanks to Joan Hartman for various kinds of support, and to the College of Staten Island for the research awards that helped me get underway. Very special gratitude to Ernest Callenbach for his encouragement of this book, his astute suggestions, his unfailing kindness. Many thanks to Leon Ablon for generous and patient giving of his time and expertise when it was sorely needed. My appreciation to Amos Vogel, and Richard Barsam, Philip Green, Howard Negrin, and Claire Sprague. Many thanks to Norman Wang of Renee Furst for his assistance, to Richard Koszarski at the Museum of the Moving Image, and to Richard Pena for his help. Thanks for various kindnesses to Gary Crowdus and Dan Georgakis of *Cineaste*. Thanks to New Yorker films, to Somi Roy of the Asia Society, to Catharine Verret at the French Film Office, to Ingrid Scheib-Rothbart of Goethe House New York, to Joanna Ney of the Lincoln Center Film Society, to the Film Forum, to Virginia Hennessy of the BFI. Thanks to Charles Silver and others at the Museum of Modern Art, which was an invaluable and inexhaustible resource for this project. Many thanks to Dennis Doros at Kino Films. Thanks to my *Persistence of Vision* comrades for their understanding, to Carol Pipolo, Linda Sharp, Lauren Hymen, Udayan Gupta, Kavery Dutta, to others whom I have no space to mention, and to Alison Bricken and Noreen Norton at Praeger.

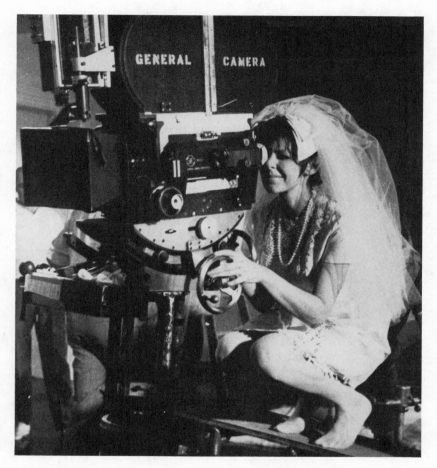

1. Elaine May in wedding dress, acting in and directing, *A New Leaf*. Courtesy of Paramount and the Museum of Modern Art/Film Stills Archive.

2. Claudia Weill's *Girlfriends* (Susan photographing Ann). Courtesy of Warner Bros.

# Women
# Directors

# 1
# General Introduction

Women directors, almost invisible just fifteen years ago, have from the late 1970s on, and especially in the 1980s, been entering feature filmmaking in unprecedented numbers. Their current levels of activity are without parallel in living memory or in the history of feature films. It is no longer unusual for five or six films by women directors to be playing simultaneously in Manhattan theatres, films as often from Europe or elsewhere as from America, since the phenomenon is international. With this veritable explosion of films, we are witnessing nothing less than a new world for women, all the more dramatic given the sad early history of women directors.

Since half the world's population is female, roughly half of all feature films should be made by women. The actual numbers, as is well known, are shockingly different. One statistic has it that between 1949 and 1979 (and this takes in the period when women started entering feature filmmaking again in numbers), one-fifth of 1 percent of all films released by American major studios were directed by women.[1] Before that, only one woman director, Dorothy Arzner, worked in America from silents and the beginnings of sound in the 1920s into the 1940s[2]—*one* woman directing in the heyday of Hollywood's productivity and power. Even in the more active years at the very beginnings of the film industry, the years that were most hospitable to women, the numbers were small.

Since women gave abundant evidence of high capabilities on every level right from the very start of moviemaking, with their work on silents, their subsequent fifty-year virtual exclusion from directorial ranks can only be accounted for in terms of what it meant, and means, for a woman to take control of and give direction to a massive enterprise. Dorothy Arzner recognized and was in fact attracted to that very power from the time she thought about going into the industry: "I remember making the observation, 'If one was going to be in the movie business, one should be a director.' He was the one who told everyone what to do. In fact he was the whole works."[3] So he was. That women directors were such a rarity historically has to be seen in terms of what so powerfully assertive an act of authority by a woman would have meant in those decades, given traditional definitions of the feminine firmly in place until very recently.

We are a half a century—and a strong feminist movement—beyond the newspaperman who entitled his 1930s *New York Sun* story about Dorothy Arzner: "She's the Boss of the Screen." And even so, it is only now, in the late 1980s, that women have begun to seriously enter upper management in corporate businesses. A very different world, and yet there is surely good reason why the change in business has occurred at the same time as the opening up of feature film directing to women. And even now, the businessmen who work with women corporate managers report complexly troubled responses, which they are advised to express openly in seminars organized for the purpose. The two major creative areas of film in which women have always had an assured and important place, acting and editing, involve women in functions entirely compatible with their traditional social roles. Woman as spectacle marks female acting performances from the very earliest cinema[4]; and editors (usually women) serve directors (almost always men), supportively helping them realize their visions. In the words of the editors themselves, they are "the silent partners of directors,"[5] "not the wife but the mother."[6] Nothing could be more different from being a director, "the one who [tells] everyone what to do."

That women directors have for so long been an anomaly has been, it seems to me, a great loss not only for those who could have been major directors, but for the culture. However much we associate Hollywood with glorious images of women, feminist film scholars have over the last decade and a half brilliantly shown us in Hollywood "classic" (that is, male-directed) cinema that those most famous of female shapes were largely shapes of male desire and fear, male fantasy. For all the input of the great stars or of women screenwriters, the voices of women went essentially unheard, an impoverishment surely.

But the new entry since the mid–1970s of women to feature filmmaking is altering that (and will do so more profoundly yet, if given the chance). In an American film industry where moneymaking is everything, the money figures themselves impressively reveal how firmly women have established themselves on different levels of U.S. filmmaking in the last few years. Susan Seidelman's *Desperately Seeking Susan* took in $27.5 million on a $5 million budget, as well as making many critics' ten best lists. Amy Heckerling's *National Lampoon's European Vacation* earned $50 million and was among 1985's top-ten-grossing pictures. And even the much commented upon cost of Elaine May's *Ishtar* at $50 million was all the more extraordinary because it was given not to Coppola or Cimino but to a woman, who could, in the new spirit of equity, also use it disappointingly.

In addition to entering the big money (though the two alas have no connection to one another—or an inverse one), some women directors are creating films as powerful as any being made now, often with a vision unlike any previously seen on screen. Because women directors' situations were severely restricted in the past, one has the sense of women's voices speaking with depth in cinema for the first time. The largest of the recent directors are engaged in the remarkable feat of building a women's cinema singlehandedly from next to nothing.

To examine that cinema is the aim of this book. The approach is through a study in-depth of what for the most part seems to me the best narrative cinema. Given space limitations, regrettable omissions were unavoidable. At the same time I have tried to communicate the remarkable range of the work being done at a time in history when women's lives have opened up to a level of possibility—and hence confusion—never before experienced. So the aim here is not a neat selection of films tightly structured to support a theory or generalization. I felt it important, at this early phase of inquiry, that the book's structure be open enough to accommodate this unruly a body of work in all its diversity of vision, personality, aesthetic forms, political values, cultural milieus, feelings about women—and to let it speak to us itself in all its rich abundance.

For this initial exploration, then, of more or less mainstream feature films (mainstream in the sense of Truffaut and Bergman as well as Paul Mazursky), I have chosen the women directors and films that are in my view, quite simply, the strongest artistically. These are usually directors with an oeuvre (though a few single-film directors are included for various reasons). And because of the quality of their work, these are directors who have generally achieved international recognition as major figures. The American chapter is the main exception, where it seemed most useful to explore the broad current range of women's feature filmmaking in this country. Even there, though, most of the directors—Elaine May, Susan Seidelman, Joyce Chopra—also come to mind when one thinks of American quality films of the last decade. On the other hand, certainly neither Goldie Hawn nor Amy Heckerling will make anyone's pantheon, although the careers of both women have a place in the American chapter, and in the larger discussion of women directors.

But if the directors and films are deliberately not pre-selected to serve some idea, I am myself struck—for all the diversity—by the patterns that do emerge, even across the widest cultural differences—and by how intensely this body of work contributes to a dialogue about gender issues. This should not surprise us if it is true of directors, as Alice Ostriker argues for writers, that they *"necessarily articulate gendered experience just as they necessarily articulate the spirit of a nationality, an age, a language."*[7] Motifs recur from one director to another, themes with variations, partial patterns, generalizations that apply to a certain number of films. There are, however, no generalizations that apply to all women directors or their films. Agreeing that "no theory, however suggestive, can be a substitute for the close and extensive knowledge of women's texts which constitutes our essential subject,"[8] my concern is to understand what women's feature filmmaking has been, and is. And the way I feel I can best do that is, again, to take a long close look at the films themselves. That then is the main business—however heterodox these days—of the study that follows.

What quickly becomes apparent is that recent films by women directors have been doing nothing less than opening up literally new worlds on the screen, women's worlds,[9] to which probably only a woman could provide entry in depth. A rich body of work for instance has developed around girls' coming of age: with Diane Kury's *Peppermint Soda* and the more rebellious fierce-willed intellectual girlhoods in Márta Mészáros' *Diary for My Children* and Margarethe von Trotta's *Marianne and Juliane*, or Joyce Chopra's rendering of American teen culture in *Smooth Talk*. In these films, though all have a claim on our attention as engaging, powerful works of film art, we see girlhoods of a kind not represented before on film, of a sort that such strong directors are themselves likely to have had, and also perhaps—thinking of Chopra—observed in their own daughters. Such films are made with the detail, subtlety of insight, metaphorical reverberations, that come from being inside an experience, to which gender is a central element. (This is certainly not to impute something permanently built into the genetic code, but a complex social shaping—that is nonetheless extremely powerful—as any clear-eyed feminist mother of a daughter of five, or eight, or fifteen years old, can testify. What our "natures" are we still know very little about, though one imagines that understanding will grow quickly, at a moment in history when gender definitions are undergoing extraordinarily rapid and radical change.)

Women filmmakers direct a different, new-to-the-screen kind of attention to older women too, not mythicizing them into sexless loving, or unloving, mothers; or vampirish threats insofar as they are seen as sexual women—but allowing them, as say Gunnel Lindblom does in *Summer Paradise*, to be defined principally as persons, friends, professional people, with passionately held points of view. There are women directors like Maria Luisa Bemberg, who place at the heart of a film an older woman's desire for a sweet young boy-man; women directors who give older worn-looking heroines an entire sympathy and a whole new lease on life, erotic as well as otherwise (as, say, in a recent odd German film *The Wolf Girl*, by Dagmar Beiersdorf, 1985). Karen Arthur, working with writer/actress Joan Hotchkis in *Legacy* (1979), skillfully shows an irritating, middle-aged upper-middle-class WASP American woman going to pieces inside the emptiness of her luxurious house and life. Made with a knowledgable mixture of sympathy, revulsion, and pity, it is sadly a kind of film unlikely to get any serious distribution here. But most taboo of all in American cinema, there are directors who deal with truly elderly, unglamorous, even severe women with the most loving empathy (from Shepitko's *Wings* to Sens' *36 Chowringhee Lane*, to Lindblom's *Summer Paradise*)—perhaps part of that continuity between daughters and mothers of which Nancy Chodorow writes in *The Reproduction of Mothering*.

In the films made by women a subtly different kind of vision is directed at everything from kitchen work, to nuances of sexual experience, to the dark areas of pornography and violence that have increasingly, perhaps inevitably, entered the work of women directors. The equation of woman with body, woman as sexual sign, the central way woman has been viewed in patriarchal films, is generally approached very differently, as one might expect, by women directors (although some on the most commercial side of Hollywood filmmaking, like Amy Heckerling, have in fact made the same kind of leering-at-female-bodies sequences as male commercial directors do, in the undisguised hope of making as much money for doing so). But a very different vision is apparent in a touching early sequence in Mészáros' *Adoption*, which simply contemplates the heroine's body in its existential being. That difference can also take the form of the intensely carpelled red flower, erotically reminiscent of the flowers of Georgia O'Keefe and Imogen Cunningham, emblematic of the plain heroine of Amaral's *Hour of the Star*, who delights in the smell of the brawny workingmen pressed around her in a crowded Brazilian subway car. A newly-lusty, open sexuality is powerfully evident in many recent films by women: from a momentary repeated vision in Varda's short, *Documenteur*, of a reclining unknown naked man, the camera moving toward his genitals, a reticent statement of the heroine's loneliness and longing; to electric moments of desire that flash between women; to inversions of the old pursuit of the virginal girl, as with Bemberg's Jesuit priest in *Camila*, or the titillation of brash older girl and shy boy in Thevent's *The Night Wears Garters*, one of a recent crop of French "art" films by women that border perilously on soft-core porn. That unabashed aggressiveness is taken to the point of a woman's not only no longer waiting for Mr. Right, but as in Susan Seidelman's least effective (and least successful) film, going out and making her own, reversal of the Pygmalion myth, reflecting women's empowerment and dissatisfaction.

Recent films by women directors rarely end with the heterosexual couple restored, a finale for the most part not desired by the heroine. Indeed, a number of important films resolve the heterosexual problematic not only not with a happy-couple ending, but with a woman, *viewed sympathetically*, killing a man, in fantasy or "reality": from von Trotta's *Sheer Madness* and Dörrie's *One Through the Heart*, to Gorris' *A Question of Silence* and Akerman's *Jeanne Dielman*. (Among numerous woman-directed silent film precedents for such violence, Germaine Dulac's *The Smiling Mme. Beudet* [1923] is the best known.[10])

The absence of the controlling male gaze, and the displacement of the man generally, from the center of many recent women directors' films has its converse in enormously compelling explorations of female bonding. A space has been cleared for women—that in classic Hollywood existed largely in the maternal melodrama[11]—for a long look at intense relations between women. In recent narrative films these are less between mothers and daughters than between sisters, friends, sometimes women lovers. In an exchange between several German feminist film critics some years ago, about the way two women characters in Márta Mészáros' *Adoption* look at each other, one critic considers that "perhaps a new kind of female eroticism and creativity can be found in films that show how women both look and return the look. This kind of relational attitude might be more subversive to the patriarchal code than any kind of terribly emancipated woman."[12] The look shared by women on the screen indeed figures centrally in a number of the most important films to be examined here. Unlike the old Hollywood gaze of male control that rendered the woman merely an object to be observed, admired, desired, women in these films give the look and return it in an equity and reciprocity where no one is reduced to object and spectacle. The act of looking is active and relational without having to do with power. This mutual gaze also unquestionably opens the way to eroticism between women—especially in the European films free if not to express it then at least to suggest it. The best women's films about female bonding have been extraordinary pioneer explorations of a profound part of many women's lives: from the idealizations of *Entre Nous* at the easy end; to the battling and embattled affection of elderly lifelong friends in *Summer Paradise*; to von Trotta's painfully intricate realities—one woman's adulation of another, or sense of the other's betrayal, or jealousy, or clinging merger, or the tortured dynamics of women's friendships in tension with the claims of the women's male partners. The list of works dealing with this material could be lengthened by many additions at this point, not the least of these on the Pop side, the deservedly long-lived lady-cop TV series, produced and written by Georgia Jeffries, "Cagney and Lacey."

That films, like other art forms, "necessarily articulate gendered experience" would seem illustrated yet again by the fact that the work of the two major European figures in this study, Margarethe von Trotta and Márta Mészáros, is haunted by what one has to call very concrete forms of women's concerns. Mészáros' obsessive subject is her struggling women characters' longing for children and for parents, their repeated involvement in her films with childbirth and issues of parenting. Von Trotta's obsession is with sisters and other similarly intense female bonds. Going the long cultural distance from the Western Europe of West Germany through the Eastern Europe of Hungary to the Republic of China, the charming prize-winning recent film *The Girl in Red* offers another instance on another level. Woman director Lu Xiaoya chooses as a metaphor for rebellion in that film a teenage girl's marking herself off from others by dressing differently, in a red tunic.

While a male director might also work with yearnings for parents, even yearnings for children, the centrality of the subject to Mészáros, the forms it takes in childbirths, adoptions, various kinds of very basic nurturing, interwoven with the other levels of subjectivity of the Mészáros heroine, mark it—profoundly recognizably—as a woman's vision. Again, it goes without saying that one does not mean something in the genes, fixed and immovable in the very "nature of women," whatever that might be; but rather "historically defined difference,"[13] part of a culturally shaped, rapidly changing experience. So too while a male director's boy hero might also use clothes to symbolize difference, the historic (and still present) weight that clothes and appearance generally carry for women, and again the particular nuance with which *The Girl in Red* works with a teenage girl's life, marks a difference.

Von Trotta's *Marianne and Juliane*, from its powerful opening frames of a woman pacing a darkened room, caught up in passionate reflection, intensely takes us into a woman's subjectivity that expresses itself strongly through writing, thinking, work. Von Trotta's Juliane is a heroine who never stops working. She shares this not only with the heroines of other important German women directors—Helke Sander's heroine in *Redupers*, Helma Sanders-Brahms' in *Laputa*—but with those of many women's films generally, from the gusto of Dorothy Arzner's woman pilot in *Christopher Strong* in 1933, to Claudia Weill's photographer in *Girlfriends*, even to Susan Seidelman's hustling deal-making Wren in *Smithereens*. That work for their heroines should be granted this primacy by women directors is not surprising, given that this has to be a major way women filmmakers experience their own lives—as largely defined by work. Nor is it surprising, either, despite memorable working women such as Hawks' Hildy or Hepburn in *Adam's Rib*, that an intense exciting absorption of a whole being in work is not primarily how men directors have experienced women.

These repeated themes, images, orientations link one woman director's films to those of others, creating a loosely (but unmistakably) shared body of represented experience. Yet to attempt to define what makes women's films different from those of men is, everyone agrees, an undeniably perilous and easily challenged undertaking. Helene Cixous writes of women's writing, where this attempt has been made more frequently and over a longer period of time, that "it is impossible to *define* a feminine practice of writing, and this is an impossibility that will remain, for this practice will never be theorized, enclosed, encoded . . . which doesn't mean that it doesn't exist."[14] Elaine Showalter argues in response, in 1981, that the process of defining is already underway, having to do with "small but crucial deviations," that require us "to respond with equal delicacy and precision."[15] A writer about film suggests that "perhaps we should be content with stating that there is a different sensibility at work in women's art which is impossible to define"[16] and that we must live with "the paradox that there cannot be any certainty about what is feminine in art but that we have to go on looking out for it."[17]

While Teresa de Lauretis, too, emphasizes the daunting difficulty,[18] the shock of recognition she reports in watching *Jeanne Dielman* seems to me the most important factor in the whole vexed issue. Speaking of watching a housewife's routine activities, and the hesitations and small slips in the process, de Lauretis notes: "What the film constructs—formally and artfully, to be sure—is a picture of female experience, of duration, perception, events, relationships and silences, *which feels immediately and unquestionably true.*" (italics mine).[19] What is more, she recognizes in "those unusual film images, in those movements, those silences and those looks, the ways of an experience all but unrepresented, previously unseen in film."[20] Similar experiences mark the films of von Trotta, Mészáros, and other women directors, with the female spectator as crucial a factor there.

Of course not all woman-oriented films are feminist. *Peppermint Soda*, for instance, is entirely focused on girl and women characters without being identifiably feminist—unless looking closely with a camera at a girl, and giving intense attention to her feelings, the events of her life, her coming of age—simply regarding them as important enough to warrant that kind of attention—is regarded in itself as a feminist act. Chantal Akerman's stirring statement with regard to *Jeanne Dielman*, quoted at the start of this book, resounds in one's mind to support that view. Still, there are directors (the Kurys of *Peppermint Soda* and *Entre Nous* is one) who seem more accurately described as woman-identified than as feminist.

There are also directors who made one or more strongly feminist films, affected by the passion of the Women's Movement at a particularly intense time (those films often coming out in the late 1970s, like Varda's *One Sings, The Other Doesn't*) while their previous and subsequent work is not feminist in our present sense of the term. To add to the confusion, there are directors who say they are not feminist when one feels sure they are, like Márta Mészáros, or Claudia Weill with reference to *Girlfriends*.[21] Feminist films themselves run an enormously broad range from a young woman's wry struggle for an independent work life in *Girlfriends* to the radical separatism and anti-male violence of *A Question of Silence*. There are films such as Susan Seidelman's *Smithereens* that would not be called feminist in themselves but that involve a vision of a woman inconceivable before feminism, though the jargon term "post feminism" seems equally unsuitable, with its implication that feminism is finished and we are on to something else. And again, *Smithereens* is a film that it would be hard, really impossible, to imagine a man making.

On the other hand, several important women directors focus principally, even exclusively, on male protagonists—and some treat those women they do include largely with contempt or sexist stereotyping. These tend to be women over 50, shaped well before feminism, such as Lina Wertmuller, or the early Elaine May. But while these directors at first seem to deal with women with no more interiority and understanding than many male directors, directors like May and Shepitko will actually use minor female figures with a special kind of tellingness—in Shepitko's case chillingly so. Further, Elaine May's largely male *Mikey and Nicky* or even Wertmuller's *Seduction of Mimi* or *Swept Away* arguably offer certain illuminations into gender because the directors *are* non-males and are situated, perhaps more than most, simultaneously both inside and outside of their own femaleness.

Even if women often take the roles of victims in these directors' films— even if the mother's voice of fear in Joyce Chopra's *Smooth Talk* is a voice one would rather not hear—at a time when women's lives reflect a radical rethinking of gender roles, a turbulence and sense of possibility as in no other time in history, the full range of women's voices needs a hearing. The melodramas that used to be called "Women's films" in classic Hollywood, "weepies" made by male directors for women spectators, with their focus entirely on the emotions of the central woman character, and themes of romantic love, family, mother love, self-sacrifice, illness and loss, were much more uniform and identifiable than the films here called women's films. These constitute no one genre, and the "female subject" here is indeed "a site of differences" not to be "again collapsed into a fixed identity, a sameness of all women as Woman."[22]

Yet there is that intriguing coherence, links that extend to the broad history of women filmmakers, and the histories of individual directors. In those individual histories, struggles for recognition are counterpointed by personal struggles with traditional demands on women: guilt over neglecting family; letting career demands take second place to finding a husband or having a child; or taking time out periodically from one side of life for the other. Latin American women directors have recently come to our attention who made their first feature film at 42 (Bemberg, who later directed *Camila*) or 52 (Amaral, who directed *Hour of the Star*), after raising very large families. But American and European women directors' lives too are simply in general more complicated than those of their male counterparts—at least at this point in history. Imagine an equivalent of the Joyce Chopra/Claudia Weill *Joyce at 34* (about a pregnant Joyce Chopra's conflict between child and filmmaking) for Bergman or Truffaut, Coppola or Scorsese! The very idea is ludicrous.[23]

The varied cultural circumstances of training, film production, and distribution with which women directors have had to deal to gain entry to directing, and to keep making films, also require examination to the extent that space limits allow. The mid–1970s through the mid–1980s are of course the decade of entry for most directors dealt with here. Since what appears on the screen is strongly shaped by whether women directors are working in an American commercial or independent context or in a European art film context (and which one—German, French, Hungarian, Czech situations each permitting very different possibilities), the directors' relations to the particular film industry they work within is bound up with every other issue. European "art" films have a special place, indeed the central place, in this study. The extent to which they have been ignored by feminist film critics is indeed peculiar, "given that it is within this genre that nearly all the feature-length films directed by women are produced."[24] It is no accident that the breakthrough American feature films that first reflected the full impact of the women's movement, and created models for those that followed, were never made in Hollywood, never could be, and were never accepted there or distributed until they won accolades at European film festivals, valued in the context of European art films. *Girlfriends, Hester Street,* and *Smithereens*—all had to be discovered in Europe before distributors here would touch them.

European art films have their own problems, of course. Von Trotta for example has mentioned having been unable to get funding for *Marianne and Juliane* from a major TV source in Germany, money that German directors heavily count on—because of that film's disturbing contents, though that was not the reason officially given. And this is true in a country unique, at least until recently, for its support of difficult, controversial, distinctive filmmaking. Still, there can be no denying that the art film has served, and still serves, as conduit for the strongest unmediated statements, at the same time as its use of narrative makes possible an accessibility and power to engage audiences, that avant garde cinema cannot rival. The circumstances under which Susan Seidelman works, now that she has become a Hollywood director, are very different from those of the European art-film directors, and the greatest possible success is unlikely to allow Seidelman to extend by much the parameters of her style and content. On the contrary, her success is moving her with each film toward greater and greater homogenization and dilution. Could von Trotta, Mészáros, or Gorris work in the United States at all without being destroyed, even if they worked on the kind of very low-budget independent productions as do John Sayles and Jim Jarmusch, with their stubborn guardedness against cooption? And even along that route, stars are increasingly required, controversial material avoided, and small companies themselves are having trouble surviving. Yet that approach continues to offer the greatest possibility for serious work. Even a film like *Smooth Talk* had to be made outside the mainstream production routes, with an independent producer, a tiny budget, and a hard struggle. The Eastern European countries represent quite another situation, affording a director like Mészáros steady, reliable support to develop a large body of work over decades, as would have been impossible for her to have done elsewhere. But that too is of course at a cost—of certain bounds not trespassed, of quite austere budgets, and in unlucky historical periods and countries, like present-day Czechoslovakia or Poland, killing constraints.

The women's cinema under discussion here has been remarkably slow to gain the attention of feminist film scholars and critics who, partly because of a long-standing scorn for representational or realistic art, have instead privileged avant garde experimental self-reflexive (and documentary) counter-cinema, and filmmakers like Yvonne Rainer, Michelle Citron, and Lizzie Borden in the U.S., and Sally Potter and Laura Mulvey in England. (Also, films such as Helke Sander's *Redupers* or Chantal Akerman's *Jeanne Dielman* are other examples. They have received extensive attention in the field, but are not included here because they do not fall within the parameters of this study.) Judith Mayne describes this counter-cinema as the reverse side of that embrace of classic Hollywood in which feminist film criticism has been locked for so long[25]—one of the dualities into which the field has been frozen.

The austere antirealist bias of the British Film Institute, which has played a very fruitful leadership role for this generation of feminist film critics, may have influenced feminist film theory and criticism in this direction. That neither major British film tradition—of documentary or realism— "possesses the qualities of attention to interiority, subjective vision, etc. which produce the coincidence between the emerging women's cinema and the traditional (male) art cinema,"[26] within which English feminist film-makers might have been able to work, helps explain the severity of the British feminist reaction against realism and its denial of the range possible within what is called realism.

Semiotic analysis has also made its own contribution to an "antirealist polemic." Christine Gledhill has expressed the entirely understandable suspicions of many feminists concerning narrative feature film,[27] seen for so long as the instrument of patriarchal ideology. But Gledhill also looks to resolve this dilemma through the idea of women's difference: women are "constructed in a set of social relations and discourses which position them differently from men in the social formation"; they therefore "experience work, parenthood, and personal, heterosexual and family relations differently from men;" and the " 'differences' . . . potentially open up a challenge to patriarchal assumptions."[28] The austere nature of the counter-cinema, extremely difficult and off-putting even for highly sophisticated audiences, has also been increasingly recognized,[29] as well as the need for the feminist film community's awareness and support to make women directors less vulnerable.

Doubtless the slowness of the field to move on to the very important work now being done by women feature filmmakers is also partly because the imaginative methodologies evolved by feminist film theorists to further our understanding of male-directed Hollywood films have not been helpful or easily transferrable in dealing with women directors. It is as if there is no language to talk about the subject. The editors of *Re-Vision*, comparing the development of feminist literary criticism with that of feminist film criticism, point out that after feminist literary critics had explored "the limitations of male-authored representations of women," they could turn to the work of women writers, emphasizing "not women's similarity to men, but the distinctive features of female texts."[30] However, "in the relative absence of a realist tradition of women film artists working both within and against a dominant male tradition, it is not surprising that feminist film critics soon seized upon methodologies that could account for the absence of 'woman as woman.' " With realist work by women film artists no longer absent, it is surely time this shift to female texts take place in film studies as well.

The field of women and film has produced, since Mollie Haskell's enormously important pioneering *From Reverence to Rape*, an extraordinary body of scholarship: "The feminist critical text, the rereading against the grain of the 'master works,' " is indeed an "original 'cultural creation' of feminism" and even more, "a new aesthetic, a rewriting of culture."[31] For this, anyone writing in the same field, even from a somewhat different position, feels great gratitude. But however valuable the scholarship on the "master works," de Lauretis' pun on patriarchal film achievement, remarkably little serious sustained study has been directed by feminist film scholars to women's feature films. When not focused on the absence, distortion, suppression of women in male-directed classic Hollywood films, recent writing has been almost entirely focused on women's films of the "counter-cinema," avant garde films.

The area of feature films directed by women, in short, is a rich body of material begging for serious attention, analysis, and, often, celebration. The following study will try to present the larger shape of this multiple experience of women as directors, as well as examine the work and development of individual directors. It is concerned with representation, what women directors put on the screen, and to what extent these directors speak through a gendered address, as women, about women, to women. Narrative cinema, long viewed as suspect by many influential feminist theorists and filmmakers, is proving itself not only viable for women directors, but the most powerful of vehicles for the expression of a woman's and/or a feminist vision. Our best women directors are using it and using it brilliantly. A richly diverse women's cinema, including work of the highest quality, is already a reality, and can only get richer still.

From America, Western Europe, and Eastern Europe, to the cinemas of India and China, women are making movies in numbers not seen before, with themes and ways of looking that form links across cultures and continents. For all the necessary diversity, an unmistakably interwoven whole reveals itself, the long silenced voice of women. The voice suppressed on the voice-overs of film noir; the voice denied to the mother (even in Michelle

Citron's *Daughter Rite*); the voice denied too to the three women who only find expression in murder and laughter in Gorris' *A Question of Silence*: that suppressed voice is finally raised in this body of feature films by women. Women directors, virtually phased out of the early film industry with the advent of sound, never had the opportunity even historically to move from silence to speech. Such is the strangeness of their history that only now can their voices be heard, for the first time telling of realities until recently suppressed from the screen.

## NOTES

1. Even in this time of much greater visibility and activity, recent statistics hardly show the balance redressed. For example, of the 8000-odd directors who worked in film and TV in the first quarter of 1985, only 3.5 percent were women.

2. More precisely, Wanda Tuchock co-directed *Finishing School* in 1934, but the exception makes the rule even more dramatic.

3. Karyn Kay and Gerald Peary, "Dorothy Arzner," *Films by Women/Chicago '74*, 6.

4. See Judith Mayne, "Uncovering the Female Body," *Before Hollywood: Turn of the Century Film from American Archives*, edited by Jay Leyda and Charles Musser (New York: American Federation of the Arts, 1986), 64–67.

5. Anne Goursaud, editor of such films as *Crimes of the Heart, Just Between Friends*, and *One From the Heart*, at a panel, "The Cutting Edge: The Art of Film Editing," at the Women Make Movies, V, Festival, Washington, D.C., March 8, 1987. The panelists, among them Susan Morse, who edited many of Woody Allen's films, and Carol Littleton, who edited *The Big Chill, E.T.*, and *Places in the Heart*, also noted that male editors are often, on the contrary, competitive with the director, and take an adversarial stance. Several spoke of feeling uncredited, and one said that the director will tell you in private that you are a genius, but in public he is the genius.

6. Melody London, editor of Jim Jarmusch's *Down by Law* and *Stranger Than Paradise*, among other films, jokingly said this on the same panel.

7. Alicia Suskin Ostriker, *Stealing the Language* (Boston: Beacon Press, 1985), 9.

8. Elaine Showalter, in *Writing and Sexual Difference*, edited by Elizabeth Abel (Chicago: University of Chicago Press, 1982), 35.

9. While Ostriker, again exploring the same issues in literature, notes that "most critics and professors of literature deny that women's poetry, as distinct from poetry by individual women, exists," she argues that the "annexing of each new province" immediately reveals it to be "different from, and more complex than, what we thought while it was a blank spot, like Conrad's Congo, on the cultural map. . . . Who would have thought little boys were so sensitive before Rousseau and Dickens? Woman in poetry for millenniums has been a sort of blank, a screen upon which the male poet could project his fantasies." "American Poetry, Now Shaped by Women," *New York Times Book Review* (March 9, 1986), 28. Obviously, in film studies *our* screen is literal as well as metaphorical.

10. Martin Norden even speculates that the many American silent-film variations on this subject may themselves have "contributed to women's eventual near-exclu-

sion." After speaking of such films as Alice Guy-Blache's *The Dream Woman* (1914) in which a man dreams he is murdered by his yet unmet wife, and then meets the woman, he comments, "Though vamp stories proved popular at the box office, the male-dominated industry may have viewed... with growing concern... such women-directed films featuring the destruction of men [as] sending out the wrong signals to the rest of society." "Women in the Early Film Industry," *Wide Angle* 6, 3, 66.

11. See Linda Williams' " 'Something Else Besides a Mother': *Stella Dallas* and the Maternal Melodrama," *Cinema Journal* 24, no. 1(Fall 1984), 2–27.

12. "From Hitler to Hepburn," *New German Critique*, 24–25 (Fall/Winter 1981– 82), 184.

13. Gisela Ecker, ed. *Feminist Aesthetics* (Boston: Beacon Press, 1985) 16.

14. Helene Cixous, "The Laugh of the Medusa," in Abel, *Writing and Sexual Difference*, 14.

15. Showalter, in Abel, ibid.

16. Ecker, *Feminist Esthetics*, 19.

17. Ibid., 21.

18. "How difficult it is to 'prove' that a film addresses its spectator as female is brought home time and again," in "Aesthetic and Feminist Theory: Rethinking Women's Cinema," *New German Critique* 34 (Winter 1985), 161.

19. Ibid., 159.

20. Ibid., 160. De Lauretis chooses to discuss *Dielman* and *Born in Flames* probably because Akerman eschews traditional narrative, as did Lizzie Borden before *Working Girls* (which title incidentally is an hommage to Dorothy Arzner). Borden followed *Born in Flames*, a film quickly added to the feminist counter-cinema short list, with *Working Girls*, which attempts, even if awkwardly, a realistic narrative treatment of the lives of prostitutes. Ironically, in doing so Borden is guilty of just that unilluminating, tedious, slice-of-life approach that feminist theorists have often invoked to dismiss many of the kinds of films that follow here. Whether the effectiveness of the film's strong anti-male ideology, and its lesbian framing device, along with the prostitute subject matter, will be sufficient to overcome the stigma of realism for feminist scholars, or whether Borden's own defection is another sign of a general opening out, remains to be seen.

21. Possibly relevent is Martha Coolidge's remembrance of being asked, before the success of *Valley Girls*, if she was a feminist. "Well, of course I'm a feminist. But I knew that if I said yes, I'd lose the job. So I said no." Richard Corliss, "Calling Their Own Shots," *Time* (March 24, 1986), 82.

22. *Feminist Studies, Critical Studies*, edited by Teresa de Lauretis (Bloomington: Indiana University Press, 1986), 15.

23. Or for Hitchcock, as opposed to his wife Alma Reville, known as a top flight screenwriter in England, who was being groomed for a director's job herself (see Donald Spoto, *The Dark Side of Genius* [New York: Ballantine Books, 1983], 72, 103) at the time she began collaborating with Hitchcock in work and marriage. She soon stopped working altogether, and ended up the somehow haunting, old woman by his side.

24. Charlotte Brunsdon, ed., *Films for Women* (London: British Film Institute, 1986), 55. See Brunsdon and Merck essays also for instances of how art films are sometimes spoken of scornfully and for further discussion of the generic charac-

teristics of the art film. For the argument that art films derive from "a common political need to maintain a local film culture capable of disrupting Hollywood's potential domination," see Steve Neale, "Art Cinema as Institution," *Screen* 22 (1981), 11–39; cited by Merck, in Brunsdon, op. cit., 215; see also David Bordwell, "The Art Cinema as a Mode of Film Practice," *Film Criticism* 4 (Fall 1979); 56–64; and Tom Ryall, "Art House, Smart House," *The Movie* 90 (1981), 8.

25. Judith Mayne, summary of the state of feminist film criticism, 1986 MLA convention.

26. Brunsdon, *Films for Women*, 56.

27. In Christine Geldhill's summary: "the insights of semiotic analysis have led into an antirealist polemic, which insists that, since representation is tied to cultural codes, the goal of feminist practice should be the deconstruction of these codes in order to demonstrate that patriarchal ideology inhabits the very tools of meaning production." "Developments in Feminist Film Criticism, "in *Re-Visions*, edited by Doane, Mellencamp, and Williams (University Publications of America, American Film Institute Monograph Series), 23. For a full discussion of the "realist debate in the feminist film," see E. Ann Kaplan, *Women and Film* (New York and London: Methuen, 1983), 125–41. Kaplan ultimately takes the argument further: "We need now to think whether it would be possible to use a narrative form that is pleasurable and that does not produce the retrogressive effects of the commercial cinema," 198, a crucial question that I believe von Trotta, Mészáros, and others have already answered in the affirmative by their practice.

28. *Re-Visions*, 43.

29. The difficulty was graphically illustrated by the 1986 MLA's special screening of Yvonne Rainer's *The Man Who Envied Women*. Despite the very strong reputations of both director and film, the audience gradually vanished, like the line of schoolboys running through the Paris streets behind their teacher in *400 Blows*. Other theoretical feminist films, it has been noted, by "destroying the narrative and the possibility for viewer identification with the characters, destroy both the male viewer's pleasure and our pleasure"; and such films "focus more on denying men their cathexis with women as erotic objects than in connecting women with each other." Lucy Arbuthnot and Gail Seneca, "Pre-text and text in Gentlemen Prefer Blondes," *Film Reader* 5 (1982), 14.

30. *Re-Visions*, 6.

31. de Lauretis, *Feminist Studies*, 10. That body of intellectually provocative and important books constitutes my core bibliography: to mention only some, work by Mary Ann Doane, E. Ann Kaplan, Theresa de Lauretis, Patricia Mellencamp, Linda Williams—earlier most valuable, groundbreaking contributions to the examination of women directors and their films by Patricia Erens, Molly Haskell, Karyn Kay and Gerald Peary, Richard Koszarski, and Anthony Slide (and other important work from England), and helpful recent work by Mary Gentile, Louise Heck-Rabi, and Charlotte Brunsdon. Mention must also be made here of important contributions in other than booklength form, often by women whose astute, passionate responses to the work of these directors have appeared in more journalistic places, such as the *Village Voice*, or more popular film magazines.

# 2
# Antecedents

## IN AT THE ORIGINS: GUY-BLACHE, WEBER, DULAC

As a result of the women's movement and the research into women's film history it set in motion, we have become conscious of the presence of women directors (and women in many other roles, including running their own production companies) in the very earliest period of cinema. Before WWI and just after it, they were an important part of the origins and growth of the infant movie industry.[1] Though one mustn't exaggerate their numbers, which were relatively small, still, a contemporary observer early in the century notes that on all levels of the production, distribution and exhibition of films, "the fair sex is represented as in no other calling to which women have harkened in the early years of the twentieth century."[2] Marjorie Rosen suggests why: "Before it became a powerful elitist operation, the industry's hunger for material and moviemakers left little room for sexual prejudice."[3]

The most famous women directors of early silents, directors as different as Alice Guy-Blache, Lois Weber, and Germaine Dulac, were unquestionably remarkable women who made remarkable contributions to early cinema. Whether or not their films were among the best of what was being done in their time is hard to determine. Many of those films unfortunately are now lost to us, damaged irrevocably, or scattered, a problem generally for early films, but less for the products of mainstream powerful companies like Edison and Biograph than of small independent companies like Alice Guy-Blache's Solax. Alice Guy-Blache's *The House Divided* (1913), and Cleo Madison's *Her Defiance* (1916), two readily available silents, look as capable as other films of their time, without being distinctive. But Guy-Blache and Lois Weber and Germaine Dulac were held in high regard by their contemporaries, they turned out a large amount of material, they were famous and successful. They could so establish themselves because they began when the new film field was entirely open, as it was also to the Jewish immigrants who became its "moguls." Access was possible in a time of great rough-and-tumble activity and innovation,[4] when no one knew the potential of filmmaking.

When that potential—especially for money and power—became clear, however, new arrangements for production and distribution took place, and complicated consolidations and shifts of power occurred. Along with a startling rise in movie production costs from 1910 to 1920, huge studios with solid control of every step of the process were seen as the way to huge profit-taking—which necessitated incorporating or knocking out small independent companies like Alice Guy-Blache's. Women directors could have some impact as long as they could create their own companies, and also as long as conditions were fluid enough within existing studios to allow actresses or women screenwriters to try their hand at directing. Given the enormous need for product in the very early years, the generally low cost of production, and the much smaller scale of filmmaking, there was little to lose. Universal Pictures, where most of the women directors—like Cleo Madison, Ruth Stonehouse, Ruth Ann Baldwin—were concentrated, was perhaps more disorganized than others, less regularized. It paid very little, and in effect anyone off the street could try her/his hand. Hence, many who later became important, like John Ford and Rudolph Valentino, got their start there. In this atmosphere even women could have full command.

But circumstances changed rapidly from one decade to the next, one year to another: all kinds of companies went under; figures successful in one situation might well appear old-fashioned a few years later. And where gifted men might weather the shifts and emerge again in a different situation further on, it was apparently much less possible for women to do so.[5]

Yet those women we know most about were impressive. French-born Alice Guy-Blache, who made her first film in 1896, is arguably the inventor of the film that tells a story,[6] "the world's first woman director and possibly the first director of either sex to bring a story-film to the screen."[7] Determined to earn an independent income, though of a comfortable middle-class background, she learned secretarial skills unusual for women of her day and became the secretary of Leon Gaumont, who manufactured film and cameras. Alice Guy found herself fascinated with the new gadgets and made demonstration films to help Gaumont sell his product. Richard Koszarski notes: "She established Gaumont's filmmaking arm, produced nearly all the films made by them through 1906 (specializing in the talking Chronophone films), and trained such future luminaries of the French cinema as Feuillade and Jasset."[8] According to Anthony Slide: "Apparently, every motion picture produced by Gaumont until 1905 was directed by Alice Guy."[9] In that year, needing additional assistance, Alice Guy hired a director, an assistant, and a writer and "with one almighty stroke, she had created the entire early French film industry."[10]

After marriage, Guy-Blache followed her husband in a work transfer to the United States, as distributor of Gaumont, and she took some time out to have two children. Soon after, she started to direct great numbers of films again with great success, under her own company, Solax, where she was noted for her intrepid behavior, burning cars for effects, having characters hang from bridges, using a tigress. But with the shift of film industry economics at the time of WWI, the Blache operation got forced out of business.

After the firm dissolved, the marriage did as well. From 1920 on Alice Guy-Blache could no longer get work in the United States. She tried returning to France but was no longer young, had no prints of her films, and was unable to make a new start. She tried to track down her old footage and found that almost nothing survived,[11] though since then, small numbers of her films have been discovered in private collections. And though in her later years she tried also "to assure herself of the place she felt she had earned in the history of film," when she died in Mahwah, New Jersey, at 95, there were no newspaper obituaries, as Louise Heck-Rabi notes, in the state where the second half of her career took place. Also, as Guy-Blache anticipated, the "directing and producing credits for her films [were] falsely assigned to her co-workers" and her name, unintentionally or purposefully, was omitted from the histories of French and American film.[12]

Lois Weber, an American director whom Anthony Slide calls "the most important of all women film directors,"[13] came from an evangelical background, a family of preachers. The impulse to prosyletize and influence is what drove her to film as a form and to the top of a long, prolific and successful career as director—in an industry itself very much involved in uplifting and assimilating the foreign hordes newly arrived in America's urban centers. She directed more than one hundred films, though most of the films themselves again have disappeared. In a familiar pattern among women directors, she began as an actress, and went on to do just about everything in film production as well. And when she later became a director, she often collaborated with her husband, actor-manager Phillips Smalley, like Guy-Blache and Dulac, whose husbands were also deeply involved in the filmmaking business, though the women again were the leading spirits.

Weber's work usually involved a serious point to teach—anti-capital punishment, anti-saloon, anti-child labor—though she could also entertain, "making morality message movies with a shrewd recognition of box-office values."[14] A number of her successes were also attributed to her directing the films "from the female lead's point-of-view,"[15] and she felt that being a woman allowed her to "intuitively bring out many of the emotions that are rarely expressed on the screen. I may miss what some male directors get, but I will get other effects that they will miss."[16] Heck-Rabi points out how in *Where Are my Children?* Weber "deftly supported motherhood while questioning its inevitability," and that she "offered her audiences, perhaps for the first time, a sober scrutiny of motherhood's alternative in everyday dress."[17]

Around 1916 she was "the most important director on the Universal lot,"[18] and had a private studio financed for her under the name of Weber Productions. However, with *The Blot* (1920) and the four films that followed, Weber revealed herself as out of step with the postwar public's tastes, and she found herself a box-office failure, unable to find work. Weber's marriage broke up, she lost her company, and she had a nervous breakdown. At the same time, Carl Laemmle, who headed Universal, where she worked for so long, expressed the highest regard for her: "I would trust Miss Weber with any sum of money that she needed to make any picture that she wanted to make. I would be sure that she would bring it back. She knows the motion picture business as few people do and can drive herself as hard as anyone I have ever known."[19] after a brief comeback—at the age of 44!—and then sad attempts to start businesses that failed, Weber died in 1939, alone, impoverished, forgotten. Anthony Slide says of her that she brought to cinema "an intelligence and a commitment that was rare among filmmakers."[20]

Germaine Dulac, well-known early French filmmaker, worked in the period of Dadaism and Surrealism, associated herself with impressionist filmmakers Marcel L'Herbier and Abel Gance, and worked closely with the theoretician of the group, Louis Delluc. She was continually engaged with material from theatre and literature, and with experimenting with mastery of the camera's techniques, "soft focus and special lighting, prisms and distorting mirrors, screen panels for split screen effects, and fast and slow motion as the integral technical means in her quest for a visual cinema. . . . She was one of the first artists to use the screen panel, along with prism, distorting mirrors and other similar effects."[21] She made critics uncomfortable, with their emphases on plot, by what "they thought to be her excessive concerns with editing, lighting, and the creating of atmosphere through visual means."[22] Cornwell comments: "Her concern with the camera itself suggests an almost contemporary sensibility."[23]

Of the thirty-odd films she made in her lifetime, most not available to us in this country, *The Smiling Madame Beudet* (1923) is the best known, a sardonic version of an unhappy marriage shot entirely from the wife's point of view, private and reflective in mood. Mme. Beudet's smiling scorn of her crude husband's exasperating daily ways is counterpointed with her own self-possessed private world of reading, playing the piano, dreaming of escape and of murdering him. Her fantasy images, and lingering shots of her—solitary and thoughtful, a startling one of her despairing face reflected in three mirrors on her dressing table—remain fresh impressionistic strokes constructing a woman as subject.

*The Soul of the Artist* (1924), a less distinctive more commercial film which Dulac directed the following year, is an instance of the way Dulac moved back and forth between avant garde filmmaking and commercial features. It works with a glorious impoverished artist, and an equally formulaic romantic story (married poet loves marvellous actress, who brings his play to public attention, he narrowly escapes despairing suicide and returns to his anguished loving wife). Still, along with its focus on a great artist woman who fights for the work of another great artist, and the alliance made between the actress and the wife, the film uses various interesting self-reflexive shots relating to putting on a production and audience response.

Dulac's *The Seashell and the Clergyman* (1927)[24] is widely regarded as the first surrealist film, its bold imagery and anti-clerical stance pre-dating *The Andalousian Dog* by two years. It has been argued that in the film's "rendering of pure, unmediated dream logic and hence . . . the portrayal of thought processes themselves," this film of Dulac's is more useful to feminists than *Beudet* in "thematizing woman as a force of desire within the products of the filmic writing itself"[25]—though the film's controversial association with Artaud raises difficult questions. *Seashell* marks Dulac's return at the age of 45 to the making of a group of pure films set to music or to Baudelaire's poetry. Directing her last commercial film in 1928, she too found her career abruptly terminated, with shifts relating to the introduction of sound into the French film industry. When work was no longer available to her, she shifted her filmmaking energies into other film-related work—cine clubs to shape audience response, the founding of a film school, a film magazine, work on documentaries and newsreels—until her death in 1942. The Cinémathèque Française's homage to her in 1956–57, for her role there during her last two years, named her "truly the soul of the Cinematheque, exerting herself for it in the most tragic hours."[26] Called the "most important and prolific French director between 1920 and 1930," her film style "proceeded from psychological realism and symbolism through surrealism to documentaries and attempts at transposing musical structures to film."[27] She has an important place in early film history as "an intrepid improviser and experimenter in film form [who] assisted in the authorship and articulation of the film form . . . 'Mother of Surrealist Film.' "[28]

These three are simply the largest careers, with the greatest longevity, among a number of women directors of silent film about whom we know much less. Remembering these particular early directors—with all their creative boldness and originality, physical daring, tireless hard work and productivity—makes the near-total exclusion of women from filmmaking from the beginnings of sound film, essentially until the 1970s, even stranger and more disturbing than it already is. There are individual reasons why these particular directors' careers were abruptly terminated when they were in their prime in their 40s; and men suffered a similar fate at a time of rapid technological change, shifting audience composition, important changes in the whole nature of the film business. The situation takes on a different coloring for women, however, because it happened to every woman director (excepting Arzner), and from those endings no further beginnings issued. Once small independent acts of entrepreneurial boldness on the margins of the industry were no longer possible for women directors, and they could find no foothold as directors on the rockface of the corporate structures that took over, they had to wait half a century until enough pressure would build for new independent efforts to create a viable narrative cinema by women again.

As for those who managed to keep on working inside the industry, it is surely significant that Arzner established herself firmly in the earlier years (while conditions were open to women), editing other people's movies in the early 1920s and moving on from there—and equally important that she did not direct her own first film until 1927, not so early that she couldn't adapt during the period of greatest upheaval. It is also highly significant that Lupino became a director through her own production company. She herself remarked that she guesses she "was a novelty at the time and it would have been difficult to become a director then if we hadn't had our own company."[29] Given the actual figures, "difficult" should more accurately read "impossible."

## CLASSIC HOLLYWOOD: ARZNER AND LUPINO

Feminist scholarly attention continues to return to and circle in fascination around the narratives of the two women who alone worked as directors in classic Hollywood cinema. Although their films largely appear to conform to the mainstream patriarchal ideology (though in very different degrees and ways), imaginative efforts have been made by reading them "against the grain" to find underlying tensions created by their directors' femaleness—even visually conveyed defiances, disguised as compliance.[30]

In America, again only Dorothy Arzner survived the transition from silents to sound, and alone directed until 1944, retiring when *she* chose to. Arzner, whose father's restaurant in Los Angeles brought her into early contact with the stars, started out wanting to be a medical student, and ended up directing seventeen features in the course of her career. While she saw from the very start that "[i]f one was going to be in the movie business, one should be a director,"[31] she pragmatically began in filmmaking with typing scripts, then serving as a film cutter, an unusually gifted editor, a writer of stories. And where many of the kinds of women who were directors in the years after WWI were put in the newly created scenario departments of the 1920s, Arzner refused that, insisting on directing, as she also later insisted—with the same strong-mindedness—on taking full responsibility for her films, with the final decisions and the final cut hers.

At the same time the uneasiness of her situation may be suggested by the fact that she was "the total professional, perhaps rarely went out on an innovative limb, but she never botched a film, lost her temper with colleagues, and could always be counted on for a clear and sleekly competent package."[32] Other kinds of uneasiness are suggested by stories of her comportment on the set, her habitual solemnity, her "non-talking direction"[33]: the very low voice in which she spoke, her practice of having others shout her orders to actors and crew, at a nod or signal from her. In a 1936 newspaper article entitled "Hollywood's Only Woman Director Never Bellows Orders Herself," the reporter tellingly notes:

Practically all successful directors are dominant people who know when to do a bit of outright bullying, and how. Players might not take kindly to bullying from a woman; they'd call it nagging. And so there's only one woman director in Hollywood.[34]

(The act of directing appears to have been even more charged for Lupino: "I don't believe in wearing the pants. . . . You don't tell a man, actors, crews. You suggest to them. Let's try something crazy here. That is, if it's comfortable for you, love."[35])

Arzner makes the uneasiness explicit when she speaks of needing to make a box-office success with each picture.

I knew if I failed in that, I would not have the kind of fraternity men had one for another to support me. No one was handing me wonderful stories to make. I was usually having actors' first starring roles, and naturally they were only concerned with their own lives.[36]

Given her own force it is not surprising that Arzner's work—however artificial some of it may look to us now—is marked by strong-willed independent central women characters, and the kinds of strong actresses who could portray them. These she had a remarkable ability to recognize when they were unknown—Rosalind Russell and Sylvia Sidney, among them— and of course Katharine Hepburn, whose career was importantly advanced by *Christopher Strong*, though it has been pointed out that Arzner is not credited with this.[37]

The woman pilot heroine of *Christopher Strong* (1933) is a strikingly bold creation, the young and just beginning Katharine Hepburn with her purposeful strides, her brusque talk of enormously ambitious feats, the extraordinarily alert and direct look she gives to the world and to her married lover as well. The schizoid nature of female social conditioning is particularly apparent in the heroine's shift of costume from down-to-business leggings, jodpurs, mannishly cut flying jackets—to dazzlingly slinky gowns and flower-bestrewn wraps. Arzner clearly felt she needed to reassure her audience that this "new woman" is still recognizably a "real woman" for all the bold courageously ambitious self-sufficiency that would suggest otherwise.

Flight as a metaphor for freedom and transcendence is as stirring in this film as in Larisa Shepitko's *Wings* four and a half decades later. The kind of gusto and love of her work that Arzner herself voiced about the various phases of her moviemaking career, she puts into Lady Cynthia Darrington's relation to flying as well. As opposed to *Craig's Wife* (1936), made from a hit Broadway play whose author, George Kelly, felt only hostility to the woman at its center, *Christopher Strong*—its script a collaboration between Arzner and a woman screenwriter she worked frequently with before and after this film, Zoe Akins—is entirely supportive of its heroine. The camera is enchanted with her, her strikingly free physical movements whether she is leaning back on both elbows or sprawled with a leg positioned in unlady-like but graceful casualness, a fire often blazing behind her in token of her passionate intensity. She not only is in the driver's seat of the car, her passenger the man she comes to love—but of the plane, *she* taking *him* aloft.

Links between women are also striking, Cynthia's with the Strong daughter Monica, and with her lover's wife, played by Billie Burke, with whom she shares long exchanges of looks in very tight closeup in a final sequence of the film. Arzner truly does show "genuine empathy with the 'womanly women' who also populate her movies—the repressed, conservative females who live in the shadows of the world."[38] Links between women, even women in extreme conflict, appear in as early an Arzner film as *Sarah and Son* (1930), where two mothers vie for a son, born to one, raised by the other. Though the woman who has raised the boy has been deceitful, in a crucial final scene she invites the other to join her—ready to share—when the barely conscious boy calls for Mother. (This is also a film striking for the numbers of women involved in its shaping.[39])

Though Hepburn's character bows out to the angel-of-the-house wife, the way she does so, even her final suicidal flight, is an active record-breaking feat of the kind that makes her convincing as a revered model for the bold young women in the film. Pauline Kael, certainly not known as a feminist, is understandably and revealingly fascinated by Hepburn/Cynthia's other act of self-sacrifice, her agreeing to comply with her lover's request, as soon as they sleep together, that she not fly in an important match.

There were many movies in the thirties in which women were professionals and the equals of men, but I don't know of any other scene that was so immediately recognizable to women of a certain kind as *their* truth. It was clear that the man wasn't a bastard, and that he was doing this out of anxiety and tenderness—out of love, in his terms. Nevertheless the heroine's acquiescence destroyed her. There are probably few women who have ever accomplished anything beyond the care of a family who haven't in one way or another played that scene. . . . It is the intelligent woman's primal post-coital scene, and it's on film; probably it got there because the movie was written by a woman, Zoe Akins, and directed by a woman, Dorothy Arzner.⁴⁰

The theme may not be unique to Arzner, but the shading is crucial, the attention drawn to the man's request, and the sense we are given of what is lost. (This offers an interesting comparison with Lupino's *Hard, Fast, and Beautiful*, and the giving up of a tennis championship there. [See p. 27.] Lupino's interviews—not to speak of her films—indicate her own profound conflicts about conventional gender roles. Arzner's relation to work is far less ambivalent than Lupino's, her male figures mostly straw men, and the concessions made to them finally less important on the deepest level, because less internalized.) Although it is true at the same time that Cynthia's narrative function demands "that she ultimately bring/restore [both couples in the film] to monogamy,"⁴¹ the patriarchal discourse seems to me not to triumph here.

Though *Dance, Girl, Dance* (1940) too is placed within Hollywood (and patriarchal) conventions, dancer heroine Judy's (Maureen O'Hara's) breaking off her performance for a direct accusatory confrontation of the male audience is "a return of scrutiny" in what is assumed to be a "one-way process," with the "effect of directly challenging the entire notion of woman as spectacle."⁴² Equally telling is the grossness in various contexts of the male spectator; and the sympathetic motherly "director" play by Mme. Ouspenskaya, who is authoritative and full of contempt for the Hollywood scene and for the gross male who has the power to say yes or no. Arzner is clearly ambivalent about the vital, glamorous vulgarity of Bubbles, the Lucille Ball showgirl—but the scorn for Hollywood implicit in the film, and for the need to be a flesh peddler to survive there, is doubtless something Arzner herself felt in no small part, in this next to last of her films, close to her retirement.⁴³ Ouspenskaya's heavily male coded clothes and appearance, her mannishly worn hair, are strikingly like those of Arzner herself in many photographs of her.

This Ouspenskaya mother figure is unequivocally fine. While the males in the film are ciphers or fools, the ties between the women are what are really important in the film. So is work,⁴⁴ for its own sake as opposed to the leering crude agent under whose male gaze the group performs. There is a powerful sense of female solidarity: Madame watches out for her girls, and Adams' (Ralph Bellamy's) woman secretary supports Judy and is the first to clap with understanding of Judy's speech to the audience.⁴⁵ The Arzner heroine is indeed a self-determined woman, who insists "on initiating and carrying out her own projects and pursuing her own desires, rather than taking her place as part of the projects of men and as object of their desires"[46]—whatever conventional capitulations to patriarchy Arzner felt compelled to have her make in the final sequence.[47]

When Arzner retired, Lupino had not yet begun, and for some years no women directors were working in America. Muriel Box, however, was getting her filmmaking career underway in England, a director whose name recurs in that country as often and in the same way as Dorothy Arzner's does here, and whose films were capable without being distinctive. But Box's casual account of how she happened to become a director is worth including here because it makes clear yet again how women's situations cross national boundaries: "I am often asked: When did you first begin to direct films? . . . I give the year as 1950 or my age as forty-five. Neither is strictly true. Both refer to my entry as a director only into feature films; I started with documentaries much earlier. . . . My chance to direct in the documentary field would not have come but for the scarcity of male directors in wartime."[48]

Ida Lupino too fell into directing in an emergency to fill a man's place, a director who had a heart attack in the middle of a film Lupino's company was producing. However, she came to producing deliberately. The "first, and probably only, woman filmmaker in a Hollywood studio in the fifties,"[49] whose father was a well-known music hall comedian, came from a family of actors, singers, writers, mimes, jugglers, acrobats, comics, and puppeteers dating back to the Italian Renaissance clown, Grimaldi, although she was the first woman of the Lupino line, "one of Britain's oldest families, to achieve international fame."[50] Her energies unsatisfied by a straight Hollywood acting career, after a decade of successful acting she began to try her hand at scripting, then formed a film production company in 1949: "Finding the glamour side of the acting life totally distressing, Ida Lupino always yearned for something more. It became increasingly urgent for her to make statements about herself and the world around her."[51]

Urging "more experimentation with out-of-the-way film subjects,"[52] her own first venture as a producer, *Not Wanted*, is about a young teenager who picks men up in bars and becomes pregnant. Lupino took on the subject of rape in *Outrage* (1950). The film's important attention to the traumatic effect of rape on a woman is, however, counterbalanced by the embarrassment of the miracle-working god–like male healer that the heroine turns to for comfort, and by the film's extreme deference, obeissance, to male wisdom and authority. The early action sequences of the heroine pursued by the rapist are as strongly effective as the portrait of the cowering girl and of her relationships is psychologically crude. So much for prejudgments about women's aptitude for emotional and psychic nuance, and relationship; and lack of aptitude for action and suspense. Lupino's kinds of skills made her a natural for Hollywood genre production.

In *Never Fear* (1950), Lupino's second film, directed the same year, she tackled the subject of a polio-stricken girl dancer. (Lupino herself had polio in 1934, at the age of 16.) There is boldness in the choice and treatment of subject, an almost documentary kind of careful attention to the initial symptoms of being stricken by polio, and the carefully delineated route of recovery, and affecting footage using real patients—despite a lacquered and willed performance by Sally Forrest, the male lead's flatness, canned dialogue, undistinguished visuals. Yet another wounded-woman melodrama, *Never Fear* reveals, in Claire Johnston's formulation for all of Lupino's work, "the mark of disablement,"[53] because it involves the "convergence of two irreconcilable strands—Hollywood myths v. the female perspective." But this narrative conveys a further sense of female disablement in that Carol, the heroine, part of a young ambitious dance team just starting out, is terribly self-critical from the beginning. Her dancing is directed by Guy, judged by him, changed by him. She herself continually voices doubts about her ability, while the man speaks only about how great they are and how they will make it big. The one public dance they do is an enactment of sexual politics and power, the partners literally fencing. The woman disarms the man, immediately discards her weapon, switches to erotic seduction, and finally puts her head on his shoulder as sign of submission—like nothing so much as Lupino herself in her interviews! Once the heroine of *Never Fear* is rendered literally helpless, her regaining of movement and assurance in no way adds up to a tale of empowerment, requiring as it does a handsome man at each critical juncture to pat her head and to urge her toward autonomy.

If Lupino's first heroines are victims, vulnerable girls struck down, she moves on quickly to more assured and ambitious stronger women, whom she then finds it necessary to reproach and diminish. The anti-feminist content of her work becomes more explicit, and the gap between what Lupino herself did and the values she promulgated more dramatic. In *Hard, Fast, and Beautiful* (1951), Lupino assaults female ambition head-on, through a mother with dreams for her tennis-player-champion daughter, herself unhappy with the banality of her life, the ordinariness of her husband. The film recalls *Mildred Pierce*, and other Hollywood films split by a conflicting American Dream. The unambitious, decent ordinariness of the average loving American family is pitted against the pursuit of the best, the competitiveness that Hollywood itself was made of, that the directors of these films lived by—and the kind of drive a woman like Lupino would have had to have. Far more viciously than in *Mildred Pierce*, the ambitious mother here, associated with career, must be denounced as a selfish schemer from start to finish. And as the aspiring woman is denounced, so too the girl denounces her career—associated with the mother—for marriage,[54] with hardly a nod to the skill, power, glamor she is renouncing—for a man who takes her over as fully as her mother did.

*The Bigamist* (1953), built around a male central figure, again allows full expression of Lupino's profound sympathy for men. Edmond O'Brien's Harry Graham seems to become a bigamist out of his goodhearted caring about women. He also is motivated by a loneliness that the film holds his original wife Eve, played by Joan Fontaine, entirely responsible for because she becomes involved, very capably, in a business the couple run together. In one sequence we see her offering an involved technical explanation of the business to two clients, who smile at her in amused wonder as though she were a talking seal. At the same time she asks, almost orders, her husband, who is miles away mentally, to get drinks. Clearly not being "womanly" by the most conventional 1950s' definition weighs heavily on Lupino and on her work. Eve's very involvement in the business is due to her inability to have a child: had she had the baby she wants so desperately, fulfillment would be hers, and her wonderful marriage remain untroubled. As Eve's business skills are a debit, not an asset, in Lupino's eyes, so her business collaboration with her husband is seen as reducing the marriage to nothing more than a business partnership. (Lupino herself was in partnership with her second husband, Collier Young, at the time, they having formed the production company together. The company produced this film and *Hitchhiker*, and Young was the screenwriter of *Bigamist*, making a strong autobiographical ingredient highly likely.) Lupino is herself cast as the "other woman," tough externally but really vulnerable. Each character has its complexity, but one is struck by the almost excessive goodness Lupino bestows on the male characters, especially the hero—though it is a nurturing, vulnerable non-macho kind of goodness that suggests a woman's sense of what is desirable (or, as in say Sirk's *All That Heaven Allows*, a man director very conscious of what an audience of women desires). But most striking is each film's repudiation of the values Lupino lived by in her own career.

Lupino made seven feature films from 1949 to 1954, and directed over one hundred television shows after that. While one may question those who claim "technical brilliance" for her work, it is certainly true that Lupino "dealt with significant subjects not overtly and frankly considered in Hollywood films up to that time period and did so in a distinctive style,"[55] to create a sizable achievement. Thus it is particularly poignant to hear Lupino, with her hard-boiled Hollywood voice, talking as though she hated every minute of it all, and totally bought the patriarchal mainstream ideology of her films.[56] She felt compelled to say that she worked only because her family needed the money, and that "I would like to be quietly, happily married and be able to stay home and write."[57] This is the same woman described as above all daring: "Daring to sacrifice security to realize a vision . . . daring to be inventive in concept and different in technique; daring to do 'A' movies on 'Z' budgets long before it was fashionable, risking unknown faces, gambling on untried subjects; daring to shoot big while shooting fast; daring to direct at a time terrifyingly tough for women."[58]

The astounding gap between what she says, disowning all personal creative ambition, and what she did, however limited her work as art, is the most eloquent testimony of all to the terrible power of gender socializing. It also, in its schizoid doubleness, suggests a little of how Lupino could have had the boldness and strength to operate all alone, one of a kind as she did, and yet the burden she must have suffered, the toll it may have actually taken on her life and her marriages, the price she must have paid in confusion and self-reproach.

## A RECENT PREDECESSOR: LINA WERTMULLER

The European women "art" directors who preceded the current explosion of women-directed films—Varda and Zetterling especially in the late 1950s and 1960s, and Wertmuller in the 1960s and early 1970s—were important figures to those of us who came of cultural age during that holding period. They were directors who gave many of us our first experience of a woman's enunciation from the screen, though markedly different in the way gender is treated from that of later women directors, who were shaped by the full force of the feminist experience. Each produced a large and interesting oeuvre, engaging, professional, and, to varying degrees, done with great technical skill. Other films and directors might also have been included here, from Leontine Sagan's *Mädchen in Uniform* and Leni Reifenstahl's *The Blue Light*, through Barbara Loden's *Wanda*, and Anja Breen's *Wives*. No doubt each reader will have other names. But given space restrictions, selections and omissions had to be made.

Wertmuller appears here among predecessors, while Varda is discussed in a later chapter on French directors. This is so even though Varda's first feature *Cleo From 5 to 7* came out in 1961, and Wertmuller's highly regarded first feature, *The Lizards*, in 1963. Wertmuller's career, having burned brightly for a few short years and attracted large audiences, especially in this country, seems essentially over now (even though she continues to make films, sadly awful films, quite steadily). Wertmuller's male identifications, her scornful ways with women characters, her jazzy superficial cooption of the fashionable, her use of political leftism—and even the most terrible war sufferings—as entertainment, have always aroused profound suspicions as to whether she believed in anything—and if she did, whether it was on the side of women.

However, the charm, life force, brilliantly entertaining showmanship, and a certain rich ambiguity in such films of her peak period as *The Seduction of Mimi* (1972), could disguise the coarseness, even the opportunism, of her vision. Indeed, surely significantly, her subject in that film, in *Seven Beauties* (1975), and also in *Swept Away* the year before (1974), is precisely a hero's opportunism, a man (or a woman, in *Swept Away*) who will do anything to succeed or to survive. It may be that Wertmuller's films, which otherwise evade clear understanding and slip away from attempts to center their meaning,[59] have that as their bottom line—an intense desire above all to please and attract attention—and therefore lack center. These days the covering devices have become thin and transparent, and each new film feels more empty. The recent *Sotto, Sotto* (1985) has the additional interest—after all her years of working through the Giancarlo Giannini character and seeming to share the male viewpoint—of appearing to focus on a relationship between two women—a relationship that is more than a friendship, that declares itself to be a passionate love, though both women are married.

Of course nothing could be further from the truth, in view of the film's vacuousness and dishonesty. Wertmuller is in no way interested in the two women, whose supposed passionate love for one another is used only to titillate. Her focus is on the farce of a husband's chasing after his wife in frenzied jealousy and disbelief. Despite the carefully cultivated appearance of being far-out and modish, the only voice in the film is not only male but sourly traditional. This attempt of Wertmuller's to jump on the feminist bandwagon at this point in her flagging career only confirms the suspectness of her more attractive earlier work.

Still, in a film like *Seduction of Mimi*, it must also be said that Wertmuller's attention to the male protagonist is far from simply sympathetic and male-identified. She repeatedly undermines Italian macho (though also part of a long Italian comic movie tradition in doing so). Not only does the hero Mimi repeatedly cry, especially in a crucial courting scene, but Wertmuller deals with male impotence with some delicacy, candor, slyness[60]—in noting that the man, in order to perform sexually, needs a sense of his own superiority, of the woman's ignorance and total endorsement, and her incapacity to judge him. At least that is what turns the tide for Mimi. The sequence certainly suggests a subtext of sardonic woman's input. She also cuts directly away from the sexually triumphant scene that follows, to Mimi the following morning in a ridiculous hairnet, primping vainly, and then uneasily, stealthily, reading a letter from his wife. Wertmuller's vision, firmly shaped by Italian comic traditions, is derisory in all directions, like Elaine May's, but other notes through the same film suggest a woman's awareness and sensibility. Even in the most famous instance of Wertmuller's contempt for women, her treatment of heavy Amalia, the viciousness seems related to Amalia's having coerced her husband into a shotgun marriage because she was pregnant—and also seems an audacious professional woman's scorn for the conventional housefrau/breeder, no doubt also a function of class contempt.

Fiore, model of a new woman, is constructed of more than a little hokum, like so much else in Wertmuller, an easy fantasy heroine, with something for everyone. Trotskyite *and* virgin, she is arty, has liberated ideas about marriage—at the same time that Wertmuller gives her a baby right away, has her look like the Madonna, places her in the home and then—not interested in being there herself—essentially removes the character from the film. (In fairness Wertmuller insists she had to make heavy cuts in Fiore's role.) Although Wertmuller allows Fiore the film's final moral judgment, and gives her the active choice of moving on, Fiore does so with another man, and the gesture like the character is more fabulous than real—in this most modern, liberated, and unequivocally affirmed of Wertmuller heroines. And of course the man's struggle, and moral corruption, is what Wertmuller is interested in, not the woman's.

Wertmuller's detachment from her own femaleness, or her old-style sense of herself as a Superwoman, allows her to treat women with more exaggerated scorn, even loathing, than most men would dare to. Yet Wertmuller's comedy is often built on gender, in her most famous films often on an exploitation of grotesque power situations between men and women. More, she generally reverses the world's actual power hierarchy, as a number of critics noted when the films came out. So in the nasty sexual politics of *Swept Away*, she imputes great wealth and power to the heroine, played by Melato, and then uses witty play on communism and class analysis to justify a brutal and intimately viewed taming of the shrew. She taps into mass ridicule of a woman as talking too much, being too willful. A woman with opinions of her own is impossible and just needs a "good fuck" and a boot in the rear to fulfill her real nature. Wertmuller's "basic pitch" here is indeed to "popular prejudice"[61] of the ugliest, most sexist kind. But *Swept Away* goes beyond pandering to authoritarian male fantasies—it cleverly works romance/sexual material in a manner approaching soft porn. (Indeed, by her much advertised and awful "updating" of *Swept Away*, namely *A Summer Night* (1987), the soft porn and the decor are all that is left.)

*Swept Away*'s statement, particularly vile for a woman to be making, is finally that a woman has all the power, and needs to be brought low, needs to be made submissive to the man by abuse—for her own happiness as well as his. That astonishing kind of dancing to the master's tune makes Arzner's compliant endings, and even Lupino's full absorption of patriarchal values, look very mild by comparison.

The monstrous woman commandant in *Seven Beauties* is another instance of unreal power imputed to a woman, given the historical facts about where the actual power was in the Nazi hierarchy. It should be noted however that a number of major Italian directors at the time of *Swept Away* dealt with Nazism through high-style fashionableness and perverse eroticism. Bertolucci's *The Conformist* is one of the most dazzling examples. And *The Night Porter* (1974) made by Liliana Cavani, Italy's other well-known woman director, at the same time as *Swept Away* (1974) and just before *Seven Beauties* (1975), is another. Cavani's kinky use of fascist concentration camp imagery and situations for a sadomasochistic love affair between a Jewish girl (Charlotte Rampling) and her torturer (Dirk Bogarde) who meet fifteen years later, is more disturbing than Wertmuller's treatment. An Italian commentator in 1974 was right to find the film "morally ambiguous and politically dangerous."[62]

In that context of female victimization, Wertmuller seems less perverse. Nonetheless the Nazi woman commandant in *Seven Beauties* is certainly not an icon of desirable power. Wertmuller puts Giannini in the humiliated position usually held by women, and has us thus identify with the man. The sexual sequences with Giannini courting and then copulating with the monstrous woman commandant, "scaling her like a fly settling on Mount Rushmore,"[63] set off curious resonances; but like so much in Wertmuller, one here has the sense of effects thrown in helter skelter that don't come together meaningfully. One might be tempted to read the film as vindicative toward the arrogant macho Italian rooster, ruling his sisters, strutting darling of women, but the film won't stay in one place long enough to permit that rendering either.

Yet however we judge her finally, Wertmuller's are the fantasies of a woman who became powerful very early in a field by and large without women, in a profoundly patriarchal culture. Who would be more highly attuned to issues of power, powerlessness, and gender, from the inside? Wertmuller uses that knowledge often to clown shamelessly from the viewpoint of the master, and for a while got richly rewarded accordingly. But finally she is herself a victim of that lack of a self, of the shape-changing in her films, of the pretense to high values—which constantly shift and are unconvincing—while ultimately pandering instead to audience cynicism, to love of novelty and, above all, to the crudest sexist notions about women.

How much of Wertmuller's vision comes out of a female self-hatred and identification with men? (Again, perhaps necessary for a woman to achieve an important place in film, at the time she did, for years as Fellini's assistant and then on her own, in a culture like Italy.) And how much of her vision is a result of deliberate manipulation, showmanship, choices made to entertain a popular audience—choices ever more attention-demanding and outrageous (especially in treatment of gender)? This will never be measurable. But the very nature of Wertmuller's brilliance—and the ends to which she put it in a desire to please and be successful at all costs, even through self-degradation—may make its own statement.

This chapter's concern has been the exclusion of women for decades from directing feature films, and the toll of that exclusion. It cost, obviously, in terms of talent struck down prematurely and never replaced or allowed development. It meant a profound immeasurable loss for film culture itself. But it took a toll too on those very few who managed to work during those years—from Arzner and Lupino on—in the various ways they navigated the patriarchal system within which they had to operate, and how they dealt with their own gender identity under such difficult circumstances.

It shouldn't surprise us that those women who undertook the struggle earlier on to make a place for themselves as directors, and to keep that place, had to identify with male aggression and power to be able to do it at all. Those rare early women directors reflected in complex ways the strains of working as women alone, in a uniquely authoritative role, in a male profession not only governed by patriarchal values but itself a major promulgator of those values. The distortions of Wertmuller's monstrous Nazi commandant are as telling a part of this story of directorial predecessors as is Hepburn's radiant Lady Darrington behind the wheel.

## NOTES

1. Useful material on early women directors appears in Kay/Peary, in Erens' *Sexual Stratagems*, in Heck-Rabi, and in Anthony Slide, among others.

2. Martin F. Norden, "Women in the Early Film Industry," *Wide Angle* 6, 3, 58. Among other women directors active in the production of silents and early talkies were Cleo Madison, Lule Warrenton, Ruth Stonehouse, Elsie Jane Wilson, Ruth Ann Baldwin, Grace Cunard, and Ida May Park, as well as actresses who made only one or two films, such as Lillian Gish, whose single attempt at direction, *Remodeling Her Husband* (1920) was "a critical and popular success though she rejected all further offers." See Marjorie Rosen, *Popcorn Venus* (New York: Coward, McCann & Geoghegan, 1973), 367. Margery Wilson, one of D. W. Griffiths' leading ladies in *Intolerance*, was active as a director in the early 1920s. Among other actresses who tried their hand at directing were Kathlyn Williams and Mabel Normand. Many screenwriters tried directing, among them Mrs. Geoge Randolph Chester, Julia Crawford Ivers, Marion Fairfax, Jane Murfin. Screenwriter Francis Marion, writer for Weber and Pickford, directed two of Pickford's films at her request, though they were not successful. Still others: Dorothy Davenport, Elizabeth Picket, Louise Long, and Nazimova. Many women stayed on the many other levels of the film business, especially screenwriting, which, though particularly powerless and badly paid, women could do at home. See Norden for a full discussion of this subject; "Women in Early Film Industry," 58. He also speculates that women very early got a foothold in editing because it was originally seen as a menial job, requiring just the following of men's directions as to the duration of a sequence or the order of shots, only later turning into a crucial role, demanding very subtle decision-making skills. Women were also involved in distribution and exhibition in the early years, and were even "occasionally found in executive positions in Hollywood producing companies." Robert Sklar, *Movie-Made America* (New York: Vintage, 1975), 75.

The important role played from the very beginning of film, but especially in the 1930s, by women screenwriters is often illustrated by Anita Loos, amazingly prolific and witty, credited with 200 screenplays made into films, though films affirming the subservience of women. Jeanie MacPherson, also a Griffiths actress, was De Mille's script writer from 1915 to 1946, writing all his scripts until her death; June Mathis, associated with Valentino's films and von Stroheim's *Greed*; Bess Meredyth, who wrote 90 features between 1917 when she started, and 1919; Dorothy Parker;

and by the early 1920s, many other women whose names are not only generally forgotten, but sometimes not even credited (see Norden, op. cit., 64), simply dropped out of history. Of considerable interest and importance are the married-couple writing teams, like Ruth Gordon and Garson Kanin, who created such feminist scripts as *Adam's Rib*, with Valerie Curtin and Barry Levinson's *Best Friends* a recent, less-glittering parallel. Leigh Brackett's work with Howard Hawks is well known, though one shouldn't too quickly ascribe Hawks' creation of bold and independent women to this collaboration—given Hawks' own belief in professionalism and toughness, extending that demand to his women characters as well, and given Brackett's worry that she was making Russell's Hildy Johnson too aggressive, despite Hawks' insistence. It is nevertheless true that "the woman's point of view was often expressed through women screenwriters, who were more numerous in the thirties than during any other period" (Haskell, *From Reverence to Rape*, 151).

3. Rosen, *Popcorn Venus*, 367.

4. Specialists such as Jay Leyda, Charles Musser, Ellen Bowser, and Thom Gunning see those very early years as a time the full experimental richness of which has not yet begun to be understood and studied.

5. For much of the information in the preceding two paragraphs I am indebted to conversation with Richard Koszarski.

6. Louise Heck-Rabi, *Women Filmmakers: A Critical Reception* (Metuchen, NJ: Scarecrow Press, 1984), 1.

7. Ibid.

8. Ibid., 5.

9. Anthony Slide, *Early Women Directors* (New York: A.S. Barnes, 1977), 15.

10. Ibid.

11. Richard Koszarski suggests that the fact that so many very early women's films do not survive is not a question of gender but of marginality. (It need hardly be added that marginality is a question of gender.) Again, the films and records that survived best were from the largest and most popular studios, which was not where most work by women directors was done.

12. Mme. Blache points to the case of her co-worker Zecca's film, *The Misdeeds of a Calf's Head*, being mistakenly attributed to her! Lacassin corrects this: "For a long time this was the only film actually attributed to Alice Guy, although by her own account it was one of the few Gaumont pictures that she *didn't make*." Heck-Rabi, *Women Filmmakers*, 18.

13. Slide, *American Film Industry*, 391.

14. Heck-Rabi, 57.

15. Ibid.

16. Ibid., 58.

17. Ibid., 59.

18. Koszarski, "The years have not been kind to Lois Weber," in Kay and Peary, 149.

19. Heck-Rabi, 64.

20. Ibid., 67.

21. Regina Cornwell, *Film Library Quarterly* 5 (Winter 1971/72), 32.

22. Cornwell, in Erens, *Sexual Stratagems*, 19.

23. Ibid., 198.

24. See Sandy Flitterman, "Theorizing the 'Feminine': Woman as the Figure of Desire in *The Seashell and the Clergyman*," *Wide Angle* 6, 3:32–39.

25. Ibid., 33.

26. Cornwall, in Erens, *Sexual Stratagems*, 199.

27. Ibid., 50.

28. Koszarski, in Kay and Peary, 149.

29. Kay and Peary, 177.

30. See Beverle Houston, "Missing in Action: Notes on Dorothy Arzner," *Wide Angle*, 6, no. 3, 24–31.

31. Karyn Kay and Gerald Peary, "Dorothy Arzner," *Films by Women/Chicago '74*, 6.

32. Rosen, *Popcorn Venus*, 398. For a fuller discussion of Arzner, see Claire Johnston, "Dorothy Arzner: Critical Strategies," *The Work of Dorothy Arzner: Towards a Feminist Cinema* (London: British Film Institute, 1975), 1.

33. Heck-Rabi, 87.

34. Ibid., 88.

35. Ibid., 242.

36. Ibid., 399.

37. See Houston, "Missing in Action," among others.

38. Kay and Peary, *Films by Women/Chicago '74*, 7.

39. Stars, author (Zoe Akins), director, supervisor, business manager, and cutter of *Sarah and Son*—all were women.

40. Pauline Kael, "Winging It," *Deeper into Movies* (Boston: Little, Brown and Company, 1973), 341.

41. Jacquelin Suter, "Feminine Discourse in *Christopher Strong*," *Camera Obscura* (Summer 1979), 142.

42. Johnston, in Nichols, *Movies and Methods*, 215.

43. A propos of the film's opposition of classy ballerina vs. vulgar showgirl, Arzner told an early reporter that she enjoyed reading, was presently reading Plato, but asked that he not mention this in the story lest it be thought highbrow. *New York Sun* (Sept. 23, 1930).

44. In this the film relates to male-directed show-business films such as *Stage Door*.

45. The film comes from a story by Vicky Baum, and so is female generated on several levels.

46. Houston, "Missing in Action," 35.

47. Feminist critics have mined Arzner's films for other resistances. Beverle Houston finds a purely visual defiance on the part of the Arzner heroine—who, in various charged situations, is allowed a final refusal on "the level of film as a system of exchanged looks," by averting her face. Houston, 26.

48. Heck-Rabi, 135.

49. Ibid., 223.

50. Francine Parker, "Discovering Ida Lupino," *Action* (1967), 19.

51. Ibid., 21.

52. Ibid.

53. For a full discussion of this approach, see Claire Johnston, "Women's Cinema as Counter-Cinema," in Bill Nichols, ed., *Movies and Methods: An Anthology* (Berkeley: University of California Press, 1976), 216.

54. For an examination of this relationship between mother and daughter, see Wendy Dozoretz, "The Mother's Lost Voice in *Hard Fast and Beautiful*," *Wide Angle* 6, 50–57.

55. Heck–Rabi, 240.

56. A much-quoted instance: "Any woman who wishes to smash into the world of men isn't very feminine . . . Baby, we can't go smashing. I believe women should be struck regularly—like a gong. Or is it bong? If a woman has a man who loves her, she better stick close to home. I've turned down jobs in Europe because I'd have to leave my husband and my daughter and my cats. I couldn't accept those jobs unless I was a guy." Ida Lupino, "Me, Mother Directress," *Action* 2, no. 3 (June 1967), 15. The conflict was doubtless a real one for a woman trying to maintain a family life in the 1950s. See Kay and Peary, *Women and the Cinema*, 178, for other similar complaints Lupino repeatedly made.

57. Rosen, *Popcorn Venus*, 379.

58. Parker, "Discovering Ida Lupino," 19.

59. Pauline Kael notes, "There is hardly any point in discussing the stated ideas in a Wertmuller film, because they can't be sorted out." "Seven Fatties," in *When the Lights Go Down* (New York: Holt, Rinehart Winston, 1980), 138. Ellen Willis has related on-target things to say about *Mimi*'s "double messages." "Is Lina Wertmuller Just One of the Boys?" in Kay and Peary, 378.

60. Perhaps the coarse humor in her work is how she adapts "male boldness," along with the bravado that she carries off, at her best, so spectacularly.

61. Kael, "Seven Fatties," 136.

62. Mira Liehm, *Passion and Defiance: Film in Italy from 1942 to the Present* (Berkeley: University of California Press, 1984), 355. Teresa de Lauretis seems to me unconvincing in her attempt to read the concentration camp as a metaphor for gender relations generally, and the situation between the two characters as above all a refusal to forget and cover over the past. See *Film Quarterly* 30 (Winter 1976/77), 35–8.

63. Kael, 137. See her entire essay for one of the best discussions of Wertmuller available.

# 3
# American Women Directors

## INTRODUCTION

In the greatest film industry in the world, in the United States, as we have seen, the struggle of women directors to gain and maintain a foothold has been difficult in the extreme, from Alice Guy-Blache onward. As for the less than a handful who succeeded, given how profoundly their unholy assumption of directorial power must have challenged the gender definitions of their time, surely it should not surprise us that Arzner chose to look like a man, or that Ida Lupino, for all her output, talked the whole while about how she'd rather be home cooking for husband and child, and how she was just forced to do this for the money. Or that the next carrier of the grail in the United States (for decades seemingly a relay race for women directors, passed from single hand to hand), Elaine May in the early 1970s, though her humor disparages everyone, aims a particular animus at her women characters and works through male protagonists.

Feminism has profoundly altered this situation for younger women directors, whether they deal directly with it in their work or not. The overtly feminist independent films of Claudia Weill and Joan Micklin Silver in the mid- and late 1970s, *Girlfriends* and *Hester Street*, marked a major shift (as did the additional impact of the numbers of feminist women working in documentary filmmaking like Connie Field, avant garde filmmaking like Yvonne Rainer, or somewhere between the two like Michelle Citron). Both Weill and Silver, after bold debuts, made intelligent, low-keyed, though also more mainstream, fairly sleek films—*Chilly Scenes of Winter* and *It's My Turn*—in an apparent attempt to satisfy their own perhaps European-oriented subtlety and sense of artistry, at the same time as they tried to appease box office pressures. They ended up with films less interesting than their early ones, that at the same time were too quiet and intelligent to make big money.

Women directors after them could move away, and mostly have done so, from directly feminist subject matter, while building their films around assumptions that would have been unlikely if not impossible before feminism and perhaps before *Girlfriends* (1978) or *Hester Street* (1975). These assumptions have to do with the seriousness with which central women characters are viewed—and with their being viewed for themselves, no longer in terms of the men they are attached to, as they seek to work out their own destinies; they have to do with how ethnic, quirky, even unpleasant a sympathetically-regarded heroine might be, and with defining heroines through their work.

If we do not quite yet have a clearly identifiable major woman director working now in this country, this decade has at least seen women slowly let in, allowed to get started, bringing some interesting, unique films to the screen, and, in 1987, two women directors for the first time positioned in major mainstream efforts, *Ishtar* and *Making Mr. Right*. That both were disappointments only confirms low-budget independent filmmaking as the most promising route—not only for entry films but for the long haul as well—despite the various other highly commercial avenues chosen by women: teen movies (Amy Heckerling), porno/horror films (Penelope Spheeris), the mass-marketed feminisms of Barbra Streisand and Goldie Hawn, and film production as a means to gain power in filmmaking.

How to sustain work of quality is increasingly the dilemma for the most promising American women directors working now. How does one, having made a *Smithereens* or *Smooth Talk*, continue to develop without becoming blandly commercial or without losing the market needed to get backing for the next work? How does one prevent big audience success from becoming an end in itself, the only end (and often, after jettisoning everything in a bid for audience appeal, losing that as well).

The most important and troubling issue in short has finally moved beyond mere entry—although entry is still a bitter struggle for many—to stickier questions, less related to gender than to the industry itself. One would not expect the U.S. film industry to be a likely nurturing place for female talent, much less art, but who would have suspected a few short years ago that the barriers would have yielded as much as they have, and so quickly? So who knows what miracles lie ahead. Doubtless some do.

## ELAINE MAY

Of the women currently working as feature-film directors in America, Elaine May is a figure of importance, both for the size of her talent and for her longevity. She is the oldest of the women to be considered in this chapter, born as she was in 1932. After the early women directors of silent films, and Arzner and Lupino, there are the 1970s and Elaine May.[1] Perhaps that very context, the totally inhospitable climate Elaine May entered as a woman feature filmmaker in Hollywood, is a partial explanation for the appalling vision of women in her work, as well as for her proclivity to work through male characters' points of view. Although Elaine May's work has no feminist content, not only is her film oeuvre an important achievement by a woman, but hers is unmistakably a woman's vision, painful aspects and all.

May's first film, *A New Leaf* (1971), which she both wrote and directed, works out of the comedic style May developed in her early improvisational theatre work at the Second City with Mike Nichols. May tried to stop the distribution of the film and to remove her name from it because of the studio's editings and overrulings of her intent, in her view turning the film into a "cliche ridden banal story."[2] But while obviously flawed, *A New Leaf* remains interesting and amusing; one's greatest discomfort with it is likely to derive not from issues of aesthetic quality but from its treatment of the rich woman at its center, played by May herself. So *Heartbreak Kid* (1972), still as striking as when it came out, is also disturbing for its own searingly negative portrait of a Jewish woman. *Mikey and Nicky* (1976) takes on important new terrain while still working within genre, this time two petty mobsters and the wet dark night streets of film noir—as *Ishtar* re-renders the male-buddies-on-the-road under desert sunlight as comedy. May has always worked within genre forms, not having come to film-making through the non-commercial route of independent cinema, as, say, Claudia Weill or Joan Micklin Silver have, nor having tried to make a success, as Paul Mazursky has done, of diluted American attempts at the European art film. She has from the start taken a broader, more unashamedly popular road, though she's taken it to surprising places.

In fact, Elaine May comes out of show biz and has worked in it throughout her life in different capacities. Her father was a well-known Jewish actor, and also a producer of a travelling theatre company. His daughter, born in Philadelphia as Elaine Berlin, began acting for him at the age of six, and her early childhood was spent on the road, continually travelling with her father and performing. She was ten when he died. She left school early, had a brief marriage and a daughter, Jeannie Berlin, and then drifted into acting, studying under Maria Ouspenskaya, formerly of the Moscow Art Theatre (the memorable coach and protector of the women dancers in Dorothy Arzner's *Dance, Girl, Dance*). May held odd jobs, was unable to get into a California college without a high school diploma, and so travelled to the University of Chicago, one of the rare schools in the 1950s that had a program for returning students without high school degrees. She attended classes without formally entering, engaged in "sharply worded intellectual debates with instructors,"[3] and encountered Mike Nichols, the leading actor in the theatrical group, forming a stage partnership with him that lasted from 1954 to 1961. When they parted ways, Nichols became a director, and Elaine May turned to other things—an unsuccessful attempt at play-writing, an equally unsuccessful second marriage, film roles and screen-writing, sometimes credited, more often not, for many films from *Such Good Friends* to *Silkwood* and *Tootsie*. She has continued to function as a valued and sought-after script doctor in the business when not making her own films, thus surviving intervals stretching even a decade. (*Mikey and Nicky* came out in 1976, *Ishtar* in 1987.) Unlike Mike Nichols, who works entirely from other people's books (and plays), May wrote the screenplay for *A New Leaf*, wrote the whole of *Mikey and Nicky* and *Ishtar*, and informs each with the strong original personality that came through in her comedy work with Mike Nichols.

What is most surprising when you re-examine the vision expressed in the films—especially from the perspective of *Mikey and Nicky*—is how much darkness underlies that delicious humor, the extent to which May's is a world of continual betrayal. In the first two films, these are betrayals of women, the funnily outrageous death blows bestowed on them by their mates: one husband literally trying to kill his wife, the other dropping his bride on their honeymoon. The derogatory images of the women them-selves do not move one to anger—as, say, Wertmuller's contempt for her women characters often does—but rather to pain, embarrassment, and sym-pathy, simultaneously. *A New Leaf* suggests that neurotic intellectual Jewish women are basket cases, grotesque to consider as love objects. May's female version of Woody Allen's persona predates Allen and is somehow much more painful and embarrassing than anything in Allen. Elaine May does terrible things to what would seem, on some level, a proxy of herself in *A New Leaf*, similar to the terrible things she goes on to do, through the complex comedic play of art, to her daughter in *Heartbreak Kid*. *Mikey and Nicky*, among its other fascinations, seems to go to the root of the love-lessness, the pain, the distrust, that lies under the humor. And even in *Ishtar*, where May attempts to stay within the confines of entertainment and com-edy, everyone betrays everyone else.

In *A New Leaf*, Henrietta Lowell is an astonishing study in incompetence, carefully deracinated. Her glasses keep falling off her nose, she spills tea and everything else, she drops crumbs all over herself. Henry (Walter Mat-thau), the film's hero, is an unlovable rich man who has spent all his money and is looking for a woman through whom to replenish his coffers. He wants a disastrous rich woman whom no one else would marry or care about, so he can kill her and get her money with a minimum of bother, and so he falls on Henrietta with glee. She is perfect, because so appallingly imperfect. He has to wipe her mouth before he kisses her. He is continually removing forgotten price tags from her clothes, and on the field-trip hon-eymoon he has to wipe her off and wash her after every meal—funny, but also incredibly infantalizing. Henrietta, trying to look sexy for Henry after they are married, can't even get her head through the right opening of the lingerie. Henry controls her, even to the point that when he tells her to let go of a log in a river, his plan for killing her, she does so unquestioningly.

Hers is the same trust as the heroine's in *Heartbreak Kid*; it can seem sweet, but also stupid, passive, masochistic. The entire household staff abuses Henrietta without her consciousness, or if she is conscious, she feels powerless to do anything about it. The man has to come in, call them on their corruption, take the reins and fire them. This is particularly sad imagery when you think of Elaine May at the reins of the film, in full authority over *that* complex and demanding enterprise. And though Walter Matthau is a most unlikely stand-in for a debonair upper-crust type who knows all the right vintages, May endows poor Henrietta with the worst possible taste and unthinkable gaucheness: namely, celebrating Mogen David and Manishevitz Malaga sweet wine. This shows she has absolutely no class, no social grace, a charge regarded with horror—with the built-in Jewish joke of that wine's association with Jewish families at holiday times. So too amid the whole hopelessly incompetent, corrupt staff surrounding Henrietta, May places as the cleaning woman a decrepit woman who looks exactly like everyone's old Jewish mother, another funny ethnic in-joke, like allusions to directors slyly slipped into nouvelle vague films!

Henrietta's glasses, Hollywood's badge of an intellectual, convey anything but competence. Even her one area of expertise, as a botanist, is so narrow as to have no relevance to anything. Still, it is interesting that May made her heroine a professional[4]—a little on the model of the Cary Grant bone specialist in *Bringing Up Baby*—with delight and excitement in her work, but a professional who is inept at everything else. At the same time, in her initial appearance she is coded, however comically, for lady-like identity, with a flower hat, even if it slips off her head at a chaotic angle, and with gloves. So she is firmly placed within conventional gender definitions—stereotyped intellectual, stereotyped woman.

Henrietta, apart from being incompetent, is also hopelessly insecure, continually listing her failings—she is so stupid and clumsy and gauche—and continually applauding Henry for his savoir faire, his self-assurance and authority. She says how little confidence she has in herself and how he gives her confidence. May makes her likable in a curious way, like the old sweet dumb blondes with empty heads; though this one has the head, she has the same sound of dimwitted ineptitude. She can also be seen as a mockery of Jewish luft-mensch types, hanging over cliffs in pursuit of unique ferns. In contrast to the positive associations with bookish types in the writing of Roth and Malamud, who make university teachers into attractive characters, here in *A New Leaf* that work is seen as an almost ridiculous thing to do.

The one other woman in *A New Leaf*, briefly characterized, is another portrait in denigration. After announcing she is a woman, she says in ridiculous exaggeration that she desires love, all the while the camera mocks her sizable belly. She pushes her breasts at Henry, and he cries out in funny alarm, "No, don't let them out," as if they were wild beasts. Granted, comedy has to make fun of people; and Henry Graham is himself hateful in a variety of ways. Still, the female portraits here run a singularly demeaning range, from ignominious neediness for love, to infantile incompetence.

*Heartbreak Kid* goes one further, with one of the most negative images of a Jewish woman on film—created by a Jewish woman, with her own daughter in the role of the offensive woman. On the other hand, with a book by Bruce Jay Friedman, and a screenplay by Neil Simon, responsibility is not easily placed. It can also be argued that as unpleasant as Lila is, the Christian girl Kelly is just as unpleasant, and that the Jewish man Len Cantrow (played by Charles Grodin) who scorns and betrays Lila for Kelly right after their marriage, bowing and scraping to be accepted by the Other, ruthless in his need to be in, is himself the most offensive character in the film. We are dealing with the not unusual phenomenon of comedy that draws blood all around. Given a comic vision that mercilessly mocks everything in sight, the male in this film can be viewed as a more severe victim of May's barbs than the women. In that case the film can be seen not so much as self-derogatory, self-hating—as merciless to the world of flawed human nature.

Again thinking of Wertmuller, with her abusive images of women, her vision of everyone as ridiculous, her male protagonists, one must suspect again that both May and Wertmuller reflect the wounds of an earlier and lonely generation of women directors. Some may murmur about May (as has actually been written about Wertmuller) that such women directors got so far just *because* of their ferocity to women, which made their cinematic visions acceptable while those of others with equal gifts are not. But the sheer talent to entertain seems more to the point in explaining the success of both.

Lila is not really stereotypical, and could be regarded as simply an idiosyncratic jerk, but her most unpleasant qualities can easily be chalked up to Jewishness, femaleness, or both: her insecurity (hallmark of Elaine May's women); her constant need to be reassured sexually and otherwise; her orality—love of food, egg salad all over her face, pushing food into the man's mouth; and her apparent unsatisfactoriness sexually. The WASP girl has everything Lila lacks, from her most Christian of names, Kelly, to Cybill Shepherd's blonde cheerleader good looks, and above all else, her self-assurance. Her continual joke is that every place on the beach is her place. She is aggressive, she marks the hero out and lures him, though one is not sure why she would want to. Nothing daunts her, certainly not the fact that he is married. At the same time, she conveys more than a touch of both vacancy and sadism, in sharp contrast to Lila's limp benign good nature, which may make her crude and foolish but at least likable—even if uncomfortably a victim. In response to the horrendous blow her brand-new husband deals her, Lila simply collapses into passive weeping, even letting the cad himself hold and comfort her.

You can read the rest of the film as Elaine May's vengeance on her hero for the evil he has done. He, like Lila, is rendered in unpleasant but surely not unfamiliar ethnic terms, of Jewish pushiness, lust for the WASP world of privilege and cool grace, a yearning for entry into its high wealth and classiness. He is beside himself to have it—shades of Norman Mailer and Philip Roth, and the non-Jewish ur-dreamer of such dreams, Fitzgerald and his Gatsby. Lila's ridiculousness is registered to us through Len Cantrow's eyes, but once she is off the scene, his own ridiculousness takes stage center, a hustler, a creep. If Kelly's jokes seem increasingly stupid to us, if she seems increasingly flat and vacuous, this reduces him too because he is cringingly in a delighted uproar over everything she says. One of the nasty jokes of the film is that he should go through so much for a woman even sillier than the one he got rid of. Finally, the governing spirit of the film is nihilistic. The upperclass grand WASP family home that spawns Kelly in its chilly elegance is finally as unappealing as the more familiar hora-dancing Jewish lower-middle-class one that produces the wedding couple. And the "cold whiteness of the Minnesota landscape"[5] not only contrasts with the warmth of Miami Beach, but both are in the end uncomfortable landscapes. Kelly's falling for Len Cantrow's "authority," the phony tone of command he puts on that reminds her of her authoritarian father, receives more of May's scorn, directed both at the man's macho games and the woman's submissiveness, one aspect of a vague sado-masochism that runs through the film.

If on one level *Heartbreak Kid* feels like a Jewish woman's self-denigration, or simply a woman's self-denigration, it can also be seen as a film that only a feisty Jewish woman could make in answer to Roth et al., a scathing portrait of those late 1950s/1960s ethnic young men on the make, who dominated the literary scene in those years. The hero who gets what he wants, who wins the blonde Other such as she is, is so ostracized, so rendered the isolated outsider, that finally he is of interest to no one, not even the children he desperately tries to engage in conversation. It is a chilling conclusion, like hell, with so thin a line between the humor, the moral attack, the pity, all of which it contains in good measure—that you are left with remarkably jangled and troubled feelings, from what appears to be a popular and funny entertainment.

*Mikey and Nicky*, also apparently a Hollywood entertainment in a familiar style (in this case the gangster and film noir genres), also ends with the same kind of jarring, haunting feeling. The film looks like it is about small time hoods and killing, and May uses the genre atmosphere persuasively, skillfully building tension and suspense, from Nick's early, wild, violent restlessness and franticness, to the final hunting down and frenzied quest to escape. But the film is really a strong complex exploration of friendship and male bonds, indeed, of any gender's sibling relationship, a very bitter kind of sibling tie. (May says the film developed from a one act play she wrote years earlier about an actual situation of people who lived next door to her, involving one brother's fingering of another—a story that long remained in her mind.)[6]

May skillfully modulates Nick's (John Cassavetes') raw terror that a contract is out on his life—using the camera with an awkward agitation that almost becomes abstract—as she later skillfully shows the two men stumbling around in dark wet city streets with a paid killer's presence a constant framing comic menace (from a blubbery Ned Beatty). But that is only one level of the achievement here. The film's long opening sequence plays with the ambiguity of the friendship, with Mikey (Peter Falk), while seeming to comfort his anguished friend, in fact holding Nick's head in what appears very like a stranglehold. Mikey's amused reassurances to Nick, addressing him as if he were a scared little boy, lead the audience to take Nick's terror as hysteria and paranoia, although the film at first gives us no context for granting belief to one man or the other. But immediately after that initial sequence May makes clear the audience has chosen wrongly, and that terror and total mistrust are the only accurate responses to Nick's reality. *Mikey and Nicky* finds underneath all that male comradery of hugs, help, shared sex talk, nostalgia, something very different: lies, hurts, resentments, jealousy, a brutality expressed in the metaphor of the hood contract killing— one friend running round and round through dark streets; and the other in a car with a gunman, looking for him, waiting to finger him.

*Mikey and Nicky* is on one level the ultimate statement on a series of male buddy films that greeted the rise of feminism in the 1970s, the film having come out in 1976, one year before the first wave of U.S. women-bonding films emerged: *Julia, Girlfriends, Turning Point*. Along with the remembering of one another's parents and dead younger brothers, of having been friends for decades, along with Mikey addressing Nick as if he were a kid, there is a general sense of men remaining on the level of boys. The film's very title uses the diminutive form of both men's names, ironically suggesting affection, but also the names of childhood. The two play kid games together in the midst of imminent murder, and Nick, in a panic and soon to die, buys candy, comic books, lollypops for himself—from a late-night candystore owner holding his own hidden gun through the scene. The world of macho-male tenderness and comradery is full of weapons, and human relations in the world of the film are marked on every side by terror, betrayal, suspicion, destruction. Taking place largely through one night, this film is even darker than most film noir, because even its sole intimate relationship ends with one butchering the other.

As the two men move through bars, buses, a cemetery, past sleazy movie houses (mostly back to origins in Philadelphia, though May was compelled to add footage shot in L.A.), *Mikey and Nicky* also works with a multitude of faces and human interactions freshly invoking city life. The interactions are only a step away from the kind of acerbic comic routines that made May famous, but they never get self-indulgent, they are quickly pulled back into the larger shape of the film. Struggles to force various kinds of rules— trying to buy cream in a luncheonette, smoking on a bus or insisting on getting out the front door of the bus—move quickly to violence, the levels of hostility among strangers extremely high. For city dwellers it is all fearfully (although in May's hands also laughably) familiar. The social network of the film, not only of friendship or of work relations but the larger, casual, yet essential public one we move through daily on the streets, is also permeated by hostility, the response of violence always a hair-trigger away. It is a very grim world on every level—and yet continually informed by humor, from the large joke of the killer's being held up by a traffic tie-up or having to ask directions, to innumerable little jokes: a mother asking her kid for his crayon to write down the new site for the killing, interactions in a black bar, or in a cemetery (Mikey's continual apologizing as he steps on graves, Nicky's yelling for his mother when he can't find her tombstone in the darkness).

*Mikey and Nicky* can be read as a meta-text on the male buddy film. Working as richly with the reality of macho maleness as the women directors discussed later do with women's bonding, perhaps May's very femaleness gives her a special insight into the nature of the male bond. She also uses classic American iconography to create a strong metaphor for modern heartless America. And because the focus is on bonding, the film increasingly turns on the character of Mikey, though it starts out as Nick's film, beginning with Nick's terror and ending with his death, literally placed at Mikey's door. The Nick who early captivates us through Cassavetes' personal beauty and charm, crazy though that also is, gradually is revealed to be a man who cares for no one, who uses people and ignores them when he is riding high, a good-time boy who humiliates everyone—his wife, his mistress. The question of how a thirty-year-old friendship could bring Mikey to the point of fingering his one and only friend is gradually answered by these recognitions, and by Mikey's resentment of Nick's having everything, having always had everything, getting it all easily, even getting Mikey's father's love as Mikey himself seems never to have gotten it.

The film's ultimate subject is a powerful one: the emotional destitution that lasts a lifetime as a result of who was the favored one, of how the parent related to the child. In having it father and son, rather than mother and son or father and daughter, May can again make it tough, not melodrama—and in a way minimize gender—since maleness translates into a universalizing of emotions that femaleness is not yet seen as allowing. Perhaps May focusses on two men because her years in Hollywood and familiarity with the industry have taught her that a serious psychological study requires framing by a genre tale, of action and excitement, at least having it look like that in the packaging. May herself, when asked publically why she works with men characters rather than with women, says she wishes she could work with women characters but that it simply comes out the other way when she writes, she doesn't know why. But it seems to me the fine feeling she has for each character and for what goes on between the two men indicates the rightness of the choice for her.

Mikey isn't fully honest about the sources of his despair but the film makes these sufficiently clear to us—wounds most human beings can only deal with obliquely. Mikey is the one not even his own father liked, let alone the Jewish hood boss Resnick. When the friends confront one another finally, who has done what, or not done what, for whom, each feels the other has given him nothing in return for what was given—a web of feelings that does exist in families and in close old relationships and is effectively caught here.

The bonding theme is powerful because these two, it becomes clear, are really all each one has, one another's only friend when it comes down to it. Nick's words about how no one else can share the early history they shared turn out to be true. Mikey, in his fancy house, with good wife and child, seems utterly isolated and pathetic by the film's conclusion. His unwavering maintenance of that isolation, his unrelenting barring of his door against Nick's imploring and banging, conveys how deep the pain and humiliation have gone. There is no ambivalence whatever in him about his friend's destruction. But we too view Nick's petitions with detachment, learning what we have learned about him. So, as in all of Elaine May's films, it is not only hard to take sides but also hard to like anyone at all. Reminding us again, as Woody Allen does too, of the pain under the comic mask, over and over she returns to themes of degradation, an unreconciled darkness under the humor.

While both earlier films, though working through the male's point of view, give women characters almost equal weight to the male hero, in *Mikey and Nicky* women have much more minor roles. On the other hand, Elaine May offers unusually sympathetic images of women characters in this film. Nick's mistress, with an odd looking, slightly beaten, out-of-focus face, to whom Nick brings Mikey, is no blond floozy, earth mother, or other usual cliche, but a distinctive person. Her dignity, her interest in the news—for which Mikey condescends to her, the pitiful insecurity that drives her to beg Nick to say he loves her, her edgy outrage as Mikey propositions her at Nick's instigation—all convey a strong sense of personhood. The sequence is characterized by humiliation, though also by her indignant refusal to be treated that way. Elaine May's sensitivity here seems related to her being a woman director. Still, the women in all three May films are disturbingly masochistic. Though the mistress in *Mikey and Nicky* does angrily accuse Nick of putting the other hoods up to trying to make her, she ends up being worried he is mad at her. Nick's other female victim, his ex-wife, another delicate though brief portrait, convincingly conveys her anger at him for years of neglect and abuse, but she dissolves into love and pain for him, and also ends up an exercise in docile female masochism— as he fast-talks and cons his way even in the shadow of death. Even Mikey's nice ordinary matron wife, though totally peripheral like the others, is like the others memorable. May manages to make her distinctive in her ordinariness, and to convey a woman who is warmly supportive without being able to genuinely understand either her husband or their life.

That Elaine May did not stay within the formulaic limits of genre predictability doubtless explains some of the difficulty this film had. (May has said the company expected a summer comedy, and not only refused to distribute the film, but entangled May in a lawsuit over it.) The film's genre surface's promise of much mindless action and violence is not kept. It has something far more intriguing in mind, working instead on an intimate personal level, to gradually, subtly, unfold the inner dynamics of relationship—a little like the structure of Mike Nichol's (Edward Albee's) *Who's Afraid of Virginia Woolf:* a stripping down, in a single night, to reveal the reality of each of the two men, their relationship, those closest to them, the nature of their lives. Vincent Canby's attack on *Mikey and Nicky*—the same Canby who loved *The Heartbreak Kid* ("a first-class American comedy"[7]) and even loved *A New Leaf* before it (a film "touched by a fine and knowing madness," hopefully "the first of many films Miss May will direct, write, and star in"[8])—seems as much a reaction to Cassavetes as to May, when he accuses the film of the "busy banality that Mr. Cassavetes' own films . . . fall into when the actors take over from the director."[9] But the style of *Mikey and Nicky* is not Cassavetes', and usurper of films as he can be (one thinks of his attention-grabbing role in Mazursky's *Tempest*), Elaine May's control, economy, and shaping are unmistakably in charge here. While no doubt some improvisation was contributed by Cassavetes and Falk, whose general territory this is, May says the film was too complicated to permit much. The screenplay was not written for the two actors, although when they were signed on to the project May rewrote lines to incorporate their speech rhythms. While Canby's devastating put-down of *Mikey and Nicky* concludes with a kind of compliment: "Miss May is a witty, gifted, very intelligent director. It took guts to attempt a film like this, but she failed."[10] It seems to me she did not fail at all, in the indeed gutsy new direction this film represents for her.

The concept of years of hurt, indifference, envy—and the comradery of irreplaceable memory (but little else positive)—constitute a brilliant angle on bonding. Such bonding—as easily that of sisters, or women cousins, or friends, or a man and a woman (critics have even suggested that the "N" and "M" of the title characters allude to Nichols and May)—is certainly a corrective to the vague idealization of friendship in a film like *Entre Nous*. It offers the ultimate (paranoid?) nightmare that those we are closest to and have deepest ties to are the ones who are bent on destroying us, all the while they smile and reassure. May commented at MOMA about the film: "Nobody fingers you but your best friend—they always do it, and they never leave town."

*Mikey and Nicky* is exciting evidence of growth and of new ambition and confidence—from a director who, though not from an independent film background, took a major risk. That risk certainly paid off richly in artistic growth. Whether May was subsequently penalized in jobs and time, as she speaks of being, for reasons of artistic courage or for other reasons, is not fully clear. What is clear is that such a difficult experience had to have a sizable impact on *Ishtar*, and on May's functioning under the pressures of that film's terrifyingly large budget. With stakes this high and with so recent and shattering an industry fiasco (though an artistic victory) behind her, the pressures must have been incredible in the direction of safe, light entertainment. Warren Beatty as producer made the project possible (his fabled acumen surely not misplaced here, whatever the outcome), his respect for May deriving from their having often worked together. (Dustin Hoffman also worked with her on *Tootsie*.) In contrast to the grandiosity that downed Coppola, May tried on the contrary to hide out(and like Nicky avoid being destroyed?)—not only giving no interviews and having nothing to do with the media, but even asking that her name be left out of stories about the film! Perhaps that very process enabled word of mouth to sentence her to a *Heaven's Gate*-style fiasco even while she was still working on the film, long before almost anyone had been allowed to see it.

*Ishtar* seems uncannily, unconsciously self-reflexive, its joke of the two men's choosing Morocco over Honduras because it's *safer* (only to be plunged immediately into life-threatening peril on every side) feeling like May's apparent opting for safety in this film by keeping it light, by keeping it busy with action and plot, by the obsessive care she brought to every aspect of the project (in retrospect the very choices that got her into trouble). Yet not only do many much worse films fail, but many much worse films succeed. *Ishtar* is amusing, has wonderful moments, and whatever its serious problems with plot-line confusions, insufficient sense of spontaneity, lack of some deeper inner coherence—its $50 million budget is what subjected it to microscopic attention and created a level of expectation it couldn't satisfy.

With the pairing of Beatty and Hoffman, who became close friends during the making of the film, May returned to the light entertainment Hollywood genre of the Hope–Crosby *Road to Rio–Zanzibar–Morocco* films, about two second-rate entertainers moving from adventure to adventure. May brings to this structure a level of high intelligence and verve that it never itself had. The genre takes May back to a show-business world she knows thoroughly, having spent her whole life in it, and she does very well with all that, especially with the collaborative efforts of the ne'er-do-well pair, from their voices creating the central song—"Telling the truth is a dangerous business"—even before the film starts, while the Columbia logo is still on the screen, through the first fifteen minutes of the film. The sequences with Rogers and Scott in New York, before the trip to Ishtar, is May in high professional form—fast witty cuts perfectly timed—humor with a dark edge of pain. The witty series of song routines, with the audience of kids looking unresponsive, even stunned (the old Hollywood putting-on-the-show film and also an expression within the film of any filmmaker's nightmare of failure, especially with the crucial youth market); the fading out of the bar with Sinatra's "Set 'em up Joe" to the earlier lives of each man; Dustin's song for the elderly couple, written by May; Weston's funny agent; Chuck's (Dustin's) windowledge despair sequence; Beatty's limpness (like an air doll, as some critics have described the understated wit of *his* performance)—this is fine, funny material. Lyle's absurd awe for Chuck is charmingly expressed in the interplay on the pronunciation of "shmuck," ending with Dustin staring intently at the persistently mispronouncing Lyle and patting him on the back with a kindly encouraging untrue "Better," and Lyle responding with a breathlessly worshipful "You really know the lingo."

The whole concept of these two, stumbling along with what a director of moister sensibility might have affirmed as an incorrigible human hopefulness, which someone other than May might even have turned into a homage to performers (as Dustin and Sydney Pollack do in *Tootsie*), is funny. Despite a history of failure and second-rateness and clear lack of talent, they persist, remain playful and upbeat, and in the face of the most terrible situations still keep triumphantly turning their most desperate experience into songs, though (wryly) songs as banal and cliched as if the two had never experienced anything other than Hallmark cards—or indeed the most trite, pop Hollywood movies. A running joke of the film is that, work-obsessed as they are, in the show-business way of old Hollywood, they keep commenting that this is their best work, even while dying of thirst in the desert, even as they are about to be killed by a charming emir, or a friendly CIA agent, or an equally friendly beauty from a terrorist group.

As in the world of *Mikey and Nicky*, everyone in *Ishtar* (named for the goddess of Love and War) is spying on one another, has secrets, is trying to kill someone else, even the beautiful girl whom the two helped, even these two best friends in the world. Despite the theme song—"Telling the truth can be bad news"—the film doesn't permit one to see the pair as innocents accidentally thrown into a shark's world, since they too deceive one another (though not for really hurtful ends). But as the beggars and passersby and passing cars all turn out to be spies, these two themselves become just another part of an entirely untrustworthy and destructive world. There are hilarious moments here too, from the generally smarmy performance of Charles Grodin, to a scene with vultures who work on spec, to Beatty's Lyle kneading Shira's breasts in amazement as she, in boy's garb, talks Third World revolutionary politics. May attempts through political satire to lampoon a larger canvas of human absurdity: with a CIA so inept that the one group in the crowd it thinks are real tourists are the ones who hold up the pair, a CIA that says contradictory things from one phone call to another right after, and a CIA that, when the Secretary of State is invoked, asks with astonishment, how would *he* know (about anything)?

Yet it is almost as if May were continually remembering to back off, not to make it too dark and astringently keen (after *Mikey and Nicky*). Perhaps the project got too vast—just reading the long lists of credits is dizzying—to fully control. (And what woman director has ever before had the resources to attempt a film on an epic scale, except Leni Reifenstahl, who with her legendary organizing energy certainly was able to hold it all together.) Perhaps the heavy plotting and action, geared to the box office, was something May wasn't sufficiently adept at. Perhaps darker notes—could she have risked them on a deeper level—might have led her to a center in herself that would have held it all together better and justified it by a grandness of design or a profound note struck. And even as the film actually ended up, were it not for the money issue, *Ishtar* would simply be a light modest May film, bearing some interesting relations to earlier May work.

As it turns out, 1987 put both Elaine May and Susan Seidelman in positions unique for American women directors, May with her fourth film and Seidelman with her third. For the first women to experience big-league mainstream American filmmaking, both attempts failed. But like Geraldine Ferraro's vice presidential campaign, the attempt—and to have had the chance to try—was itself exhilarating and a major gain. Nothing is more bizarre than the promise of that big league, looking like everything is possible, offering what appears to be the most open opportunities, but actually fraught with severely mutilating limits and dangers.

Both the gain of having broken this final barrier, and the upshot (dismaying both for box-office failure, with its possible impact on future works, and for the quality of what was done) again suggests perhaps that freedom really lies in keeping the stakes smaller. Both women made much better films when they had less to do with them, and therefore needed to reach only smaller-than-blockbuster audiences.

Elaine May's past achievement as filmmaker is larger than most remember; and her potential for creating more important films remains large. One hopes she can in future make films that allow her to grow—perhaps low-budget films—not as Coppola is doing, almost as if his spirit has been destroyed in the process of reduction, but as a viable way to keep that spirit venturing.

# THE FIRST FEMINIST MAINSTREAM FILMMAKERS: JOAN MICKLIN SILVER AND CLAUDIA WEILL

At a women directors' film festival in New York not long ago, Joan Micklin Silver and Claudia Weill appeared on respective evenings following screenings of *Hester Street* (1975) and *Girlfriends* (1978). As noted earlier, each spoke of her work on these films as out of another time altogether, a time totally impossible for women. Both directors talked independently about the ordeal of doing what they did when they did it, as if astonished at this bold, absurdly innocent, younger self undertaking such an impossible task. They conveyed a poignant sense of themselves as having no idea what they were getting themselves into, of how the industry worked and what it wanted, just doing their project and then finding that no one would touch it. Both spoke of staggering under debts and money problems, saved only by prestigious foreign film festivals' acclaim—and European distribution money in Silver's case—which allowed them then to open in New York. When they then went back to the American film industry, armed with that European recognition, they had to fight bitter struggles (Silver describes one over even the name of *Chilly Scenes of Winter*) against the attempt to turn their work into the standard product again.

## Joan Micklin Silver

Joan Micklin Silver's debut film, *Hester Street*, came out in 1975, before *Girlfriends*, its feminist content less clear, its impact less startling, because more disguised under the historical ethnicity of its subject matter. But the choice of so Jewish a subject matter, and the use of Yiddish through much of the film, was itself bold and startling. It is in fact intriguing that the many women directors included in this chapter are almost all Jewish—Elaine May, Weill, Seidelman, Chopra, Heckerling and Gottlieb, Streisand, and, alas, Goldie Hawn. If that Jewishness figures in their films, it tends less toward the satirical treatment noteworthy in the work of Jewish male writers and directors (with May's *Heartbreak Kid* an exception), than toward sympathy or out and out celebration, as in Silver's *Hester Street*.

With *Hester Street*, Silver thought she might only have the money to make one film in her life, money gathered by her businessman-husband acting as producer—and she wanted that one film to be a homage to the beautiful strong women in her family, both of her parents' Russian-Polish immigrant generation, and that of her grandparents. *Hester Street* from Abraham Cahan's *Yekl, A Tale of the Ghetto* (1896), instead of turning envyingly toward the gentile world like *Heartbreak Kid*, turns back toward the traditional world of European Jewry in a way unusual among American Jews. It celebrates *shtetl* values above the new American values, which are seen as materialistic, placing a peddlar above a yeshiva *bucher*. The heroine Gitl affirms those traditional values, from the married woman's wig, to salt in the pockets to ward off the evil eye, to her admiration of Mr. Bernstein for his learning and his writing of commentaries after his day at a sewing machine. She respects Bernstein for teaching Joey the Hebrew alphabet, as Jake teaches him to play baseball and to be a Yankee.

Yet no one is idealized in the film, certainly not the women. We see the divorce rabbi's wife making sure she gets money from Jake, and fussily picking hairs off her abstracted husband's jacket; we see the mean crowding of living conditions; and those who have lived in America for a while mocking those just coming over. To Mamie, alone in a foreign country, is attributed a calculation and unpleasant satisfaction with money-saving and the guarding of her nest egg, though she also has her own strength.

While the Cahan story was about a man who came to America, Silver was more interested in the woman's story, though Carol Kane's Gitl, despite a fine performance, is too fey for the earthiness of the women of that world. (The Cahan story describes Gitl as swarthy and peasant-like.) Gitl tries in every way she can to please Jake and continually fails, until, releasing herself from the confines of her corset, she laughs with pleasure over what she sees in the mirror and over the ridiculousness of her struggle. Starting out powerless and bewildered as a stranger in a strange land, Gitl develops a sense of her own dignity and increasingly shapes her own life. It is she who decides that she does not want Jake anymore, that she has had enough of him. It is she who makes the overture to Mr. Bernstein, she who gains a tidy sum from the divorce lawyer through her poise, enabling her to buy a store and make it run, while Mr. Bernstein gives lessons and studies Talmud. So she continues to live out the old values, but also gives the film a feminist emphasis, although the actual historic patterns themselves reveal strong women who took care of the worldly struggles and were dominant in the practical world. The women also show a solidarity, Mrs. Pochovny helping Gitl transform herself, like a mentor or mother, and fighting Jake for her as he gets unreasonable and unpleasant.

The other side of women's skill in handling the world is that the less macho man, gentle and always formally dressed, usually sitting and reading, is by far the more attractive man in *Hester Street*. (Streisand's casting her male lead in *Yentl* as appealingly sexy as a hip Hollywood actor involved no such risk). The character of Bernstein was a large risk for Silver. So, too, Claudia Weill's heroine Susan represents a risk in *Girlfriends*, not to speak of Eli Wallach's middle-aged rabbi, cast in that same film as Susan's romantic interest. There was, it needs to be said, an unembarrassed courage in both directors about these strongly ethnic castings. Silver has spoken of *Hester Street* as the result of total ignorance. In narrow commercial terms of what is likely to sell in the film industry, and perhaps also in some technical areas, this may be true. But though badly lit and overacted in places, *Hester Street* is a fine debut film and it says something about the new opening up of the 1970s that, given all the Jewish input into the film industry from its origins to its present, this may be the one film one thinks of that celebrates the Jewish immigrant experience.

The other two feature films Silver went on to make show her range to be surprising, in a quiet way, apart from the gains she made in technical skills. *Between the Lines* (1977) is a charming, winning comedy about a late 1960s' counterculture Boston newspaper, *The Backbay Mainline*, its demise the demise of a time (well before *The Big Chill*, that slick Hollywood rendering of related material, and before *The Return of The Secaucus Seven* as well). Silver catches the high spirits and idealism of the 1960s without portentousness, keeping the tone light and human, with a nice flow and an effective use of music. And while the book and screenplay are the product of men, the film sounds some interesting feminist notes. Silver surprises with the terrific way she films a striptease, and by following this sequence with a charged interview with the stripper by a couple from the newspaper, once romantically involved—Harry, sensitively played by John Heard, and his ex-girlfriend photographer Abbie (Lindsay Crouse). With several astute touches Silver conveys the struggle of wills between these two, Harry's fury over Abbie's telling him to take off his jacket, or over Abbie's too aggressive questioning of the stripper, moving in on his turf, and her arguing he is threatened by the rapport she establishes with the woman. These sharply accurate interplays extend as much sympathy to the man's sense of things as to the woman's self-assertion; indeed the man is the one who has the serious work crisis in the film.

Yet the two women in the film who are involved in couples have their own important dramas as they continually fight for their own place. Laura, also on the *Mainline* staff, is played by Gwen Welles (the film's casting is an appealing and sensitive mix of fine actors who convincingly convey a 1960s' community). Laura lives with an unsympathetic reporter, now writing a book, who makes traditional demands on her, writes too slickly—for the movies!—and who uses lovemaking to keep her from work. There is a good small scene in which Laura tries to inject her voice as Michael, full of himself and his book contract, speaks for her, to her visible dismay; and in the end Laura decides to follow Michael to New York even though she feels she shouldn't—situations sharply observed by a feminist director who at the same time does not give the film as a whole a polemic tone. The good couple (Heard/Crouse) resolve their differences. Silver opts for couples though subtly cognizant of the difficulties they pose, especially for women— which is really a major subject of each film. She also opts for gentle, intellectual men, John Heard a charmer in the central role here. While only lightly political, the film evokes memories of the joy of 1960s' activism, and the sadness and loss in this little world with its passing; and it offers no easy, upbeat closing sense that the private world really consoles for loss of the public world. Its comedy works well too: the incorrigibly hustling

Max (Jeff Goldblum); a final ribbing of his complacency and also that of a young, foolishly solemn would-be muckraker, both basking in small moments of celebrity; a funny set-piece spoofing conceptual art; and a general texture of quiet wittiness and buoyant joking. The film is pleasurable for its intelligence and literacy, though the film industry seems to regard these qualities as having as limited an audience as a black and white film in Yiddish coming out in 1975.

For her third feature film, *Chilly Scenes of Winter*, Silver worked with a novel by Ann Beattie, herself doing the screenplay, and with women in a number of the production roles. *Chilly Scenes* is a love drama, glossier than Silver's other work, doubtless to demonstrate bankability, but again gracefully, intelligently made. It focuses on the male protagonist, the attractive John Heard again, the camera looking at the world from his side, in terms of his need for and obsession with the woman, Laura—although Laura is also important to the film, and considerable sympathy is extended to her. This time there is no visible feminism. Laura's major quality is a lack of self-esteem; the older women in the hospital are competitive and savage. But this capable, even touching, film can convey both real whimsy and spontaneity, difficult to communicate without strain; and it is also full of a growing pathos and pain of loss, everyone's broken-hearted fix on someone they can't have, waifs seeking nourishment. The tone is one of whimsical desperation, of people on the edge, and yet it is light and funny—no small feat to catch such a note. But most special of all is the film's way of dealing with the interpersonal textures of daily life, the moment by moment texture—just what American directors usually can't do—of what passes between people, through their eyes, bodies, tiniest gestures, the subtlest interplays in the quietest ways.

Silver continues to work productively, directing in theatre and TV drama: a filmed version of F. Scott Fitzgerald's "Bernice Bobs Her Hair"; "Finnigan Begin Again" with Robert Preston and Mary Tyler Moore, about a middle-aged love affair; other theatrical film projects in the future. Seeing her films again is a reminder of how much spirit and intelligence is in them, of Silver as a valuable national source of the precious adult film art we need and lack here.

### Claudia Weill

Claudia Weill made *Girlfriends* in 1978 after a decade of working as a camerawoman, in itself an unusual role for a woman, and of directing short films, primarily documentaries: her half-hour *Joyce at 34*, in 1972, with Joyce Chopra, about the situation of a pregnant director—Chopra herself—trying to negotiate a personal with a professional life; her documentary on China, "The Other Half of the Sky," for Shirley MacLaine. *Girlfriends* began shortly after that project, first as a documentary about growing up Jewish in New York City, funded by grants, and then as a ten-minute fictional short from a script Weill wrote with Vicki Polon. In the end distributed by Warner, yet with all the integrity of the independent film it was, *Girlfriends* made a mainstream impact partly because of its quality, and partly because it appeared at exactly the right moment. Mazursky's *An Unmarried Woman* came out at the same time, after a decade during which Hollywood gave us only male buddy films, all the ferment of feminism apparently having scared the men in the industry away from that material. Like most of Mazursky's work, *Unmarried Woman* is a decent film that explores a woman's situation with seriousness and honesty, but with an overlay of Hollywood smoothness and with patriarchal premises still underlying the film, despite the director's attempt to confront those.

*Girlfriends*, on the other hand, talked with a surprising new voice that even now feels fresh, distinctive, disarmingly personal. First, the subject was striking and genuinely feminist: Weill's young heroine struggles to shape her professional life as a photographer. And then the attractive New York Jewish quality of its central figure is very different from standard film images of young Jewish women (*à la Heartbreak Kid*), less stereotyped, more unique and appealing, at the same time ethnically recognizable. Further, the look and implied personality of Melanie Mayron, who plays Susan Weinblatt, is central to the film—her wild hair and unfashionable glasses, her too-round face and irregular teeth, her attractively clumsy gait, her intelligence, lovely whimsy and hunger for life, and intense work ambition—and the fact that all this makes her beautiful. She is full of a precious individuality unusual in film, and rooted here in the particularity of her New York Jewish origins.

The film is about work, an area of life that American films generally do less well with than, say, Italian films.[11] Weill begins *Girlfriends*, after a series of still photos of the two friends' faces tight in a series of frames, with Susan behind a camera, in the darkened room where her roommate Anne is still asleep on a mattress on the floor. The next scene, in the rabbi's office, again begins with Susan behind the camera photographing a bar mitzvah boy shaking hands with the rabbi. Her character is thus defined above all through her work, as a woman with a camera. Further, that beginning sequence of one woman taking photographs of another, leaning over her sleeping form with a camera, with intensity and intimacy and total concentration, is again the paradigm of woman looking at woman in these films. The film as a whole is after all Weill's examination of the development of her central woman character, and of the relationship between the two women and their struggles, but especially Susan's struggle, the center of our interest, to launch herself professionally. If *Smithereens* is Portrait of the Filmmaker as a Young Girl being initiated into the hustle, *Girlfriends* is as well, less ambiguously, with more realism and less sense of the dirtiness.

Not that Weill glamorizes work. She honestly pictures what it is to work hard, to learn to push oneself and promote one's work (in this film's particularity, in Soho galleries), to cope with competitiveness. She portrays having to do time-serving jobs that you dislike just to survive, having to lie to get past the front desk, having to keep your antennae out and ask everyone about work, having to accept unsavory compromises—a magazine editor (obviously even more usual an experience in the film business) who alters your work in a way that makes it no longer yours and yet the beginner's being afraid to say so lest the editor not take it at all. Anyone who has done work—particularly work about art, with integrity—in the real world has experienced some of this, and Weill's incorporation of all these small truths is what gives the film its fine texture, detail, authenticity. She shows the disappointments, the loneliness, the joy of finally getting through, of achievement and recognition.

The film begins as though focussed on a close friendship between two women, and does hold that thread and return to it throughout the film. It genuinely evokes shared moments, of poems read aloud for response and support, of the pain of not getting that, of work triumphs shared, of fears and jealousy, of a sense of betrayal through the placing of friendship very much second to marriage claims, and always of loyalty. Still (and Weill herself speaks of this), the director is not very much interested in Annie as a person. The character ends up serving mainly to dramatize the conventional course of life Susan repudiates, and the changes underway in recent America that make even such a woman uncomfortable within the conventions. Yet even with Annie the issue of work is raised at the very start, through Annie's reading her poetry to Susan, and not being able to deal with her critical response. But mostly Annie's life changes allow Susan to raise questions in the film about getting married and having a child, to greet both of Annie's announcements with deep disturbance—perhaps for the first time in American film history?—because they mean forgoing her writing. Susan, scornful of the old "gracious living" marriage ideal, is like one of her photos, glimpsed fleetingly, of a girl turning away from the bride, the bride herself totally covered as within a white shroud. Susan jokes about dropping the bouquet.

Yet the film harbors no cliches. If all the marriages in the movie are floundering, living alone is not idealized but seen as painfully lonely. Viewing the film again after a decade during which so much has happened, one is especially struck by Susan's vulnerability, by how much of a struggle it is for her to tolerate being alone and on her own, by how much she collapses. Susan thoughtfully says to Annie that she likes living alone, with an immediate cut to her picking up the stray girl Celia, an action that obviously says the opposite. One of the refreshing things about the film is that it makes no attempt to bridge these moments, doesn't even draw attention to the discrepancy, just lets it sit and assumes our intelligence in making the appropriate surmises—an intelligence on the film's part, and an understatement, that is integral to the film's quality. Yet for all Susan's loneliness (struggling with bars over her window, crying alone in front of the TV— or after her disappointment with the rabbi, walking down a street past a kissing couple) there is also her fierce struggle to maintain her self, the crucial other side of the equation, as when she gets into a fight with Eric because she won't give up her apartment even though he thinks it silly to pay two rents.

The final crisis of that issue occurs after she has spent the night arguing with Eric about their relationship, and then realizes she forgot to supervise her first gallery show. She cries out in frustration at again losing herself. The struggle for selfhood in these terms seems very much to belong to the early years of feminist films—and Weill's unwillingness to call this a feminist film is puzzling, because if this isn't one, what would be? At the same time, Susan's struggle for individuation applies not only to the love affair, but to Susan's friendship with Anne—and her ultimate capacity to allow Anne a separate life with which she can share her.

The film extends considerable sympathy to men. The boyfriend Eric is charmingly rendered, especially through the playfulness Weill is very good at. Susan's yearning for a father seems to underlie her interest in the married rabbi, played by Eli Wallach with the touching passionate yearnings of a respectable, humane, middle-aged man. The two share collusive winks and jokes about the Jewish world they work together in, from Jeffrey's pushy mother to chicken-liver Torahs, though the humor is strikingly gentle and affectionate, with no contempt for the Jewish world of weddings and bar mitzvahs that is so easy a target for various (again largely male) writers and directors. But gentle as is the film's humor toward Jewish excesses, at the same time the feminist point is made that Jewish women could not talk to God. The feminism in *Hester Street* accepts the traditional definitions of women's strength in the Jewish world and does not begin to engage that issue.

Most striking and fresh about this film, though, was not only the kind of female central figure it focuses on, and not only its interest in her work life, as opposed to her love and sex life, but also her friendship with another woman, itself even more unlikely a central subject at that time for an American film. Despite the old Hollywood showgirl films like *Stage Door* (using the glamour of showbiz to portray the bonds among a community of women), despite occasional glimpses of women supportive of one another (like Mildred and Eve Arden's Ida in *Mildred Pierce*), the women we are most likely to remember from classic Hollywood films are the Bette Davis–Miriam Hopkins kind of old friends in *Old Acquaintance*, each forever envious of what the other has, particularly of The Man. If they sit face to face in the final sequence, it is only through the defeat of the whole world's having moved away and left them to each other. In *Girlfriends*, with the two friends struggling to share their lives despite separation, and Susan remembering her friend at her moment of work triumph (her first show), the final scene before the fireplace—which is surely an homage to *Old Acquaintance*— is, more, a reminder of the immense difference. The two women laughing together, in an intimate bond that excludes the entering husband, have earned their friendship, which is not just the last resort of two old maids, but an achievement, gained over obstacles and differences, a yearning to celebrate and commiserate together, something won, not lost. It is in fact one of the momentous gains resulting from women's altered sense of themselves as a result of feminism.

The closeness between the friends is carefully placed on heterosexual ground when Susan rejects the sexual approach of a drifting waif of a girl, Celia, whom she takes into her apartment. Indeed, the line separating really close bonds of friendship from erotic attraction is an issue that haunts this book, recurring almost as often as the motif of deep bonds between women recurs in these films by women directors. Weill, when queried about this treatment of a lesbian, speaks instead of a spectrum in the film of ways in which women are open to new experiences, with Celia more venturesome than Susan. Even Julie, the older, more experienced photographer in the film, is emerging from a divorce. A mentor, she gives Susan advice on how to operate in the art world, admits jealousy as Susan learns, and the two women finally help one another. Susan, after her own photos are accepted, is able in turn to help Julie, conveying a sense of women networking. When Julie is involved in setting up her own show, the brisk professionalism with which she takes charge of her own situation is clearly meant to contrast with Susan's leaving it to the others, first deliberately and later unconsciously, and then being anguished because the show did not turn out as she meant it to. The caring between women extends to Susan's gentleness toward Celia's fragility and neediness, though that is never sentimentalized. Celia's irritating ways are also clearly revealed; her lack of a self is what most needs exorcizing in Susan.

On the other hand, over-professionalism as a problem becomes a subject for Weill's second film, *It's My Turn*, as she examines the double pull of professional commitments and yearning for a personal life—the two necessarily conflicting in real life in so all-consuming a work as film–directing is for women. This time with a $7 million budget (as compared with the $140,000, painfully strung together over a long period of time, with which Weill made *Girlfriends*), and with a screenplay again written by a woman, Eleanor Bergstein, *It's My Turn* is the glossier film Weill got to do for Columbia as a result of *Girlfriends'* success. Through Jill Clayburgh Weill creates a far more homogenized heroine in her bid for larger audience access, as well as a romantic male lead (Michael Douglas) who is a baseball player. Despite these concessions to commercial survival, the film is done with wit and charm, a winning, lively pace, even a waywardness full of light quips that reminds one of *Girlfriends*. The heroine here is again dealing with advancement in her profession, this time as a university mathematics professor—perhaps because the problematic issue is her detachment. Her real restlessness though concerns a long-term relationship—with a jokey Charles Grodin—that lacks commitment and that she feels she must change. The wedding of her widower father, to whom she is deeply attached, and her attraction to the son of the woman her father is marrying, all set in process a kind of life crisis for the Jill Clayburgh heroine, a questioning of her values. Asked by a *New York Times* interviewer whether she and Eleanor Bergstein were telling audiences, and women in particular, in *It's My Turn* that feminism has gone too far, that the liberated life isn't all it's cracked up to be, Weill answered:

The film isn't meant to hit you over the head with a message, though there's a message in there somewhere if you can decode it. It's about a girl who has negotiated her personal life around the idea of space rather than intimacy, to accommodate her career more than try to forge an emotional connection, a family connection, in her life. There are people . . . so involved in cultivating themselves or their career or their place in the world that they are totally incapable of dealing with another person, of listening to another person, of forming any kind of binding love relationship or . . . nurturing relationship. And so to me that film is about the need to pay attention to that side of things as well, not one at the expense of another.[12]

Whether because of this need in Weill herself—opting to tend to her private gardens for a while, or the fact that the box office returns of *It's My Turn* were insufficient for the big studios (despite good reviews, despite its having earned nearly $2 million in its first three weeks of release, and its being such a capable film for all its compromises)—Weill has been noticably absent from feature filmmaking the last few years, spending them instead directing several plays by other people in New York, getting married, having a baby. However, she is happily in process of return, back making a film—but on the West Coast, suggesting major changes underway. She speaks of working with genre ideas, on a thriller with heavy plotting but subtle texture as a way of getting a vision in, while also trying for action and suspense. She doubtless is coming back into a more supportive climate, with many more women directing than when she started. Her first two films, despite their different levels of expressiveness, have the autobiographical underpinning of an interesting woman's development, and hopefully her next project will permit her to create something real, and thereby permit us to watch her further development. There would be a satisfying justice if the new opening out that both she and Joan Micklin Silver were instrumental in beginning were to allow both of them to fully realize what their earlier work promised.

## SUSAN SEIDELMAN

Susan Seidelman's *Smithereens*, in the fresh conception of its central female figure and its visual vitality, is another independent debut film that announced the presence of a major new woman director. It is not surprising that it was the first American independent film accepted for official competition in the history of the Cannes Film Festival, despite its low-budget look and some flat stiffness in its acting. The film gives us a heroine who never stops moving, skinny and fragile-looking but full of explosive nervous energy and relentlessness, very unpleasant and wonderful at the same time. There is humor throughout the film, and humor in her, even in the terrific outrageous punk-rocker get-ups she wears, very short skirts, odd tops, bright colors, wild black-and-white checkered sunglasses, red converse sneakers. She is always busy, in the opening sequences plastering images of herself all over subway cars, involved in self-promotion, talking the language of dealmaking, appointments, L.A. trips. Indeed, the character suggests the grimmer aspects of what it must feel like to be a filmmaker trying to break in, seen with harsh honesty.

It is in many ways not a pretty picture. Seidelman has Susan Berman play Wren flat and hard, mouth a slash of bright red lipstick, nothing gentle or tender ever visible in her, her relations to people built only on using them, to further her career or simply to enable her to survive. At the same time we soon understand that she is busy with nothing at all, that her hustling is built on nothing. In that important way and some others she is clearly not a Portrait of the Filmmaker as a Young Woman—but nevertheless the connection to the movie business seems to me very much there and much of what gives the film its power, and the character her poignance for us. Because the truly remarkable thing is that we care about her, we are very interested by her, all through the film. She keeps our concern through all her manipulations, and by the film's conclusion she moves us to feelings of pain for her as a lost one, one who will never make it anywhere. So in this odd way, though the character does nothing, the film is above all about a woman whose work is everything, and for whom love—again refreshingly—means nothing at all. She is a heroine who is, as Carrie Rickey notes,[13] like no heroine we have ever seen in the movies before; she is a weasel, in the tradition—as Rickey also rightly notes—of such unsavory figures as Scorsese's heroes (e.g., the de Niro character in *King of Comedy*).[14] Seidelman's character is perhaps even more complicated because one feels tenderly toward her, at least as a woman spectator; one is in some way charmed by her, even though the film makes no obvious attempt whatever to charm us. It is a feat to work on all these levels at once, and to manage not only not to alienate us, but to hold our sympathy.

I think it has to do with the degree to which Wren is active, a feisty fighter—and her unabashed self-advertising in a zany New York street way (without at all feeling derivative) like the posters she pastes up everywhere, or the red spray paint with which she paints her name on walls with arrows leading to it. Or the idiosyncratic ways she shows what appears to be jealousy, or at least wanting a woman out of the way, by burning off half of someone's picture of a couple. It has to do with her chutzpah, pushing and bluffing her way into the Peppermint Lounge, maneuvering to get people to let her use their apartments, pleading but in a flat affectless way so she never sounds in trouble but like she has a million other resources, which is in fact what she is always saying. There's something that seems valiant about that, or about her loony bright plumage, struggling through all the perils of Lower East Side New York all on her own, through those dark mean streets, trudging tenaciously with those wild little red sneakers and crazy outfits. The valiant feeling of this film is related to that of the woman drifter in Varda's *Vagabond* (or the heroine of Bette Gordon's *Variety* who stalks 42nd St. sex shops at night)—the sense of a vulnerable woman entirely exposed to the harshness of the world: in *Vagabond* to the worst that nature, in the form of winter, can do; in *Smithereens* to the worst that human society can do, in the form of New York sleaze. However, for a New Yorker the film's treatment of all that is almost unbelievably benign:[15] (What sweet Montana boy would ever survive sleeping in an unlocked van in the isolated street lots that the character Paul sleeps in?) The valiant feeling also comes from the quality of the humor, a strung-out prostitute who gets into Paul's van with him, offers him a series of erotic services for descending prices, and finally offers him her chicken salad sandwich and reminisces about the clay turtles she liked to make in school. It's a zany humor that keeps light, doesn't insist, never feels forced. Again, when Wren seeks Paul for one last time, only to find his van filled with a strange assortment of prostitutes, a pimp, a very gay man—as Wren walks away they are listening to one person reading movie-magazine gossip aloud, in *True Romance* cliches, just barely audible on the soundtrack, about Candice Bergen, and about Louis Malle having a lot to recommend him to any girl.

Part of Wren's poignancy comes from her aloneness. We know she merits that aloneness by the unscrupulousness with which she deals with people. It also results from her having turned her back on her family, full of contempt apparently for the New Jersey backwater she comes out of, ethnic and working class, this in itself an important change for a number of heroines in recent American women's films.[16] Marriage is totally rejected here, represented through the comic-strip ugliness of Wren's sister and brother-in-law's marriage, constant fighting, the woman smoking away in haircurlers, the man engaged in obsessive car-polishing. These are perhaps cliches but they express Seidelman's very strong revulsion toward the only form of being "settled down" that is visible in the film.

The only other character who is stable and fairly normal is Paul, the boy from Montana. As in so many of these films by women, the men chosen as leads are enormously, unerringly attractive—both the good boy and the bad boy in this film. At first Paul and Wren seem the opposite poles of the world of the film. (*Desperately Seeking Susan* is built around the related, though different, pairing of Susan and the suburban girl.) Then *Smithereens* further develops the opposition that interests Seidelman when Eric, played by Richard Hell, comes on the scene with his slightly, excitingly, decadent and mocking face that makes Paul's decent good handsomeness seem too straight and boring, even on a simple physical level. And this is so even though we see that Wren and Eric are one of a kind, and that their sort of "using" behavior may even be built into the business they are trying to enter. Eric too lives in other people's places, is a parasite, marries someone apparently to get money from her. He gets money from Wren as well through a bizarrely funny incident of robbing a solid-citizen jerk, a man waiting until 11 p.m. to call his wife (for the rates to go down) or the cozily familiar way Wren recognizes a photo of "Jane and the kids" among his possessions after she and Eric have robbed him. Eric lies and betrays, but is nonetheless appealing. Paul cares about Wren, he's gentle and nurturing, he takes care of her wounds, he is goodlooking, but at the same time the director accepts, understands, her total indifference to him except as a last resort for a place to sleep. His idea of moving on to New Hampshire is exotically alien to her, as it would be bound to be, creature that she is of nighttime Lower-Eastside milieux that the film works with so beautifully: the streets like a bizarre painted landscape, the lights, the tenement fronts— all done stylishly with brilliant, wild, often primary colors and camera movements that are continuous engaging. New York City is Wren's context, the only world she could belong in, though Seidelman also makes clear that Wren's course is not a lifeward one. She has funny but apocalyptic dreams of the whole earth (except California) falling into a crack, and TV screens throughout the film are used to make a continual statement that the world is going to pieces, to Smithereens, as Eric's poster proclaims, though whether this condition applies to just Wren's life, or the whole milieux she is part of, or, as one of her dreams tells her, the whole world though they don't realize it yet—is not made clear by the film.

Wren's name also seems to suggest that she is as common as can be, a small ordinary bird, nothing special. Not one of those who can make it, but one of the many ordinary ones who will fail for the few who get through—and we witness her chilling decline. The final line of the film, spoken to Wren by a man trying to pick her up from a passing car, "Got anything better to do with your time?" is particularly disturbing, directed to someone who has so relentlessly hustled from frame to frame, has bouncily trudged on with those tenacious little red sneakers—and later on in the film, though weighed down by two big shopping bags containing all her possessions, has still kept moving. Indeed, through the later part of the film she seems a thin line away from being a bag lady. *Smithereens* is finally an exploration of the classic American theme of making it, and of failure, but transformed here, partly because seen through a woman's eyes, a unique vision of a woman's experience.

With *Desperately Seeking Susan*, Susan Seidelman's second film, we have the familiar situation of the poignant charm of the first film, done on a shoestring as an independent production, earning the director a second shot, more entertaining, but also more homogenized and bland, playing it safer. Seidelman in fact makes a charmer of her second film, and perhaps does as well as it is possible to do while still achieving a large success. She says of *Smithereens*, released five years after she graduated from New York University film school: "If I hadn't done *Smithereens*, it probably would have taken 10 years until I got to do a movie like *Desperately Seeking Susan*—if I'd get the chance at all. By nature, I'm impatient, so I decided to go out there and make a movie myself. And then I hoped that film would help me get other work."[17]

With *Smithereens* Seidelman gave every sense of having a distinctive vision, with themes of some depth, and at the same time the capacity to draw a wide youth audience to meet the necessary American box office demands. She bided her time before she chose her second film, although she was "sought out by Hollywood with offers to do dopey teen-age comedies."[18] Her second film, *Desperately Seeking Susan*, though it doesn't much extend our sense of what Seidelman can do, mines *Smithereens* and changes it, with a broader accessibility and acceptability in mind. The unpleasant, conventional New Jersey relatives are upped in class, less stylized, more smoothly caricatured. They become the heroine's—Roberta's—Spa-king-of-New-Jersey husband, Gary, and his sister—though indeed there's a comic book/fable quality about both films, which Seidelman is entirely conscious of. She says she worked for a tone in *Susan* that was not too serious and "not too cartoonish either"[19]: "You don't want it so unreal that it's like a total cartoon, but you don't want it so realistic that it loses the imaginary fable-like qualities . . . "[20] The double heroine (Roberta the suburban wife, played by Rosanna Arquette; Susan, the wild one, played by Madonna) is a kind of composite Wren—Roberta's fragility and commonplaceness, Susan's stylish way-out-ness; or they can be seen as foils in the way Paul and Eric are in *Smithereens*. (The film is full of such funny juxtapositions, as of the husband Gary in his sensible beige suit and tie in the elevator of a dance club surrounded with every kind of wild weird hairdo and get-up, the elevator constriction—and the subsequent spilling out—of the human multiplicity, adding to the absurdity, which you can laugh at both from the clean suburban side and the hip New York side.)

Seidelman asserts that casting is "crucial,"[21] and Madonna was in truth an inspired choice, an exotic queen acquiring odd clothes, jackets with gold triangles on the back, bright gem-studded boots that she must have—like Wren's inventive punk clothes in *Smithereens*. Madonna carries that off with flair, even if her not being an actress shows through here and there. But she's a witty and plausible casting as a wild thing, though at the same time really quite as endlessly preoccupied with acquisition—in the way young audiences also are—as Roberta's super-straight husband Gary, whose kitchen, archetypically clean-white-surfaced and jammed with appliances, wittily features Julia Childs on TV directing the evening meal.

The film carefully attends to the accoutrements of "image," codes of dress and behavior, as the two women (superficially) exchange clothing and lifestyles. The straight life folds easily enough, with Gary giggling over marihuana, about being the spa-king of New Jersey, and his sister Leslie fighting a losing battle as she tries to navigate the increasingly, amusingly turbulent waters that shake up her notion of normality. But Leslie, who at the beginning asks the hairdresser that Roberta's new hairdo not be weird, and who laments when she sees the contrast between Roberta's wedding shot and her later mug shot—what New York has done to her—is an exaggerated voice of convention. Even audiences in the suburban malls can laugh at Leslie, and yet Roberta in her liberation ends up in a place they can find non-threatening. Roberta's going to work and earning her own money by joining a magic show, which is part of her odyssey into new selfhood, has a touch of the performer—as well as many allusions to film-going, from *The Lady Vanishes* to Fellini. Roberta may be a more klutzy/magical/conventional performer than Madonna, but she gets it together, makes her own living, doesn't, for instance, live off Wes' projectionist job.

Among the film's particularly wonderful moments are the opening ones, while the credits are going on, with quick shots of beauty parlor activities, women under dryers, cut hair swept up from the floor. The music on the soundtrack is used very effectively; and there is the excellent basic idea of the film, of an ordinary housewife becoming fascinated with the wild life of a rock star. In that way *Desperately* is a coming-of-age film—a young woman's *Saturday Night Fever*, with yearning New Jersey housewife staring out at the twinkling George Washington Bridge, and then making the trip across—even if done entirely in terms of style, Roberta moving from an easy-to-put-down straight suburban life, to a funky though modified punk. Susan is the Real Thing, so with her the stakes are higher, mob killings, real life/death danger, promiscuity, a boyfriend who is a musician and much further out than Dez, the good, solid, sweet-looking film editor with whom Roberta links up.

But romance has a centrality in this second film while one of the nicest things about *Smithereens* was that it was entirely offhand about sex and about couples, both of which hardly happen at all but insofar as they do, do so casually, truly of no moment. *Desperately Seeking Susan* is in danger toward the end of turning into just the complacent kid movie for the teens in the malls that Seidelman scorned, as the two couples lean back cozily and laugh, with even the wild girl domesticated—just as we thought we were watching the domestic one become wild. Seidelman, having left Wren pitifully adrift at the end of *Smithereens*, with nothing more irrelevant than a man for her at that point, chose with the ending for this new film to stay much closer to old patriarchal formulas, and to resolve everything through the couple.

It is clear from Seidelman's talk about her two films and how she shifted her ground that she knew exactly what she was doing. Her shaping of the film, to make it popular and commercial, went strongly against the original script and scriptwriter Leora Barish's vision—which intriguingly focussed more strongly and complexly on the relationship between the two women. In interviews Barish saw the film as less about people moving out of suburbia than about "imagination and how it could save anyone."[22] She gives the sense of having a far more ambitious design than Seidelman would trust to the screen for that crucial second film that can make or break. Further, to move from the *Smithereens* budget of $80 thousand, to the *Desperately Seeking Susan* budget of $5 million, must in itself give pause, even to a high-spirited desire to take risks. People indeed asked Seidelman if she made the Susan character more sympathetic because she was making a studio movie, though she insists in return—accurately of course but really beside the point—that "I liked Wren's gutsiness," and also liked the sexiness of aloof Eric and the niceness of non-macho Paul.

The greater conventionality one feels in *Susan* may have had to do with external pressures as well as self-censorship. Orion, which Seidelman praised for the freedom it gave her, did not give her final cut, and seems to have required compromises. For instance, while one may regret the obligatory linking up of couples with which *Desperately Seeking Susan* ends, the conclusion also shows us the two women receiving medals of honor for the return of the Egyptian earrings, both raising their arms in triumph. In *Ms.'* coverage of the making of the film, the emphasis is on the "rarity" of "the two female characters go[ing] off into the sunset together—an ending the producers [both female: Sarah Pillsbury and Midge Sanford] had to fight for."[23] Pillsbury notes further that "the guys [that Susan and Roberta] are with probably won't be the guys they'll be with forever, while the friendship will probably last." So, despite the fact that "the studio was worried that homophobic audiences would Jump to the Wrong Conclusion, the film's ending has been shot as it was originally written." But this applause seems to have nothing to do with the film we finally see, where the women have no friendship at all, sharing only one momentary very fleeting look after Roberta hits the villain over the head and saves Susan, a look that stays in the mind because it is so unusual a moment of intimate contact. The *Ms.* story speaks solemnly of the "frank female-centeredness"[24] of the film, but how much frankness is required here? It is also disturbing that an independent company as generally highly regarded as Orion should have been so uneasy and intrusive on this issue. Much of the responsibility for the dilution of the original screenplay may not be Seidelman's, but have to do with what it means to make a film in America—namely, compromises that alter one's original vision beyond recognition.

Considering what gets done in the United States to actual scripts one knows of, that attempt any degree of bravery and unconventionality, especially about closeness between women, it is remarkable that woman/ woman films have gotten made at all. That they have gotten made probably has less to do with greater general progressiveness than with the particular independent-film circumstances in which each came into being, from *Girlfriends* to *Desert Hearts*, or even Marisa Silver's *Old Enough*. Whatever its own problems, the European film situation has allowed for more possibility, from Kurys' *Entre Nous* in France to von Trotta's and Mészáros' work (though each has complained about intrusions and limits), to the strangest anomaly for effortlessly attracting funding, Gorris' *A Question of Silence*. That so much has gotten through, and that so many taboos seem to have fallen so quickly, does not mean that the situation can only get progressively better. In America, at least, what got through feels rather a triumph of specific women's tenacity of purpose, willingness to sacrifice outside the usual channels, at least for a one-time attempt, or special circumstances or sources of support that may not be there in future. Though successful precedents have opened many doors to women directors in the industry, and while the success of a number of new independent films gives hope that the money people will notice that going outside the safe formulas can also be lucrative, the pressures the other way are formidable and it is a mistake to minimize them.

And again Seidelman carried it off well, and made *Desperately* with wit and flair within the constraints. It is not for nothing that Vincent Canby (though more sanguine than he should be) wrote of Seidelman's move to her second film: "With *Desperately Seeking Susan* . . . Miss Seidelman successfully takes the long, potentially dangerous leap from the ranks of the promising independents to mainstream American movie-making, her integrity, her talent and her comic idiosyncracies intact."[25] The crucial next question was whether the large success Seidelman realized with that film would enable her to avoid serious future compromises, which *Making Mr. Right* answers, unfortunately but not unexpectedly, in the negative.

The central character of *Making Mr. Right*, a woman again although ambiguously named Frankie Stone, is a professional image consultant whose job is to give an android a public image, to mold and socialize it/him.

She finds that having had a bad history with men, the challenge is taking a blank slate of a man and turning him into what she thinks is the perfect guy. Professionally she's quite fulfilled. In a way, she's become the man she always wanted to marry, and now the question is: after you've reached the point where you're happy in your work, how do you integrate that with having a personal life and having relationships with the opposite sex at the same time, because the politics between the sexes have changed?[26]

The idea of a woman's having become the man she always wanted to marry is truly what makes this time extraordinary for women, and it is a shrewd idea for a film to focus on. However, in the terms of Seidelman's film, it applies only to Frankie, since the other women characters seem not to have work at all, or else not to take it seriously. The only other character who brings a genuine passion and creativity to work is the man scientist and he is scornfully viewed like an overgrown "nerd" from the youth movies. There are good moments around Frankie's work situation, another of the opening sequences Seidelman does so well, with Frankie putting herself together for a conference, almost making *herself*, as she drives along a freeway in her little red convertible. Red is also the dominant color of the film, not only because of the loud, tacky Miami setting but because of the aggressiveness (here feeling like crudeness) of Seidelman's women. As Frankie arrives, though, and is flanked by her assistants, she gives an appealing sense of being a woman in charge, a woman directing, taking in information, giving instructions back.

Seidelman does less well with Frankie as reverse-gender Pygmalion. Frankie does teach the android, Ulysses, a little about social relations, about how to look into a woman's eyes and make her feel as though what she says matters intensely. But the possibilities for wonderful satire in that education, like the several wonderful ideas around which the film is built, go nowhere. Worse, the general dilution or absence of freshness applies to the heroine too, who—despite Ann Magnuson's talents, and Seidelman's casting her for levelheadedness—is so much blander in this role, so much more flattened out and homogenized, than the earlier characters of Rosanna Arquette and Madonna, not to speak of Susan Berman's Wren.

The men are a sorry group, in keeping with the film's premise, but again too cartoonishly grossly so, in a way that doesn't allow for subtle nuance or metaphoric suggestiveness—from the sullen, alienated scientist, to the sleazy and unfaithful politician boyfriend, to Trish's long-haired soap-opera-star husband who also sleeps around, to the slick, lecherous, Indian supervisor of Chemtech. On the other hand, the ideal Ulysses is a basket case, sweet, totally malleable, infantile, liable to fall apart in demanding situations (usually sexual)—and apparently (though the film seems unclear itself on this point) only minimally understanding—although looking like he understands. His little moralistic speech about humans being the ones who can't deal with love, the ones who live like machines, is another idea that could have had impact but has none at all because nothing is explored with any subtlety.

For the women the moral seems to be that something is better than nothing, whether that something is Trish's husband, or Ulysses. (Ulysses is reminiscent not only of the hero of *Being There* but of the *Purple Rose of Cairo*'s old-movie hero, especially in the jewelry-buying scene.) The film's fun—with Yuppy-buying, Miami Latins, various kinds of crass Jews—is as uninspired as its future-tech sets. But worst of all, the film's ending is entirely conventional, built around the old magical kiss and magical love, even if Seidelman can cleverly rebut such a charge by arguing that the film is in conception really anti-romance and anti-male. The best thing about *Making Mr. Right* is in fact that conception, but a brilliant conception is hardly enough to carry a film.

Given that Seidelman is the most powerfully placed young American woman director at the moment, it is painful to see her films in a steady line of descent, into more and more standardized work, that contains less and less of what made her so appealing to begin with. It surely doesn't make one overly hopeful for the future to think that Seidelman, at this point in her career, is where just about everyone wants to be. What kind of place is that? If she has been operating, as one would guess she has, with the box office principally in mind, that strategy interestingly hasn't worked either. The popular fable structure she has lighted on for her films offers a first-rate vehicle for both wide accessibility and the possibility of considerable metaphorical density and depth. Woody Allen's films are similarly constructed, though the softness and vacuousness into which his recent work—untethered from anguish—has drifted too is becoming increasingly obvious and distressing. Seidelman in turn has gone too far toward comic-book simpleness; she is too pragmatic. What her work needs is an infusion of genuine content, intelligence, vision—enough substance to match the marvellous ideas around which she constructs her films.

## JOYCE CHOPRA: *SMOOTH TALK*

If the 1980s are witnessing the debut of numerous new women feature film directors, in reality the "new" is part illusion, concealing in many cases long years of experience in film work, often in documentary filmmaking. So Joyce Chopra, who many of us remember from *Joyce at 34*, which she made with Claudia Weill during an on-camera pregnancy fifteen years ago, is, at 49, with her first feature film *Smooth Talk*, one of the most promising "new" directors around.

*Smooth Talk*, very highly acclaimed by Vincent Canby and most other critics, has come under attack from a number of feminists, most notably Ruby Rich, whose highly intelligent critical voice always deserves an attentive hearing. Rich strongly praises the first half of the film but attacks Chopra for having in the second half returned to a regressive sexual double standard. Calling *Smooth Talk* less a post-feminist film than "a belated pre-feminist one,"[27] Rich argues that this "48-year-old mother of a teenage daughter" has "made a movie with a message for teenage daughters everywhere: keep a lid on your sexuality, don't you dare express it . . . or . . . Like a grownup bogeyman Arnold Friend will come and get you."[28] Rich thus conjoins Chopra's own biological daughter (fifteen at the time of the film), the daughter in the film and, by further extension, the feminists of the 1980s whom Rich, herself speaking with the voice of a daughter, clearly feels this feminist of the early 1970s is betraying.

Rich makes a strong case, and there is no question but that the film is problematic for the terms in which it casts a sexual initiation story (though the original Oates story, "Where Are You Going, Where Have You Been," is central to that discussion). But all the same, *Smooth Talk* is one of the finest of recent American films and one suspects it is so in no small part as a function of Chopra's much-cited age, and equally much-cited status as mother of a teenage daughter. She is able to hold in complex balance a sense of the young girl's dazzling sexuality, the lit-up joy that Connie walks around with through the film, and at the same time an equally sympathetic hold on the mother's disgruntlement, love, and sense of danger. Chopra certainly feels for the mother and gives her a voice, surely an antidote for that lack of women's voices not only in classic Hollywood, but even in a feminist exploration of mothers and daughters like Michelle Citron's interesting avant garde film, *Daughter-Rite*, where the mother's side is again left out, silenced, and only a composite daughter voiceover is presented to us by the young woman director. For all the accusations directed at the mother in *Daughter-Rite*, she is never allowed to tell her story, while one of the nicest things about *Smooth Talk* is that the mother's voice is very much present.

As a result, there is a much more complex balance of affiliations at work in this film, all of the layers creating richness. Chopra is intensely, affectingly, with the girl too, understanding her joy, her wanting to "have it all" as her sister says, her wanting to know everything, as Arnold Friend says. Chopra even understands the uneasiness and need to please suggested by her constant smiling. Such details of response and interaction, most intelligently shaded, catch with keen accuracy the reality of a young adolescent girl, of a difficult, spoiled American puberty. Mining her earlier documentary on 12 year-old girls in Waltham, Massachusetts, as well as her own life, Chopra also keenly catches a teenager's self-absorption, narcissism, indifference to the adult lives around. Surely women directors have to be allowed to voice those feelings since they too are real—as well as to have a woman walk boldly through 42nd Street porn shops and stalk deserted night streets, as Bette Gordon did in *Variety*. It is true that few subjects demand more of an "overhaul in social and sexual perspective since the late sixties than the prospect of female sexual awakening,"[29] and slowly that process of overhaul is underway. But that sex can be dangerous and frightening, as well as liberating and pleasurable, is incontrovertible; and to treat as retrograde and verboten a woman's sense of the dangers of sexuality for young girls is to be proscriptive in a way that is dangerous for art. That *Smooth Talk* is more than meanly punitive toward the sexual woman, in the manner of *Looking For Mr. Goodbar*,[30] is indicated by the complexity of its vision, given the sadness of the other family members, the ambiguities of the film's ending, the persistent radiance of Connie, which makes her shine among the others.

Connie's dazzle often takes the literal visual form of backlighting her hair, as in one close-up with Connie polishing her toenails, her thick very blonde hair shining brilliantly around her head as she bends over her task. The early part of the film, as it establishes that radiance, presents a series of wonderfully accurately observed teenage-girl rituals, especially of the three girlfriends continually grooming. One terrific sequence involves very fast cutting—to James Taylor's song "Is That the Way You Look?"—through a series of movements, hands putting on bracelets and necklaces, painting eyelids, belting, unzipping. Oates in her stunning story writes of Connie: "Everything for her had two sides to it, one for home and one for anywhere that was not home"[31]; and the girls very quickly and efficiently transform themselves into their sexual out-of-the-house selves. This kind of sequence is fast becoming obligatory in film, especially women directors' films, even cliche—with elements of it in *Old Enough*, the opening haircutting sequence of *Desperately Seeking Susan*, even European films like *Diary for My Children*. But given the centrality of such activities in young girls' lives—the endless working away at appearances, largely to attract men, feminism or no—its recurrence in film is not surprising, and is especially well done here by Chopra.

*Smooth Talk* manages to take the speech and general interactions of the flat-surfaced all-American malls and fastfood diners and to invest them with a subtlety, rich tension, size, at the farthest remove from youth-film banality, just as it takes the sex-and-virginity subject matter of those films to a whole new level. Chopra's film works wonderfully with omnipresent transistor radios and music everywhere, daughter/mother conflicts, and the intensely provocative sexual behavior of young girls. Chopra does this last by making the exposed carnality and beautiful shapeliness of body almost overwhelming, at the same time that she does not leer at it, roll over it, fetishize parts of it, as a male director might. The combination of beautiful, aggressively seductive body and the virginal white bathing suit/shorts (Oates has the girl dressed in green in the story) with which Connie goes with Arnold Friend seems just right for conveying the mixture of sexual woman and innocent girl.

Connie's youthful beauty is itself breathtaking but also just right, in that she is not beautiful in any strict sense. She is more ordinary than that, though with something different and far more interesting in her than in the other two blonde girls she seems interchangeable with as the film opens.

In that very first sequence, when the three girls are lying sunbathing on a blanket, the camera's angle viewing them is such that it is only Connie we see, with other mysterious limbs curled someways behind her, with the sexual suggestiveness of the image placing the subject of Connie's sexuality before us from the start. It is a subject amplified in various ways throughout the film, with the beautifully rendered excitement of roving the shopping malls, the passionate neckings in cars, and Connie's utterly happy statement to her sister June about how very nice the boys are.

The response Connie's sexuality elicits from mother and sister, in its sourness and even inappropriate lashing out, suggests not that the film is loaded toward mother and against Connie, that the film doesn't like the young, as has been argued, but on the contrary, it conveys how threatened the others are by Connie, a subtle view and one reason why seeing the film only in terms of fear and negativity toward adolescent sex is to flatten it out. Connie's confiding elicits a strikingly harsh response from June, the sexual jealousy of the stay-at-home sister for the pretty younger one, like June's feeling scandalized by the positions Connie puts herself into. So too Connie's mother's permanent look of sarcastic peevishness seems to come as much from the presence of Connie's blinding radiance, as from a mother's middle-aged sense of being the expected drudge in the house, and being in some drab way trapped in that house, though also struggling with it by continually trying to rework it and adorn it. As both mother and daughter dance to the same James Taylor song in separate rooms, the sequence serves less to emphasize the distance and antagonism between them, than to create the tones of different life stages, the wistfulness and gravity of the older woman, who has seen disappointment and limitation, and the hopeful ebulliance of the young (and ignorant). But Connie moves out of it all in effect, she opts out of the household in characteristic adolescent fashion, refuses or forgets chores, her mother asking the classic question, "Don't you ever think about anybody but yourself?"

The mother also suffers from a keen sense of loss over her daughter's refusal to do things together any more, another part of the entry into adulthood, even to Connie's shrinking from being hugged. The sadness of the mother, who has spent fifteen years of her life intimately involved with Connie, is real, the film bringing a rare kind of sensitive intelligence to the situation of an older woman. She deserves sympathy too, achieved through freshly observed and instantly recognizable details. A lovely sequence that holds all these elements is when Connie offers for once to help her mother with the painting of the house, starts painting erratically, like doing a dance, and then grows pensive and drifts apart, motionless, lost in thought: the girl's self-involvement is touchingly conveyed, as well as the affection and bemusement of the watching mother. While Connie's perception that her mother is out to get her is often borne out by the way the filming is done, and Oates speaks of the two having an ongoing irritation, the mother's annoyance also often seems justified, the voice of the worried mother again an important voice to include.

On the other hand, it must be said again that a film that starts out seeming a definitive film about female sexual initiation but turns out to be about rape, is unquestionably disturbing. The character of Arnold Friend creates a genuine uncertainty about how the sexual initiation, how sex itself, is regarded in the film. Is he a force for punishment? *Is* this an indictment of sexual girls? Is the film saying that any beginning sexual experience has a terror and sense of the unknown, of something brutal and alien? That it does metaphorically turn your parents' house to cardboard, that it does necessitate that on some level you leave that house for good? The Oates story to which the film is remarkably faithful, and from Ruby Rich's perspective is "the predictably nasty JCO story" — can also be seen as a virtuoso stunner of a tale that hits one with the same kind of apocalyptic impact as Flannery O'Connor's *A Good Man Is Hard to Find*, though one need not share the sense of total destruction around the corner that O'Connor voiced there, herself mortally felled by lupus, to be staggered by the power of the story's vision. Such impact does not come from a commonplace acceptance of the fiction's vision as a guide to the conduct of daily life; it is closer to what Oates writes about the film *Smooth Talk* and her discomfort in seeing her work taken out of its "contexture of language": "All writers know that language is their subject; quirky word choices, patterns of rhythm, enigmatic pauses. . . . Of course we all have 'real' subjects, and we will fight to the death to defend these subjects, but beneath the tale-telling it is the tale-telling that grips us so very fiercely."[32]

Chopra does make major changes of course, because she is less interested than Oates in the metaphysical reverberations of the tale, but rather in the realistic nuance of a young girl's rite of passage. Citing her early documentary, *Girls at 12*, as the source of much of the material of *Smooth Talk*, Chopra said recently, "My true interest is in the behavior of young girls."[33] Hence all the beautiful realistic detail she added changes the tale from an allegory, entitled by Oates "Death and the Maiden" in an earlier version of the story and haunted by an actual mass murderer reported in the newspapers—to a more ordinary pubescent young girl's experiences. Perhaps this very shift in emphasis invites moral application and hence attack. Chopra's changes in fact move in the direction of the girl's survival and even empowerment. Connie's being driven back by the apparent rapist is a surprise, if we remember Oates' beautiful dire words implying Connie's doom and death (though again Oates' sense of a death is metaphorical, while Chopra's treatment is more literal). Chopra's handling of the ending, the evasions of its silences, are perhaps due to the director's own uneasiness with this material, her own ambivalences, which led her to refuse to suggest the girl's destruction, though she is unsure with what to replace that outcome. But to have dropped the whole conception of Arnold Friend would be to destroy the link to the story altogether. Rich effectively points out that the powerful visuals all victimize Connie, who directly preceding the rape is continually shot in "close-up, tightly, claustrophobically, with no space around her, pinned into that tiny unmovable frame," while giving massive space around Friend "in middle-shot, framed against an ample landscape, lots of space around him, master of the territory."[34] But, for all that, surely we do not come away from this film the way we do from *The Birds*, Tippi Hedren first confidently venturing forth, and gradually being reduced—in a familiar Hitchcock mode—to a mother-dependent zombie.[35]

The world is undeniably a dangerous place, and more dangerous for girls, especially when they give off simmering signals without understanding their own power. So on the one hand, Connie *is* asking for it, in her bare halter and her suggestive, flagrant talk and movements. Her seductive aggressiveness toward male strangers and their "buns" gives us a heroine as sexual in fact as young men in films have always been—the film "post-feminist" in how it takes for granted that females are sexual, and can chase men this way. At the same time, inside her large beautiful grownup woman's body Connie—and her friends—have little confidence, talk young girls' group slang, giggle and play nervous if also cheeky games, seeing it as exciting and pleasureful without a full sense of what they are dealing with. The darker side of things, which no woman can deny exists, indeed involves running into strange menacing hulks in the mall, or the weird driver the girls pick up at the start who looks at them too intently, or a foreboding walk for Connie down a dark deserted road all alone late at night, when clearly anything could happen. There is an ascending order of trouble in the men who take Connie euphemistically for a ride. Rape is real, and girls *are* victimized by the violence of men, rarely the other way around, though homosexual violence also makes clear the dangerous risks men run from other men through casual sexuality.

The reconciliation that Connie seems to reach with mother and sister at the end of the film, returning to the arms of each, also has drawn criticism as "an old-fashioned mother's dream: fleeing the consequences of her sexuality, Connie returns to the bosom of her family, to the literalization of mama's arms. That's what Joyce Chopra might call a happy ending."[36] Certainly the family holds a positive value for Chopra, though she surely did not mean this reconciliation to forever foreclose the outside world—of sex, love, adult open experience. It is rather a vision of reintegration after earlier ruptures, which is often the actual curve of maturation; a vision of separation—by an adolescent torn both by the need to set off over the boundary, and by an inner voice still calling "Mommy"—and later a return on different terms but still as a part of the family on some level. If the film opts for the family, Chopra has her right to that value.

Yet, again it is held complexly, the home rendered not very attractive, with quarrels over the demanding father's tuna fish, and mother and sister reading women's magazines in often darkened interiors. There is a sense of family pleasures and comforts but more of something depressed and un-realized, and hence excited—even if also made jealous—by Connie's ven-turing forth. Her delight in putting home behind her seems understandable, among other levels, because despite the mother's scorn for Connie's having only a bunch of trashy dreams in her head, nobody else in this house appears to be interested in much, from the father's well-meaning self-satisfaction and blindness, to June's just hanging around the house, to the mother herself with little to do but talk to her sisters, despite the restless dissatisfaction with that life and desire to change it implied by her continual house-fixing.

The unfinished house is used skillfully in the film, in itself and given all the associations of houses, as in Emily Dickinson's poetry, as metaphor for the female self (as well as the family nest from which Connie must be expelled, as in Doris Dörrie's *In the Belly of the Whale*). So the house also offers a parallel and appropriate setting for this unfinished girl, waiting for completion of some sort. The film takes for granted that Connie will triumph. Her cringing in terror, in foetal position, when she must leave her parents' house, is regressive, but only momentarily so. She will take her leave, as we all must, and come out on top of it all. Chopra attempts (however admittedly ambiguously) a feminist ending in giving the sense of Connie's passing into womanhood and control over her world. *Smooth Talk*, though undeniably problematic, is a compelling film—and also unimagin-able through the eyes of a male director, as it undertakes to examine a girl's rite of passage that few if any films have really looked at before, however numberless many have leered at pubescent girls.

## THE YOUTH MARKET: AMY HECKERLING, LISA GOTTLIEB, AND MARTHA COOLIDGE

A number of recent women directors have entered the industry through films for the teen audiences which constitute a large part of the current U.S. film box office. Indeed, there is almost no way in the United States not to make films with this audience in mind, even films like *Desperately Seeking Susan* and *Smooth Talk*, though those films clearly had much more on their minds than box office returns. But even the directors of the flagrantly commercial films run a range: Amy Heckerling seems to have walked right out of film school into movie-making through this route, while Martha Coolidge has been a serious director, knocking on doors for a long time, and finally finding entry in this way. It is as if with the decline in quality and maturity of American films, a new kind of equity is possible, barriers are lowered, young men directors with unknown names come and go, and a new kind of access is also possible for women.

The films produced by this group of directors, however, are for the most part truly standardized "products," with their only aim the capturing of the kid market at the malls. At best they are quite professional, pleasant, formula-filled entertainments, often high school comedies with the usual issues of virginities lost and nerds vs. hulks, such as Heckerling's *Fast Times at Ridgemont High* (1982), or Lisa Gottlieb's *One of the Guys* (1985). Amy Heckerling talks about feeling "a lot of pressure . . . I see male directors who can do one bad movie and then a second bad movie and then a third before they finally succeed. And then they're hot directors. I haven't seen a woman do that yet. I always feel that I can't stop, because they'll forget me if I do."[37] Her eye is entirely rivetted on the box office: "You know what would be great? If there was a female who could do what Lucas and Spielberg do: make tons of money. The best and the worst thing about this industry is that that's the bottom line."[38] As a group these directors' films have done as well as most, and those that failed at the box office did not necessarily fail because the work was bad—Heckerling's *Johnny Dangerously* (1986), for instance, a good-natured, enjoyable spoof on old Jimmy Cagney tenement dramas.

The films deal with boys and girls mostly as though there were a male eye behind the camera, often a leering one. In *Fast Times*, what little character development there is goes to the male characters, and the girls are concerned only with how they look and which boy is cute, with Heckerling exploiting female bodies, parading them around in bikinis, moving her camera over them as they lie by pools, or on beds half naked while making phone calls to one another. Though ultimately, despite all the sexuality, there is a sense of innocence and fun in this film, it is also shocking that during interactions between two girls, a woman director should be focussing on them as bodies, not for each other but for the spectator. On the other hand, though sex is quite casual, it is seen in the film as only sex, and the girl wants romance. The sleazily macho guy is repudiated for a sensitive Woody Allen type, uncertain of himself, fleeing the girls' sexual aggression. Heckerling's *National Lampoon's European Vacation*, uneven technically, though generally pleasurably entertaining, feels a bit of a send-up of the patriarchal family, with Chevy Chase its cheerful, blundering fool of a father who is always telling everyone what to do and who understands nothing. The women, however, wife and daughter, are utterly inane.

While teen films by women directors seem mostly geared to looking like the male product, or at least following whatever the successful formulas may be, one way gender does figure is in a film like Lisa Gottlieb's *Just One of the Guys*, which plays with sexual inversion—as many others have done, from *3 Men and a Cradle* (men watching over an infant), *The Night Wears Garters* (woman as seducer), and *In the Belly of the Whale* (woman on the road). In what seems a rather witty feminist spillover, the heroine of Gottlieb's film, feeling she is not taken seriously because she's cute, and that she'd get a more serious chance at a journalism prize if she were male, masquerades as "one of the guys." This involves her in all manner of discomfort, a kind of humor most familiar from Shakespeare's comedies of sex disguise, with direct borrowings in the film from recent commercial work like *Victor Victoria* and *Tootsie*, and most fully and shamelessly from *Yentl*. In *Just One of the Guys*, however, the material is fairly stale by comparison, as well as having an unpleasant victimizing edge (though this too is teen movie cliche) toward the high school kids who are a little intellectual and hence seen as weird.

But most striking when compared with *Yentl* is how little feminism actually figures in this film. After its first few minutes *Just One of the Guys* completely drops the issue of Terry's writing, her ambition and belief in her work, and turns into a mooning teenage love story—wanting him, his not knowing, his making out with someone else at the dance as she watches, the sex-obsessed kid brother. This film too treats us to lascivious slow pans over Terry's beautiful curvacious body; though presumably justified in terms of the issue of sex change, it is again a woman director producing leering cheesecake for the market. The film may appear to put the disguised Terry in the Pygmalion role of teaching the boy she likes how to dress right, and urging him to ask a girl to the prom, hence the girl taking an active, aggressive, director's role in her own life. By the film's end, however, she is back in demure feminine clothes; she asks him to go out and he says he's the guy and it's for him to ask. And calling to mind Arzner's *Christopher Strong* more than 50 years back but how much further ahead, he will ride with her as long as he can drive (her car). Not only does Gottlieb's film leave us with the couple restored, but with all the old roles firmly back in place.

Martha Coolidge, having made, among other films, a well-known feminist documentary about her grandmother, *Old Fashioned Woman*, and a 1976 film about rape, *Not a Pretty Picture*, then turned to Hollywood, where she directed two commercial feature films, *Joy of Sex* and then *Valley Girl* (1983), which made back $17 million for an investment of $350 thousand. Her most recent film, another one for the youth market, *Real Genius* (1985), about mostly male scientific whiz kids, "broke through a well-established sexual barrier that had roped off boys, science, and (perhaps most importantly) multimillion-dollar special effects budgets as male turf."[39] Coolidge herself says she "was attracted by the chance to do men dealing with men, because women bring a fresh perspective to male characters. I'll opt to show them as more vulnerable than a male director would,"[40] an impulse she shares with directors like Doris Dörrie and perhaps Elaine May.

The most important element of *Real Genius* that sets it apart from the other youth films is that it is built around respect for mind, work, skill— which the film translates into high-tech magic light games, and "hackers" cracking government codes to get information. The characters are half fraternity-horsing-around kids, and half scientists, intensely at work on teams with high excitement, trying to solve problems. The film may also be full of spoofs of the academic, but the pursuit of mental conquest is what has all the emphasis and it is seen as power, fun, something to be respected above all. There is wonderful fantasy, a touch of Spielberg's magic and more, of C. S. Lewis' children's book, *The Lion, The Witch and The Wardrobe*, especially in the character Laszlo Hollyfield in the film. A 1960s' style intellectual who keeps vanishing into the back of the wardrobe, his name doubtless an homage to *Casablanca*'s white knight, he is a touching creation, destroyed as he is by the destructive uses to which the government has put his work. Coolidge brings him into the 1980s with newly discovered material needs, and yet he is the means of thwarting one more destructive weapon. So while the film is not solemn, it takes on serious issues and expresses a distrust of the uses of science by the world of male power.

Again in this film the director's sex appears to be irrelevant. The narrative almost entirely concerns males. However, the one female among the geniuses is conspicuously neurasthenic, a nonstop talker, and in her first words to the hero she offers to make a bed for him. Unsure of herself, waiting for the hero to find her appealing, she even knits him a sweater. The film also offers an orgy of girls from a beauty school making the apparently obligatory display of female bodies in bathing suits. Still, the hero chooses the smart girl over a blonde bimbo; the film is itself obviously not lecherous in its look at the world, but rather imaginative, and strikingly without cruelty or violence. Its small male hero's oddly androgynous look perhaps betokens the woman-presence in the film indirectly.

Martha Coolidge alone conveys a creative dimension beyond the youth-market formulas she too feels obliged to employ. A major figure behind a network created to give aspiring East Coast filmmakers the kind of connections when they go West that California film school graduates have, Coolidge was touchingly quoted in a *New York Times* story as hoping to spare others from her own experience of wasting years just trying to get started. One of the most depressing statements I know is Coolidge's discussion of her film *The Joy of Sex* a year and a half earlier, and before *Real Genius*: "It's my first studio picture, my first union picture, and my first picture as a member of the DGA. . . . It's taken me 18 years to get where I wanted to be. Now what I have to do is make films I really want to make."[41] And alas, *Real Genius* followed. One hopes that Coolidge, now firmly established through the access made possible by the teen movie (and the other women directors who likewise gained entry that way) will indeed be able to turn the opportunity into a more ambitious and important achievement, earned as it has been at so fearsome a cost.

## THE NEW LESBIAN MAINSTREAM FILM

A major concern in recent women's films is love between women—a closeness between sisters, mothers and daughters, friends—that also forms the central content of one of the most influential women's studies texts, Nancy Chodorow's *The Reproduction of Mothering*. The point at which love between women turns into a lesbian experience is a complex issue[42] and "lesbian criticism continues to be plagued with the problem of definition."[43] Adrienne Rich's solution, the notion of a lesbian continuum, would in fact include many of the filmmakers in this study.

I mean the term *lesbian continuum* to include a range—through each woman's life and throughout history—of woman-identified experience; not simply the fact that a woman has had or consciously desired genital experience with another woman. If we expand it to embrace many more forms of primary intensity between and among women, including the sharing of a rich inner life, the bonding against male tyranny, the giving and receiving of practical and political support . . . we begin to grasp breadths of female history and psychology which have lain out of reach as a consequence of limited, mostly clinical, definitions of "lesbianism."[44]

Bonnie Zimmerman worries that this definition, by its breadth, risks "blurring the distinctions between lesbian identity and female-centered identity," and prefers the definition by Lillian Faderman: " 'Lesbian' describes a relationship in which two women's strongest emotions and affections are directed toward each other. Sexual contact may be a part of the relationship to a greater or lesser degree, or it may be entirely absent. By preference the two women spend most of their time together and share most aspects of their lives with each other."[45]

Obviously both of these passages apply to relationships between women in the work of a number of the most important European directors included later in this study, like Margarethe von Trotta, Márta Mészáros, and Diane Kurys. Though these are directors who generally work in a heterosexual context, their films include sequences between women with an unmistakable erotic charge and intimacy.

This has been a taboo area until recently in American films, with an independent film about close women friends like Claudia Weill's *Girlfriends*, as earlier noted, careful to explicitly repudiate homosexual content. This is not to mention films of the same period by male directors, like *Julia*, in which a remark suggesting lesbian feelings between the two women friends is responded to with a bizarrely outraged fury. But with John Sayles' independent *Lianna*, as well as some less than fully open approaches by European films, the way was eased for Donna Deitch's *Desert Hearts* (1986), which she made because "there hadn't been a story about a love relationship between two women handled in a frank and real way."[46] The film is made in the manner of a commercial Hollywood film, with no art movie aspirations/pretensions, highly enjoyable to watch, thoroughly professional in pacing and performances, and shown not in a marginal theatre but a good sophisticated but mainstream Manhattan cinema. Deitch, who is 40, is another "new" director who has been making commercials and documentary shorts for many years (on women's societal roles; on the mile-long mural in Los Angeles' Tijunga Wash), starting with *Berkeley 12 to 1* in 1969. It took her six years to get *Desert Hearts* made, though only 31 days to shoot it. The raising of the necessary $1.5 million was of course itself an enormous undertaking, though she managed it partly with a National Endowment grant she received for another purpose. Deitch made the film all by herself,

because I wanted to do it so badly. It's very difficult, if not impossible, to get a job directing features. So, the only way to do it was to do it myself. I just figured I'm going to go out and use all this energy, and I could put it into trying to make the film through a studio and wind up not getting anything. Sometimes even if they like the film, they take it away from you and make you an associate producer or something, and I wanted to direct. Now I'm probably going to give the studio setup a try. I can't go on raising money like that.[47]

This is of course a familiar story.

Set in the 1950s, the drama concerns the love between two women, a wild Western dark young one, Cay—a potter of some kind, sensitive underneath, not drawn to men though a handsome one pursues her; and an older blonde sophisticate from the East. Vivian, supposed to be some kind of intellectual, is most unconvincing as an academic, characterized largely by convoluted formal speech, but (played by Helen Shaver) she wears a wonderful period grey suit and has a charming way of holding herself and moving. She has come to Reno for a divorce, her choice, out of her need for a big life change, with no children to complicate things. Part of the film's interest lies in the wooing of an apparently straight woman, the older one, who is also resistant and uninitiated in the way virgins used to be, with the narrative excitement deriving from breaking through all that. Ruby Rich, commending *Desert Hearts* for daring to "deliver what some of us, growing up culturally bereft in the 1950s and 1960s, have always been waiting for. . . . a lesbian heart-throb movie,"[48] notes that the film "manages to convey the particular atmosphere and intensity of women falling in love with each other for the first time—not the coyness of the sexy but voyeuristic *Entre Nous*, not the punish-me morality play of *Lianna*, not the dead-end neurosis of *Another Way*, but the heady pleasure of an emotional drama allowed its physical consequence."[49] The film places this drama in a bold Western milieu, big astonishing landscapes around Reno, Nevada. Again Rich comments that the film "embodies a wonderful sense of female adventure, acknowledging that the greatest adventure for women may still be romance but refusing to give up the wide-open spaces. Deitch takes the landscapes along for the ride, degendering the pitch-perfect country-western music . . . that fills the soundtrack, creating an expansive world outside the domestic sphere for women to inhabit."[50]

The great adventure for women may still be romance in this film though conspicuously not so in most others by women in the last few years. And perhaps even *Desert Hearts* is not fully at ease with romance, hence its looking to Douglas Sirk-style melodrama to convey it—even to family relations, though here an odd, broken, and not quite blood family. Vincent Canby was disturbed in his *New York Times* review by what seemed to him the dead, canned quality of the dialogue, lines like the older woman, Fran, saying she loved Cay's father "because he reached in and put a string of lights around my heart." Canby writes, "It's the sort of film in which everyone, including the English professor, talks as if she'd grown up inside 'The Life of Helen Trent.' " But while everything in the film is a little overblown and excessive, from the landscape on, it all works, within its form. And even the line that Canby cites is effective in the context, especially when Cay uses it later for *her* feelings about Vivian. The film also puts subsidiary characters and the general pop-art gaudiness of the backgrounds to effective use.

*Desert Hearts*, set in 1959, before the freeing 1960s, is a tale of liberation through a warm loving relationship between two women. Lesbian love-making frees a woman seen almost in caricatured terms as uptight, cerebral, formal, loving of order, stilted in speech, all connected to the East. She has left her marriage and her heterosexual life, and come to the place of gambling, to take her life risk, as the two women talk about risk-taking and unrealized ambitions. This tale of liberation is set in a particularly uptight time, the pastness established through the big blowsy country love songs of the period, the music all of a piece with the visual style and the conception of the whole. Rich also sees the film's being set in times past in terms of the "immense difficulty confronting any project bent on putting women's love for each other up on the screen," meaning not just the problems of getting such a film made, but "what happens to self-hatred when the lights go down? What movie theatre is ever safe enough to allow women to relax and not go tense when Cay and Vivian first kiss or at last make love? Deitch has made her task easier by locating the dynamic in the past, when the barriers were more obviously exterior than interior and discrimination was overt rather than veiled."[51]

Above all, like the old Hollywood melodramas, *Desert Hearts* is entirely focused on women's emotions. The camera watches the women eye each other, watches Cay dance with Darrell but look at Vivian the whole time, the male gaze of no import here, everything framed instead by women looking at women, yearningly, affectionately, sensually, affectingly. The actual physical wooing sequence between the two women, in a car, builds the tension of physical closeness, a delicately awaited consent, sensitive to nuance, never a sense of imposing wills. The lovemaking is handled in graphic sexual images, focusing largely around mouths, desire enmeshed with contact between the lovers' eyes, a complex range of emotions on faces. Vivian's uncertainty as to what literally to do constitutes a new turn on the female initiation film!

Vivian's misgivings about this new sexual experience also relate to the serious issue of her becoming an outsider as a result, looked down upon automatically through any erotic involvement with Cay. Cay dryly says to Vivian: You are just visiting, this is where I live, in this outlaw world of the lesbian. The sexual sequences end with Vivian not wanting to leave the bedroom at all, partly, it would seem, judging from what happens later when they do, out of fear of the new social situation.

But nicely there is no simple melodrama in the rejection Vivian suffers from those in whose house she has been staying. The mother surrogate Frances is seen as jealous of anyone who would take Cay away from her, Cay being all she has left of the man she once loved. Frances' son, young Walter, takes a fancy himself to the professor. Thus, the recoil of the two from Vivian's involvement with Cay is not only because of how the straight world looks at lesbian love but also involves thwarted desire, self-interest. The film concludes with acceptance by both characters, in fact a blessing form the proxy mother Frances, which Cay has waited for. Cay in turn reassures Frances she will always be there for her. The mother/daughter interface is thus also affirmed at the film's end.

Formally simple, a stranger arriving by train and then departing, the ending leaves open whether the two women will continue together or not, though they part lovingly. The film's hearty affirmation of lesbian love, an affirmation explicit and unambivalent, is very hard if not impossible to find in other earlier films. Frankly treated lesbianism that also doesn't require heavy suffering can be read as a sign of a new climate or only an accidental missive slipped through to us by Donna Deitch's skill, tenacity, and devotion. The film plays with funny lines like having a ranch hand say of Cay and the women who come to her bed: "Beats me how you get all that traffic without any equipment"—which got an enormous laugh from an audience full of lesbian couples that I saw the film with when it first opened in New York, a humor clearly built on affirmation. It will be intriguing to see what kinds of films Donna Deitch goes on to make, since the sheer entertainment skills shown in her directing of this film should open a Hollywood career of some kind to her. It also remains to be seen whether more serious, more complex lesbian films lie ahead in the near future, whether the severe restrictions of Hollywood will allow anything to follow from this.

Certainly on the evidence of a small, flawed, but very nice Canadian debut film that comes to us a year after *Desert Hearts*—*I've Heard the Mermaids Singing* (1987), directed by Patricia Rozema—there would appear to be real change in the air. Of course Canada is not Hollywood, and given the intense feelings of Canadians about their separate cultural hegemony, apologies are in order for placing a Canadian film in an American chapter this way, for lack of time and space to give a full chapter to Canadian women directors. *I've Heard the Mermaids Singing* is interesting as, among other things, an affirmation of lesbian love, more obliquely than *Desert Hearts*, with a very light touch, but entirely comfortably, and solidly within art film/mainstream conventions.

The film's heroine is a kind of female Billy Liar, a somewhat flakey but ordinary secretary, unsuccessful in the world of work and human relations, no longer quite young, who develops a crush on the sophisticated older-woman art gallery owner with whom she works. While that attraction seems largely a matter of mentor/heroine worship, we suddenly become aware as Polly does that the woman has a lesbian lover. The film, which also mocks art-world pretentiousness, has our Polly relating to much of the world vicariously—by repeatedly fantasizing herself into mastery of enormously demanding situations—scaling Toronto tower blocks, conducting a Beethoven symphony to thunderous applause—and through her photography. The film distances itself through self-reflexive play with images, as with its inventive use of grainy, blurry, videotape segments interspersed through the narrative. Polly is also placed on the outside of the two women's relationship, fascinated by it, with a range of feelings toward each of the two. In the film's last frame, realism suspended a final time, Polly follows the two women out of her door, into a magically radiant natural place, barely glimpsed by us (which is presumably where following them will lead). Though too cute and naive, with a few recognizable borrowings, *Mermaids* is an engaging first feature, an initiation film, a woman's belated coming of age, seen entirely in terms of women (with the only men in it pompous or jealously bitchy). And with barely an explicit show of physicality, the film is also a celebration of lesbian love and love for women, and suggests that perhaps it is true that this material, without needing to be sensational, is finally entering the discourse of film.

## HOLLYWOOD POP FEMINISM: BARBRA STREISAND AND GOLDIE HAWN

With Barbra Streisand and Goldie Hawn we turn to insiders in the film industry, women with great power, who are also strong feminists, each with her own distinct persona and following, the films of each reaching very large audiences. *Yentl* seems to me a far more interesting effort than anything Hawn has produced, perhaps partly because of its literary source in a story by I. B. Singer, and also because of its ambition in addressing the whole issue of women's position in the traditional Jewish European *shtetl* world, with its reverence for learning, from which women were excluded. It was a project that Streisand sought to realize for many years, to the amusement of some in the profession "at the hubris of a forty year old actress/singer/producer/writer playing an eighteen-year-old girl playing an eighteen-year-old boy."[52] Equally ambitious are Streisand's explorations through the film of questions about the role and "nature" of a woman, relationships between women, even the admirableness of the traditional woman, to whom Amy Irving's Hadass is in some ways a homage. *Yentl's* use of sex-disguise creates odd reverberations of feeling between the two women, which make one wonder what was accidental and to what extent Streisand, whose only film this is, knew what she was doing. But compared with the richness of this material, and the issues it raises, films like *Private Benjamin* or *Protocol* seem simply silly.

With *Yentl* Streisand also provides another instance of how a seriously feminist film can work entirely within the established structure, be slick, middlebrow, undistinguished visually, and yet moving, with an audience impact of a breadth no film by von Trotta—let alone Helke Sander!—could ever have. In questioning "traditional sex roles and cast[ing] doubt on other cherished assumptions as well," *Yentl* "makes accessible to a large audience ideas that have previously been broached only in the works of 'serious' female fiction writers and academic feminist theorists."[53]

That it may be threatening for the same reason is suggested by *Yentl's* having been nominated for no Oscar, and by the paucity of writing about it despite its status as "the first major American film directed, coproduced, and co-written by a woman—who is also its star."[54] The crucial, though perhaps unanswerable, question, raised by Pauline Kael: "When a woman takes such control of a mass-market film, is the resulting work substantially different?"[55] elicits in the *Film Quarterly* review I am quoting from, by Fernley and Maloof, the view that the film contains a kind of revolutionary content within its popular context.

*Yentl* alters the feeling tone of Singer's story sufficiently to have evoked Singer's strong opposition, a troubling note because the Singer family, which produced three famous writer-brothers, also produced a promising and brilliant sister, said to be the model for Yentl. Like the stories of other such sisters—such as that of the invalid Alice, sister of Henry and William James, for one—that of this Singer sister, Esther Streitman, is painful and now deeply revealing. She wrote only one novel in her life, a life marked by unusual sufferings, breakdowns, and despair. The novel, *Deborah*, was published in 1983 through her son's actions in London, where Esther lived most of her life, having been married off to a totally unsuitable, crude, and rather brutal man, whom she accepted as a way of getting out of the hopeless confinement, for a girl like herself, of the Eastern European world she grew up in. Her novel conveys just this sense of yearning, frustration, exclusion, of a highly intelligent and gifted young girl in a rabbi's family. That *her* sailing away did not give *her* the "more" that Yentl seeks, perhaps involved many factors, even bad luck. But Esther Streitman's poignant story makes especially harsh Singer's irritated dismissals of Streisand's strong, honest attempt, in her own pop style, to tap into those same yearnings and dreams (though probably without ever knowing anything about Singer's sister or her book). This was no commercial enterprise for Streisand but a fifteen year obsession, completed despite all obstacles, indicating something of what it meant to her.

What is particularly strong about the film is the yearning to know, which Streisand focusses on from the start and never turns away from. The heroine's desire for sacred books, rather than the storybooks that are for women; her interest in books rather than carp; her hopelessness at fulfilling womanly duties like cooking; her father's pride in her, and her own joy of achieving, talking, arguing about ideas—all that is powerful feminism, and it does not get corrupted or diluted or betrayed by the popular form in which it is presented. Even the final song, which Yentl sings as she leaves the life she knows for a new life, about being able to see only a piece of sky—and then "I stepped outside and looked around,/I never dreamed it was so wide/Or even half as high"—sounds oddly like imagery from von Trotta's *Sheer Madness*. The fact that it is popularized in the artificiality and over-sweetness of a Streisand song does not rob it of value, or make it mean less to a spectator, though surely more to a less sophisticated spectator. Even the final imagery of flying carries echoes from Arzner to Shepitko to Erica Jong!

The Fernley and Maloof article makes a strong case both for the appropriateness of *Yentl*'s contested ending and for the film's homoeroticism, between the two women, Streisand's Anschel and Amy Irving's Hadass. Again linking girl-child development to close merger with the mother, as in Chodorow's *Reproduction of Mothering*, the writers argue that erotic love between women is a natural development for women: and concluding that Kael was right in feeling that a film so extraordinarily controlled by a woman would be different, they locate its difference primarily in the covert, devious, but unmistakably recognizable love (romantic love) that exists between the two women. To anyone who has watched the film closely, with all its disturbing cross-sexual currents, this is not a viewpoint to be hastily dismissed.

But going no further than the generally tender emotions between Streisand and the more conventional woman, these also take us again to that no-man's land (literally) of woman's respect for woman. Yentl herself yearns for a wife like Hadass—who wouldn't want such caring attention, she tells herself. At what point all this intense emotion can be called erotic attraction is a question again raised by this film. The authors of the article argue that perhaps our being heterosexual or homosexual distinctly and entirely is itself the notion that needs revising. Certainly this study of women directors points in that direction.

Of course, Yentl's tribute to Hadass can be seen more simply and cynically as a mass-art strategy to please everyone, Streisand's reassurance to those many of her fans who live conventional lives. They can feel then that the film is not reproaching, but rather accepting, their lives, even if Yentl herself is rebellious and demanding. It must be added though, and again one can't be sure how consciously Streisand did this, that Hadass also looks pitiful in her vacuity—as she constantly changes her shape, her opinions, to please the male, constantly checking whether this or that is to his liking. The vision of the "real woman," in her pretty sweetness, with her beautifully prepared food and her pet-like deference, strikes one finally as repellent, the character revealing the full emptiness of traditional ideal woman as nothing else that comes to mind. If one indeed experiences Hadass this way, presumably Streisand is expressing more than Yentl's loving attraction to her—and the emotional landscape of ways of being a woman becomes remarkably complex.

The ending of *Yentl*, with the heroine refusing marriage to the really appealing good man, opting instead for an open-ended future, is not unique in the last few years. It still feels bold, however, especially in the context of all the obligatory returns, through film history, of women to their men, whether suitable or inadequate. If Yentl married Avigdor, he would want her to give up learning, or to study covertly at home. He expresses his views in exactly the kindly, humanistic way of shtetl tradition, telling the woman that children are more important than Talmud, and that a wise woman knows everything without opening a book and that's a greater miracle. Yentl, not enticed, goes off alone to America, to a life of possibility, the boat journey a metaphor for a new social place. Mazursky ends *An Unmarried Woman* on a related note, but he leaves the charming prince close at hand (though temporarily removing him physically). So does Gillian Armstrong in the Australian *My Brilliant Career*, a film that when it came out looked bolder than it really was—in less-than-good-faith dangling of a romantic match before us through the whole film, though Armstrong really means in the end to have her heroine go off alone to her writing. *Private Benjamin* also ends with Judy's stalking off in her wedding dress, miming the ending of *The Graduate*, though Judy's gesture seems largely silly rhetoric. But it is not rhetoric when Yentl sings, "Papa, I have a voice now,/ Papa, I have a choice now." It is feminism, it is the American Dream; Streisand does it well and moves very large audiences with it, and more power to her.

As *Yentl* got made because Streisand cherished and promoted the project for fifteen years, a sizable number of other women too have had an impact on the U.S. film industry not as directors but as producers. Jane Fonda created her IPC production company so that a film would be made about Vietnam that involved women, and also because she was concerned that good roles disappear for actresses once they enter their forties. Among IPC's credits are *Coming Home*, *China Syndrome*, and *Nine to Five*, one of 1981's biggest money makers (though it is hard to feel enthusiastic about that film either for its comic art or its feminism). Other well-known actresses like

Jessica Lange (*Country*) or Sally Field (*Places in the Heart*) have fought for projects, carried them through to fruition (sometimes with the special support of a woman executive within the company), and often played the heroine as well. Jessica Lange has written exuberantly about her role in *Country*, not only as the central character, a farmer's wife, Jewell Ivy, but as the force behind the project: "It's hard for me to separate the playing of the character from the making of the film, because it's my film. It sprang out of the knowledge I had of what was going on in rural America, and I co-produced it."[56] She speaks proudly of how the film, "a good, small, honest film—not sentimental, not romanticized,"has been used to organize farmers and educate them, and how audiences of farmers have stood up and cheered at the end. Her commitment to the project was passionate and personal also in the way she drew on her whole family in rural Minnesota for her part, "to convey the tremendous strength and tenacity of these women in balance with a heartbreaking vulnerability."[57]

This access by women to a kind of power male actors like Warren Beatty or Paul Newman have long had, is heartening, though in the energetic instance of a figure like Goldie Hawn, it can be equally disheartening. Hawn's intense activity in recent years promoting projects, or actually serving as producer or co-producer of a number of the films in which she has starred, culminated in her creating her own production company, the Hawn-Sylbert Movie Company, with Anthea Sylbert. It was Sylbert, whose credits go back to May's *Heartbreak Kid* (as designer), who was a Warner Brothers executive when *Private Benjamin* was in production; who as vice-president at United Artists in charge of production put *Swing Shift*, a longtime project of Hawn's, into development; and who went on to serve as executive for other films, including the supervising of *Yentl*.

Hawn and Sylbert formed their partnership in 1982 following the success of *Private Benjamin* (which took in $175 million in ticket sales). *Swing Shift* was underway at the time, although neither Hawn nor Sylbert were involved as producers with that film (which was marked by battles between director Demme and Hawn, and ended up making less than $7 million). The first full-fledged production to appear under the aegis of the new company was *Protocol*, which grossed more than $26 million, followed by *Wildcats*. A future film, intended for Hawn and Barbra Streisand, *The Sisters Project*, intriguingly has the two actresses playing sisters and may also involve Streisand's own production company.

Hawn's might seem an enterprising and exciting career were the quality of her work higher. *Private Benjamin* has the appearance of a feminist fable for the masses, as well as a light and pleasing entertainment: "JAP" gets turned into a "mensch" by the Army, someone who can take care of herself and who is no longer a spoiled, self-indulgent woman who lives only to order furniture and to satisfy men. So profound is her transformation in the course of the film, we are told, that she finally walks out on the man who is everything a girl like her would ever have wanted, a young, handsome doctor with a beautiful house, and the bonus of old European class and elegance, as well as wealth. In her wedding gown she walks out of the house and up a road, without a future, without anyone else in her life, accompanied only by her sense of her own dignity and a refusal to accept what degrades her.

Apparently a stirring moral. Why then does the film feel like a crude, slick TV sitcom, which *Yentl* avoids being? Both films work with classical aspects of the Jewish milieux, the shtetl, the JAP. Yet the crassness of the world Hawn depicts is in Hawn's own sensibility, so somehow the definition of the strong accomplishing woman in this film seems entirely off the mark: learning to march with the pack in the army and follow orders to do punishing deeds of great physical endurance, and be praised by authoritarian army papa for doing so; getting invited into the equivalent of the Green Berets; comradery and solidarity illustrated by swapping tales about orgasm with the rest of the gals. These seem stupid extremes for a laugh, without relevance to real life, not resonant in larger ways, a peculiar way to define a woman's making it. In the later scenes at SHAPE headquarters in Belgium, Judy seems to be just a glorified secretary looking glamorous in picturesque Europe.

That there is no serious work alternative in the film is one indication of its vacuity and lack of real seriousness. So too is the fact that the only other important woman is the heroine's arch enemy, out to get her, competitive bitch-fighting straight out of old Hollywood. Comedy of course can chronicle the developing and struggling self—as Woody Allen's does. Hawn may think that this is what she too is doing, but she is really only toying with feminism while still being a kewpie doll, her scripts without intelligence, her films without invention or freshness or reality. The reasons why Judy walks out of the last marriage—unlike Yentl's desire to be free to develop her mind and be more—are also too familiar, conventional ones, like a womanizing man and his old girlfriend.

*Swing Shift* is an even more startling case in point, since it works so closely with the material of Connie Field's feminist documentary. *Rosie the Rivetter* (1978). Not only is that film shockingly not credited in *Swing Shift*, but the spirit of the film was altered almost beyond recognition. Since we are not dealing with some great classic novel, it may be unfair to ask *Swing Shift* to show fidelity to *Rosie*. But the changes from passionate feminist documentary to Hollywood feature are instructive, even with a powerful and supposedly feminist woman as a main architect—though again Hawn and director Demme were at loggerheads. Indeed, it seems significant that so good a director as Demme walked out on the film with his editor, "rather than participate in work we didn't believe in: There was a portion of the footage that I didn't care for and didn't want to shoot, but I did it anyway. The script I agreed to do was first and foremost the story of a friendship between two women during the war years. Those women's relationships with the men in their lives were not supposed to be what it was all about.''[58]

But that is exactly what the film is about. Hawn's role as Kay was expanded to suit Hawn, as was a subplot about Kay's husband's return from the war, and *Swing Shift* spends an enormous amount of its time on male–female relations, extensive footage on Hawn's uninteresting husband and the sweet guy who pursues her endlessly at work, with his funny motorbike, and his jazz and black musician colleagues, and the sadness of his heart trouble—doubtless all to disqualify him as a future marital possibility, lest we wonder why anyone would let him go for a husband like Kay's. This, and Kay's endless guilt over being unfaithful to her husband, are the major interest of the film. It deals only summarily with how the women were drawn to factory work by war propaganda, and the work itself. Even the final judgment has the women consoling themselves with ''We showed them'' (their men, that is)—thus themselves restoring the patriarchal power eroded by the war. The film retains only the most minimal sense of Kay and Hazel sharing their lives. And *Rosie's* deliberate addressing of truly diverse people is reduced in *Swing Shift* to a couple of black women visible on a line, and—almost an offensive joke—a midget among the women rivetters, a Hollywood-style token for all the human difference left out. In short, the mere presence of a powerful woman actress/producer shaping projects doesn't mean either that those projects will be of any interest artistically, or that they will necessarily be less cynical and degraded in their visions of women than the male-produced commercial product.

*Protocol*, the first film of Hawn's new company, is even more disheartening than her earlier two films, a shameless vehicle for placing Hawn at the center of everything, Barbie doll perfection of hairdos and clothes styles, a silly pointless comedy, with the whole world loving the cocktail waitress Sunny who becomes part of the State Department. The film draws heavily on Frank Capra films, though fatally without Capra's passion and vision, obviously hoping to tap into the new American patriotism. The worlds Hawn is drawn to, the Army, the protocol of the State Department, are never seen critically, they are just background. And Mr. President's call in *Protocol* is received by her heroine with just the same goggle-eyed reverence and satisfaction with which she responds to the green-beret leader type in *Private Benjamin*, authoritarian daddies patting her on the head as she continues to be the silly dizzy girl-child. It is not surprising that Hawn ends the film with a dedication to Daddy. But it is also again significant that the only other major woman character, the strikingly handsome Gail Strickland who plays Ambassador St. John, a woman with great power and a pro, gets struck down in the end, and more degradingly than the men sychophants, as she sprawls on the ground, backside up, in our final view of her. It is exactly the fate of the commanding woman played by Eileen Brennan in *Private Benjamin*. The spirit behind these projects is entrepreneurial and self-adulating, certainly not feminist, not even just genuinely respectful of women.

Sunny, like Judy, is everyone's darling, and though she is a scatterbrain, we are meant to feel that underneath there is a great deal more to her. With her loud portable-radio "box" among the fancy Washington types, she is a populist heroine, stopping an assassin, triumphant in her bid for political office, which everyone begs her to make! At the same time she has husband and child—in short, everything. At the same time Sunny's accomplishments amount to nothing. The film's point is unclear, vague, but unobjectionable, something tagged on about how we should vote and keep an eye on government.

*Wildcats* is the latest installment in Hawn's cinematic argument that women can be as tough as men any time, a kind of macho competitiveness. This film again draws, Capra-like, on popular material—football, cute little blonde taming the black ghetto beasts that set everyone else cowering, the magically strong individual who makes miracles happen, who out of her tough tenacity and grit gets all us Americans, black and white together, working in harmony in the end for that touchdown. The whole idea of proving to others that you can do it—which fuels the film—seems sad, as it seems far too late in the day to ask us to believe in the kind of liberalism voiced here, even in a fairy tale. Hawn conveys only the surface of the world her heroine has to conquer, keeping a good distance from any real characterizing of the blacks in the film, or the whites, falling back on slapstick and action shots whenever possible. Janet Maslin, talking about the predictability of Hawn's repeated redoings of the "iron buttercup roles in which [she] has been specializing," hits on the principal evasion:

However dogmatically attuned it is to sexism, "Wildcats" never acknowledges any possibility of racial tensions between the dainty blond coach and her mostly black football team; when Miss Hawn is seen venturing alone into a tenement . . . she seems almost willfully oblivious of any potential danger. Perhaps some of her confidence grows out of the fact that the players, for all their rudeness, are essentially so tame. . . . The team's cheerleaders . . . are a good deal raunchier than the players themselves.[59]

Feminist statements appear at several crucial points: the heroine assures her younger daughter that she can be a helicopter pilot or anything else she wants. And the heroine's determination to go ahead with the coaching is accounted for by all the years of her marriage she had her husband's opinions, now finally wanting her own. But again the extremity of the life change makes it silly and not to be taken seriously on any level.

Despite some courage in dealing with such charged material, though softened by many evasions, the lack of intelligence and freshness remain major problems. Hawn is one of the few Hollywood women with real power. It seems, at least to one with the luxury of watching from the sidelines, obscene to use this power to such trivial ends, geared only to the making of money through banal cheap patriotism and through a kind of pop feminism that looks half the time like its opposite. Yet perhaps Hawn has been able to achieve the power she has just because this is what she is. Any woman's increased power in Hollywood is bound to open doors for others, some of whom will surely make more substantial use of the opportunity. Still, the career of producer Goldie Hawn makes clear that the simple empowering of women, plus apparent good intentions, do not necessarily constitute improvement—possibly instead even a corruption of feminism.

## NOTES

1. In June of 1980, a committee of women members of the Directors Guild of America presented the following statistics to a meeting of studio and TV network executives: "Of the 7,332 feature films . . . released by major distributors during the last 30 years, only 14, or two-tenths of 1 percent, were directed by women." Also, out of 65,500 hours of national TV during the same period, only 115 hours or two-tenths of 1 percent, were directed by women. And 35 of those 115 hours were directed by Ida Lupino. Louise Heck-Rabi, *Women Filmmakers: A Critical Reception* (Metuchen, NJ and London: Scarecrow Press, 1984), 246.

2. Sharon Smith, *Women Who Make Movies* (New York: Hopkinson & Blake, 1975), 51.

3. Ibid., 50.

4. Marion Meade makes the contrary argument—in breezy journalese, with clever points that also show their age a bit—that Elaine May turns traditional sex roles inside out in *A New Leaf*, because the woman is economically independent, and passionately interested in her work, work which is not a dilettantish diversion, and she is not in pursuit of a husband. She argues that in Henry she gets what she needs, a wife, someone to take care of things for her, "run her house . . . make sure her clothes are presentable, and accompany her on field trips." However, Meade does notice that "the intensity of male contempt for women is staggering" in both the May film and Barbara Loden's *Wanda*, and wishes that both directors' "little-girl women could have shown a touch more spunk." "Lights! Camera! Women!" *New York Times*, April, 25, 1971, 11:1.

5. Lester D. Friedman, *Hollywood's Image of the Jew* (New York: Unger, 1982), 255.

6. This statement, and others in this essay generally ascribed to May, was made on November 17, 1986, during a question and answer period at the Museum of Modern Art in New York, following a screening of *Mikey and Nicky*, part of the Directors Guild of America's 50th Anniversary Tribute in honor of Elaine May's achievement.

7. Vincent Canby, "*The Heartbreak Kid*", *New York Times*, Dec. 18, 1972, 56:1.

8. Canby, "*A New Leaf*", *New York Times*, March 12, 1971, 28:1.

9. Canby, "*Mikey and Nicky*", *New York Times*, Dec. 22, 1976, 34:4.

10. Ibid.

11. See Elizabeth Dalton's work on working women's films.

12. Carey Winfrey, "Claudia Weill: It's Her Turn Now," *The New York Times,* 15.

13. Carrie Rickey, "Where the Girls Are," *American Film* (Jan./Feb. 1984), 53.

14. Ibid.

15. Seidelman, speaking now about "filming in the Lower East Side junkie heavens in the dead of night," adds, "We were so stupid, never thinking about being robbed or shot." *Moviegoer* (November 1986), 7.

16. See Rickey, 68.

17. "A Blow for Independents," *New York Times* (Jan. 27, 1985), 17.

18. Ibid.

19. "NYU film school graduate desperately seeking success," *Washington Square News,* 19, 21.

20. Ibid., 5.

21. Ibid.

22. Leora Barish, *Film Comment* (June 1985), 16.

23. Lindsy Van Gelder, "On the Set of *Desperately Seeking Susan,*" *Ms.* (April 1986), 114.

24. Ibid.

25. *New York Times* (March 29, 1985), C5.

26. *New York Times* (May 3, 1986).

27. Ruby Rich, "Good Girls, Bad Girls," *The Village Voice* (April 15, 1986), 89.

28. Ibid.

29. Elayne Rapping, *Cineaste* 15, no. 1 (1986), 36.

30. See Kaplan, *Women & Film,* 73–82.

31. Joyce Carol Oates, "Where Have You Been, Where Are You Going?" *The Wheel of Love* (Greenwich, CT: Fawcett, Crest, 1970), 115.

32. Joyce Carol Oates, *New York Times* (March 23, 1986), 22.

33. *Boston Sunday Globe,* (April 13, 1986), B8.

34. Rich, "Good Girls," 89.

35. See Bill Nichols, *Ideology and the Image* (Bloomington: Indiana University Press, 1981), chap. 5.

36. Rich, "Good Girls," 89.

37. Elaine Warren, "Amy Heckerling," *Moviegoer* (January 1985): 11.

38. Ibid.

39. Zina Klapper, "Movie Directors: Four women who get to call the shots in Hollywood," *Ms.* (Nov. 1985), 62, 65–7.

40. Ibid., 65.

41. Ellen Stein, "Careers in Movieland," *Ms.* (July 1984), 98.

42. "What Has Never Been," Bonnie Zimmerman, in *The New Feminist Criticism: Essays on Women, Literature, Theory,* edited by Elaine Showalter (New York: Pantheon Books, 1985), 200–24.

43. Ibid., 205.

44. Ibid.

45. Ibid., 206.

46. *Boston Globe* (April 13, 1986), B1.

47. Ibid., B8.

48. B. Ruby Rich, "Desert Heat," *The Village Voice* (April 8, 1986), 72.

49. Ibid., 71.

50. Ibid.

51. Ibid., 72.

52. Steven Bach, *Final Cut* (New York: William Morrow & Company, 1985), 390.

53. Allison Fernley and Paula Maloof, "Yentl," *Film Quarterly* (Spring 1985), 38.

54. Ibid.

55. Ibid.

56. *New York Times* (Sept. 16, 1984), H19.

57. Among many other instances is the actress Mary Steenburgen's collaborative project, *End of the Line*, with herself producing and a young film student directing, her encouragement having led to his screenplay. " 'It happens that both of our fathers worked for railroads.' The film is about railroad workers in Arkansas, which is where both she and the young director grew up, and 'The film is a real labor of love.' " *New York Times* (Aug. 22, 1986), C6.

58. *New York Times* (May 4, 1986), C8.

59. Janet Maslin, *New York Times* (Feb. 14, 1986), C5.

# 4
# Western European Women Directors

## GERMANY

### The Development of a Major Director: Margarethe von Trotta

*Von Trotta's Achievement*

Margarethe von Trotta—who over the last decade has directed six films, all good and two first-rate—must now be counted among major directors. She had made this leap so quickly and so recently that it is strange to find her only mentioned twice in passing in a book like Timothy Corrigan's *New German Cinema* (1983). Her work is also of special interest because it is a woman-centered and woman-affirming cinema of a kind still a rarity—women looked at with intensity and love by the woman behind the camera, by one another on the screen, and by women like oneself in the audience, to whose eyes the whole is directed; and because of the visual and dramatic bounty of metaphors and ideas with which von Trotta turns this into art. Von Trotta is engaged in the immense task of creating a major women's/feminist cinema where so little that is helpful existed before by way of model.

She has had to rely most on what she has learned from men, like Schlondorff and Bergman, which she then has put to her own uses. Though von Trotta's films use some traditional devices to create a cinema art that is relatively accessible, gripping, pleasure-giving, they never look like conventional traditional realism. Still, one is reluctant to call hers either a women's or a feminist cinema: she does far more than merely center on women characters, and yet, while she raises issues that are feminist, views women in ways one must call feminist, one hesitates to sum up her cinema with a word that suggests something ideological, programmatic (however appealing the ideology and the program). Von Trotta often gives us responses that feminists may find dismaying—showing us, for instance, in *Sheer Madness* that the freeing of one woman, shackled by heterosexual dependency and subordination, through the love and support of another woman, can lead to murder, or the dream of murder. While the moral of the film is certainly not that women are better off left undisturbed in their self-hatred and helplessness, you come away with uncomfortable and jarring questions, as you do from the sound of the boy Jan's voice commanding Juliane to begin at the end of *Marianne and Juliane*. Hence, despite von Trotta's opting to, and her capacity to, create illusion and identification with characters, audience identification in her case does not lull and close off thinking, and certainly does not bind the spectator more closely to patriarchal ideology—the main grounds for the strong opposition to narrative on the part of feminist film theorists over the past decade. Von Trotta communicates a radical content through a richly engaging and highly professional narrative form. And through the strong narrative involvement into which they draw us, the films disturb us deeply, leave us each time—but especially in *Marianne and Juliane* and *Sheer Madness*—with anything but emotional closure, raise in us questions, and contain values that would be anathema in more conventional cinema. One is grateful that von Trotta is too complex, too ambiguous, to fit into any ideology; that she draws her vision from deeper, wilder places—more paradoxical, irrational, intransigent sources. Hers is a women's cinema, *and* a feminist cinema, and more than these.

### Von Trotta's Career

Von Trotta—who spent a number of years collaborating with her husband Volker Schlondorff, as actress, screenplay-writer, and eventually co-director—with *The Lost Honor of Katarina Blum* in 1977 sufficiently defined herself or felt enough confidence in her own powers to no longer find that arrangement workable. Conflicts arose between her and Schlondorff over the shape *Katarina Blum* was to take, he choosing to focus on external action and she wanting to work further with motivation (no surprise if you consider that film in relation to, say, *Marianne and Juliane*). Von Trotta concluded some years later: "You can't co-direct. It's a hypocritical term. All I did was work with actors. Volker was in charge of the technique, the artistry, the way the film finally looked. As a director I make the decisions myself. I've watched and collaborated enough."[1]

The route von Trotta took to her own directing is by no means a privileged one but very familiar from the biographies of women filmmakers, a remarkable number of whom are or have been married to directors, from

Maya Deren to Agnes Varda to Larisa Shepitko; others have worked with husbands in some kind of film partnership, like Muriel Box the English director, or Mai Zetterling. Sometimes the man, like Schlondorff, is initially more famous than the woman (Mészáros and Jancso are another obvious example), and can be the woman director's entry and her mentor, or an advocate, or at least a supportive comrade-in-arms doing related though different work. Acting and screenplay-writing too are frequently paths of entry for women directors (Diane Kurys is one of many examples here, or Elaine May, or Ida Lupino and Mai Zetterling of earlier generations).

There are those who grumble about von Trotta, perhaps unduly influenced by such an unbalanced, unconvincing attack on her as feminist critic Charlotte Delorme's review of *Marianne and Juliane* in the influential *Frauen und Film*.[2] There is perhaps the feeling that she has had special access through a man, (perhaps also involving disapproval of Schlondorff's own fairly commercial movie-making style)—and through money, especially given the bitter struggle of other German women directors for funding. (Márta Mészáros with her characteristic forthrightness summarily commented when I interviewed her[3] that those complaining German women directors don't get funding because they are not good! Whereas the good directors, like von Trotta, Helka Sander, and Helma Sanders-Brahms, keep getting the money they need.) But women directors in Germany have created a lively and fertile feminist film culture over the decade, have fought for and, to a remarkable degree, won an enlargement of possibilities.[4] That so many feminist film directors have been able to work in Germany, however difficult the struggle for funding, is unprecedented and unequalled anywhere else in the world, and makes for an excitingly abundant soil for any woman filmmaker to work in. But since her first solo film, *The Second Awakening of Christa Klages*, von Trotta has evidenced a growth that has set her far beyond anything coming from other German women directors.

Comparing von Trotta's work now with the films she did with Schlondorff indicates the extent to which she is working with earlier themes and values, and what she learned from Schlondorff and adapted to her own distinctive uses: most importantly, perhaps, his deliberately turning radical politics into accessible populist film forms; his having through thriller genre techniques and other means tried to render that material engrossing and available to broader audiences. But no one could mistake von Trotta's films—which take us to dark disturbing places that open our fundamental values to question, with their haunting psychological content—for conventional films.

### The Von Trotta Heroine

Repeatedly drawn to activist heroines, von Trotta for her first independent effort, *The Second Awakening of Christa Klages*, chose for her central character a woman who resorts to violent anti-social action—robbery—for money to sustain a childcare center, at once creating exciting drama, raising a central feminist issue, and making a social critique. In addition, the matter of state-subsidized childcare for single mothers may well have had particularly heavy personal import for von Trotta, since in interviews she has described her own childhood as a hard, poverty-stricken one, living in near squalor in one small room with a Russian unmarried mother, from an old noble family, who went to work as an office clerk while the very young child begged on the street for money for food. That von Trotta would move from figures like Katarina Blum in her last picture with Schlondorff, to Christa Klages on her own, on to the terrorist Marianne in *Marianne and Juliane*, as well as feminist activists like Juliane in the same film, and like Olga of *Sheer Madness*—to her perhaps most ambitious heroine, the heroic revolutionary figure of Rosa Luxemburg—conveys a strong continuity of concern. At the same time, the differences among these central women characters record a shifting development of values that invite exploration.

What is most striking when you compare von Trotta's work with Schlondorff—say, their last film together, *The Lost Honor of Katarina Blum*—with von Trotta's own treatment of terrorism, *Marianne and Juliane*, is the superficiality of Blum, a conventional kind of woman, pretty, captive of the love dream, hounded victim of all those patriarchal males of the ruthless yellow press, the fascistic police, and the other anti-establishment cliches (whatever truths they may also contain) of the lying, murderous institutions of society. The film as a whole is built on external, thriller genre techniques for creating suspense—and Katarina Blum is like a shadow of the man she gets implicated with, he the active one, she getting into it vicariously, standing for little in her own right. She and the heroine of *Coup de Grace* can't begin to be compared in interest with the later von Trotta women characters, in films which genuinely center on the female psyche and female action in the world, the woman herself the fully individuated person at the center, the fiercely committed one. In *her* treatment of terrorism, von Trotta considers Marianne with all the tensions of dialectic, sees her from many refracting angles, dramatic fragmented meetings, memory images, a pastiche of other people's responses. The sum is highly critical of the terrorist (this is clearly the real reason for Delorme's distorted attack, a fury at social democratic values) but complex, as the best art must be, working with the self and the political together, with no easy polemic anywhere. While Juliane is our center, and she repudiates the values Marianne lived by, the terrorist is her sister, a part of her. Serious political concern, in this case a highpower dialogue on the Left, constitute one of the continuities of von Trotta's work. And though Marianne's political position is not clearly defined, a more specific mapping of where exactly on the extreme Left she is is not information crucial to the film, because it is political in a broader way—as well as being able to rely on the nation's recent memory of the Red Brigade, the Baader Meinhof gang, and Gudrun Ensslin herself, model for Marianne.

Von Trotta's first two heroines, too—Christa Klages, and Maria, of *Sis-*

*ters*, before Marianne—are very distinctive women, and in *Marianne and Juliane* and *Sheer Madness*, not only are Marianne and Juliane, and Olga, and even Ruth, the centers of interest but also the active forces, powerful even if the real power is what they are engaged in struggle with. Von Trotta's turning then to the figure of Rosa Luxemburg is continuous with her political commitment, but also involves an interest in a woman of great public power and effectiveness, who is also an intellectual. Stanley Kauffmann, though he raises questions about *Rosa Luxemburg* in his *New Republic* review (aptly headed "A Large Life"), stunningly calls von Trotta "arguably the best filmmaker now at work," addressing a subject that "only an artist of her talent and intellect would attempt."[5] Von Trotta was drawn to her for the many layers of her personality, not only the politics but her artistic leanings, her humanity, and her being able to be a woman among men without giving anything of her womanness up, which von Trotta said was very important to herself, understandably given her own position as a major woman artist in an arena of men. Whatever the film's flaws, and it is certainly more flawed than those that precede it, it is moving for its ambition, in taking on a figure—especially in these conservative days—whose whole life was committed to changing the world. And it is moving simply to have an epic film built around a woman, an intellectual political heroine defined by intelligence, strength, courage, highly respected even to adulation. Yet the film creates this portrait without sentimentality, even if it provides a softer, less deeply complex, less sharp-edged and vital sense of this remarkable person than one could have wished, perhaps because of the massiveness of the materials.

In keeping with the way women save other women in her work, von Trotta spoke when I interviewed her of "Rosa" in a very intimate, almost mystical, way as having helped her in her struggle to shape the film ("She gave me a lot. . . . I sometimes had the feeling [of] internalizing her, that I became her. . . . that she was present. . . . I had the feeling she really wanted to let me know things about her that were not yet known.") For all her willingness to take on a really whole woman, von Trotta has not exhausted the theme of sisters, with everything it has meant for her in terms of women struggling for autonomy, and struggling to become whole through incorporation of some buried part of the self. Her projected next film is about two close women friends yet again, one of whom gets cancer, she thinks because she took away the other woman's boyfriend. The sick woman is certain that only her friend, who has since become a doctor, can save her. So the enmeshment of two women, despite separation, the capacity to curse and to save the other woman, still remains at the center of von Trotta's imagination.

### Christa Klages and "The Look"

At the heart of her first solo film, *The Second Awakening of Christa Klages*, von Trotta places a long highly charged look between two women, her heroine bank robber and the woman bank clerk who Christa held up. It is almost as if von Trotta were directly responding to the issue of the famous Laura Mulvey male gaze. Everything hangs on this look, the whole film builds to it, Christa's future—freedom or imprisonment—depends on it. Conformity and marginality also confront and come to terms with one another across that exchanged look, but what makes a bridge possible between the two characters is finally their alliance as women. The mysterious bank clerk chooses to release Christa, refuses to find her guilty for her antisocial act, endorses her or feels at one with her, crosses over. Von Trotta's profound involvement with pairs of women, her own passionate gaze behind the camera repeatedly fixed on two women looking, has one of its most moving expressions when Christa Klages and the bank clerk exchange this look at the film's conclusion, a look frozen and held a long time through the final titles. If "the image of woman [has] always look[ed] through the mediation of the male,"[6] according to Judith Mayne, in this scene the looking pointedly excludes and rejects the intrusive male intervention. An exchange between two German film critics about Márta Mészáros' *Adoption*, in which a middle-aged widow yearning for a child takes under her wing a troubled young woman from a nearby foster home, applies repeatedly both to von Trotta's work and to other, later, Mészáros films:

*Lennsen*: But we don't visualize them in terms of mother and daughter...The women's identities are much more complex, and they are fluid in relationship to each other. Both of these women present their bodies; however, they present them not to the camera, but to each other.

*Fehervary*: In most films women either look or are looked at. The fact that the two women in this film really *look at each other* is what makes it so explosive, I think. When I saw the film it occurred to me that I had hardly ever seen this kind of imaging on the screen. It was then I realized why the women's buddy films, like *One Sings, the Other Doesn't* or *The Turning Point* have been so disappointing to me: Two different types of women are displayed, almost "served up" to us to be consumed. As images they exist separately and interact only through the eye of the director or the camera.

*Lenssen*: I like the underlying homosexuality in male films about men, the so-called buddy films and many of the Westerns...I think [women] should use [these conventions] for our purposes.

*Fehervary*: Perhaps a new kind of female eroticism and creativity can be found in films that show how women both look and return the look. This kind of relational attitude might be more subversive to the patriarchal film code than any kind of terribly emancipated woman.[7]

The male gaze of classic Hollywood, with its voyeurism and fetishism, may have reduced women to spectacle, object, absence. But under the differently attentive eyes of women film directors, especially the best of them, like von Trotta and Mészáros—from the very early stages of their work in feature films their central characters are women defined as active, looking subjects, and that subversive relational attitude between women is at the heart of these directors' visions.

### Christa Klages: Other Central Notes Sounded

Christa is a most attractive figure, and von Trotta bestows on her an anti-social action of a forgivable sort, for an end hard to fault. It is even compatible in an odd way with traditional maternal female roles, since Christa commits this criminal act in behalf of children, to protect them. Even within so helpless a constituency, Christa is further concerned with the most powerless, the foreigners, the children of welfare families, children who would end in institutions otherwise. The issue of care for the children of single parents, or for working women generally, has of course always been important to feminism. A critique of capitalism is also implicit in the sense of outrage that wealthy societies are not willing to support such childcare centers as the one Christa has worked so hard for, while early in the film, a child reads out the astronomical prices people are willing to pay for luxury cars. So Christa's crime is sympathetic from a feminist perspective, a left perspective, and in terms of general compassion.

Still it is a crime and von Trotta, after beginning with the drama of the act itself, goes on to undercut our negative judgment in many ways: having no one get hurt, making the police very unsympathetic, but mainly through the pastor, Hans, to whom Christa and Werner, her partner in bankrobbing, go for help. The young pastor, a somewhat idealized man who looks more like an intellectual or artist than a pastor, becomes taken with Christa and, despite his moral horror when he discovers that she and Werner have committed a robbery, continues to help her and to find her highly sympathetic, thus disarming us of our moral censure of Christa. Indeed, in a church sermon, he associates her act with the heroic deaf and dumb Katrin in Brecht's *Mother Courage*. The repeated crosscutting to close-ups of Christa's face during this story makes clear that von Trotta, through the pastor, finds Christa's act a Christian one. (The character's name speaks for itself.)

Christa, while in some ways a sweet forerunner of Marianne—leaving her child behind for radical action that involves a risk of imprisonment, even death—and for a trip to a sunny revolutionary country (here Portugal, there Lebanon) is more ordinary, hearty and warm, motherly, than Marianne. With her partner and sometimes-lover Werner we see her protectiveness, given his neediness, his own bad experience with an institutionalized childhood providing another motivation for saving other children from similar harm. Christa is the strong one. The act she commits is full of risk, and though she commits it with males, she does so not as the males' helper or accomplice. It is *her* crime, hers the strong sense of motive, she the one with fierce authority. She gave everything to her childcare work (that work ethic is unwaveringly strong in every von Trotta film) and won't give it up. She is a fighter, brave and fearless—for which her friend Flo admired her at school as a girl. (It is not surprising to read that the situation within the film was an actual one and that at the time of the film's release, von Trotta "was herself imprisoned for a day for interrupting a trial connected with this case.'"[8]) At the same time Christa is not idealized. Though strong, she is also a modest character, impulsive and not thoughtful, becoming paralysed for a while. When asked in revolutionary Portugal to sing a song to her workmates, she rejects various suggestions, including a famous leftist song of triumphant struggle, choosing instead a plaintive song about Little Jacob who went into the woods and was never heard of again, even though his brother and his sister continued to call "Where is the Little Jacob?"—another fine instance of that unpredictability in von Trotta's art that one prizes. No socialist-realist-type poster figures in von Trotta, or whatever their 1980s feminist equivalents would be.

The film's male characters are generally sympathetic, with the exception of Flo's husband, away in the army during the week, bat-hunting on weekends, the reason for Flo's nightmare terrors. But the two central male characters, Werner and the pastor Hans, are seen as good men. Werner, however, is pitiful, uneducated, jealous, sad as one of life's victims, viewed with compassion but also seen as not interesting—though he is decent and protective of Christa as she is of him. The pastor, though, reads Yeats and Brecht, brings the coffee and is otherwise a nurturer, and seems to prefigure the later character of Juliane's Wolfgang. Both Werner and Hans are found sexually attractive by the women. The film subtly charts wayward erotic currents running four ways, through the four central characters, mitigating against stable, enclosed, exclusive paired partners (as is true of von Trotta's later films in different ways): Christa and Hans embrace under Werner's jealous observation; Christa's friend Flo and Werner are drawn to each other while Christa soberly watches but accepts.

But the real passion of the film is in the relationship between the two women, Christa and Flo, the delight they feel in one another's company, their joyful reminiscences of shared school experiences. When Werner, feeling excluded, thrusts his presence between them, it is an intrusion—a triangular emotion repeatedly examined and developed in later von Trotta films. But in this first film both kinds of loving seem to sit relatively comfortably side by side. When Werner is gunned down, Christa's anguish immediately enlarges into a grief for him shared by the two women. As Christa comforted Flo through her nightmares, so Flo comforts Christa through hers, and the film then casually moves the friendship between Flo and Christa into a lesbian love, as it casually allows these women love either for men or for one another. The connection between the two women flowers when Flo joins Christa in Portugal, itself deep in revolutionary change, though they are later asked to leave partly because people are conscious there is something special between them. The revolution has no room for woman-love.

The release through Christa of a woman locked into an oppressive heterosexual relationship that gives her nightmares, is the situation of von Trotta's later *Sheer Madness* seen from the other side, through the strong liberated one's life and point of view—as if through Olga and not through Ruth—though *Sheer Madness* works the other way, and though the material gets far richer and far more interesting by the time von Trotta made *Sheer Madness*. Without pursuing the question of where the breaking out leads the two women who break out, *Christa Klages* gives us the emergence of both Flo, and of the bankteller as well, both through Christa's strength and boldness. The theme of the magnetic attraction between two women is of course crucial to von Trotta's vision in every one of her films, as is the heroine's being a strong and sturdy fighter. It is interesting that Christa adopts an obvious male look during the Portuguese sequences, with her cap, pants, and general manner, though Flo is given a more conventionally "soft," "feminine" style. So, earlier, Christa notes that Flo is the kind of woman men want to marry, while Christa is not, is too independent. In *Sheer Madness* Ruth wears dresses and Olga pants, but the imagery there has more fluid import. Von Trotta never names the love between Christa and Flo; and though in general she establishes her heroines as all primarily heterosexual, and though in general sex in her films is very reticently handled, she also seems careful to keep what happens between the women just this side of explicitly sexual. She presents it as just naturally shading from intimacy and pleasure into sexual closeness, almost as if not worthy of making a fuss about.

Von Trotta's viewing the world from a female perspective begins with the narration, the first words of the film being a voiceover of Christa telling her own story, and reminding us of all those classic American films whose women characters are repeatedly presented to us through male voiceovers, like *Double Indemnity* and *Vertigo*, or whose stories are otherwise not in their own hands, like *Mildred Pierce*. Recurrent von Trotta images and themes are sounded when we see Christa first in front of a window (which is how *Marianne and Juliane* and *Sheer Madness* begin as well) talking about how she had to create her own jail before she realized what had happened to her, an imprisonment motif that also figures centrally in the films that follow it. The odd-looking bank clerk, whose usual punctuality and rule-following is suggested by how her single lateness astounds her office mate, and whose tight boyish haircut makes her look like the epitome of repression and control, begins a series of von Trotta's boxed-in people.

The bank clerk character can strike one as a genre contrivance to generate excitement, this sinister-looking woman with mysterious purposes who seems clearly to represent the other side. But even early in the film, before she knows anything about Christa, she is pointedly evasive about the photograph of Christa the police show her; and in her solitary room she places her own photo face next to Christa's, seeming drawn to the other woman with a secret link. The final sequences of the film orchestrate the suspense of who she really is, this stranger moving through the sites of Christa's world—the childcare center, Christa's mother's place, Christa's friend Flo's place—as later heroines also live one another's life, cross over the boundaries of self and other. The film's conclusion is prepared for by the bank clerk's disturbance at finding the childcare center being evicted, and by her aggressive and disapproving questioning of the landlord, who justifies his action on the grounds that the childcare center created a pig sty. The comment of one of the center's women that a sex shop is his idea of clean leads the bank clerk to join with the others in their scorn—for a society that finds sex shops okay but childcare centers not worthy of support. So when the bank clerk is asked by a group of men in the film's final scene to identify Christa, the intense look that the two young women exchange is not only very moving, but carefully prepared for. The film closes with the camera resting at length, through the credits, on Christa's face, showing, while trying not to expose to the observing men—pointedly evading the male gaze—the surprise and delight of her second awakening, an awakening (as in *Marianne and Juliane* and *Sheer Madness*) not in the time-honored way to a man, but to a woman. And to a woman not only in the one-to-one way of Christa with Flo but in the larger, more political, feminist way of solidarity of women with women—as well as an opening of one part of the self to another, a conversation within.

### The Sister Films

The three films between *Klages* and *Rosa Luxemburg*, the three "sister" films (though *Sheer Madness* is actually about intimate friends who are like sisters) now would appear to stand as a self-enclosed unit, steps in an increasingly complex exploration. The first of these, *Sisters*, or *The Balance of Happiness* (also called *The Balance of Fortune*), gains greatly by being considered with the two extraordinary films that follow it, *Marianne and Juliane* and *Sheer Madness*, containing as it does important ideas and images that von Trotta further orchestrates later. First, all three sister films have a kind of fairytale archetypal dream-like structure, doubtless related to the primacy von Trotta places on the subconscious and the unconscious and her own reference to the alter-egos in her films as "shadow selves" or "dream selves." The recurrent image of the movement into the bare-trunked woods, for instance, works like a fairytale archetype, which is the way it is actually used in *Sisters*, a "Once Upon a Time" into the woods of human mystery, turbulence, danger, confusion. Several times in *Sheer Madness* Olga suddenly appears before Ruth, in a way that is entirely improbable as realism, that feels like dream.

The woods image, with its feeling of pastness, of old tales, relates to the use of memory flashbacks, also recurrent in von Trotta, beginning in *Sisters*, which opens with a flashback, of a fairytale read by the two sisters as children, ur-narrative to start *this* narrative, as the ur-relationship of a shared childhood underlies their present relationship. The two young girls are often tightly set within a frame together, reading, putting on makeup together, endlessly reflected back in mirrors, sharing a past, although given much less time and more simply structured here, than when von Trotta uses it again later in *Marianne and Juliane* where the delicately complicated time layers form a major part of that film and make all the difference to it, humanizing the difficult and severe character of Marianne, deepening ideological discourse and relating it to both a personal and national past, explanation and distancing that serves to make the present more comprehensible and more sympathetic. In *Marianne and Juliane* the memory images are linked with Juliane, in *Sisters* with the dreamy artist sister—both rememberer and storyteller—who seems caught in the past as part of something regressive and pathological, a refusal to grow up. In *Sheer Madness* the device is used still differently again, less for memory than future images and fantasies, mostly Ruth's of herself hanged, in a lurid black and white, within the color of the present-time film.

The sense that the discourse of von Trotta's films is conducted by women and for them is further augmented by the striking use of song in the films, largely a woman's operatic voice, to accompany and intensify, add grandeur, to moments of immense pain. The sound has the effectiveness of another kind of heightened voiceover, woman-mourning and woman-comforting, woman-sorrow. This is important, from Christa's cantata, through the singing accompanying Anna's worst times of pain in *Sisters*, to the woman's voice, rich with tragic emotion, that contributes so much to the scene in *Marianne and Juliane* after Marianne dies, when Juliane is on a stretcher, hysterical with anguish, crying "When will there be another face like that again?"

But the most important common element in all the sister films has to do with the theme of freedom, of being locked in and trying to break out or lead someone else out. *Sisters* works with confinements of the human spirit, is filled with images of enclosure, walling Maria about at work and Anna at home. These strongly link to the prison confinements of *Marianne and Juliane* and the domestic confinements of *Sheer Madness*, barriers—with windows out to the world—that often operate in the films on a level that is subconscious and dreamlike. Even in *Rosa Luxemburg*, where the heroine through her life is confined in one prison after another, the literal sense of imprisonment is continually supplanted by a metaphorical sense, especially in several specific sequences: a series of silent shots of prison environs; a scene of women prisoners hurrying to a gate where they await release; and an image of Rosa sitting in her little garden within the prison courtyard.

In *Sisters* each sister feels boxed in: Anna continually positioned in front of a glass tank (for salamanders), her face frequently framed behind its glass rectangles; Maria equally boxed in, in long shot, by the sterile modern rectangular office partitions of her work place; and each sister by the other and by the needs of her own psyche.

As always in von Trotta, the public and private interweave. Critics have spoken of von Trotta as alternating between making personal films and political ones, calling *Sisters* one of the personal ones, but she is herself more precise about her practice when she says that no separation between the two is possible; and even *Sisters*, an apparently exclusively, even claustrophobically, private film, has its oblique commentary on a capitalistic technological world. Images of the practical work world are oppressive, the young lack enthusiasm for entering it, Maria's writer friend speaks scornfully of the self-packaging that goes into gaining success in this world and more than anything, von Trotta's own images of Maria's office, its inhumanness, long shots of a secretarial pool where all work like ants, makes its own indictment. But there is no keeping the public world out. When we for the first time watch Maria come home from the office, from public to private world, while she prepares dinner and her dark sister Anna comes toward her for the first time, a male radio voice is talking about how tests have just shown that rats could survive a nuclear war.

The vivid wonderful song sung several times in the course of the film, by a man who works in Maria's office, is a kind of personal journal-poem that regards getting through the day as an act of survival. It speaks of loving as well as eating out of a can, and voices the dream of bursting out of the confines, knocking down the facades and taking responsibility, yearning to feel life. This song provides the setting and correlative for Maria's new romance, very short-lived, with Maurice, her boss's son, but it is an existential and general social statement as well, and not an optimistic one. At the line: "If you do what you want, you're living in danger," Maria turns to Maurice with a large smile of recognition. And the lyric continues, that you can only be free if you do what they want you to. As it applies to Maria's life, the breaking away is both from the tie to Anna, which is suffocating to her, and also from larger social confinements.

## The Issue of Merging Identities

But while the public world is unpleasant and difficult, most threatening is the interior world in *Sisters*, because identity itself is continually at risk. The merging of identities is also a powerful preoccupation in *Marianne and Juliane*: the merged faces of the sisters in the mirrored glass of the prison present a disturbing image of Marianne's disintegration and perhaps Juliane's too; as does Juliane's acting out of Marianne's forcefeeding, and even her acting out of her sister's death. Parallel and equally chilling in *Sisters* is Maria's seeing her dead sister's face and not her own when she looks in the mirror, her identity supplanted—an engulfment conveyed not only through that image but through the whole film, which gives a sinister general sense that Maria's life is possessed, in some terrifying way, by Anna, by this Other. The merging theme, and the exchange of identities, someone haunting someone else's private space, done chillingly, but beyond mere genre chills, evokes that thinness of boundary separation Nancy Chodorow, in her important book about female development, *The Reproduction of Mothering*, notes as special to women.

Miriam serves as yet another instance of one woman inhabited by another. She is just the right addition to the film's blend, with her "feminine" charm and wiliness, her hustling eye on the main chance—namely a rich husband to marry. She is entirely different from either of the other two central characters, and even a relief for her lightweight soul. But just that appealing liveliness of hers, that sprightly and more "normal" quality, makes all the more terrifying her becoming possessed by the spirit of the Other, her gradually turning inward and growing immobilized. No doubt much of the terror, of essentially a vampire theme, derives from being in someone else's control, one who takes away your autonomy.

That lack of defined boundaries—at the very center of film after film by von Trotta—is an area not only of threat, to an endangered ego, but of extraordinary empathy, which von Trotta as a person herself often communicates even to people who have just met her. The touching, even strange, way she speaks of Rosa as with her, helping her, in the struggle to shape her film, is another form of the same theme. The merging of selves, von Trotta's most distinctive theme, von Trotta herself views as deriving ultimately from her own intense relationship with her own mother, though in interviews she also points to other biographical sources for various films: a friendship of hers for *Sheer Madness*; the actual Ensslin sisters, one of whom became von Trotta's friend, for *Marianne and Juliane*; a sister she feels she was subconsciously aware she had, even through *Sisters*. In any case, von Trotta's preoccupation with merging identities, though grounded in the peculiar realities of her biography, coincides with a differentiation issue central to women generally.

It is so central that Nancy Chodorow places the issue at the heart of *The Reproduction of Mothering*, where her thesis—well known by now since her book is deservedly widely referred to—is that the enormously formative process of being mothered is experienced very differently for a child of the same sex as the mother, and a child of the opposite sex. Boys, to establish themselves as male, have to turn away from their profound love for the mother, to identify with the father, and so make a sharp and final break from that early total love. This is a process that endows them with strong ego boundaries, as well as making them shun the empathetic, and other functions that would mean a regression to mother love, threatening to their whole sense of themselves as male. Women, Chodorow notes, who obviously don't have to make that kind of shift—and who therefore never make a final break, are continually concerned as a result with the issues of establishing a separate identity, with problems of autonomy and dependence, of experiencing oneself as a separate person.

The issues Chodorow identifies as crucial to women, like those at the center of von Trotta's films, are above all related to merged identities. In pre-puberty, Chodorow writes, "a daughter acts as if she is and feels herself unconsciously one with her mother,"[9] and mothers, because they are the same sex as their daughters, tend to experience the daughter "as an extension or double of the mother herself."[10] Chodorow notes that "the ease of this [gender-role] identification [with her mother] and feelings of continuity with her mother conflict with a girl's felt need to separate from her and to overcome her ambivalent and dependent preoedipally-toned relationship."[11] Her relation with her father, however important, can never have the same kind of impact on her, "as the earlier relation to the mother, since it does not concern whether or not she is a separate person."[12] Noting the way both boys and girls look at the culture for males or females to identify with beyond their father or mother, Chodorow writes that they do so for different reasons: "The girl is not trying to figure out how to be feminine, but how not to be her mother."[13] Often she turns to close friendship with another girl because it "permits her to continue to experience merging, while at the same time denying feelings of merging with her mother. . . . A girl alternates between total rejection of a mother who represents infantile dependence and attachment to her, between identification with anyone other than her mother and feeling herself her mother's double and extension."[14]

Certainly this material from Chodorow about the "tendency in women toward boundary confusion and a lack of sense of separateness from the world,"[15] applies almost exactly to each von Trotta film, even if translated there to sisters and friends, making a little more distant and equal the relation between the two women than would be true of a mother and daughter. The primacy Chodorow gives this issue in her analysis of the shaping of the psyches of women within the sex-gender system, perhaps explains why this material, given the same kind of primacy in von Trotta's films, has such a haunting impact, on this spectator at least. That impact has to do not only with von Trotta's skills, which are considerable, at building disturbance through thriller-style narrative codes, but more importantly, with her reaching deeply into central material, especially for the female spectator, relating to that original bonding and to problems of differentiation and of guilt at going one's own way.

While Nancy Chodorow argues that that kind of merging of personality is mainly an issue of female development, of incomplete separation of mother and daughter, of course certain male directors—most notably Bergman and most brilliantly of course in *Persona*—work intensely with merged selves, lack of clear boundaries, schizophrenically-split selves. Although von Trotta herself has reservations as to the extent of Bergman's influence on her work—aptly noting that his name is continually evoked with hers because he is one of the few male directors who has worked closely, for his own reasons, with pairs of women—still, her debt to *Persona* seems reflected in all three sister films, even in the virtuoso ways she visually handles two faces in closeup. The confusion of boundaries, a female propensity to merge that sometimes seems to become psychosis, fills *Sisters* with the horror of looking into the mirror and seeing the other one; of guilt at trying to separate from the other one; of suffocating under the burden of the other's total neediness.

That this area is especially charged and obsessive for von Trotta also derives from yet another odd biographical note. Von Trotta has spoken in interviews about the strange experience of discovering that she herself, who had been brought up as an only child of a single mother, with whom she was extremely close and shared everything, had an older sister whose existence her mother had kept secret from her. This discovery, made after her mother died, and after she directed *Sisters* and appeared on German TV to discuss it, was so traumatic that it precipitated a breakdown. So perhaps the film, and even those that followed, issued from fantasies that consciously or unconsciously grew from the buried knowledge of this reality, perhaps throughout von Trotta's growing up.

Beyond this, the great closeness between von Trotta and her mother, living alone together in one small room right into the director's adulthood, suggests the kind of symbiotic cocoon the sisters form. While von Trotta only works in the films with mother–daughter material peripherally and rather minimally, again the intricate choreographings of close bonding relationships in these three films are, among other things, displacements of that original mother/daughter bonding. Von Trotta speaks of the relationship as strengthening, not restricting: "She gave me every freedom; nothing was impossible. But when I went out into the world, I started bumping up against boundaries and restrictions. I realized not everyone considered me an equal."[16]

It is significant that by the time of *Sheer Madness*, the two women are *not* sisters, there is more separation between them than that. Though they share the usual deep bond, and though they are very important to one another, identity itself is not in danger. It is the *male* force in that film that is the threat to Ruth's identity—and the other woman strengthens her autonomy. Although Ruth is suicidal, her fantasy of killing the man can be seen as a gesture, if regarded metaphorically, of self-realization. But certainly it is crucial that by *Sheer Madness*, von Trotta is no longer engaged with the exploration of merged selves, the danger of losing one's self—but rather with learning to move strongly into the world.

*Alter-Egos—Two Parts of the Self*

In returning repeatedly to the sisters, or two women, motif, von Trotta is struggling not only with the issue of women-bonding, but also with the split self, different aspects of a single person—even perhaps a cultural split, between a dreamy melancholy Russian self and an efficient German one. The two parts of the self in von Trotta's films often are too extreme and incompatible to live together, or even to live. This is most obvious in the first sister film, *Sisters*, where the outgoing sister, Jutte Lampe's Maria, the working sister, is characterized as rather harsh and cold, at odds with the dark, soft, recessive Anna who can hardly function at all, while Maria functions very effectively but lacks a soul. Maria is in constant motion from home to office, and derives all her prestige as an executive secretary from serving the most powerful male's wishes and needs.

As von Trotta goes on, however, she expresses less ambivalence about the hardworking effective autonomous women so central to her films—like Juliane in *Marianne and Juliane*, or Olga in *Sheer Madness*—than she showed toward Maria. For one thing, the later active heroines serve desirable ends and act in the world as counter-figures, Juliane the feminist activist/journalist, Olga the teacher/feminist in *Sheer Madness*, Rosa Luxemburg a revolutionary seeking to overthrow a world of pain and injustice (unlike Maria, the handmaiden to patriarchy and capitalism). Still, Maria's employer is no George Grosz caricature, though he is a pointedly capitalistic corporate figure; acted by Heinz Bennent, he seems intelligent and humane, which means kind and respectful to his servant. It always being important to notice who serves the coffee, here Maria does all the serving, the film cutting from her making food for her sister Anna, to her preparing a Danish-and-coffee breakfast tray for her boss. In the power world of the workplace he alone is endowed with humanizing images: the overbearing painting on the wall behind him, of a large black purposeful ship, makes a statement about dark, almost sinister power, but also the relief of the outside world of nature, even something romantic, against all the cold anonymous functional office angularity.

As Maria's great energy and effectiveness in this world is both respected and also seen as coldness, so von Trotta's other efficient working women are also often cold, aloof, hard to know. This film's generally troubled sense of Maria's hardworking efficiency seems also a repudiation of the New German Reconstruction, of a national set of values—apart from its functioning on a personal level as a pathological proficiency that drains other people by infantilizing them. One critic even says of Juliane—in von Trotta's next film, and perhaps her most appealing heroine—that she would seem brusque if Marianne weren't so much more brusque.[17]

Maria is the one who gets things done but her severity is underlined by her appearance, the kinds of man-tailored suits and pulled-back hair that the old Hollywood codes signaled for a career woman who had lost her "womanliness." Contrariwise, when she gets involved with a man, and generally moves toward a breaking away from the cocoon, she wears her hair free, her whole look softens, and her clothing also gets freer in the style of Miriam, with pants, vests. So von Trotta has a problematic relation to so work-driven a figure at this point in her own career, sees her as needing softening, and also freeing. In this regard (and also remembering Christa's need to express her strength and bold freedom by mannish gear in *Christa Klages*) von Trotta's remarking, when interviewed, on the importance to herself of Rosa Luxemburg's having been a "real woman" has a special import. She notes that though Rosa was "a very intelligent woman and a very fighting, polemic woman too. . . . in the Social Democratic Party . . . the most important writer and thinker," yet "she didn't give anything away from her womanness." However appropriate to Rosa, as a statement of von Trotta's own development and in the context of the history of women directors, these comments are not only interesting but full of poignance.

At the same time, the endorsement of work is never open to serious question for von Trotta. Maria fiercely argues that Anna's prolonging of her student life was a way of avoiding dealing with the world and that who a person is, and what he or she is worth, comes from work. Her friend Fritz after Anna's death dismisses her words as nonsense, but it's Maria's view that remains with one and carries conviction. And whatever the questions von Trotta may have had about this vision at this time in her career, as evidenced by the way she frames Maria in this film, to feminists for whom work and achievement have become so central a value, the equation of "polar bear" and work commitment has almost the feeling of the classic Hollywood's *Woman of the Year*, with its equation of the Katharine Hepburn professional woman's competence—actually brilliance—with total human and female failure and "unnaturalness." Still, the public world and public self are cold in *Sisters*.

However, the world of the home there is equally troubling in an opposite way, dark and womblike, warm reds and browns that feel oppressively enclosing, and of the body. As Maria's coolness is underlined by her constant association with white, especially white clothes, Anna, withdrawn, identified with the house, is always dressed in black or dark colors. One recalls Bergman's dark red body/interior atmosphere in *Cries and Whispers*. (Von Trotta's use of contrast between the dark womb-like home imagery and bright airy work space recurs importantly, as we will see, in *Sheer Madness*). In *Sisters*, the recessive Anna is hard to accept as a scientist—aesthetic, ethereal, with her long free hair and liquid melancholy eyes. Von Trotta's melancholy alter egos have been intriguingly remarked to appear Jewish[18] and often to have Biblical Jewish names (like Ruth), in contrast to the blonde more Teutonic women of the pairs. Anna is identified with art, imagination, artiness—with more dreams, her mother says, than could ever be realized;

and with total self-involvement, as Maria says of her. The organic oppressiveness of the home in *Sisters* is also contributed to by the strong presence of plant leaves, and a glass tank containing a pair of exotic little animals, too obvious a stand-in for the sisters, like Laura's glass creatures in *The Glass Menagerie*, or the fish tank in *The Graduate*. (There are a variety of other echoes of the two sisters through the film, like the two old sisters Anna works for, or the writer living with his sister, a small indication of how carefully von Trotta crafted her work from early on.) The dark recessive sister who nests in this lair is dependent as a child, almost like a foetus, clinging to Maria, literally leaning on her back, waiting for her to return, with great spiritual beauty but death-like inertness—the secret sharer, the dark side of the self. In what von Trotta calls "these mirror films," with "one character reflecting the other," she speaks of "the night and the day character, your shadow following you, a confrontation with your own shadow."[19]

When the second young one, Miriam, takes Anna's place in the apartment after Anna kills herself, von Trotta through her shows the genesis of Anna's, and Maria's, trouble. Miriam lightens the flat on every level, paints everything white, opens windows and lets in light. However, her normality makes all the clearer Maria's role in Anna's malaise. The bouncy Miriam's growing lassitude as she allows Maria to take care of her, suggests that Maria's overwhelming control was responsible for Anna's infantile incapacity, paralysis, lethargy. There are strong suggestions in these symbiotic relationships of a powerful mother caretaker, and the dependent child waiting in terror for mother to return, for her undivided attention. Even before Maria's relationship with a man begins to shake Anna's world, she is shown waiting at home for Maria, who is working late at the office, hugging herself and rocking, a pathetic image of child-need, child-terror, and self-mothering. She adores and clings to Maria's strength, but also resents her mother-tone of martyrdom, Maria's irritation that she has to do everything herself, though she insists on doing so. The younger, needy one rightly recognizes that Maria needs to be needed in this way. The film succeeds in conveying the poignance from both sides: the younger one's terror of separation and abandonment; and the older one, whose desperation to be free is expressed obliquely by her playing at running Anna over on the road to their mother's house, and during the fierce fight they have during their visit.

Von Trotta conveys the ambiguity of who dominates whom in this relationship, the interchangeability of mother/daughter roles. The dark womb-like enclosed world of this symbiotic relationship between the two women also carries some quality of film noir—and Anna at various points seems an oppressive, menacing presence herself, long before her death with its curse of vengeance. Often her form encloses Maria's in a frame. Anna sits at her desk working, her back occupying the large foreground on the right, with Maria turned away over a book, smaller in the background, our image of her framed by Anna. In another sequence, Anna, having fallen asleep over her books and then come into the bedroom, stands in the doorway arm extended, back to us, her front visible in a mirror across the room, with Maria rising from bed drowsily in the background, enclosed in the frame by Anna's arm and body. Noir and thriller codes are used after Anna's death to keep her presence ascendant in our consciousness and Maria's: Anna's angry curse hanging in the air, she sitting ghost-like white at a table, doors mysteriously opening, the agitation of her felt presence in the night, and the most terrifying of all, her reflection in a mirror when Maria looks at herself—all devices for making a spiritual inhabitation physically compelling. So in *Marianne and Juliane*, Marianne's enormous continuing impact, after her death, on Juliane's life is translated into a pursuit and sorting out of clues as to whether that death was a suicide or not. Von Trotta prolongs what might seem unpromising material in the most adept and exciting way by using the strategies of thriller/detective genres to convey that one sister, even after death, remains an incubus of the other. This kind of anguish and loss of identity occurs even in *Christa Klages*, but then von Trotta did not yet tap into the visceral dread of deeper psychic levels. But Anna's face in the window, Anna waiting up at night, as both mother and abandoned child or lover, is chilling on a different level, as is Maria's assuming Anna's role later on, trying to keep Miriam home at night and away from men.

In *Sisters* the man is sacrificed not for the work but for the sister, the other woman. In making this sacrifice, Maria seems to express a mother's or daughter's intense guilt about her own sexual departure. The lure of men, and hence of Marie's own adulthood, is experienced as an act of betrayal, of the bonds of loyalty and desperate need between women. Anna's anguish over the information that Maria is dating someone, the bitter fight this precipitates in the mother's house, her despair waiting home for Maria to return, Anna's own steering clear of men who we see approach her, even her tormented cry over her journal that she is going against the laws of nature in having the intense woman-centered, or sister-centered, feelings she does, all suggest the ties between these women are seen as opposed to adult development, whether or not as lesbian or incestuous. After Anna kills herself, Maria feels she must repudiate the man altogether, although she need not—except out of an implicit sense of guilt that her being a sexual woman, drawn to men, has killed her sister. She appears to conclude that she should not have attempted to go beyond her original nuclear family, except in the compartmentalized autonomy of her super-efficient work persona.

The man in *Sisters*, however, is so little characterized that we have none of the sense of a loss, a sacrifice, that makes *Marianne and Juliane* so affecting. There Wolfgang, with whom Juliane has lived for so many years, and who she gives up too after Marianne dies, is a most appealing figure, gentle, patient, nurturing. Long before he actually leaves, though, there is the growing sense that her bond to her sister is so magnetic that it takes entire precedence over her tie to him. If we regard the sister as a part of the self, the working out of an internal struggle, then the heroine places that struggle for her own identity, her selfhood, far above caring for the man or the relationship—or at least having a magnetic claim that dwarfs every other claim—again an unusual course. As Wolf is appealing, even in *Sisters*, Maurice is the one who brings Maria the coffee in bed when they make love, a coming together linked, as noted earlier, to the cabaret song about becoming free and tasting life. That this film sees the link of heterosexual ties as an opening out into life, a freeing—a very different vision from that of the later *Sheer Madness*—is further borne out by Miriam's being the one who gets to take the little Miss Liberty statue, the "normal" girl who is forever fussing with her hair and her makeup, and who dreams "Someday He'll Come Along," preferably with money.

So while in both the later films, *Marianne and Juliane* and *Sheer Madness*, women choose women over men, and the pull of the sister is profound, there is not the same sense of it as going against nature as there is here. This is true even though the men in the later films certainly resent the women bond, because it removes them from the center of female attention, because it displaces them from authority. Also perhaps they recognize an erotic component of which they should feel jealous, since that also involves a displacement of themselves. In *Sisters*, Maurice repeats the same loving gesture of embrace of Maria from behind, as Anna had made earlier, suggesting that these are equivalent, hence rival kinds of love. It is possible that the shift of emphasis in the later films occurs from the feminism being more deeply experienced, as is the sense of how women get pushed out of shape by men's need for dominance and possession. Also, if the early struggle for autonomy is seen as waged in the original household, the household of childhood, against the pull of the mother, and also against that part of the self that wants absorption in the mother, that wants to be taken care of by her—von Trotta's vision of a later, more adult struggle for autonomy, such as we witness in *Sheer Madness*, is against the husband and the shackles of the next household. Like Nora in *Doll's House*, moving from parent's house to husband's, but still the child of each, from Anna to Ruth, von Trotta's woman struggles hard to inhabit herself.

Though the point of view is not held consistently throughout, *Sisters* is finally Maria's film (as *Marianne and Juliane* is Juliane's film), however fascinating and central the dark melancholy passionate one—and it is Maria who has to achieve the final act of integration of self. She has to come to terms with Anna, in order to complete herself: by yielding up some of her own overbearingness, excessive responsibility and control; and by making contact with her own dreaminess, vulnerability, terror. The film insists that you can't kill (repress) the dark death-involved dreaming self without murdering the achieving self at the same time; that if you deny that other self, it will be the face you see in the mirror. At least in von Trotta's economy, the one depends on the other, and she has her heroine finally struggle toward incorporating both, with a hope of reclaiming some wholeness that way. At the film's near-end the nightguard at the office building tells Maria, with Anna dead and Miriam gone, that he is missing a piece of the sky of his jigsaw puzzle, a lovely metaphor; but Maria, like the guard, has the whole night to find her own missing piece of sky.

She does so by making a final entry in her dead sister's tormented journal, in the concluding closeup. She will try to dream the course of her life. She will try to be Maria and Anna together. The film concludes as it opened with the image of the forest identified with memory, childhood, and because of the association with fairytales, with imagination and art. The image comes through the film from Anna's mind, but at the very end it issues from Maria, now the source of the narrative—which tells us that indeed she will change, and will accept, reclaim, the dreaming melancholy self that she also contains. An earlier science lecture hall sequence, apart from establishing Anna's student life, involves discussion of the idea of every cell containing within itself the capacity not only to specialize, but to replace the entire mechanism, if it needs to do so—since, the lecturer maintains, every individual cell contains the code for the whole. The specialized parts of the divided self need to become more whole. It is that quest for wholeness that is the preoccupation of von Trotta's entire sister series.

*Marianne and Juliane*

*Marianne and Juliane*, one of the masterpieces of the new women's cinema and of feminist filmmaking as well, would assure von Trotta a permanent place among major filmmakers if she never made another film. Working from an actual situation (as she did with *Klages*, and again with *Luxemburg*) of great import for Germany, von Trotta waited from the late 1970s, the time of the actual events, as the film indicates by an opening pan over dated files, until the early 1980s, for her treatment. This time lapse provided some distance—that wasn't possible, say, for the segments of *Germany in Autumn*—allowing the complex mixed response to the terrorist sister, of aversion, anger, grief, admiration, and love, that makes the film so rich an experience.

The social correlative vaguely present in *Sisters* finds brilliant articulation in this film through images that evoke the charged German past and present. The long row of grand statuary busts that line Juliane's route to Marianne are like a florid wreckage of the grand German past, patriarchs on pillars, all jammed together, at the end of which we so dramatically first see Marianne's extraordinarily intense face, those figures seeming visibly to lead directly to her, she the product of them, like a wild avenging angel. It is a marvellously economic visual statement with which to introduce Marianne, to give her that context. But objective correlatives throughout enrich the film's statement: the golden, winged, warmly-lit statuary within the museum that frames the sisters' first encounter, sitting over cocoa and remembering their childhood; the pastor father's showing of *Night and Fog* to the two daughters in adolescence, each of whom in later life heeds his moral imperative in a different way; crucifixion allusions; such devices as the photo story about Nazi mothers on which Juliane is working; and most of all, the angry ideological exchanges of the two sisters ("Your bombs spoiled *our* work, not *theirs*")—most effective ways of imaging a social and political past and present. (Von Trotta uses other inventive devices in *Sheer Madness*, among them classroom lectures as in *Sisters*, and slides, to convey women's history.)

But von Trotta does as well with private worlds, between the two women, and in this film—as opposed to *Sisters*—between man and woman as well, with Juliane and Wolfgang. But again what is particularly remarkable is the intensity with which we are thrown into a passionate relation of a woman with a woman. The somber mood of the opening, with Juliane reflecting and pacing, pausing to make notes—her thoughtfulness and personal force as an intellectual itself exciting—all moves us toward the photograph of Marianne, an image that from the start dominates the film as well as Juliane's consciousness. Von Trotta has found a perfect embodiment for trying to come to terms at once with a political conflict and a personal linkage of women, a linkage astonishing in its intensity, and the totality of its woman-centeredness. In the same way, *Sheer Madness* has as its central magnetism, that between the two women, one mysteriously drawn to the other even though a stranger, finding her as through a mystical force—like nothing so much as the old love stories, in fact, were one of the two a man. And as in romances, one woman comes and saves the other, literally from death, and in a more general way as well (or tries to, dreams of it, as in *Marianne and Juliane*). The question of erotic attraction is not raised by *Marianne and Juliane* because the two women are biological sisters, because of the prison confinement, and because the contentment and attractiveness of the relationship between Wolfgang and Juliane make one less likely to pose such a question here.

In addition to the extraordinary degree that *Marianne and Juliane*, and *Sheer Madness* after it, are women-centered (and not by paring down, as in *Jeanne Dielman*, but maintaining the full richness of political and cultural worlds), the kind of women focused on are extraordinary too, with large, strongly-defined intelligences grappling with the world, again, in the most active way (as of course is true of Rosa Luxemburg). Juliane herself is immensely appealing for her engagement as a force in the world, and in her magazine (especially given the kind of magazine it is), her input in shaping its policies, her activism at the abortion rally—activities not critiqued, as some have argued, but strongly affirmed.[20] Von Trotta speaks of herself, and her friend Christiane Ensslin, as living lives of serious political commitment and activism, though neither countenances terrorism. Juliane again is no poster Strong Woman but both attractive and flawed, vulnerable, real. She is self-sufficient, yet capable of loving involvement. She takes charge of her life, chooses not to be married, chooses not to have children, chooses to place work at the center of her life. Yet her engagement with work, so intense that she seems often not to have time to eat, is very differently treated from Maria's work ethic in *Sisters*. Again, it is not meaningless, alienated corporate office work— work that in Maria's case is not even her own but as a secretary, no matter how high powered, facilitating the male authority's ends. In *Marianne and Juliane* the work is significant in itself and is done with other women, who appear to work in a non-hierarchical manner, with autonomous self-containment. It is also part of something much larger, furthering the interests of all women, Third World women, even German women, by shedding light on the buried history of Nazism, the repressed terrible story, examining women's complicity with that history and victimization by it.

The film not only explores history through women, but moves across the generations of living women, by showing the touching impact of Juliane's strength on her mother. We see the older woman's secret vicarious pleasure at the young girl rebel's dancing without a partner, she who wears pants, defies the father, rejects all conventional gender expectations. Later on we see mother and daughter, as they wait in the prison, reach a kind of understanding, even complicity, about the egotism of the father, as the mother struggles to fathom what is beyond her in her daughters' lives. The mother has declared herself—and we never get close enough to her to test this seriously—as unquestioningly obedient and trusting. Hers is perhaps too heavy-handed and easy a portrait, but the girls clearly live out not only the father's fierce moralism and severity, but the mother's own repressed need to go her own way.

Mothers in the other films make a minimal contribution but are often present, asking for conformity in *Klages*, the opposite in the *Marianne and Juliane* dance sequence, but rarely seen as powerful, rather seen as sad and defeated, serving food, in lonely circumstances—with "the helplessness von Trotta's mothers always show."[21] The visit the sisters pay to their mother in *Sisters*, which anticipates a scene in *Marianne and Juliane*, has the mother as stunned witness to the anguished fighting between the sisters, and to Maria's assertion that there must be some way they can each live their own lives. The siting of the scene suggests an indirect breaking away from the mother as well. In *Sheer Madness* the mother communicates possessiveness of Ruth, and duplicates everyone else's hostility to the friendship between the women.

Beyond working with women's relations to their mothers, von Trotta does interesting things with women's relations to their own younger selves—the film a large canvas covered with ambitious women's issues. One of the finest contributions *Marianne and Juliane* makes to the pool of woman images in cinema is the young Juliane, a fierce, rebellious young girl-intellectual reading Sartre, stealing a smoke behind a school pillar, challenging a teacher—aptly, but also to be provocative—to talk about Jews rather than safely melancholic Rilke poems. It is a touching portrait of awkward pretentiousness and daring, a kind of gawky bravado, and the adolescent Juliane's dance alone is a great enrichment of the film. Perhaps one day von Trotta will take this further, a fuller development of a young defiant intellectual girl. One hardly needs to be told, but von Trotta notes in an interview about *Marianne and Juliane*, speaking of Christiane Ensslin on whom Juliane in the film is roughly modelled (and to whom the film is dedicated): "Like her too, I was rebellious, a non-compliant schoolgirl."[22]

Not only Juliane, young and full grown, but Marianne herself provides exciting and unique images of strong intellectual womanhood in this film, for all the mixture of emotions with which Juliane views her. Although von Trotta speaks of her own political anger, and her sympathy for those who have the "courage" to act on that, full of moral horror at the world's brutality, she also locates herself without hesitation with Juliane, for whom Marianne's means, her self-righteousness, the ruthlessness of her sacrifices, are never admirable. As has been pointed out earlier, von Trotta has been sharply criticized for not clarifying what Marianne stood for and what she did in her revolutionary life. Juliane tells the boy Jan at the end of the film that his mother never threw bombs, though we know the Baader Meinhof gang *was* responsible for deaths, and Juliane herself speaks to Marianne of "your bombs" as "ruining our work." In any case, Marianne is no victim like Katarina Blum, who was almost an innocent bystander; Marianne engages in the most serious actions, takes full responsibility for herself, takes the world on with ferocity and boldness and courage, however much one may disavow, with Juliane, how she does so. She is given the respect of a serious figure.

It is also part of the paradoxical nature of von Trotta's customary vision that Marianne is also seen largely as a victim, imprisoned almost from the start, doing subtle battle with the prison guards, suffering the ordeal of solitary confinement, and finally enduring a horrible death. And because von Trotta set up her incarceration so early, much of the film's sympathy for her has to do with her in this brave but helpless circumstance, rather than as an active force, allowing the film thereby to essentially dissociate itself from her as political figure in viewing her with compassion—since she has been permanently removed from action. The first meeting between the sisters is full of raging conflict over basic life values, and Juliane has to leave because she is so upset. But once out of the prison she turns back toward it and her comment is a pitying flashback memory of the young girl Marianne reciting a Rilke poem, the words like her own forlorn sentence of doom, that he who is without a home will never have one. The other continual flashback images from childhood are also used to humanize Marianne.

On the other hand, the extent of Juliane's involvement in Marianne's pain suggests that the guilt Marianne wants her sister to feel for living a "normal" life—actually hardly a conventional life, though not a self-destructive one—is guilt Juliane does indeed feel. The extremist is a part of herself she has not lived out, an experience many here shared in the late 1960s and early 1970s, though the violence and fanaticism of the Weatherpeople made it hard, if not impossible, to feel their actions as a moral reproach. It is interesting that von Trotta can maintain a feeling of strength about the two women, as not victimized, though they are both caught in a massive machinery. But we don't experience them as helpless at all, perhaps because of the passion of the engagement between them, their ferocity with the prison people, Marianne's belief in self, her issuing commands not requests, the power she has over Juliane, the whole way she maintains herself through her ordeal with will, strength, authority, on center stage, the sheer verve of the performances given by Barbara Sukowa and Jutta Lampe, and finally the authority and purposefulness with which von Trotta keeps the dramatic tensions building.

Von Trotta's skill in handling the prison sequences is striking, considering how static and bleak an environment the camera is largely confined to for much of the film—relieved only by the frequent cutting away to childhood and adolescent flashbacks, and to Juliane's fast-moving home- and work-life outside. Juliane's first visit involves a careful documentation of oppressive security outside and in, of endless doors clanging shut, uniforms, darkness, ritualistic search and strip carried out with brisk impersonality. She surprises us by having Marianne refuse the visit the first time, then receive Juliane—von Trotta using abrupt, dramatic cuts through the sequences. She also manages very effective intercuttings from memories to present time: for example, from the girls, especially the younger Marianne, crying in the bathroom after the terrible images of the heaped dead of Auschwitz in *Night and Fog*, with the voiceover "Who is keeping watch," following them—to Marianne in the prison, in black, eyes again red, though hopefully the parallelism does not mean an equating of the two kinds of suffering.

This last sequence also begins the trajectory of Marianne's visible decline from visit to visit. The two women exchange sweaters, and there is some sense of exchanged lives, or at least of Marianne's appropriating Juliane's life. The most stunning moment in the film occurs in a new prison, which adds the final level of imprisonment, a barrier of glass between the two women so they can't touch, and a confusing sound system that makes them unable to hear, or speak to, one another. In this the final scene of their encounter in present time, their faces blur and merge in the glass, suggesting merging personalities, and deteriorating identity too, Marianne visibly going to pieces, and Juliane's life dissolving as well.

Von Trotta's use of the two-sister bond in *Marianne and Juliane* is not primarily, as in *Sisters*, as two sides of a personality, either one of which is incomplete without the other. She does turn back to that in *Sheer Madness*, but the two-women theme here works rather as two sides of politics on the Left, with no synthesis possible but rather the national psyche needing to recognize and accept the repressed and banished one for its health, and for the sake of the wounded young, Germany's future, made palpable in Marianne's mutilated son Jan, with whose helplessness and vulnerability von Trotta works poignantly, if economically.

Of all the ambiguities of the film, perhaps the most fundamental one has to do with Juliane's adoption of Jan, given her feelings about not having children and about Marianne's dumping her responsibilities on her. To underline the discomfort further, von Trotta concludes the film with the boy's male voice, not gentle, not grateful, not even sad, but harsh and peremptory, commanding her to begin, to narrate Marianne's story. At the same time Jan is the concrete and innocent embodiment of all the hurts in the film. (In point of fact, Gudrun Ensslin's actual son suffered much more severe disfigurement from an acid attack, but von Trotta modified the incident to place the emphasis more on the internal wounds and scars.[23])

The same kind of profound ambiguity arises from Juliane's ever-growing, and finally all-consuming, involvement with Marianne, both alive and after death. Is this a healthy coming to terms with something, a solidarity between women and an act of love beyond all differences, a final lifeward gesture? Or is it a pathological involvement, Juliane's becoming dominated and manipulated by Marianne in just the ways she at the start of the film angrily vowed not to be, until her very life is absorbed by the dead woman, her hard-won control and space invaded, her identity lost? Von Trotta herself remarks, after saying she was not making a film about terrorism: "What I do describe is a very close relationship between two women that is nevertheless full of contradictions and contrariness, two sisters who react to and take action against the conditions in the Federal Republic of Germany in quite different ways."[24] From the rivetting power of Marianne's photo over her desk, to Juliane in the end tending the boy as she tended the others as a girl in her large early family: is she returning to old domestic shackles, or living as an engaged human being? That two such totally opposing possibilities could be supported by the film is a fascinating index to the complexity of von Trotta's vision, though it points to no sense of confusion in that vision.

The measure of Juliane's dissolution is Wolfgang, the believably forbearing, loving man Juliane lives with. The two are work comrades, sitting at nearby desks, each at his/her task. So Rosa Luxemburg's relationship with Leo Jogiches, lovers and comrades together from youth to older years, speaking the Polish of their youth to one another in a German-speaking world, is also a strong element of that film. In *Rosa Luxemburg*, though, Jogiches is barely characterized, another serious problem of that film—as is the omission of the fact that both were Jewish, a very disturbing omission from the characterization of Rosa herself. Stanley Kauffmann also registers disturbance, finding it "hard to think of her as other than a prototypical turn-of-the-century European Jewish revolutionary. This is important historical datum, and this Sukowa cannot suggest. In fact, no word about Luxemburg's Jewish background (or that of her lover-colleague Leo Jogiches) is spoken in the film; no Jewish epithet is flung at her, or could credibly be, with Sukowa in the role."[25]

In *Marianne and Juliane*, in Juliane and Wolfgang's household, traditional home roles are often inverted, he offering drinks, slicing and stirring dinner, she upstairs typing or working. This strongly contrasts with Marianne's late-night arrival with male terrorist companions, specifically seeking coffee, a scene which places strong emphasis on Marianne's doing the preparing and serving, and the men waiting to be served, surely one more critique of the terrorists, and of Marianne's self-righteous certainties about the total rightness of her way. Wolfgang, on the other hand, patiently accepts not going to a lecture, rather than go ahead without Juliane; and when Juliane is overwhelmed with grief over Marianne's death, there is a lovely intercutting of Wolfgang outside by the piers, and she grieving alone in a hotel room, the angle of his head conveying that he is at one with her grief. So when he gradually finds her behavior excessive, feels he can no longer go on, that she doesn't even know he is there any more, we don't experience that as a wounded patriarch angry to lose the woman's attention to another woman, and a dead one at that—although that *is* indeed the emotional climate of *Sheer Madness* and there *is* a suggestion of this here too. But mainly we take it as a measure of how far away Juliane has gone, yet without finding either her or him at fault.

The intercutting mentioned above is one of many instances in the film of the power of von Trotta's visual aesthetic. Her images can be beautiful in unexpectedly wayward ways, akin to her tapping into dream and unconscious levels—like the sudden unexplained appearance of a bride coming out of a hotel as Wolfgang stands waiting to hear from Juliane the crushing news that her sister is dead. Why there? Speculation about the end of Wolf's dream of marriage is too heavy an approach to the lovely strangeness of the moment, which at the same time does not feel forced or clever. There are numerous other small, easily overlooked evidences of von Trotta's attention to detail, like Juliane waiting for a train on the return from a prison visit, fleetingly seeing a mother and two girls across the train station platform; or like some schoolboys near her in the train waiting room who subtly evoke Jan without drawing attention to that.

The structure of *Marianne and Juliane*, like that of *Sisters*, builds to the death of one sister, and then dwells through the long second half on the impact of that death, the way the remaining one is haunted by it. Von Trotta's heroines are generally death-haunted, in a way that feels pathological and morbid at times, perhaps partly a function of a German attraction to the gothic and the ghoulish: the bleeding ghost of a sister, the ghastly details of a burnt child's body, the equally grisly details of hanging (though both based, again, it should be noted, on perhaps more violent realities). Juliane's somewhat bizarre pursuit of proof that Marianne was not a suicide keeps us engrossed, and keeps the link between the two alive as Juliane participates in her sister's death by trying to recreate it, even to the disturbing extreme of putting a like noose around her own neck. The strong heroines seem haunted by a sense of responsibility and guilt—or an attraction to suicide, to death, themselves, their dark sisters proxies for their own death involvement. Von Trotta importantly extends this connection from the personal to the larger national level when she remarks of Juliane: "When she takes up her investigation, she performs a labor of mourning; it is almost the work of a gravedigger. This 'labor of mourning' can be related to a person, but also to a country. It is something of which we Germans after 1945 were not capable. We were quick to push aside guilt and responsibility."[26]

Juliane's sense of responsibility takes other forms as well. "I dreamed I set you free," says Juliane to Marianne at the beginning of their last encounter. The theme of freedom as has been noted as so important in *Sisters*, is even more important in the two later sister films. Marianne is of course literally a locked-up woman, the imagery of walls, bars, enclosure obviously crucial, oddly reaching its climax in that final prison encounter where, separated by glass, sight and hearing and contact itself is almost fully cut off, at the same time that, paradoxically, a total merging of identities is suggested.

*Sheer Madness*

The confined woman, a woman with a noose around her neck, one woman freeing the other, these are where *Sheer Madness* begins. Ruth, a fragile death-drawn painter, stands by a window at the start of the film, and windows in von Trotta—though like the walls and gates that surround other characters—still show possibilities, let in light for seeing, are like eyes or camera lenses, present the other world, can be opened. But Ruth at the film's beginning, standing at the window with her back toward us, hazy rainy image unfocused outside, her hand hanging limply out the window, is faced toward possibilities that can't be made out, and reaches for nothing. Others know what she will say, others hold her life's script in their hands, control her discourse. Consequently she will not speak. "Hope is death," she says, and lies down like a dead woman. In the next sequence she actually goes off into the night to kill herself. And the rest of the film is regularly punctuated with her fantasies, in black and white, of her hanging herself from a rope.

The narrative action of the film gets underway when Olga, a sturdy, energetic professor of women's literature played brilliantly by Hanna Schygulla, comes with her husband briefly to visit the house of relatives in Provence, a house in which Ruth (also very well played by Angela Winkler) is staying as a guest. Never having met Ruth, Olga instinctively makes her way to the room in the house in which Ruth is painting. The evening of the same day, when Ruth bolts from the dinner table into the night to kill herself, Olga alone is able to find her, moving through the darkness, through ruins, cave-like forms, arches, until with the concentric circles of light from her flashlight, she reveals Ruth sitting, a rope around her neck, and brings her back. This haunting core image, recurring several times in flashback, again has an archetypal feeling, the stuff of myths: Proserpine and Pluto, Orpheus and Euridice—entering the underground world of the dead and bringing someone back to the living. It also evokes the birth process. Visually the sequence, with its curved, cavernous, in fact vaginal, shapes, calls to mind various forms—of Georgia O'Keefe paintings, Lee Boticeou's canvas constructs, Ruth's own paintings with their circles of bright light at the center of cosmic darkness. The images not only have visual beauty and authority, but are excitingly metaphoric as well. Olga increasingly leads Ruth back into life, like a mother, a daughter, like an older sister—and, again crossing gender as the film itself does, like a white knight.

The theme of the dark sister brought into the light of self-trust, autonomy, and friendship underlies that recurrent evocative image of a woman looking out a window at the world. In its opening use, with Ruth looking out at the rain, she seems to have had a breakdown. After Olga first enters Ruth's room, and then leaves it, there is another powerful image—dreamlike—of Olga outside the house, her back to it, looking toward us, and Ruth behind her, behind glass, framed and barred by the window, which is made busy and a bit sinister by leaf shadows, through which she looks sadly out toward Olga. The image goes beyond the pathological and personal to a touching feminist vision: a woman confined and yearning outward—out of all those houses and interiors that women and women's bodies have been associated with, out of all those narrowed possibilities.

Ruth, like the von Trotta heroines who precede her, is imprisoned, her imprisonment internal, a combination of personal neurosis and social forces, which for von Trotta are interconnected: "How we behave, react, think, which feelings we show and which we hide . . . none of this is accidental. The society in which we live influences us every day through its rigid structures and mechanisms, which may give rise to conscious or sub-conscious neuroses which carry over into our private lives."[27] The relationship between Olga and Ruth that releases Ruth really gets underway when Olga accidentally comes upon Ruth in a museum copying a painting. Ruth's art consists only of copies, black and white copies of the masters. It takes her a long time before she will risk a more direct relation, her *own* relation, to reality—"a chilling metaphor," as Molly Haskell has noted, "for a woman's lack of a confident, original voice."[28] When Olga comes upon her, Ruth is copying a painting of the back of a woman, looking out of a small casement window, from the darkness of her house, into the openness of the outer world, in which a boat is just barely observable. Her body leans toward the small opening, as Ruth, looking at the painting, leans toward the painted figure, who is leaning toward her freedom. Ruth's inviting Olga to her house for the first time significantly comes out of this encounter.

The film explores the deepening intimacy between these two profoundly enmeshed women who are magnetically drawn to one another from the start—to show Ruth getting increasingly strong with Olga's support, and to show the impact this has on those around them. The two women watch each other across tables in an outdoor cafe, the day after the initial rescue, with the intensity of lovers. They complement each other, as close friends often do—although again they can also easily be seen as two sides of a single self. Olga gives off boldness and competence in the world, she works hard, we see her authority in the classroom, her life force, a kind of confidence that looks like serenity. The blondness of her short, vaguely punk-style hair is echoed by her outfits, cheery pale yellows and whites, relaxed and sophisticated, usually pants. She is akin to Maria but as a working woman she is seen as far more attractive, in no way severe looking, the work commitment no longer involving sacrifice of other crucial humanness, though there remains some ambiguity surrounding what her powerfulness does to others, a suggestion of something overpowering. Mostly, though, Olga is identified with the light that that woman in the painting is straining toward, the freedom and power of that ship outside. At the same time it should be said that Olga is not a full character; she remains somehow remote, partly because this time the film focusses mostly on the dark self's subjectivity. It is rather the complementary two women, combined, that create the feeling of fullness. The acting here, like the performances von Trotta usually gets from her actresses, is first-rate.

As Olga is associated with brightness, von Trotta contrasts her light sophisticated clothes with Ruth's almost invariably black ones, which underline her melancholy, as their demure cut also suggests something regressive, subtly unsuitable, a girlish style for someone who is no longer a girl but a woman. So the dark, confined, recessive one, waiting in enclosure, here does not any longer have qualities of life, as the home did in *Sisters*, however stultifyingly, however claustrophobically. In *Sheer Madness* the place of withdrawal has become literally a world of darkness, colored the black of black leather furniture, the womblike world more forcefully and unambivalently associated with death now. There is one quick cut in the film from

Ruth's house to Olga's, showing Olga's rooms by contrast full of bright space, music, books, life. Most important, the furniture in Ruth's flat is pointedly not chosen by her but by her mother-in-law. Ruth repeatedly copies Olga, in her art she copies other paintings, she possesses little of her life. But if others have the script to her life in their hands, the narrative of the film shows her taking possession of her own narrative.

The film proceeds to follow Ruth as she moves out into that light, as she achieves that self-possession, through her friendship with the other woman. But as it shows her getting stronger, more animated, more confident in her own powers, at the same time it conveys the stake those who "love" Ruth, principally her husband Franz, have in keeping her as she was. Olga's classroom teaching is an inventive way of drawing early attention to the larger feminist perspective at work here, both in rendering Ruth's dilemma and in pointing the way out of it. As we watch Franz's mounting distress over Ruth's growing health and capacity to create and be autonomous, it is impossible to see Ruth's deathwardness as merely a private morbid drama, or simply more German pathology. Through slides and historical references, Olga documents the suppression through history that has been suffered by women. With ambitions and desires identical with those of men but thwarted, creative women of the past either got buried in hidden collaborations with husbands and lovers, men whose names became famous though their nameless women may have done much of the work; or may, through the frustration of their situation, have been driven to suicide. Through the ongoing intellectual commentary, which von Trotta handles inventively, Olga teaches *us*, too, to see the larger feminist context. The teaching impulse, in fact, has an uncomfortable missionary, colonial aspect, carried here to the Third World, those two emancipated German women carrying the Word to the oppressed women of Egypt.

However, their own sophisticated European men are all disasters, and the film offers a most damaging vision of heterosexual politics, the film's anger released as Ruth releases *her* anger, at least in fantasy, at the film's conclusion. In *Sheer Madness* the heroine is not tethered to an infantilizing mother or powerful sister, but to an infantilizing male. The woman tie now is only liberating and strengthening, and destruction now comes from woman's submergence in man, and the male need to dominate, jealous of the woman's powers and trying to stop their development. Ruth's husband Franz (Peter Striebeck) is the most blatant example, horribly proprietary of his sick wife, controlling her relationships. Von Trotta characterizes him as a strong opponent of rearmament and the nuclear threat, and eminent enough to say so on television—but whether his helping Ruth to survive is a metaphor for his own struggle against the pull toward global death, or whether, more likely, his public life lends ironic bitterness to his secret need to keep Ruth helpless and death-turned, is not clear. It is again part of the richness of the film to keep such questions open. Ruth runs to Franz like a little girl, he scolds her like an angry parent, and his possessiveness and sexual jealousy mount savagely, but believably, as the two women grow more involved. Now it is *he* on the other side of the glass, through which he watches them laugh and talk intimately. Von Trotta deliberately toys with sexual provocation in this context, by calling attention to Olga's bare legs in one such sequence and having Ruth put her head into Olga's lap— and in another sequence, having Olga in a bare sundress so that Ruth's repeated touching of her must suggest something erotic as well as generally warm and loving. (However, von Trotta herself denied this content when I interviewed her, speaking instead of "a sort of attachment" or "fascination for another woman". . . . "to be very close to her thoughts and her soul and all that but it has nothing to do with sex. You have no sexual relationship to your mother but you like to touch her, so it can be just a friendship. I think for *Sheer Madness* that's the sort of relationship to disturb men." Arguing that "sexuality practically always goes together with power games," she looks to women's friendships "where you don't want to prove all the time that you are the best, and you are more and stronger than the other.")

Franz's need to regain control is so powerful that it leads him to a series of brutalities. He tries to stop Ruth's career and to stop her friendship. When he tells Ruth that he asked Olga to be her friend, the camera pans around Ruth in anguish, positioned near an agonized Christ head—and watches Ruth carefully cancel out the point of light in the darkness of each of her paintings, themselves an eloquent metaphor for the merest step before nothing, blackness with a mere center of light, of white. Ruth also tries to cancel out her own light by taking her life—not because a man doesn't return her love but essentially because she is led to believe a woman doesn't. Or because the relationship that she thought was her own achievement and desert, apparently was made for her by a man. Franz's reaction to her near-suicide is as repellent as his previous behavior, outrageously taking over her life while refusing to take moral responsibility for his own.

But von Trotta is aiming at something larger than one particular unhappy pair, one unpleasant man—nothing less here than the oppressiveness that is built into the social construction of heterosexuality, at the cost of the woman. The father on his patriarchal pillar is a nightmare in *Marianne and Juliane*, but Juliane's Wolfgang balances that as a nurturing and appealing male figure. In *Sheer Madness* all the men are outrageous, not only he who tends the sick Ruth and needs that control over her, but those who feed off the strong Olga and then call her suffocating while they leave her their bills to take care of. If Ruth's weakness must be maintained, Olga's strength is abused, by her Russian emigre pianist lover, and by her husband Dieter (Franz Buchrieser) from whom she is separated. Although Dieter is celebrated as a theatre director, he cannot seem to do his work without Olga's help. (She is apparently herself one of the uncredited collaborators she lectures about.) His hostility toward Ruth, toward the closeness between the women, is nicely balanced against Ruth's mother's equally shocking hostility toward Olga in the previous scene. The women's friendship appears to threaten everyone.

That threat is greatest when the two are closest, during and after their Egyptian trip, separated from their usual lives and their men, and touchingly intense in their talk and in their yearning to find some way to make this last longer. When they return to the Provence house and their regular lives, they glow with their experience, Ruth full of a new lust for life, continually touching Olga, a strong physical attraction and closeness suggested between the two. The tensions this sets in motion between Franz and Olga explode in a ferocious argument. In the course of it, even their host, Franz's brother, pater familias of what seems the most normal and ordinary household in the film, becomes himself implicated in the general oppressive male condition. When Olga confronts Ruth's husband Franz, the host's wife surprises us by joining in about *her* husband, furiously speaking of how everything is his, *his* orchard, *his* children—only for cooking is her place recognized. So when Olga takes Franz on in a powerfully dramatized battle, fighting back as Ruth does not, refusing to be silenced, telling him he can't bear the competition because "she might be better than you"—Olga is presented by von Trotta as battling for all the women in the film, who share, with variations, a common fate.

Olga however hardly fares happily for all her spirit, although, as far as one can see, through no fault of her own. In the party scene at the height of Ruth's expansion, Ruth unexpectedly leaves her black clothes behind to appear in a sexy red party dress, while Olga is for once in black—though with a linking patch of red. In a surprising sequence at the piano, Olga, dramatically backlit, a send-up of Marlene Dietrich and Fassbinder as well, sings with wonderful dissonance, "Will you still love me tomorrow?" directed both to her lover Alexej, and to Ruth. Alexej won't, of course, despite everything she has given, hence the painful undercurrent to the scene along with its deadpan drollness.

But for all the seeming victimization of women in all this, they do fight back, they are in their struggle very much the subjects of their lives, they are much more active forces than sufferers, and in the film's shocking ending, ambiguous on first viewing, the refusal of victimization is most strong. With the black and white of the final sequence signalling yet another of Ruth's fantasies, this one has the animus for once directed not at herself but against the man. Ruth dreams she has destroyed Franz, either his actual person or his power over her, because he destroyed her friendship and all it meant in terms of her own growth and capacity to operate in the world. As Haskell notes, "She finds her 'self' and voice, but at the expense of her marriage. The only way she can survive as a person is to annihilate her 'keeper'."[29] The film asks, Haskell goes on to note, whether we have the right to urge "other, more hidebound women to renounce oppression, to give up their romantic dependencies . . . and thus their husbands, their lives, the only selves they know?" And speaking of our ideal: "to combine commitment to self and career with a 'great' (i.e. equal) relationship," Haskell points out that, "given the intransigencies of custom and the male ego, isn't this possible only under exceptional, rather than ordinary, circumstances?"[30]

But this act of annihilation, or at least the ability to imagine it, to desire it, is meant by von Trotta as Ruth's achievement. Hope is no longer death, at least not her own death. In *Sheer Madness*, von Trotta's two split selves now consist of the dependent one, seen as the maker of art; and the other, trying to sustain her in beautiful and unambivalent feminist terms. It is not just a matter of paying for school courses, as the older sister does in *Sisters*, first for Anna and then for Miriam, with uneasy implications of control; here it is in terms of serving as the light through the window. The light leads to Ruth's anger, with the fantasized act of murder representing an emergence from victimization, from depression, from the violence against the self—as we saw it earlier in von Trotta's Anna or here in Ruth in the first part of the film. Obviously murder is never a desirable resolution, but in film fantasy (and even beyond, the fantasy that every film is) given what depression has meant to women historically, it is a large step to have this anger directed not inward at the self but outward, toward the source of the oppression. This trajectory could easily lead von Trotta to Rosa Luxemburg, relating too to the respect von Trotta shows for Marianne and the metaphor of the revolutionary or political activist as vehicle for expression of anger, and struggle for change.

But whatever one's rendering of this complexly suggestive ending, and however feminist one's reading of Ruth's development, *Sheer Madness* does not offer a happy ending for the freed being, or for the woman reaching out the window for the light. It sets in motion a process in that direction, but maintains a sense of tragedy, of human consciousness as twisting in unpredictable ways, viewed with an intellectual complexity—agitated contradictions that ward off the reductive and that make for paradox and rich art.

That same sense of tragedy contributes to *Rosa Luxemburg* its strongest element, the use of flashback. The anguished heavy figure of an older imprisoned Rosa, whom we see first, frames the film, with a counterpoint throughout the rest of the film between the worn and painful end of Rosa's life (she in somber black against snowy prison courtyard walks) and various earlier points of her life. This is not the subtly controlled and nuanced flashback that creates the brilliant layering so important to *Marianne and Juliane*. (The narration of *Rosa* is generally more conventional in feeling than is true of von Trotta's other work, even lushly commercial at times, especially in the use of music and pretty landscape—probably in an attempt to hold audiences for the relatively austere nature of the material.) But the use of flashback in *Rosa* works principally to temper all hope and effort with something meditative and full of a sense of tragic limitation. If Rosa's speeches in the film were more successful in transmitting the burning singing revolutionary fervor they were intended to convey, more of the passion of the public world, the effect of that worn older self would have been even more powerful. There are other moments through the film that sound that double note—a New Year's celebration welcoming 1900 with hopeful words about the promise of the twentieth century, that ring bitterly to an audience that knows what the century has brought us.

Rosa's periodically powerful statements that a world has to be overthrown are matched by sentiments of anguish—over an oncoming war, a premature revolutionary battle begun uselessly, even the pain of an abused buffalo dragging a cart. It all adds up to a believable and affecting grief for the world, though perhaps more the world of the Greens than of the Communists. Rosa is the only genuine character in the film but a remarkable character, and unique because a woman: a woman of great authority and humanity; with a most difficult life, constant flight from place to place, (unstated) loneliness despite her gift for friendship; yet trying to nourish life on every level. All this comes together in the strongest image in the film: a fleeting view of Rosa sitting on a chair in the middle of a tiny square of garden in that last prison courtyard, the flower garden she was finally able to cultivate in the forced leisure of imprisonment; sitting in semi-darkness in that little garden with massive sterile prison walls on every side. Whatever does not work in this remarkably ambitious film, such a moment and such a heroine surely vindicate the attempt.

In view of that, and with *Marianne and Juliane* now carrying the weight of a classic, and with *Sheer Madness*, described by Molly Haskell as "one of the most extraordinary, the most disturbing and terrifying, women's films ever made,"[31] Margarethe von Trotta has established herself as a major director, and is tapping into material simply not approached before. Hers is not only a women-centered cinema, but a feminist cinema, passionate without ever being doctrinaire, working a terrain that is central for women spectators, with a largeness of ambition and an intellectual excitement that is yet never divorced from the most intense emotions, engaged in the outside world as well as the inner world. Von Trotta herself has defined a women's aesthetic as primarily identified by its not separating ideas and feelings, by the willingness "to stand up for things we believe in," as well as by "the choice of the subject and . . . the attention, the respect, the sensitivity and the care with which we approach the people we are depicting.[32] Her work has the magnetism of strong narrative without being formally conventional, and is particularly rich in powerful metaphors for women's experience. What she has learned from Schlondorff, she has put to her own uses in carving out a women's cinema of distinctiveness. That this excellence is not only the work of a woman, and not only work about women, but work strongly marked by feminist consciousness, is a major development in the experience of women in film, an experience that goes back to the earliest years of film history but that is still, given its peculiar development, just beginning.

### Doris Dörrie

The "stunning box-office success of *Men*," the *New York Times* announced when Dörrie's third film opened in New York, "has catapulted [Doris] Dörrie into the front rank of West Germany's post-Fassbinder generation of young directors."[33] And so it has. But even her first two films, which had very brief showings in the New Directors series at MOMA, made clear that from the beginning this was a director to be taken very seriously. Both *Straight Through the Heart* and *In the Belly of the Whale* represent a high level of filmmaking, each production full of authority. From early on her work revealed a strong personal vision and voice, and an ability to captivate—even with the stranger, more alienated material of the earlier work.

Yet *Men* is not as shocking a shift as it would seem in tone and point of view from the quite tormented dramas of young women heroines struggling with older men in the first two films. These have their own kind of charm and flair and memorable moments of whimsy mixed in with the pain; and they also extend enormous sympathy to the uptight, troubled older men in those films, even while the director works there through female characters' eyes. *In the Belly of the Whale* is particularly interesting for its mix of humor, violence, and luminosity.

Dörrie—who is only 31, born in 1955, and very productive—offers in her oeuvre a striking contrast with von Trotta, centered as her films are on young women drawn to authoritarian older males, father figures whom you would be tempted to call fascistic if they were not themselves seen as so sick, vulnerable, and anguished. Dörrie's subject matter can seem a regressive hearkening back to old heterosexual romances of spontaneous yearning heroines and severe, unavailable men—though *In the Belly of the Whale* starts to feel like a critique of this material. As von Trotta's work has at its center intense relationships between women, and heroines making their own way in the world, often with strong left political values, Dörrie's drama is that of young women drawn to "straight" males, and if the films have any politics, it is an ambiguous, dark, sexual politics of heterosexual power, submission, abuse. By the time of *Men* this seems to become a good-humored endorsement of capitalistic materialism and what used to be called Establishment values, although Dörrie insists the film is satiric of those values and of the opportunism of the characters.[34]

*In the Belly of the Whale* (1984) is about a girl's coming of age, entering puberty, cast in terms of male authoritarianism and female masochism, and a struggle to go beyond these. The heroine, fifteen-year-old Carla, like Joyce Chopra's heroine in *Smooth Talk*, has to move out into the world, out of her original household. But if violence marks the passage in Chopra, it does so far more profoundly in Dörrie. In fact, Dörrie's work generally has a strain of violence that is striking even in a changing context of women directors implicated increasingly in the violence of the general culture. In Dörrie, the usual perversity of German filmmaking takes the form of the disturbingly masochistic position in which she puts women (though in another paradox they don't aim their own violence at themselves, as is usually the case with von Trotta's women, but at men). All this made her first feature *Straight Through the Heart* (1983) an uneasy experience; but *In the Belly of the Whale* is particularly interesting because it addresses the issue directly, it gives it center stage as the film's very subject matter.

The shocking opening of the film presents the female as a hunted, beaten animal, someone crouching, only a hand and shining eyes visible, under a staircase, and then found by a pursuing male, dragged out, and beaten. The relation between the two characters is deliberately ambiguous in this opening sequence; the two could easily be lovers but are revealed to be father and daughter, a daughter who is almost a woman, a father who is holding on to her unnaturally, with no other women in his life in the ten years since he divorced her mother. His violence, expressed through his position as a cop, is early vented in a particularly brutal way on another victim as well as his beautiful daughter, Rick Wummer, whose girlfriend has thrown both him and his possessions out of her house (a scene repeated in *Men* with Stefan). The whole film circles around male/female couples and shows them as mostly impossible, with one of the two always victimized.

Rick, looking a bit hippy-ish and played by the charming, gentle actor Eisi Gulp (the "sugarbaby" in the Percy Adlon film of that name), at first appears ready to revenge himself on the daughter for how the father beat him. But he and the girl instead form a touching alliance as the girl runs away from home to find her mother, and Rick picks her up. The result is a female road movie, the girl the wanderer—in one more of the reversals the new women's films have given us—as the father remains confined to the house, and obsessed with keeping it neat. (So the two men in *Men* are confined to domestic space and the woman, Paula, there is in a sense the wanderer, freewheeling, twirling her tie provocatively on the paternoster.) The girl's quest, on the road, is indeed the strongest part of *In the Belly of the Whale*, because both actors, with great skill, create a playful and affectionate sanctuary between them from the harsh punishing experience that is called love in the outside world, a kind of sanctuary that exists again in *Men* between the men. Rick is perhaps too idealized a figure, in the abandon of his own despair over his rejecting girlfriend, Holly, entirely at the disposal of the young girl, Carla, but his kindness and caring is so jauntily handled as to never seem unreally good. One of the strongest sequences of their experience together is a near drowning, visually very well done, with Carla vanishing beneath waves, Rick realizing and struggling to get her out, the camera leaving us unsure whether or not both are gone. Indeed, both characters have trouble keeping their heads above water in their lives, and in some way are trying to save themselves and one another on this journey.

The on-the-road parts of the film are also strong because of the effective trajectory created by the girl's moving toward her long-lost and unknown mother, and the mother—who we see is at loose ends herself—awaiting the daughter's approach. This archetypal women's-film motif promises for a while to be an important variation on the theme. The mother has been kept from her daughter for ten years by the father's refusal to let her see the child—deriving from his rage against the mother as a whore, a slut—although it is unclear whether his prime concern is that she was involved with other men or that she is slovenly, both given seemingly equal weight. The cop father is a man obsessed with order, at the same time in an unstated way with eroticism as well. He gives his daughter a virginal white dress, wants her to be a respectable woman, and finds her changing into something he doesn't know. This, and his frenzied screaming at the girl for the mess of her room, eliciting classic adolescent responses (it's her room, she can deal with it, she wants nothing from him) takes the usual parent–adolescent encounter to an extreme point, a kind of madness.

The girl resists of course. After the initial scene in which she is beaten, there's a zany moment in which she drowns a little Mickey Mouse in a sink, with a rope around his neck as well, with nutty sounds of drowning to accompany the action. She play-acts shooting with her father's gun in front of a mirror, herself decked out in black leather, overly made up. And she runs away, helped and nurtured by the gentle male her father saw as his enemy. Surely the film goes well beyond one adolescent daughter's struggle with a strict father to something far more ambitious, an attempt to deal with German male authority, seen as fearsome but also extremely troubled, and, it turns out, powerfully enticing, a national family drama not to be simplified. The father is kept by von Trotta at a great distance, in *Marianne and Juliane* for instance (though in *Sheer Madness*, male attitudes come in for profound assault for the ways they infantilize, drain, bury women)—while the mother fusion is presented over and over again in von Trotta's women/women intimacies. In Dörrie the father is the center, the problematic, what her women get wrecked on.

The mother, we discover, needs the young girl as much as the girl needs her mother. As the girl traces the mother it is clear the mother too is a victim of men, not only of her cop husband but of the lover who suddenly got rid of her, the boss who fired her, her not wanting to tell anyone where she moved to because she knew she would then sit all day waiting for a phone call from Him. Yet her end-of-the-line apartment is no simple cliche, nor is her current Italian boyfriend, who seems kind and nurturing; at the same time, she is a barmaid and clearly not in firm possession of her life.

The two women's destinies finally about to cross is one of the promises the film makes but then withholds. Carla, with a minimum of clues, finds the mother almost mystically, magically, like the bright blue color Dörrie bestows on everything surrounding the questing characters. The blue seems related to the sea, present throughout the film, to the mother's living by the sea, the only real clue to her location. Blue colors the clothes the girl and Rick wear, the reflected light coming into the mother Marta's room, or reflected on faces, the color of the strange vehicle carrying the whale exhibition that gives the film its name. But the yearning toward one another of the two women is never realized. And the final scene between the parents, the rhythms of which don't quite work, conveys as much violence on the part of the mother as the father: she toys with a huge kitchen knife, plays with accusations of murdering him, full of a sense of his having humiliated her in the past, and finally actually cuts him and locks him in the bathroom. It is she, however, who is destroyed in the end, by gunshot, in a way that presents the father as partly innocent, though it is not clear why he should be.

What the film loses through these sequences it regains in its conclusion, with the father taking the body of the mother to a bus stop bench to leave her there, Carla discovering the blood left behind, finding her dazed father, and shouting out in front of a mass of people that he's a murderer. The tables are in a way turned, as they were between the man and his wife earlier, when she holds him captive. But in both cases the women gain power only to fall back to a lower level. When the father starts to cry and fall apart, the daughter promises not to tell, and taking his gun, holds off the approaching crowd—Rick along with the others. She is herself now identified with her father in a frame, spatially and psychically as well. From taking the role of accuser on behalf of her mother, from her anguish over the final loss of the mother, who is now removed from her forever, the film's ending, as shocking as its beginning, puts her again in the violent power of the father, for all her struggles to move away and into her own sphere.

The whale motif, which the film sounds from early on and throughout, suggests a foetal existence—in Dörrie's own view, the safety of being inside the family.[35] To be swallowed up in such a huge and phallic shape also suggests, biology to the contrary, being held in a male enclosure rather than a female one. Since Jonah does come out, the image also holds the promise of birth. The whale image appears to us first with extraordinary beauty and strangeness (and Dörrie's command of visual effect in each new film is very strong, both in itself and with the sense of her own vision). From the first scene of violent beating of daughter by father, and the girl left bloody, weeping, crouched foetal-like inside a shower stall, Dörrie cuts to an amazing, eerily gorgeous shot of a bridge softly curving in the darkness, its sinuous shape outlined by romantic lights, and a strange flaming beacon passing over this high-up shape in the darkness, later seen to be a whale exhibit carried in a long vehicle. Surely it is not only the security of confinement that is presented with such joyful luminosity, but the promise of freedom and birth that Jonah represents.

The tormented man-woman nexus of Dörrie's films is announced in her very first film, *Straight Through the Heart*, a more limited and in my view less interesting film perhaps because it takes us back to the old heterosexual romance of the man filled with terror of anyone getting close to him, and the utterly needy woman whose masochism draws her to such a man—a kind of female entrapment one would hope the Women's Movement has helped move us beyond. The situation in *Straight Through the Heart* is pathological although not remarkable in the peculiarly tormented context of the New German film generally. The pretty heroine Anna Blume conveys with her bright blue hair a flakey bravado and at the same time a frailty. She is at once tough and a pathetic waif. Fired from her job at a supermarket checkout counter for giving food away to kids and women, she conveys something anarchistic, impulsive, mildly lawless, all of which attracts the utterly blocked and conservative dentist Armin to take her into his life. There is between them also the economics of his affluence and her resourcelessness, a hint of the pull toward material luxury, that people sell themselves for, with no moral compunctions raised about this. Dörrie's blue-haired heroine reminds one a bit of Seidelman's Wren in *Smithereens* though Wren is a more affecting heroine because of her hustling, her fight—however demented and illusory—to make a place in the world. With Anna, on the other hand, we are back with woman's desperate neediness, wanting *him*, increasingly wanting nothing but this man, a man who can't give, willing even to give him a child even if that's all he wants from her, willing to do anything to make him like her. Armin expresses disgust over these emotions, and they *are* disgusting, at least troubling, to the female spectator as well. Yet because Dörrie takes this material to such a hallucinatory place, because she handles it with such visual and dramatic skill and has shown by her return to it that it is an obsessive core theme—feminist disapproval is finally beside the point. This is true especially as we see in *In the Belly of the Whale* the illuminating places this road can take her, and especially as we see her heroine struggling in the most life-and-death ways against her bonds, a paradigm then of one kind of woman's struggle.

But for all the empathy with the young women questors, charmers who don't take themselves too seriously, both films carry a heavy feeling of the poignancy of the man, who is more trapped than the woman. This is particularly true in *Straight Through the Heart*, where the man is entirely caught, though he has the trappings of power with his money, his professional status, his seeming control over the situation with Anna, his being a good deal older than she and she even calling him Daddy. But the patriarchs, real fathers and proxy ones in Dörrie, are deeply ailing, and though they are power figures, utterly impotent. They are in deep trouble, male trouble of denial of affect and spontaneity, patriarchal trouble. Armin's own desperate entrapment is never in doubt, seen as that by Anna who wants to liberate him, though by an apparent fatedness she ends by destroying him in the process. For all his pinstriped conservative suit and solid furnishings, his dream image of himself is as a black butterfly on a hat—his doomed soul, perhaps. To envisage a cop in similar terms of sympathy, as trapped victim—as Dörrie does in her next film, *Belly*—although he brutalizes both his daughter and a young male stranger, is a harder task but Dörrie does that as well. So again it is no great surprise to find her in *Men* shifting sympathy and focus entirely to the male characters. Indeed, with the "straight" man of the pair in *Men*, Daniel Arbrust, Dörrie now drops critical perspective—it seems to me, despite her vehement denial—for what feels like a pretty unambiguous, even complacent, embrace. In this sense one can indeed be troubled about the confluence of narrative enticements and ideological statement, and wonder which in fact was the primary factor in the film's success. It is fair to ask whether it is an accident that the two come together so neatly here.

In *Straight Through the Heart* the focus, as in so many women's films, is on interrelationship, on connecting, and Armin is so cut off that he plays chess by long-wave radio communications with a man in Osaka. At the same time, the women, who are capable of connecting and look generally more whole, are destroyers in both films, and the male fears of rendering themselves accessible seem valid. This is true even though in *In the Belly of the Whale* the man actually kills his wife, and not she him—but she tries, she cuts him. The daughter too—the object of violence earlier—poses in a mirror with an aimed gun, though it could be argued that given their relationship, she'd be better off with a gun than with the daughterly loyalty and love she ends by affirming. The murder in *Straight Through the Heart* is committed with the man in a strikingly vulnerable situation, sitting naked in a bathtub, his back to the heroine, electrocuted. She in the final sequences, seen carrying the child she kidnapped, among immigrant workers, is as alien as ever, her newly dyed blonde hair setting her as much apart from these darkhaired people as her blue hair did before. While they pass food around among themselves, she remains the hungry one too, even though finally they offer her some. *In the Belly of the Whale*, for all its promise of release and birth, ends with a shocking commitment by the girl to her patriarchal imprisoner—and with its two male characters, the hippy and the fascist father—it prefigures the direction of *Men*. It prefigures *Men* also by catching the charm and light, witty spontaneity of Wummer, not easy to do, as easily as both the brutality and the anguished impotence of the cop father. But the loyal filial anguish of *In the Belly of the Whale* is quite different from the endorsement, however charming, in *Men* of West Germany's corporate hustle for more money and more things, with the hip artist Stefan revealed to be as materialistic as anyone, no different after all—like the wife Paula, like everyone else, apparently. In this comedy of total accommodation—which, for all Dörrie's talk in interviews about the humorlessness of Germans, has a beautifully paced humor that is almost never forced—all have succumbed to the accumulation of wealth, through endless work, with Armbrust having learned nothing from his respite from this life.

One can imagine how bitter Dörrie's enormous national and American success must be for the many struggling German feminist radical left filmmakers, who often attacked von Trotta, a passionate leftist and feminist, as too slick and politically unacceptable. They will doubtless chalk Dörrie's success up to a slickly conventional narrative style supporting nasty patriarchal capitalist values. (At the same time, Dörrie's immense success is bound to have great impact on the nature of films being made by German feminist directors.[36]) But Dörrie's two earlier films are compelling pieces of work, that would never reach a wide audience—she was good then and is good now!—as the films of other less well-known German women dirctors with more commendable values are frankly often less interesting.

Dörrie is clearly not a feminist, though she makes Paula jaunty, and gives her a far greater dignity than the husband is given for his little office liaison. The subject of women working is not of interest to Dörrie, most unusual among this group of women directors. And relationships seem happiest without a sexual ingredient, as with Carla and Rick in *Whale*, or the cozy domesticity of the two men in *Men*, an unusually tender instance of male bonding not covered over with the heavy macho paraphernalia with which American male directors, or even Elaine May, treat such relationships.

*Men*'s most important function may be the ensuring of Dörrie's future funding and distribution, because Dörrie's talent is certain, though the ends to which she will continue to put it remain to be seen. She speaks scornfully of the American film industry for its concern with commercial hits only—"If films can only be like 'Pretty in Pink' or like Spielberg and 'Rambo,' then in the end film is going to be worth only as much as a Big Mac"[37] and this is a very good sign for her future. So is her telling me she loves Susan Seidelman's *Smithereens*, but likes *Desperately Seeking Susan* much less because it is slick. Her relation to uptight establishment German men provides her an important subject matter that I think she could take much further than she does. It is clearly a love/hate experience for her—the uptight male protagonists most identified with the traits she regards as German are the characters who get all the sympathy in her films, and at the same time the interview she gave the *New York Times* concluded with her saying that before, she could only think of returning to America, but now she is "really proud to be a European—but not a German, never."[38] After the success of *Men*, Dörrie went from a budget of $400,000 to $1 million for her fourth film, *Paradise*, but more important still, the film sounds like a return to the themes and tone of the preceding two, which is where her talent and future development would seem to lie. *Paradise* concerns a married dentist who falls in love with a young woman, and it ends violently, though "it starts out very funny" in Dörrie's words, a mixture of tones she does very well. However Dörrie's future young women fare, and however far she can take a unique exploration of the German male psyche she has already begun, Doris Dörrie gives every promise of being one of the major European women directors to be reckoned with in the future.

## Other German Women Directors

German cinema, as has been noted, has been unique for the large number of women directors active in it through the 1970s into the 1980s. The list of names is long, among them Ulrike Ottinger, Jeanine Meerapfel, Elfi Mikesch, Jutta Bruckner, Ula Stoeckl, Friederike Pezold, Claudia von Alemann, Heidi Genee, Pia Frankenberg, Dagmar Beiersdorf, Helga Reidemeister, Austrian Valie Export. To seriously examine this body of work (and the circumstances under which it was created) would constitute a book in itself. Choices had to be made, and regrettably omissions occur—of films like Helke Sander's *Redupers*, a central film in the feminist film scholars' canon, or the interesting work of Helma Sanders-Brahms, who has come increasingly and deservedly to international attention. Her first film *Germany Pale Mother* (1980) is a haunting work about mother-daughter bonding in the tragic circumstances of wartime destruction. *The Future of Emily* (1984) works interestingly with three generations of women. Sanders-Brahms' *Laputa* (1986) is a love story about a Polish woman photographer who meets her married French lover between planes in Berlin; like *Emily*, it is focussed on a dynamically work-oriented heroine. Despite various problems here as in the earlier two films (with the central metaphor, for instance), *Laputa*, like *Germany Pale Mother*, is intriguingly engaged in studying the national visage.

*Laputa* is not only dominated by a woman's sensibility, but powerfully catches the harried, tormented sense, known particularly by women—and women now especially—of being torn by conflicting claims of important work, family demands, and even the pull of a passionate love life. Though not distributed theatrically here, doubtless because of problems posed for spectators by their slow pace and their artistic incompleteness, Helma Sanders-Brahms' films are among the more intriguing and satisfying of a wide range of films currently being produced by German women directors.

## FRENCH WOMEN DIRECTORS

### Agnes Varda

Agnes Varda has been making films for over three decades now, starting out at a time when less than a handful of women were directing. Varda's longevity as a serious filmmaker, her capacity for survival, is in itself moving, as other august figures have come and gone, their trajectories played out by death or burnout in one form or another. Varda—born in 1928, four years older than Lina Wertmuller and Elaine May, since 1962 the wife of director Jacques Demy—made her first short, *La Point Courte*, in 1954. She made her first feature, *Cleo From 5 to 7*, in 1961, and it is not hard to remember how dazzling that film looked when it originally appeared, or *Le Bonheur*, for that matter, in 1965. Varda has come in for her share of criticism but, forerunner and "mother" of the New Wave, she continues to work and grow, each new film a bold new direction, even though each— for all Varda's past achievements and feisty energy—involves a massive struggle for financing to get off the ground.

Varda's first feature film, *Cleo*, focussed on a woman alone, in quest, wandering through (urban) space; her most recent film, *Vagabond* (in French, *Sans Toit Ni Loi*, "Without a Roof or a Law") again centers on a solitary woman moving through (rural) space. But Varda's relationship to a woman as subject generating her own story is a complex one. On one hand, for all her apparent unconventionality, she is one of the pioneer generation still very much shaped by traditional gender roles and values. Varda's own personal originality, courage, and aggressiveness as a filmmaker contrast poignantly with the conventionally pretty blondes whom she makes her central women characters, who dream of wedding gowns, and whose forays beyond the domestic world are largely encounters with painful solitude, suicide, death. For Varda, she who is *sans toit*, without a roof, homeless, is out in a very cold world indeed.

At the same time Varda in her very first feature film self-consciously works with femaleness. *Cleo* follows a pop singer for two hours, in more or less real time, wandering through Paris, waiting to find out if she has cancer. Her confrontation with death alters everything she sees. The kind of heroine Varda chooses is almost shocking for looking so much a bonbon, blonde and busty, tight bodice and very flared skirts, stiletto heels, with a sweet mannequin look. It is intriguing how such a Marilyn-Monroe style of sexy "femininity" has attracted a number of women directors who in their person seem as foreign from it as Dorothy Arzner looks in a photo talking with a young Lucille Ball at her satiny gaudiest. (One also thinks of Joan Littlewood's memorable British *Sparrows Can't Sing* [1963] with its own variety of sexy blonde bird, English working-class style; Chytilová's *Daisies* [1966]; and the even stranger comradery of Simone de Beauvoir writing with enormous sympathy about Brigitte Bardot at the height of Bardot's "sex kitten" days.) The sexy women, almost exaggerated into caricature, are used in very different ways by each director, but informed by a woman's inside knowledge. So Varda has her heroine try on lovely poofs of hats, or has her compose her smiling face for the man approaching her from across the room, under the rivetted eye of a camera that refuses to cut away in the usual mode of a two shot.

Cleo's world—as one of appearance, surface, narcissism, women's involvement with their reflected image in the eyes of others—is established by extraordinary visual effects, beautiful and intricate in their own right, that Varda gets with mirrors and shop-window glass, superimposed reflections, exciting multiple visual planes, throughout the first part of the film. The heroine's continual looking at herself in mirrors; her saying nothing to her absentee lover of her illness, presenting only a pleasing front; her joy in adornment and in her own beauty; her sense of power as she sees men on the street taken with that beauty—are finally given the lie by the shadow of death. For us as spectators, too, with our sense of Cleo's imminent mortality, the importance of daily sights and events is everywhere altered with the thought of their temporariness, which is of course the reality of our condition anyway. The film even seems an essay on the pitfalls of French stylishness, the prettiness that is so striking not only in other lighterweight French women directors discussed later but, in her own way, in Varda too, about whose films' over-prettiness critics have always, and with reason, complained.

Cleo's discontent, her growing dissatisfaction with the pretty facade as a major value, her acute awareness of mortality making everything else shallow and silly—is clearly at the center of the film. And the terms of the whole drama are very much gender defined. Cleo is even grateful her probable cancer is in the stomach area since it won't show, either so she can continue to be beautiful, or because she is a person who doesn't expose real feelings, a person who (as she tells us) finds illness indiscreet.

The feather-trimmed queenly white robe Cleo changes into to sing with her two musician collaborators maintains her aura as a confection, for a while. The song lyrics the three sing are a little survey of the range of pop stereotypes of a beautiful woman like Cleo—at the same time that they are yet one more form of unreality and mask. Like Cleo's various other confrontations throughout the film, they reveal a self-consciousness about the nature of being a woman and the functions women serve. One of the songs is about a gold-digger, the second a woman who plays the field, neither of which could be further from Cleo's actual preoccupations with mortal illness. But the third, the only song Cleo sings alone, concerns being a vacant house, being dead, alone, and ugly because the singer has no love. The song is a foreshadowing of the film's conclusion, and perhaps main theme—the lack of love in Cleo's life. Her living space with its eccentrically, baroquely regal furniture, placed in bare, bright white, loft-like spaces, combines Varda's usual aestheticism with a starkness suggesting a paucity in the life lived there. The film charts a quest to find love.

Varda clearly means for Cleo to become increasingly real as the film progresses. In the latter half of the film Cleo finds surface and pretence intolerable, and when she takes off her wig and changes into black, she looks stripped down and bereft but a person, no longer an adornment. In a cafe she sits next to a pillar that is a mosaic of tiny mirrors, emblematic perhaps of her nacissism now in fragments, or of her now fragmented self. Her second wandering the streets, alone, shows her the swallowing of awful things, live frogs, and bodily mutilations—paralleling her new awareness and future condition, what she has to assimilate, in place of frothy hats. It also takes us through the feel of streets and faces, through environs, that Varda does so very well, with wonderfully alive and expressive camera movement throughout.

Cleo finally tells the soldier she encounters at the film's end, who shows genuine concern for her, that her real name is Florence. As with her hair, we are surprised to find out her name is not her own: Cleo—from Cleopatra, pointing to her archetypal glamorous woman mask. Cleo increasingly shows more of herself to people, as she goes to find her woman friend—an artists' model in a school's sculpture studio—where all is stripped down to woman's naked body, the core of the truth, no longer covered over. Cleo tells her friend of her illness soon after, as their car goes through an underpass, the screen rapidly going dark—the visual, as often in the film, an effective metaphor for inner mood.

But this friend can only empathize with Cleo to a degree. The final encounter between Cleo and the soldier locates the deepest possibilities for empathy in the couple.[39] As a result of this relationship Cleo thinks she is no longer afraid, she thinks she is really happy, although simultaneously we hear the doctor's confirmation of the cancer diagnosis, and the need for radiation treatment, presenting a very uncertain future. The tentativeness saves the ending from being as conventional as it might. The soldier may even be killed in the army when he returns to Algeria. Despite the existential slipperiness of our lives, Cleo no longer wants to worry, simply to enjoy the man for the short time he is there, an existential act of acceptance that for Varda turns the crisis around.

So the film moves from a sense of Cleo's finding little that is real in her life, crying out that she still looks like a doll, with nothing showing of the pain she feels—to a stripping away of narcissism and unreality, to a bond of some sort. There is a sense of going a full circle from *Cleo*, Varda's first feature, to her most recent film, *Vagabond*, 25 years later. Cleo, in her growing anxiety, restlessness, terror, moves through a series of encounters in a rather shapeless picaresque structure similar to that of the later film, and as a death overhangs both heroines, so there is a loneliness of each woman wandering alone. But *Cleo* leaves a promise of a new beginning through love. This promise is underlined by sights seemingly in passing in the last part of the film: a baby in an incubator, a pregnant woman. Cleo finds everything made new. By the time of *Vagabond*, the prettiness, the "femininity," and also the hope are gone.

It might easily be argued, however, that this change relates less to the likely disillusionments of age, than to the greater freedom available to a woman director who has spanned the decades Varda has. Asked in a 1970s interview if producers want her to make love stories because she is a woman, she says no, rather "because they only want women to be involved with love in a film. . . . And if I could make *Cleo* about femininity and fear of death, it is because the girl was beautiful. If you told the same story about a 55-year-old lonely woman, who would care if she were dying of cancer and who would come to see the film?"[40] When I interviewed Varda after the success of *Vagabond*, she said she was "amazed" that she did it "with no compromising at all," and still people were "touched and intrigued."

Varda's second feature film, *Le Bonheur* (1965), created controversy for its ambiguity, from its apparently ironic title, to the seeming detachment with which Varda presents a happy family into which the man, Francois, brings his new love for another woman. His wife Therese immediately drowns herself; the new woman Emilie replaces her in bed and as mother to the small children; and with this reconstitution of the family, serenely observed by Varda's camera, happiness appears to be restored, and the natural cycles of life accepted. The judgment of *The Oxford Companion to Film* on Varda's films, that they "combine a rich visual texture and elegance with deliberate coldness and a disconcerting quality of abstraction,"[41] seems particularly applicable to *Le Bonheur*. The film appears to dispassionately observe two people whose happiness is at cross purposes, each with his/her own persuasive logic. However, early on, after Varda has just introduced this picnicking happy family that loves nature, she has them visit a relative, a knitting housewife watching television. On the TV screen a patriarch-philosopher under a tree is exaggeratedly served by a pretty young thing who runs to bring him a drink and tell him how much she loves to hear him talk. He complies with a pronouncement that happiness may consist in submitting to the laws of nature, a statement that might be taken as the philosophical text of the film (and was by several critics at the time) were not the tone of the sequence so bristling with sardonic mockery, a mockery of female deference to guru male, and of male self-satisfaction.

*Le Bonheur* is as painful and disturbing to watch now as it was when it first came out, but what has become stunningly clear is that the disturbance comes from the unacknowledged presence of rage and pain under a surface of the loveliest color and nature imagery, handsome characters, beautiful children, sunny family scenes. (Without directly addressing this particular issue, Varda in a 1970s interview speaks explicitly of how things feminism has now made clear "were not so clear ten years ago when I made *Le Bonheur*."[42]) The brief TV sequence is one of the very few narrative moments that allow us to see below that placid surface, a surface intact largely because the women, especially the wife, do not tell their own story. The film is shot from the man's point of view and gives us no access to the women's subjectivity. Indeed, the wife seems to have little access to her own, as we witness in rapid succession her tentative acceptance of the husband's admission of a new love, her telling him he is her happiness, her allowing him to make love to her, and her drowning herself immediately afterward. The sequence makes for a violent indictment that renders everything that follows—especially Francois' restored pleasure and guiltlessness—intolerable, monstrous, under the curse of the drowned woman who never uttered a word of reproach, unless in the old language of martyrdom, of woman's masochistic self-victimizing as a punishment of the man.

Woman as martyr and sufferer plays a large role in Varda's work, as do other kinds of conventional female roles, graphically conveyed in *Le Bonheur* by a montage of the wife Therese's activities: childcare, kneading dough, cutting patterns, sewing, watering plants, providing nurture in other ways, and continual deference to the man's needs and desires. These are repeated later almost exactly with a parallel montage of Emilie's activities when the second woman replaces the first; and Emilie in the film's final sequences is bent over Francois' children as Francois walks freely about, his face full of the pleasure of the fall woods. The importance for Varda of the domestic, the family, is doubtless part of what moved Claire Johnston to denounce Varda as "reactionary" for an oeuvre that "celebrates bourgeois myths of women,"[43] and to see *Le Bonheur* as "facile advertising-style daydreams" and Varda as placing "woman outside history." But the parallel montages of wifely activities, which foreground female gender roles, convey a detached, intense, consciousness of a sort far more uncomfortable and alienated. And the film, looked at now, can also be seen as very much a product of history, in the way, for instance, it buries the wife's rage in martyrdom.

The saccharine, overly-pretty celebration of the family seems to me ironic, with an edge of bitterness, though also a celebration. Varda does position Francois firmly in charge as *pater familias*, with his house carpentering, his overseeing of end-of-day household tasks, his affection for his children, over which Varda lingers. Varda cast the actor's whole family as the film family in order to get just that visceral connectedness they do convey. Varda's camera does careful and true things with those children, charming, also pitiful as they sleep and then wake, seeking a mother forever gone. Varda also enjoys extended family gatherings, neighbors, ordinary people in a small town, a background of women pushing carriages, couples young and old, pregnant women again—part of Varda's vision of the flow of life, like the flowers through the film, and the countryside. Francois' wife makes gowns for brides, related to the sense of couples in Varda's next film, *Les Creatures*, as an imperilled sanctuary, under attack and fragile. And yet the sardonic coloring marriage and the family take on in *Le Bonheur* as a result of the wife's suicide is akin to how the imminence of cancer renders the whole facade of femaleness an absurdity in *Cleo*. Both films, even if they have led to more perplexity than inquiry, seem constructed to raise basic questions, about women's lives especially.

In *Les Creatures* (1966), about a writer and his wife who retreat to an island, the woman character (played by Catherine Deneuve) is particularly vulnerable, pregnant and suffering from a muteness ambiguously brought on her by her protector husband himself, as a result of his reckless speeding on the way to the island. The muteness, a conception that interestingly came to Varda in recurrent dreams, is the more fascinating given our current concern with female discourse, and women robbed of their voices and control over their own stories, and also given the fact that Varda herself is a great talker. This film also has in common with Varda's earlier two the striking blondness of its heroines; indeed, the Other Woman, the really desired woman in *Le Bonheur*, is the blondest of blondes, unnaturally—almost horribly—perfect. The wives are also overly pleasant, Varda seemingly appropriating the most conventional view of the time as to what constitutes female attractiveness—like a visiting anthropologist surmising what the "normal" woman/wife is. Varda's own expressive looks, by way of parentheses, are conspicuously dark, and her enormously vital and charming manner anything but sweet.

*Les Creatures*, with its plot about an evil genius with a machine that makes people express their subconscious feelings, was received largely negatively, as too much the product of a cerebral ingenuity (as much of a danger for Varda as prettiness). However, seeing it again recently, one is struck by the vitality of Varda's filmmaking, her aesthetic sureness, the film's bold visual beauty, and by something touching as well as technically impressive in the film's vision as it moves from a sense of private happiness between husband and wife, to the mindless hurt and evil that goes on outside their moatlike fortress house. The clever science-fiction machinery of the game between the writer and the evil genius involves not hokum and mystification but a genuine sense of the mysteriousness of things and the sinisterness of forces all around. The stakes of the game are the beautiful mute wife, and victory in this game means one couple who can stay together no matter what, no matter what destructive forces the evil figure brings to bear to make lovers turn against one another.

Repeated rapid crosscutting from seascape images accompanied by very taut, high string music, to the domestic interior, the wife breaking eggs or rolling dough, effectively creates a sense of mystery and danger. The wife, characterized in entirely traditional terms, never even wants to go out, though the restless tormented writer-husband (played by Michel Piccoli) is continually taking long walks. She swells with pregnancy, always sweet and loving, though unable to speak. She bakes and cooks and embraces her husband, the creative one, the one writing a novel, the one struggling with the demons—that seem outer demons but are increasingly clearly inner. It is a strange conception of a woman, given all Varda's work-directed energies, and again only the evil women in this film are dark. Yet the wife, with all her seeming happiness in her domestic role, and all her charm, in having no voice of her own seems Varda's way of indicating that this wife is mutilated in this situation, can't express herself, though she tries and practices. Yet that it is with the birth of the child, the baby boy, at the end that her voice returns, again underlines Varda's deep, if highly ambivalent, relation to traditional female roles.

At the same time, although it is the complexity of the man's fantasy life Varda enters, *Les Creatures* seems strongly female in its orientation. It is attentive to women, who throughout seem for the most part to have things taken away from them, one's purse robbed, the other nearly losing her husband sexually, even the hotel proprietess, elegantly played by Eva Dahlbeck, feeling that her married doctor-lover takes from her but gives her little back. The threat that makes Piccoli stop the game is the danger of rape to one of the young girls. That the intolerable should take this form perhaps suggests a woman's sensibility. Still the film's drama is set up as a male fantasy, male terrors high in a very phallic tower. The film also works with the tenuous line between art and "reality," events in the writer's novel happening in "real life," so that the evolving stories we see are possibly all in the writer's mind. It makes the toying with even fictional fates seem enormously dangerous, standing above the miniature couples on a chess board and planning their next moves for them. While the actual evil forces are rendered rather crudely, *Les Creatures* is intriguing, especially if seen as about marriage and its dangers, the menacing outer world a projection of the inner difficulties that endanger the relationship.

The family nests of Varda's films gets a 1960s' hippy translation in *Lion's Love* (1969), by the trio of Viva and the co-authors of *Hair*, lolling in bed or hugging, polymorphously perverse, in an L. A. pool. The film's cuteness and prettiness are even more uncomfortable now than they seemed originally, not the first film by a European director working in English and in Hollywood that badly misfired. But it is interesting that the one venturer outside the decorative huggy home/nest in this film is a visiting woman director, played by Shirley Clarke, who is asked by Varda to commit suicide. Clarke balks, refusing right on camera, insisting she would never kill herself over not being able to make a lousy film, only maybe if something were to happen to her daughter—a refusal one wishes the wife in *Le Bonheur* had made as well.

The best of the films Varda has made since are marked by far more painful visions—of women outside domestic safety trying to maintain themselves— making for some of the strongest work in Varda's career. In Varda's most affecting short, *Documenteur* (1981), a French woman in L.A. with her young son, her husband having left her, is lost in labyrinthine streets and in her own loneliness. Genuinely working through the woman's point of view, the film also conveys her sexual yearning, through a several-times repeated image—from memory or fantasy, we are not sure—of a prone naked man, the camera panning in, through several movements, toward his genitals. The image takes one by surprise, with the force of another taboo broken, [44] in the representation of female desire. (At the same time Varda has not on the whole been an erotic director, despite the striking series of nude tableaux of lovemaking in *Le Bonheur*, and even more, a subliminal series of brief jumpcuts when Francois first comes to Emilie, through which Varda enters very effectively into the creation of male desire.)

*Documenteur* in retrospect seems deeply related to *Vagabond*, Varda's most recent film, in which a woman's freedom is truly a catastrophe. In between, in *One Sings, the Other Doesn't* (1977), Varda attempted a feminist celebration of two active young women bravely shaping their own destinies on their own in the world. Nothing could make clearer that artists have to follow their own deepest voices, which choice and will cannot influence. *One Sings* was universally and rightly panned as too willed and neatly schematic in its upbeat, sunny, positive thinking. Hence Varda's one outright feminist film, which should be the center of this discussion, is not. Yet is is a pleasant film—about two friends who go different ways, one a singer, the other later involved in a birth control clinic, with Varda's own daughter Rosalie as a representative of the younger generation. As elsewhere, Varda narrates her own film, her voice directing our sense of things here as male voices always have done. With this film, Varda deliberately sought a large audience and also chose to affirm the fact of being a woman. Yet *One Sings, the Other Doesn't* is forgettable as *Vagabond*, about a young woman drifter, with a dark severity in its beauty, is not.

The power of *Vagabond* comes in part from how the stark harshness of subject and setting precludes any temptations to sweetness. The film begins with the stunning pain of coming upon a young woman dead and frozen in a ditch, through flashbacks and documentary-style commentary then creating the journey that led her to such a miserable death. But Varda sees Mona not as a victim, but rather as someone who says no to everything so totally as to look like independence itself. Mona's is an intriguing presence (with an extraordinary performance by Sandrine Bonnaire) that one never gets bored watching, unpredictable, affecting in both her tough resourcefulness and her vulnerability. The film's original title, translated, "Without a Roof or a Law," alludes first to the pitiful condition of living outdoors in an unbearably cold winter, but alludes second to caring for nothing and nobody—a freedom so total that it is the same as total loneliness, as one of the film's characters says. Varda has Mona give off a self-sufficient strength; she mostly can take care of herself, scrounge for things to eat, fend off unwelcome questions, evade the police, find various forms of shelter, even draw occasional lovers and then get rid of them. She gives a sense of being freewheeling and able to cope, though we know how much pathology must underlie her behavior.

The film takes care never to romanticize her situation or her character. Various good people offer her a chance to settle down into a more comfortable situation, most vividly a hippy-style goat farmer and his wife, but Mona's unwillingness to work, in the midst of the couple's energetic industry, makes the philosophically inclined farmer comment on the emptiness of a freedom so total it leads to self destruction. At the same time Varda, moving back and forth between normal people's lives and Mona's, offers an implicit critique of respectable normality and even shows Mona envied by lonely wives. But Varda herself clearly does not see Mona's freedom as in any way enviable but rather as terrible, even if conventional lives, lived inside houses and comforts and couples, are also profoundly unappealing.

The film raises philosophical issues as naturally as it creates images of great though austere beauty. It also creates through Mona a kind of prism through which to look at a wide range of characters, people tenderly protective of her or guilty about not involving themselves further. Varda refuses to take sides, and creates complexity by laying different attitudes and perceptions side by side.

There is a profound ambiguity in the film's being centered on a female sensibility that is really not there, that is truly an absence. We too remain outside this character, who does not have a language, or even a willingness, to reflect on herself, generally turning to a car radio or a television set when her current ride or otherwise benefactor asks her questions about herself. There is ambiguity in her self sufficiency, which is suicidal—at the same time that she moves us in her willful insistence on doing things on her own terms, moving through various landscapes with her bold stride, boots and backpack, hair long, uncombed and unwashed, but with a quite beautiful face. But it is a bold stride to nothing, to death, or simply Away From. Varda handles these contexts with the beauty she retains from her first vocation as still photographer. Her camera often tracks to allow us to pick up all kinds of visual detail about an environment before and after we get to the main character's actions, creating a continual beauty for the eye that at the same time is never gratuitous here but tied closely to the narrative. The film also uses nonprofessional actors, ordinary people, in whom Varda has long had a special interest.

The film brings together what Agnes Varda can do best and shows her as skillful and intriguing a director as ever, in presenting a life—with an extraordinary mixture of compassion and toughmindedness—seemingly far removed from that of her own indefatigable productivity and purpose. It's a life that shows a freely wandering woman, without a roof or a law over her, as in very big trouble. Varda, when asked in an interview years ago, about the dearth of women film directors, answered: "Prejudice, I suppose . . . not men's, it's women's. Women think it's not feminine to be strong. How silly that is! A strong woman needs protection just as much as a strong man does." The unprotected woman is the subject of Varda's most eloquent moments, with the pain that accompanies that condition. Varda was the earliest of the current major women directors, out there struggling by herself long before others were, and shaped by an earlier world—though, in becoming a woman director in the 1950s, at the same time uniquely defining herself. For us in the United States with a film industry that is all compromise and box office, a director like Varda who works out of a larger vision of what filmmaking is about, that she has lived out all these years, with all the difficulties involved, in itself represents a most important kind of survival and triumph. But when in addition we consider what visions of women Varda worked out of, that achievement seems a far more impressive triumph still, painfully hard won as it must have been, and nonetheless bravely pursued.

### Diane Kurys

Diane Kurys has been able to reach a much broader audience than Mészáros or von Trotta are ever likely to do. Her first film, *Peppermint Soda*, was the largest grossing film in France in 1977 and was awarded the Prix Louis Delluc as Best Picture of the Year. *Entre Nous*, her third film, also did very well, in the United States as well as in France, earning kudos all around from New York reviewers, and prompting the *New York Times* to call her, among other things, a "major new filmmaker."[45] Her subject has largely been initiation, rites of passage, to greater or lesser degree through the eyes of girls or women; and also friendship, the friendships of young girls in *Peppermint Soda*, of a trio of adolescents in *Cocktail Molotov*, of two adult married women in *Entre Nous*. This material, and Kurys' very effective presentation of it, her charm and humor, a visual appeal, make her films very pleasing. At the same time she reflects only the sweet side of Truffaut, clearly her major mentor; there is something too easy in Kurys' work, too fast-moving and superficial, too pretty.

Kurys' most successful foray into female initiation terrain is her first and best film, *Pepermint Soda*. The film was a revelation after years of watching, apparently without gender consciousness, Truffaut's *400 Blows*, Menzel's *Closely Watched Trains*, Olmi's *The Sound of Trumpets*, and numerous other cherished films charting a young man's coming of age. *Peppermint Soda*'s simple existence made one notice that there were next to no films about female initiation experience; that watching young girls was a wholly different experience, moving in another and much deeper way because about oneself; and that unbelievably, through decades of film viewing one had never consciously noticed these distinctions. Just the early sequence in *Peppermint Soda* of the girls' return to school for the new school year was extraordinary when first seen in 1977, watching girls coming together after a summer apart, their joyful greetings to one another, their kissing and embracing, noticing this one's tan and that one's haircut, excited talk. For the woman spectator there was the stunned sense that one had never before seen a camera focus with this kind of attention, time, care, truth, affection and interest on young girls this way. And simply to look at them at length, in their exquisite bud-like beauty, continues in itself to be moving.

The school sequences move along with speed and charm. A high overhead funny shot has the girls in a series of lines in the courtyard, each one with a teacher calling the class roll, all the voices calling names at once. Classroom sequences (a girl getting ink on fingers and lips, other mischief) remind one again of Truffaut, Vigo, others, for the vision of the girls' anarchic, joyous free spirits yoked in by authoritarian, dried-up teachers, dreadful oppressors of these spirited girls. The line between autobiography and fiction that Kurys continually plays with is extended even to her having shot *Peppermint Soda* in the same lycee she and her sister attended as children, using 300 girls, none of whom had ever acted professionally, and from whom Kurys gets beautiful performances.

Kurys works with first menstruation, with sex talk (through a running joke of a misinformed girl), and with first love. In one of the most memorable sequences of the film, Anne, tagging along with her older sister to a dance, has her first encounter with a boy, their awkwardness and shyness wonderfully caught, but at the same time a funny poise. Anne tells the boy to get her a drink and then remembers to ask him to bring back cookies. After the dance, in a beautifully understated scene at the railway station, she remembers to lift her coat a little to show her leg to the boy—details that really catch the texture of being a girl that age. Anne's older sister Frederique, 15 to Anne's 13, well into the adolescent mysteries Anne is just entering, has a really full-blown romance—but ends up telling Anne, in a shared bath, that she's tired of the boy. Anne bursts into tears, her response conveying a lovely sense of youthful pain, especially in a child of divorce, at the fragility and transience of relationships. Love doesn't last, there's no solid ground. What seems a small thing for one girl, ready to move on, is heartbreaking for the other. Such moments are special, and when the film first appeared (this is happily no longer true, another measure of how much has changed in a decade) it was not easy to remember another film with intimacies exchanged by two sisters, or different phases of development measured in two girls by their differing responses to such an event, with this kind of delicacy.

Anne, the hanging-on younger sister, is fascinated with Frederique's affairs, even to the point of steaming her letters open. She wants pantyhose desperately in a bid to be older, she lies to get them, putting them on in the hall, convinced they will make all the difference, in the way girls that age do. Watching the intimacy between Frederique and the mother, Anne resentfully feels left out, full of a competitive struggle for the mother's love and of the sense that the other one is more loved. She peeps through doors, forever trying to see into her sister's life. At the same time the two girls are often in collusion, Frederique leaving the door open at night for Anne, a tacit understanding between them. More often, though, Frederique feels burdened by her younger sister, and is bent on keeping her own older-sister's privileged place, by pushing Anne away as too young. She does this most unfairly in the scene that gives the film its name and nicely summarizes Anne's struggle through the whole film to move into puberty and adult-hood: the scene in which Anne orders a "diabolo menthe" in a coffee shop with her friends, and Frederique humiliates her publicly, proclaiming her too young to be there—declaring that this is forbidden, still just beyond reach, as if Frederique won't let Anne grow up.

This issue is addressed by the very first opening image of the film, Anne with difficulty trying to push open a door, though it is a boy that actually opens it for her. (Again the feminism of this film, if one wishes to see it as feminist, consists in the simple attention to women, to their interactions with one another, sensitivity to their feelings, all the closeups that often make words unnecessary, as well as the girls' and mother's struggles to define their own lives.) Anne's pushing the door is like the fumbling into adulthood, through the funny misconceptions, the disillusionments, the obstacles. And surely the number two painted on the train door and else-where is not accidental, the important sibling factor in her struggle.

While Anne's friendships are used mostly for comic ends in the film, Frederique's bondings are more serious, especially since she is attracted to two difficult students, one of them Muriel, whose mad mother killed herself, and who says "shit" to the whole school as she whirls around in the school-yard, repudiating the suppression that goes on in that mass of confining compartments through which the ebullient spirits of the girls are funnelled.

After Muriel runs away from home and school, Frederique turns for friendship to Pascale, a politically engaged girl. During a class outing se-quence to a romantic historic nunnery, filled with legends of obeisant and self-humiliating women, the two girls—far from the others—look intensely at one another, an erotically charged look, a strong sense of a sexual pull between them, which Frederique quickly moves away from. It is an im-portant moment—prefiguring *Entre Nous*—that Kurys here simply includes and moves on from, perhaps suggesting the way such moments can occur in a life. In another, possibly related, touch, Frederique and Pascale appear shortly after, toward the film's ending, in male costumes for a Moliere play. (Kurys' theatre acting background enters each of the films with brief stage sequences of one sort or another.)

Kurys later plays in other ways with female dress—Anne's boyishness in

*Cocktail Molotov*, strongly contrasted with her well turned out, "feminine" looking mother, or the lady-like conventional appearance of Lena in *Entre Nous*, fur coat, pearls, earrings, deliberately contrasted with Madeleine's freer dress, in pants often and in black, with upturned collars. Kurys playfully caps the ambiguities of gender codes by having Lena's husband in *Entre Nous* tell his kids a bedtime story about a woman with a beard.

Fathers figure importantly in Kurys. Muriel's father's brief entry into Frederique's life is handled with quiet subtle reticence, the older man's loneliness and self-denigration clearly reminding the girl of her own father. His gentle decision not to "take advantage" of such a young girl, his daughter's age, is again nicely done in its quietness. So are the two Weber sisters' feelings about their own father, their embarrassment at his picking them up at school, and over his less than romantic looks. The father himself is a truly conveyed mix of good devoted dad, and a modest timid person, unromantic, caring, telling jokes his daughters don't get, trying his best. Anne's ability to manipulate him into taking them skiing, and more, her relentless persistence until she overcomes his opposition—seems accurate for that age, and also seems a possible portrait of the artist, the filmmaker, as a young girl, with the kind of relentlessness any filmmaker, and particularly a woman filmmaker, must have to survive.

Anne, an unusually beautiful girl, walks through the film in red cap and red scarf, conveying intensity, passion, anger—the redness even suggesting the body/self. Though she is obedient to her mother, especially in contrast with Frederique's rebellion, her charm can lead one to overlook the extent to which she lies, cheats on tests, does badly in school, steals. Both girls are more rebellious and problematic than one might notice, an important theme in *Cocktail Molotov*. But it is the affectionate seriousness with which the director takes the growing up of young girls that makes *Peppermint Soda* stay so strongly in one's mind.

*Cocktail Molotov* is built around a strong conception, a girl and two boys who miss most of the 1968 student uprising in Paris because they are travelling on the road. The girl, Anne, has run away from home after a bitter battle with her mother and she has taken the two boys with her. But though Anne has missed the larger event, she has her own personal student uprising, going off on her own at 17 with a boy her mother opposes because he is working-class, experiencing first love, first sex, abortion, young wandering and hitchhiking.

The battle that sets this off, between Anne and her mother, in which Anne hits her mother back and says horrendous things to her, is a shockingly dramatic opener for the film, a brutal encounter in an extremely affluent house. But the film doesn't work on the two levels it addresses, the understanding of the 1968 events or the personal story of Anne's development. A voiceover at the end tries to bind the two with words written in script across the screen, like a final personal message whispered in our ear—a technique Kurys uses also in *Peppermint Soda* and *Entre Nous* to create an intimate autobiographical connection between the film and its audience. The final words here—"They said it was all over but we knew it was only the beginning"—are written over a freeze-frame of the car, the liberation car with its love/peace graffiti message. But beyond rhetoric, we do not know what is beginning, either in the larger world—or that of Anne and her two friends.

Most damagingly we don't have a sense of Anne evolving. She is an indistinct character, though more distinct than the two boys with her. Though Kurys is never good at character creation, she handles parent/child relations well, and the fight here between daughter and mother is unusually real in catching the girl's adolescent arrogance and hostility. The utterly adoring father again is a bit pathetic in his vulnerability and his willingness to do anything at all for Anne, without a moment of judgment. And Jewishness figures in each of Kurys' films. But *Cocktail Molotov* needs more intelligence for dealing with the ideas it sets in motion, and despite its greatest strength, its capacity to evoke a sweet sense of youthfulness, the film lacks the effectiveness of *Peppermint Soda* and *Entre Nous* that derives from their being interestingly directed from a female point of view.

*Entre Nous* works well as narrative, and as entertainment, in its focus on women's lives. It gives pleasure simply on the level of watching two women friends walk and talk together, plan, investigate a shop, speak about husbands and sex and about their bodies, as they are also continually called by children—children having fevers, bickering, getting lost—at the edges of their discourse. It even gives pleasure on the more trivial level of watching their clothes, their period activities, eating bon-bons, pinning dresses, going to a fashion show. Kurys focusses on the intensity and intimacy between the two women: Lena's casually confiding to Madeleine, in passing, that through her long years of marriage she never had an orgasm, as she did in one brief encounter on a train with a stranger soldier; Lena fighting her way to Madeleine when she hears she's had a breakdown; Lena reading a letter from her friend with such absorption that she doesn't notice a pot boiling over.

However, it is an intensity and intimacy limited by the limits of Kurys' capacity to create character, and by her way of cutting away from passion and staying on surfaces, so that finally her work lacks that sense of women looking at one another in the way of von Trotta or Mészáros, not allowing in the end for anything so intent and lingering. On the other hand, in focusing on a relationship that goes beyond friendship into lesbian love, Kurys takes elements suggested in Mészáros' most intense films about two women, and von Trotta's as well, and pushes them further. Since all three of these directors have created work in which heroines' love of men is a powerful force, such feelings seem often to live comfortably in women with heterosexual feeling. The dethroning of patriarchal centrality, and the shift to woman/woman intense involvement and importance, appears to also re-direct the flow of sexual energy, or at least to break down the taboos forbidding its flow toward other women.

Kurys has spoken in interviews about *Entre Nous'* links with her mother's life, and about her own reluctance to have *Entre Nous* billed as a lesbian film, "suspecting it would narrow or skew her audience and blind viewers to the nuances of the story."[46] She instead created sexual encounters with men for both women, while indicating their passion for one another, in which, Kurys herself says,

there was something of madness . . . I remember it as laughs all the time, complicity, intimacy. I have their letters; they were passionate. My mother said they tried to have sex but it didn't work—they just laughed. Later, they both found other men . . . I wonder if it wasn't the pressure of the period and the gossips that prevented anything more. Maybe today they would've run away and lived together. It lasted 25 years and there wasn't a day when they didn't see each other, not a day.[47]

The difficulty in getting financial support for *Entre Nous* had to do with the backers balking "less at the sexual innuendoes than at the presence of two women without a leading man." The bond between the women in the film often excludes or puts down husbands—or other men, as when the two women dance together in front of two ogling men, and by their amused, ridiculing comments and laughter, objectify the men in turn. Since women are always fair game for male intrusions in public places (one thinks of Doris Lessing's story "Woman on the Roof," or several strong scenes in Mészáros), there's a pleasure in some reversal here. The fullness of the women's friendship underlines the inadequacy of each marriage—and war-time upheaval serves as an easy shorthand, but surely not a necessary one, to explain mismarriage. The husbands are seriously flawed but human. Madeleine's ne'er-do-well husband Costa is the simpler of the two, a study in ineptitude, a source of humor. Michel, Lena's husband, is controlling but sympathetic, his scenes with his little daughters enchantingly tender, much more than the feelings the women show their children. He is hard working, responsible, has no interest in books, and falls asleep during plays or calls them vulgar. The director clearly knows him from inside and em-pathizes with his pain, as is clear in the final tableau by the sea. It is the one totally arresting image in the film, it alone having that magical coming together of all elements that bespeaks a genuine vision: wife and husband below, he weeping and saying "What a waste," with the younger daugh-ter—the director as a child—above them in the beach house, looking out at them and beyond.

Still, Kurys also identifies with the mother in her feistiness, prepared at the start to walk off alone, once released from the prison camp, because her new husband's name is more dangerously Jewish than her own, Weber.

When Michel, controlling and autocratic, objects to the tightness of her dress revealing her panties, she removes her panties and stalks out alone. She learns to drive, decides to work so she has her own income and options, and looks the ignominious vassal only when she must appeal to Michel for money. His jealousy, his hurt and rage, are understandable but the violence he unleashes against the shop is also hateful, especially given Madeleine's fragility.

The nature of Madeleine's breakdown is not at all clear to us, but the relationship is rendered more easily acceptable to a wide audience in this film because the husband Lena flees from is impossibly unreasonable to live with, and the woman she goes to is in pathetic trouble and desperately needs her. But the vagueness of Madeleine's characterization is not merely strategy; all the characterizations except the father Michel are superficial, Kurys again not analytic, neither exploring characters as individuals nor in terms of the dynamics between them. That approach worked for *Peppermint Soda*'s archetypal moments of initiation but with these full grown women the lack of a more intricately detailed reality is more apparent. We know very little about Lena too and about what matters to her. And not only is the crisis that produces Madeleine's breakdown even less defined, but her emotions generally are kept at a remove from us. The film repeatedly cuts away from opportunities for passion, or even knowledge, and opts for a cool, quick moving, highly controlled surface.

Kurys' visual style too is full of bold leaps between images, and cuts away, her camera at once economic and fluid: the rapid counterpointing of the two young women's lives during the war; the sexual sequence on the train done with a quick series of shots, Huppert in elegant period dress, the two surreptitiously observing soldiers, all very skillful. The film's handling of history, of prison camps, refugee railway confusion, victory parties, is also adept, but somehow at the same time shallow, not quite felt, thin. So with the costumes, the interiors, even the values of a 1950s parental world— well done enough to give audiences the sense they are getting a two–generation thumbnail social history of women's lives but all on the surface. Even the film's ending carries an inappropriate sense of tease in that final song, "I wonder who's kissing her now," loud and brash and period, that takes to an extreme the sexual ambiguity of the whole film, but with a kind of seductiveness and wryness to no clear purpose, moving from the father's anguish to such a cute question.

*A Man in Love* (1987) is Kurys' most disappointing film to date. It appears to be a bid for full commercial success, while at the same time attempting to maintain a European art-house cachet by the continual evocation of so unique a figure as Cesar Pavese. The use of Pavese for the sensationalism of his suicidal end—which is not merely the first aspect of him dwelt upon by Kurys but apparently the primary aspect of his life of interest to her— indicates the level of bad faith in the film. Further, to invoke Pavese as a figure of eroticism, for hot sexy scenes—the film's true primary interest—can only be grotesque.

The film's title suggests that a male sensibility and subjectivity is at its center, though the young heroine Jane (played by Greta Scacchi) is the person the camera follows from beginning to end. However, we enter neither character's being at all. The structure of the narrative, counterpointing actors' work in a production with their personal involvements, has been used most memorably in Truffaut's *Day for Night*, the luminosity of which is as different from this film's banality as indeed day is from night. No doubt Kurys' long experience with theatre and film might have informed this material with insight and feeling, but one is instead struck by the absence of all intelligence and subtlety.

We recognize familiar Kurys notes: the importance of father, mother, original family; the loyalty and protectiveness shown to that father yet again; and the circular self-reflexive ending that adds a sense of surprise auto-biography, which Kurys depends upon in place of depth. In this film the great experience is for the heroine to move on from acting to writing—writing this very film, *A Man In Love*—and the ending implies that it is made possible through the love affair Jane has with Steve (the actor who plays Pavese), as well as through her mother's death and the strength she feels is passed on to her from her mother. However, nothing at all in the film has suggested that Jane even wished to write, and there is certainly nothing to justify the grand sense of achievement asserted by the film's final swelling shmaltzy music.

The only affecting material in this film relates to the closeness between Jane and her mother, played by Claudia Cardinale; the film's most moving line is Jane's final voiceover, speaking of realizing when her mother is dying that "no one would ever again listen to me with that kind of attention." *A Man in Love* has little to offer beyond this: some exciting sexuality, manipulative slick photography, beautiful lovers, and the pretentiousness of an arty, pointless, double plot. Not only is the film in no way feminist, but Kurys' shooting of Greta Scacchi's lovely body and face makes her as much a passive female sexual object and adornment as any male director would, and the jealous-wife subplot also brings no sensitive woman's sensibility to bear on that familiar material.

The characters generally are ciphers; the film business is used to no purpose; and the film suffers badly from the not unusual difficulty of a European director's making a film in English—with the language, however familiar to the director, somehow continually sounding wooden, its cadences and rhythms wrong and unnatural. Clearly meant to chart another young woman's coming of age, with the mother's passing on linked to the daughter's fully maturing, the film doesn't come together intellectually or emotionally. Diane Kurys has at her best beautifully conveyed women's initiation rites, done with a charm that has earned her considerable box-office clout. But

*A Man in Love* is a saddening film from a director who, like Susan Seidelman, had in her previous film a very strong commercial and critical success, which should have encouraged her to celebrate and risk a little. One hopes that for Kurys' next project she can use the freedom her success has won her, although this is perhaps a very hard request to make of this first breakthrough group of broadly appealing women directors, tasting what must feel like a particularly precarious success.

### Other French Women Directors

While new women directors (and producers) have been emerging almost as rapidly in France as in the U.S.—with the help of various tax related policies that support filmmaking[48]—their work is as smoothly, even slickly, commercial as that of German women filmmakers has been largely associated with the alternative cinema. Coline Serreau's *3 Men and a Cradle* is an obvious example. An immense success in France, nominated for an Academy Award for Best Foreign-Language Film (and later made into an enormously successful American film), the film takes what might seem a silly premise—three men with good jobs, living a hedonistic bachelor life, suddenly having to take responsibility for an infant—and makes something funny, tender, and ultimately serious, out of it, all the time looking like a quite conventional commercial comedy. Recalling a somewhat related film by one of the very few English women directors, Wendy Toye's *Raising a Riot* (1955), Coline Serreau in effect argues that men become better human beings by opening themselves to the love and nurture of a child. Her film also asserts the need for this caretaking to be shared, since it is too hard for women to carry it all themselves, when they are trying to keep a work life going as well, as an everyday thing doing the kinds of balancing these men do for a brief and temporary time, at least until they choose otherwise.

Still, the new crop of French films by women directors seems lightweight as a group—striking, less for intelligence, seriousness, artfulness, than for stylishness, and even for crossing a line into pornography of sorts, and violence. *Black and White* (1986), a debut film by 31 year old Claire Devers, honored at Cannes, takes the new interest in violence to nasty extremes, through two men, one of whom seeks physical punishment from the other, in the form of increasingly violent massages (culminating in death).[49] The director's involvement is not at all in bonding (like May's in *Mikey and Nicky*) but rather in violence, battering in a vacuum, with no point beyond itself, and no illumination to justify itself—like watching a one-sided cock fight. Or rather, the interest is in the utter total passivity of the masochistic victimized white accountant. While these traits have often been ascribed to women traditionally and are evoked by any battered wife's story—and hence the accountant is not a surprising figure for a woman director to focus on—

the film disturbingly goes no further than to watch him presenting his body again and again to be destroyed piecemeal by a black masseur.

Another "art"-style film bordering on pornography—Virginie Thevent's first feature, *The Night Wears Garters*—is also one of a number of women's films that negate love. With the reversal of its virginal boy lured into raunchy sexual vistas by a somewhat older girl, its audacity can be seen as charming and disarming, or as shallow, empty, sensation-mongering, or both. This material is also doubtless part of the deluge of erotic films and pornography produced in France currently.[50] It may be that the Thevent film, under its continental sophistication, is on exactly the same level as Amy Heckerling's teen movies here. As those films seem, for all their obsessive, gross insistence on sex, to be an odd harking back to the young-on-campus formulas of 1940s' June Allison movies, so the French counterpart perhaps works with its own indigenous convention of older woman initiating sweet young boy. Whatever one's misgivings, there's a pleasure in the idea of a woman having made such a film, the barriers toppling on every side. And given how brief a time women directors have been an active presence, we are witnessing a remarkable leap into the boldest sexual territory, done with notable stylishness, as in other recent films, like Joy Fleury's *Sadness and Beauty*, an updated "women's film"-style melodrama, and Caroline Huppert's well done *Sincerely Charlotte*.

There are also more familiar kinds of coming-of-age films, like *The Red Kiss* (*Le Rouge Baiser*, 1985), a debut film set in 1952 Paris, directed by longtime producer Vera Belmont, that works with the initiation material of a young politically-conscious 15 year old girl of Polish Jewish Communist family background.

Though the work of neither is much known in this country, Yannick Bellon and Nadine Trintignant are veteran directors, and both have had recent films shown here. Bellon's fifth feature film, *La Triche* (1984), deals with an affair between a police inspector, married, highly respected and respectable, and a young homosexual musician. Trintignant's most recent, *Next Summer*, suggests why she has been able to continue to make movies for over twenty years but also the limits of those movies. The film takes us through the ups and downs of various couples' lives, affectingly conveying some of the reality of middle-aged marriage, its loyalty, disillusion, acceptance; but it is no feminist film, built instead on age-old French truisms about unfaithful husbands, men and women's needs for one another, and the battle of the sexes. It does remarkably little with the central middle-aged mother and wife (Claudia Cardinale), who conveys only vacancy, with much reassurance from others about how beautiful she looks and how young, as if those are the only or the central issues for an older woman. Dino/Fanny Ardant's grief over the hero's brain disease feels uncomfortably like an exploitation of her relation to Truffaut at the end of his life.

All in all, left to choose between the would-be shocking and commercial new young women directors, and the more humanistic undistinguished veterans, one feels only a measured enthusiasm for the actual work being done now in France by women directors, but a great deal of enthusiasm for the fact that it is being encouraged and made, and finding success.

## ONE OF A KIND

Among striking individual works by directors who have either not gone beyond a single film (not uncommon among women directors until recently, given the obstacles placed in their paths), or whose later films fail to achieve the same level of interest, Gunnel Lindblom's *Summer Paradise* and Marleen Gorris' *A Question of Silence* deserve particular attention. Both are polemic films, the first preceding feminism, the second the most fiercely extreme ideologically of the feminists films discussed here.

*Summer Paradise* (1977), from Sweden, is the first film directed by Gunnel Lindblom, from a novel by Ulla Isaksson. Long a theatre director in Stockholm's Royal Dramatic Theatre, Lindblom is best known as an actress Ingmar Bergman cast in many of his most painful and strange roles for women, and Bergman in fact produced this film. *Summer Paradise*, though flawed, conveys a great deal of personal passion. It is interesting less for the polemic at its heart (which luckily Lindblom doesn't chain the film to, so it has a larger life) than for the women characters who constitute its fabric—especially two older women friends, around sixty, Katha a doctor and Emma a social worker. Their friendship frames the film, opening and closing it. It also frames the plight of the troubled young. In the generation of Katha's daughters, the promiscuity of the unmarried daughter Sassa, and the adultery and misery of the married Anikka and her husband; and among the very young, murderous anger and suicide. The film at its center poses a social problem: what will happen to our young, who are being poisoned and destroyed, and whom nobody takes care of any more. Young Tomas' unexpected suicide at the summer house illustrates that thesis perhaps too neatly. To further underline the point, the film concludes with the broken-hearted elderly Katha and Emma getting into their car to leave the summer house, and in the process themselves overlooking the oddly draped figure of the troubled young boy King, left behind unnoticed.

The passionate feeling with which this theme is treated makes the film moving at times—its tormented worry about the future of children itself of particular concern to a woman director and to women spectators. But the older women are what really make the film a powerful experience. It is powerful because of the richness with which their friendship is conveyed, and the unusualness of looking at heroines with elderly, lined faces and bulky bodies, who are strong, struggling women in their own right, not in the role of mothers or even of professionals—though Katha is a mother and both are very much professionals—but simply as people. It's astonishing to recognize that *Summer Paradise* is stirring partly because this is so unique an experience in film.

It is also stirring for the seriousness with which the two women friends take each other, the contrast that is developed between them: Katha the doctor with her bourgeois cleanliness, order, perhaps a little self-satisfied; and Emma the social worker with her fierce passion, sloppiness, helplessness. Both are women without men, Emma never having married, Katha's husband having long ago left. Katha carries it all, the big house, the full family spanning four generations, all by herself, and feels able to—and also has a delicious capacity for delight in her precious summer world. However, she is still vulnerable, disturbed about the nearly psychotic boy, King, somewhat guilty for not having him and his mother Ingrid back to the summer house, because she yearns for peace.

Because Katha's is such a susceptible, aware sensibility, Emma seems not fully fair in speaking several times of Katha's self-protectiveness. But Emma herself is a complicated case. With all her social passion and social anger, she (who is given the polemic voice in the film) is unmarried, messy, somehow childlike and needing to be taken care of. Her passion seems necessary to Katha, and she accepts Katha's staunch mothering as if it is coming to her. There's one scene with Katha on her knees removing Emma's wet shoes that is especially affecting. Their complementariness is caught with wonderful clarity, showing why two such different women would be friends. The film also respects Emma's understanding and passion at the same time as it takes in her despair, the fact that she hardly has the strength to survive herself, subject to deep depression, heavy drinking, and, after the boy's death, needing to be helped simply to stand up. Whatever the differences between the two women, they give precious comfort and support to each other. Emma almost operates as the doctor's emotional life, her passion; but even there, the doctor is a person who serves in her own right, a woman with her own commitment to healing. What's at work seems largely the extreme social guilt of a uniquely comfortable country, Scandinavian decency and discomfort over having things, self-laceration as much as genuine conscience.

The two elder women, without any relation to men, are seen in their full individuality: both their values as they fight for ideas, and also their personalities. The sense of a precious, messy, lifetime link that goes deep, between two older women whom no male director would ever put at the center of his work, is in itself extraordinary. So in one sequence is the simple view of Emma taking her clothes off, unceremoniously, because she has just come in from the wet. The body we are shown is just an older woman's body, without West Coast tannings, tightenings, diet spas; yet nothing to be leered at or mocked; just looked at as we look at ourselves.

In another sense, males are at the center of the film. Both male children are in dire straits, and the film is focussed on the need to save them. A

particularly strong scene has elderly, big-bodied Katha following the frenzied almost psychotic boy King up a steeply rocky incline and then holding
him, over a precipitous drop, as he fiercely flails to get away. King's mother
has equally dark possessive feelings for Katha's daughter Sassa, and jealousy
of Sassa's involvement with a young man named Kiss. The film treats the
beautiful bodies and the sexuality of Kiss and the photographer daughter
with equal handed explicitness, and in this enlightened, liberated Scandinavian world both of Katha's daughters are professional people.

Yet all these interesting, and even melodramatically violent, themes matter less than the love between the older women, who are also endlessly
doing battle with one another as well—and not just battle for battle's sake
but because there are really deep differences between them. All the while,
the film has its pleasures, the sensuous domestic pleasures of beautiful looking food, the loveliness of the natural landscape and the summer house, the
freshness of linen and its smell, a general delight in living processes. In all
these ways *Summer Paradise*, whatever its limits, stays in one's mind with
pleasure and a sense of something original, and something distinctively
female.

*A Question of Silence* (1982), a more recent film from Holland, gives us
women relating to women in more disturbing ways. It expresses an angry,
uncompromising feminism at the same time very effectively using the tools
of mainstream narrative cinema. Marleen Gorris made *Broken Mirrors* since,
but this, her debut film, is by far the more effective. Gorris' subject is the
spontaneous, seemingly gratuitous murder of a man by three women who
are strangers to each other and to the man, but who are bonded through
the shared experience of female humiliation and oppression. Gorris' women
are not typical heroines any more than Lindblom's are: one is a hefty,
middle-aged, working-class waitress (Nelly Frijda) whose heartiness is a
familiar style pushed into something acerbically unnerving; the second is a
washed-out housewife (Edda Barends), odd-looking and stiff moving, silent
to the point of catatonia; and the third (Henriette Tol) is a pretty and
extremely capable secretary who is scathing in her articulateness.

The drama of *A Question of Silence* resides primarily in the question of
the silence of all three women—and, by implication, of all women—a silence
even when they speak, because they are unheard, not listened to. The
secretary's skills are recognized by her executive boss, but her analysis and
recommendations at a business conference get praise only when a man offers
them after she has already done so and been condescended to and ignored.
Liberties are taken with her, in small bitter ways to which no man in a
business setting would ever be subjected. The feisty waitress taking sexist
abuse disguised as humorous banter all day long from male workers; the
domestic isolation of the poignant housewife, buried in a numb despair—
if these portraits are somewhat familiar and schematic, they are nonetheless
touching for the realities they evoke. The characters may not be richly

individuated but they don't need to be for this film's purposes, in order to have a strong impact.

The three women, strangers, come together in a women's clothing boutique by chance, though Gorris' choice of that setting, with all its associations for women, is of course significant. The three women share a commonality of lives lived in the same desperate, suppressed way only for the reason that they are women, and so become linked around the housewife's defiant shoplifting. After they join in the killing of the shopkeeper, they go separate ways to various acts of festive celebration, each carrying her blood-red boutique bag as a kind of banner.

Gorris uses a variety of effective devices to have us accept, on some level, the violence into which this desperation explodes: by discrediting the men who dismiss the three as crazy and unlike other women; by having a group of other women—a very ordinary looking and representative assortment—present in the boutique at the time of the crime, calmly witnessing the killing and, by not reporting it, tacitly participating in it; and by the changes the psychiatrist (Cox Habbema), whose job it is to judge whether the women are sane, undergoes—as she touchingly loses her professional detachment. A married, professional woman, she starts out pointedly heterosexual, and grows increasingly agitated, distanced from her husband, more and more deeply connected to the women, climaxed in the intimacy of intensely shared looks and a mimed embrace. The film's conclusion positions the psychiatrist heroine between her husband, impatiently beeping his car horn for her to follow, and a group of women—identified with the three principal women—with whom she lingers and, again, exchanges a long, intent look, through that shared look in effect indicating her choice.

All the most affecting moments of *A Question of Silence* have to do with feelings of solidarity among and between women. In a strong courtroom scene, the solidarity that Gorris envisages expanding, does so movingly as the three defendants share intense, sympathetic looks with the four observers scattered through the courtroom like invisible partisans. While the psychiatrist is trying, futilely, to make herself heard by the male lawyers and judge, a bitter, chilling, liberating laughter rises from the defendants in response to the idea that three women killing a man is the same as three men killing a woman. We need only consider the numbers of news stories of each sort to recognize a reality so commonplace and accepted that we rarely think about it, and all that it implies about men's daily brutalizations of women. The laughter of recognition that is picked up by the four women spectators, and then by the psychiatrist, presumably reaches into at least part of the movie-going audience.

Yet while one can say that this film is really about women's silence, anger, and solidarity, it is not so easy to step around the violent act at its center—which we are not actually shown but which is vividly communicated to us—from the broken glass weaponry, to the report of mutilated genitals. The boutique owner who is killed by the women in *A Question of Silence*, it is made clear, is culpable only because he is a man. He has an unpleasantly smug, superior smile, and quietly objects to having his merchandise stolen, but is otherwise—insofar as we know—no more deserving of a horribly violent end than the next guy. Yet the film expects us to view his killing with the calm acceptance of the other witnesses. That Gorris gets us to accept as much as we do speaks for her directorial authority and the genuine ways her film taps into issues of women's pain, anger, and the bonds between women.

## NOTES

1. *Newsweek* (international edition, May 3, 1982), included in New Yorker Films press material.

2. See Charlotte Delorme's "On the Film *Marianne and Juliane* by Margarethe von Trotta" in *Journal of Film and Video* 37, no. 2 (Spring 1985), 47–51. See also Ellen Seiter's "The Political Is Personal," in the same issue, pp. 41–46, in which she attributes von Trotta's recognition in the United States as Germany's major woman director to "von Trotta's collaboration with Volker Schlondorff, her association as an actor with the New German Cinema, the production of her films by Schlondorff's company, Bioskop-Film" (p. 41), everything in short but her talent and the power of the films themselves. See also E. Ann Kaplan's "Discourses of Terrorism, Feminism, and the Family in von Trotta's *Marianne and Juliane*," *Persistence of Vision* 2 (1985), 61–62.

3. "I've quite often discussed this question with German women directors where I have to hear that they are very badly treated. . . . I have to admit that I am not surprised that they are complaining, these women directors. Even for those bad stories they always find money to make. And those German women directors who are very good, like Margarethe von Trotta, Helke Sanders, and Helma Sanders-Brahms, they always make films. It's simple mystification, just because we are women." From an interview I did with Mészáros in 1984.

4. For the specific gains of German feminist filmmakers, see H.B. Moeller, "West German Women's Cinema: the Case of Margarethe von Trotta," *Film Criticism* 9, no. 2 (Winter 1984/85), 56.

5. Stanley Kauffmann, "A Large Life," *New Republic* (May 18, 1987), 24. He also notes that given the "profusion of ideas" and the "multiple currents of personal life" involved, "a full account is impossible. . . . Honor, then, to von Trotta for making Rosa Luxemburg as well as she did."

6. Judith Mayne, in *Re-visions*, edited by Mellencamp, et al. (Los Angeles: American Film Institute, 1983).

7. "From Hitler to Hepburn: A Discussion of Women's Film Production and Reception," *New German Critique* 24–25 (Fall/Winter 1981–82), 184.

8. John Sandford, *The New German Cinema* (New York: Da Capo Press, 1980), 163.

9. Nancy Chodorow, *The Reproduction of Mothering* (Berkeley: University of California Press, 1978), 136. Chodorow later quotes both Fliess and Balint, on the issue of boundary-blurring. Balint speaks of those feeling a lack of self, or emptiness,

as likely to be women feeling "they are not being accorded a separate reality nor the agency to interpret the world in their own way. This feeling has its origins in the early mother-daughter relationship [involving a] distorted projection of what the mother thought her infant daughter's needs should be" (p. 100).

10. Ibid., 109.

11. Ibid., 136.

12. Ibid., 129.

13. Ibid., 137.

14. Ibid.

15. Ibid., 138.

16. *Newsweek* (international edition, May 3, 1982), in New Yorker Films packet.

17. Janet Maslin *"Marianne and Juliane,"* *New York Times* (April 22, 1982), C19.

18. Undated and uncredited interview in the New Yorker Films press materials for *Marianne and Juliane*.

19. In an interview I did with von Trotta in 1986.

20. See Kaplan, *Persistence of Vision*, 61–68, especially 64.

21. Kaplan, *Women and Film*, 109.

22. Interview, New Yorker Films packet.

23. Von Trotta in a discussion of the film at Goethe House, New York, January 13, 1987.

24. Interview, New Yorker Films packet.

25. Kauffmann, *New Republic* (May 18, 1987), 24. In seeing the issue here as Sukowa vs. Jewish identity, and thus as "one more hard choice von Trotta had to make," Kauffmann is more accepting of this omission than I myself am, although he does delicately note von Trotta's recognizing "that it was a sensitive decision for a German director" (p. 24).

26. Interview, New Yorker Films packet.

27. Ibid.

28. Mollie Haskell, *"Sheer Madness,"* *Vogue* (December 1983), 57.

29. Ibid.

30. Ibid.

31. Ibid.

32. Von Trotta, interview with Carol Bergman, *Cineaste* 13, no. 4 (1984), 47.

33. James Markham, "Behind 'Men' Stands a Woman With a Sense of Humor," *New York Times* (July 27, 1986), 19.

34. Doris Dörrie, when I interviewed her shortly after *Men* opened in New York, said repeatedly that *"Men* is a film about German opportunism."

35. Dörrie calls it "a metaphor for being safe at home and happy in the past with her family when everything seemed to be alright."

36. That impact is already evident in a film like Pia Frankenberg's *Noisy Martha* (1985), which spoofs the German feminist film world by having an outlandishly arty film critic—who reads *Frauen Und Film*—ask the central character/director various questions throughout the film about her relation to feminist aesthetics and theory. The director, who summarily says she has none, keeps moaning about her own superficiality.

Another recent German film, *The Wolf Girl* (1985) by Dagmar Beiersdorf also goes very much its own way, with something of Dörrie's whimsy. What starts out as a seemingly wayward *Desert Hearts*, with an attraction between Mascha, an older filmmaker, and a very beautiful, nearly mute, wild-haired, dark-skinned girl, plus a transvestite man-friend named Marilyn, turns out to be an idiosyncratic, appealing film about self-renewal.

37. Markham, "Behind 'Men,' " 19.

38. Ibid., 25.

39. Varda notes in an interview over a decade later that when she started making films, "It was very rare . . . to question the idea of the couple." Jacqueline Levitin, "Mother of the New Wave: An Interview with Agnes Varda," *Women & Film* 1, nos. 5/6 (1974), 66.

40. Ibid., 64.

41. *The Oxford Companion to Film*, edited by Liz Anne Bawden (New York: Oxford University Press, 1976), 725.

42. "It is true that I can now see my own films with a new vision because of things which have happened . . . because I did a kind of self-education on feminism, which we all do now, because we have opportunities to do so. Things are clear now. But they weren't so clear ten years ago when I made *Le Bonheur*, even though I had already read Simone de Beauvoir, and had discussed these things, and had fought for contraception, sexual freedom, new ways of raising children and alternatives to the usual form of marriage." Levitin, "Mother of the New Wave," 64.

43. "Women's Cinema as Counter-Cinema," in *Movies and Methods: An Anthology*, edited by Bill Nichols (Berkeley: University of California Press, 1976), 216.

44. This is so, notwithstanding such early sexually and artistically avant garde films as Carolee Schneeman's *Fuses*.

45. *New York Times* (February 12, 1984), H20.

46. Marcia Pally, "Come Hither—But Slowly: Dessert with Diane Kurys," *Village Voice* (January 31, 1984), 52.

47. Ibid.

48. Judith Miller, "Tax Shelters, May Aid French Films," *New York Times* (July 5, 1986), 11.

49. Among still darker porno/features are such films as the German directors' Elfi Mekesch and Monika Treut's *Seduction: The Cruel Woman* (1985), a more extreme example. Placing a woman in a totally autocratic position, bizarre and cruel but all powerful, even over camera angles and movements, the degradation here is directed at males, a sadomasochism open to the charge of simply reversing male pornographic fantasies.

50. A representative of the government-supported Maison des Femmes, arguing that France has reached "the saturation point of eroticism," complained about the exploitation of female nudity in French ads. "It's a cultural problem," she says, "because French women are still taught that they must be submissive and seductive, that their primary function is to be beautiful and to please men." Judith Miller, "French Tolerance of Eroticism Fades," *New York Times* (Nov. 26, 1986), C7. This attitude is particularly apparent in the work of the older women in this chapter— although something very different (it's not clear yet whether better or not) is conveyed by young women filmmakers.

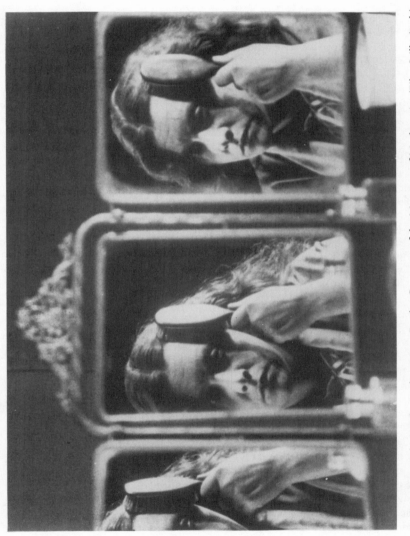

3. Germaine Dulac's *The Smiling Mme. Beudet*. Courtesy of the Museum of Modern Art/Film Stills Archive.

4. *Christopher Strong.* Courtesy of the Museum of Modern Art/Film Stills Archive.

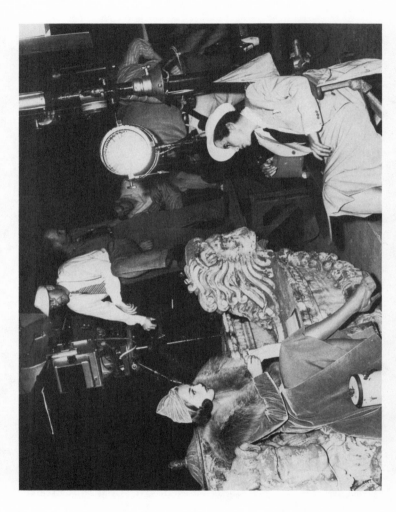

5. Dorothy Arzner, with leading lady Joan Crawford, on the set of *The Bride Wore Red* (1937). Courtesy of the Museum of Modern Art/Film Stills Archive.

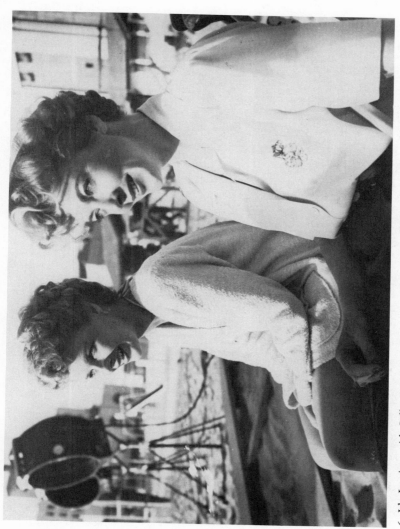

6. Ida Lupino with Sally Forrest, *Never Fear*. Courtesy of the Museum of Modern Art/Film Stills Archive.

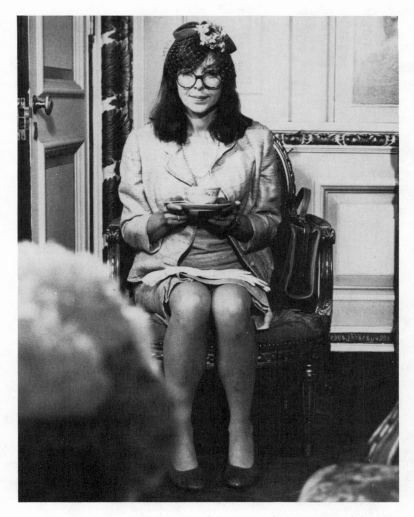

7. Elaine May as the heroine of *A New Leaf*. Courtesy of Paramount and the Museum of Modern Art/Film Stills Archive.

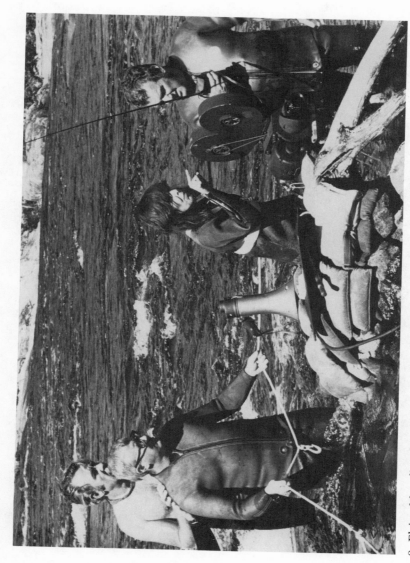

8. Elaine May directing *A New Leaf*. Courtesy of Paramount and the Museum of Modern Art/Film Stills Archive.

9. Joan Micklin Silver's *Between the Lines*. Courtesy of Midwest Film Productions, Inc.

10. Claudia Weill's *Girlfriends*. Courtesy of Warner Bros.

11. Susan Seidelman's *Smithereens*. Courtesy of New Line Films and Susan Seidelman.

12. Joyce Chopra's *Smooth Talk*. Courtesy of Spectra Films Inc. and the Museum of Modern Art/Film Stills Archive.

13. Barbra Streisand on both sides of the camera, *Yentl*. Courtesy of MGM, UA Entertainment Co., and the Museum of Modern Art/Film Stills Archive.

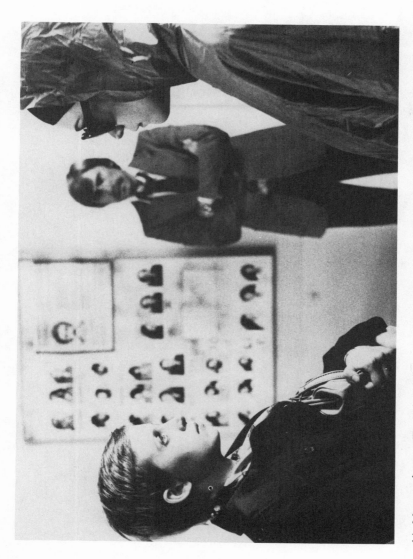

14. Margarethe von Trotta's *The Second Awakening of Christa Klages*. Courtesy of New Line Films and the Museum of Modern Art/Film Stills Archive.

15. Von Trotta's *Marianne and Juliane*. Courtesy of New Yorker Films.

16. Von Trotta and her two actresses: *Marianne and Juliane.* Courtesy of New Yorker Films and the Museum of Modern Art/Film Stills Archive.

17. Doris Dörrie's *In the Belly of the Whale*. Courtesy of the Film Society of Lincoln Center.

18. Agnes Varda's *Cleo from 5 to 7*. Courtesy of Zenith Films.

19. Agnes Varda with the leading actress of *Vagabond*. Courtesy of the International Film Exchange.

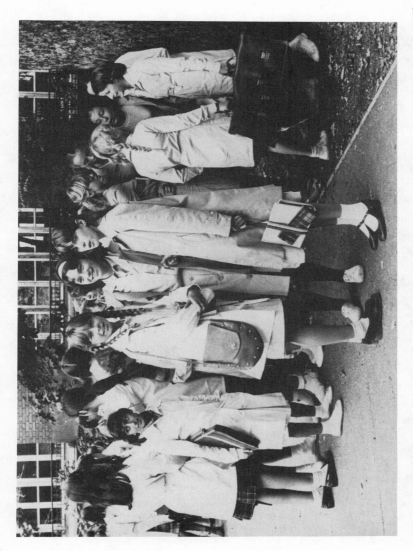

20. Diane Kurys' *Peppermint Soda*. Courtesy of New Yorker Films and the Museum of Modern Art/Film Stills Archive.

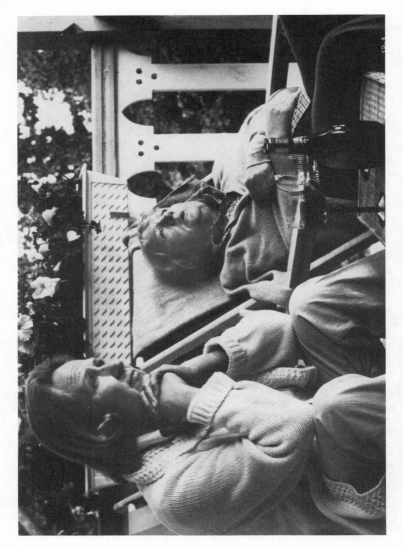

21. Gunnel Lindblom's *Summer Paradise*. Courtesy of Almi Pictures, Inc.

22. Marleen Gorris' *A Question of Silence*. Courtesy of Quartet and Castle Hill Films.

23. Márta Mészáros' *Adoption.* Courtesy of Kino International.

24. Márta Mészáros' *Nine Months*. Courtesy of New Yorker Films.

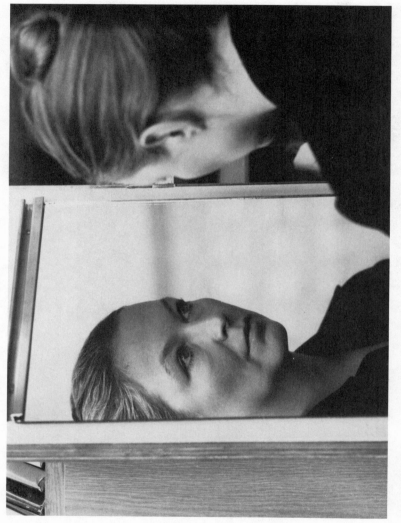

25. Márta Mészáros' *The Two of Them*. Courtesy of New Yorker Films.

26. Larisa Shepitko's *Wings*. Courtesy of the Film Center, Art Institute of Chicago.

27. Shepitko on location. Courtesy of the Film Center, Art Institute of Chicago.

28. Věra Chytilová's *Daisies*. Courtesy of Films, Inc. and the Museum of Modern Art/Film Stills Archive.

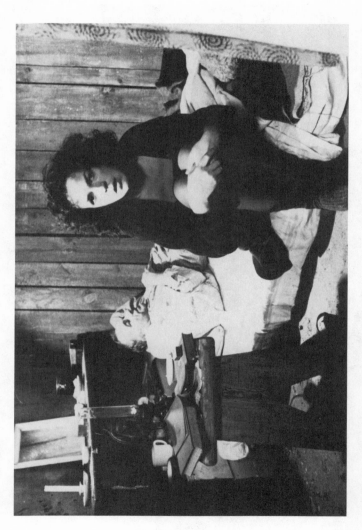

29. Agneiszka Holland's *Angry Harvest*. Courtesy of the Film Society of Lincoln Center and the Museum of Modern Art.

30. Euzhan Palcy's *Sugarcane Alley*. Courtesy of New Yorker Films and Orion Classics.

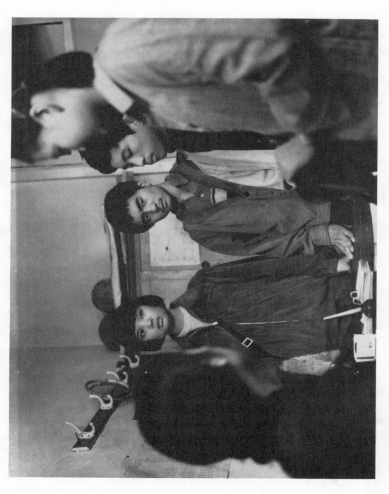

31. Lu Xiaoya's *The Girl in Red*. Courtesy of the Asia Society.

# 5
# Eastern European Women Directors

## INTRODUCTION

Of the major women directors to come out of contemporary Eastern European cinema, Larisa Shepitko (USSR), Věra Chytilová (Czechoslovakia), and Márta Mészáros (Hungary), with all the extraordinary talent they represent, are a tragic group. Shepitko was cut down by fate, not politics, killed in a car accident at the very moment her filmmaking, powerful from the start, came with true fullness into its own. We have four films of hers, and an excruciating promise of greatness destroyed. Being Russian, the extent to which she could venture aesthetically and politically was severely delimited, though she still came in for official reproach for following her own questing vision, as did her husband, director Elem Klimov, for his earlier satirical work. Věra Chytilová, one of the boldest and most brilliant of the directors who constituted the Czech New Wave before the Russian invasion of Prague in 1968, was cut down just as surely, but entirely by politics. After a seven year enforced silence through the 1970s, she now continues to make modest films inside Czechoslovakia. What is striking is how strong, original, and uncompromising both of these figures were, how much they asked of themselves, the extent to which both pushed their art to the limits and past the limits. Where could they have gone if their art could have developed on its own terms through a lifetime?

Mészáros alone works at full strength, very productive. She has been amassing a large body of work over three decades of filmmaking, supported by a climate in Hungary that allows more latitude of expression than elsewhere in Eastern Europe. Stylistically in no way as innovative as Chytilová was, nor grand with something hallucinatory around the edges like Shepitko, Mészáros' realism carries surprise and revelation and is not plodding. Her eye is both on the drama of women, and recently also on the tragedy of history, a tragedy that is hers in the most personal of ways, she having been orphaned as a small child by Stalinism.

There are other figures as well. Russia's women directors go back to Esther Shub and Olga Preobrazhednskaya in the 1920s, through a sizable number of recent directors whose films we simply do not get to see,[1] as we do not see those of such Hungarian women directors as Judit Elek. Neither Czechoslovakia nor Poland has offered fertile ground for women directors—despite Chytilová (and Krumbachová), and Agnieszka Holland—though Poland also has surprises in its past, like the remarkable Wanda Jacubowska, a Jewish Polish woman director who was imprisoned in Auschwitz and went back in 1948 with an all-women crew to make a powerful film, *The Last Stop*, about the camp and the solidarity of the women there.[2]

However miserable a situation the Eastern European state film industry has created for many directors, paradoxically—because it is not commercial and cut-throat competitive in the same way ours is in the West—it has also been able to offer a relatively hospitable nurturing ground for a director like Mészáros. It offers the precious assurance that she can steadily continue to make her films, without constant hustling for money, without constant awareness of the box office—though competition for funding is at the same time keen in Hungary because that country overproduces directors.[3] While the censorship apparatus there was dismantled in 1967, J. Hoberman notes: "The strongest censorship in Hungary, everyone agrees, is self-censorship," and quotes the Hungarian writer Konrad: "When your fancies touch barbed wire, the bloodhounds that protect you from yourself begin to bark."[4] Mészáros denies any problem of censorship, noting that making a film about lesbians would be much harder to do in Hungary than anything political. International co-productions, especially for Hungarian directors, have allowed for some expansion of possibilities. On the other hand, in countries like Czechoslovakia and Poland especially, political restrictions are of course grimly constricting, and can make questions of gender pale next to the common enemy faced by both men and women, which makes honest art hard, sometimes impossible. Still, the world of women's lives and the experience of gender is important for all these filmmakers. Mészáros and Chytilová ground their vision in it; and though Shepitko does not, one of her most interesting films has an intriguing heroine, and those films built around male central characters still use women in profoundly evocative ways.

## THE DEVELOPMENT OF A MAJOR DIRECTOR IN EASTERN EUROPE: MÁRTA MÉSZÁROS

Márta Mészáros' films are among the most powerful and important to be discussed in this study. She is also one of the world's handful of living, working, women filmmakers who have been making films for three decades. She has a full oeuvre to her credit, beginning with some twenty-five documentaries, mostly made early in her career, although also such recent documentary shorts as the very touching *Ave Maria*, about the world's refugee women and children, for the U.N.; and fourteen feature films: *The Girl* (1968), *Binding Sentiments* (1969), *Don't Cry, Pretty Girls* (1970), *Riddance* (1973), *Adoption* (1975), *Nine Months* (1976), *The Two of Them* a.k.a *Women* (1977), *Just Like At Home* (with Anna Karina, 1978), *On the Move* (with Delphine Seyrig, 1979), *The Heiress* (with Isabelle Huppert, 1980), *Mother and Daughter* (1981), *The Land of Mirages* (1983), *Diary for My Children* (1984) and *Diary for My Loves* (1987). Luckily, though a number of her films are unavailable here, the best and most mature instances of her art are in distribution in the United States.

Mészáros' long apprenticeship in documentary filmmaking is evidenced in the feature films in the alert, curious, plainspoken way her camera looks at the truths of people's lives, their work places, their faces, their bodies, and of course their inner beings. But along with that general clear-eyed examination there's the constant, sometimes astonishing sense of the eye of a woman watching women in ways that we have not experienced on screen before. Mészáros has noted that in her films "the leads are invariably women—I portray things from a woman's angle"[5]; elsewhere she remarks: "Ever since my first film, *The Girl*, was made, I have with the obstinacy of a mule, pursued my attempt to study the characters of types of women with a strong personality and capable of forming decisions for themselves."[6] Mészáros' films indeed have at their heart a girl or a woman, struggling with a serious decision she must make in working out her life. Her women are usually strong, independent, often going against authority, though also often very needy of the men in their lives. Mészáros works from "a woman's angle" from her very first feature, *The Girl*, even literally opening with frozen frame after frame of the heroine's head—though Mészáros deals with men characters with considerable compassion, also frequently seeing the world through their eyes.

The trauma of early orphaning that Mészáros suffered as a child is at the core of her work, reflected in many ways in her questing women. When asked if *Diary for My Children* was autobiographical, she said, "Not just this film; I tell my own life story in most of my films. The search for Mother and Father is a determining experience in my life. The concept of the child left on its own or abandoned is something that has excited me in almost all of my films."[7] The whole issue of parents and children runs through the center of her films, again hauntingly sounded from her very first feature, *The Girl*. There a young woman raised as an orphan sets out to find her parents, particularly her mother. In the most searing moment of the film, when Zsonyi first encounters the mother, the two women exchange a long silent look across a high long fence that Mészáros pans along—with a beautiful use of space and motion—token of the separation the girl must finally recognize as permanent. She is never to have the mother she hoped to find, nor the father. Often in Mészáros' films an older woman parents a younger one (and is parented by her in turn), as in *Adoption* or *The Two of Them*. Having a baby is also the central issue of *Adoption*, and *Nine Months* concludes with a stunning live childbirth sequence. Even Mészáros' awful French co-production, *The Heiress*, is built around an absurd triangular situation with a pregnancy at the center of it, one woman having a baby for another who cannot herself be pregnant.

The little girl in *The Two of Them*, who at first appears to be a minor figure, gradually becomes a central one, a crucial though largely silent presence in that film. Zsuzsi has parents but somehow is usually forgotten by them, often looking abandoned. As we watch her, in her grave delicacy quietly cleaning up the bottles after her drunken father, trying to make order out of the general disorder of adult lives, she seems barely a child, more a little parent herself. In the watchfulness of her tiny face through the film, she sees terrible things, watches a father not be a father, fall apart, as she is also intensely pulled by love and loyalty to him, sensing his presence in the midst of partying noise and music, and running purposefully straight to him as though by magnet. Her eyes frame whole sections of the film and though apparently on the sidelines, she—in all the vulnerability, help-lessness, truthfulness of childhood—is a major part of what makes *The Two of Them* such a strong experience.

Not only does that child grow in importance in that film, but the child actress, Zsuzsa Czinkoczy, moves to the center of the Mészáros films that follow. She is the central character of *All the Way Home*, as a ten year old girl who forms a deep bond with a man. She is the heroine of *Diary for My Children* (and *Diary for My Loves* after that)—there an older but not yet adult girl, Juli, whose orphaning is for the first time directly described in the painful autobiographical circumstances of Mészáros' own. The question of Juli's being adopted by her aunt Magda is also important in this film; and young Juli is often seen as a little girl in flashbacks, and sometimes appears at once as both little girl and older one, layers of the self in time, the hurt child ever present.

These are birthings of the self, attempts perhaps also to go back to that fearfully wounded child and heal it, to raise the fledgling self. One of the girls from another home for abandoned children in *Adoption*, the beautiful Anna, tells Kata the heroine, who wants to adopt a child, that she should not, because abandoned children are profoundly and permanently wounded people. But the central events of the film have to do with Kata's going ahead with the attempt, first spiritually adopting Anna, acting as her mother, and then actually adopting a baby. So too Kata replants pots of geraniums growing outside, a metaphor for her attempt to give Anna more earth to grow in. Relatedly, the strong and struggling heroine of *Nine Months* si-multaneously is about to give birth and also gets a job working on an experimental farm-irrigation project, metaphor for her own life as an experimental force for change, growth, nurturing. Children and childbirth are central on many levels to Mészáros' questing heroines.

In charting the journeys of these heroines—and in Mészáros' first very powerful film it is literally a journey—Mészáros is by no means wedded to dogged realism.[8] For instance, when Zsonyi in the opening sequences of *The Girl* flees in disgust from a luncheon reunion for orphans, for solitary anguish, she is followed by a sixteen-year-old boy. This boy's unexplained appearance—at three particularly lonely and despairing points in the film—suggests that in his seemingly whimsical impulsiveness he is her suicidal alter ego, what lies beneath her composure and competence, what she attempts to heal throughout the film. The very structures of Mészáros' films convey a sense of rambling, almost improvisatory, open-ended inattention, even indifference, to the sort of tight seamless narrative that tries to create an illusion of verisimilitude. While Mészáros is wedded to the moment by moment textures of her character's life, she can be impatiently terse, fragmented, even sloppy if judged in realist terms, because her preoccupations are, happily, elsewhere.

Indeed *The Girl* seems akin to abstract musical movement. The film begins in the orphanage, the heroine's face framed within the tension of her holding an arrow in a bow, poised, as a series of other girls release theirs. That sense of a directive headed in the most purposive and singleminded way to an end, the tension of an unreleased trajectory, is really the essence of the whole film and the heroine. Only after she moves through her obsession with each of her lost parents, is she released into the adult world of heterosexual love. At the same time, Mészáros even in this most youthfully romantic of her films, with the girl ending up in the arms of a wonderful looking stranger who is magnetically drawn to her, concludes on a dissonant note. As Zsonyi enters this new love, the suicidal boy dances around her; strange-looking rock musicians sing a wonderful song in odd falsetto; and the final freeze frame of the girl—all leave us with offbeat, bittersweet reverberations. The heroine's movement from quest for a mother to entry into the unknown of man–woman adult love has an archetypal quality. So realism seems an inadequate category to describe other memorable moments in other Mészáros films, like the panning around the wedding table at the end of *Adoption* as a metaphor for young hopes breaking down before our eyes, presented with an almost avant garde condensation of statement.

The repeated associations in Mészáros' films of women with birthing and mothering functions by no means represent an affirmation of traditional female domestic roles—rather the very opposite. In *The Girl*, Zsonyi's quest for her mother takes her to a traditional woman in a mountain village, as shrouded in black modest peasant garb and kerchief as any Muslim woman behind the veil. Serving and clearing food, the mother and *her* mother look like chattel, and the mother gears her behavior entirely to the continual orders of her patriarch husband. In another extraordinary image, at a village dance the mother immediately joins a long row of darkly shrouded women seated on the sidelines, all looking old, while the young girls dance. (The ferocity of the mother's closeup, agitated, jealous pacing makes the sequence even more disturbing.) The trousers, short hair, bold movements, and other suggestions of rebelliousness, of the young heroine from Budapest bespeak a dramatically contrasting independence, as a TV show of Miss Universe and the French can-can also suggests feminist ironies. So do the continual male intrusions on the girl, violations of her, intensely engrossed as she is through most of the film in her quest. In one affecting frame Zsonyi stands as if magnetized, watching the retreating mother—her modest encumbering garb cancelling her out—take food away. The woman holds Zsonyi's passionate attention in the frame, not the young-man son who is intently watching *her*, nor the male world around the sexy TV show that the mother's husband urges the girl, entirely uninterested, to enter.

Mészáros' next major heroine, Kata in *Adoption*, may look lonely at 42 by herself, in her wood workshop, but her self-sufficiency is also clear and attractive. In one interesting sequence Joska, the married man Kata loves and wants a child from, takes her into his home by way of justifying why he says no. His wife, domestic, bland, conventional looking, does not appear in the least enviable. She voices her own dissatisfaction with her confinement to the house, though when Joska says he wants her home, she timidly echoes his words and disowns her own feelings.

The feminist note in Mészáros gets sounded even more strongly in the later films, *Nine Months* and *The Two of Them*. (*The Two of Them* is known in this country as *Women*, though the European title, a direct translation from the Hungarian title, seems to me preferable because more precise.) There domestic confinement is almost tantamount to imprisonment. Juli resists a marriage in the first film, and Mari destroys one in the second, to get release. There is never an interest in the actualities of child care or cooking or other home processes in Mészáros' work, and those who pride themselves in such activities, like the boy's hostile mother in *Riddance*, are often unpleasant. The most memorable instance in Mészáros of a woman laying the table and putting out the meals is significantly in *The Two of Them* when the heroine almost hits her husband with a frying pan of eggs in her desperation to make an impact on him, on his distance from her and his scorn for her sense that *her* work is also important.

If the domestic doesn't interest her, the processes that really do interest Mészáros are work processes, and her films—from *The Girl* and *Riddance* on—use factories and other kinds of work places in striking ways. A string factory with its droning noise and geometric spools figures in *The Girl*, a weaving factory in *Riddance*, and in *Adoption* there are fine sequences of women working in a woodworking factory, the camera intent on the sanding motions of the workers, or the way sawdust coats the fat arm and elbow creases of one of the women. Her old documentary training doubtless coming into play, Mészáros in fact went back to documentary in 1971 to make *Women in the Spinnery*, about factory girls in work very like that of her early heroines. In *Adoption* Mészáros clearly likes the look of wood pieces piled in interesting formations, or the machinery in Kata's own home workshop, the handsaw hanging on her wall. *Nine Months* too has memorable sequences in the iron foundry in which Janos and Juli work, and even in *The Two of Them* the workplace, the workers' residence, gets at least as much attention as the home does. Even sequences that don't seem work-related, like the medical check-up Kata has early in *Adoption* to see if she can still have a child, reveal an affecting interest—through the tightest possible closeup—in medical hand on body, professional attentiveness, the blood pressure machinery, but most of all the mortal human machinery, somehow deeply touching in its vulnerability, veined arm extended, hand opened for pulse reading, heart beat on the sound track. Before we know anything about Kata as a person, there are these sequences of the animal self, the most basic self, without words, of the body arising from sleep, coughing, stretching, opening the shutters to a new day, showering, at work, and in its nakedness being examined by other hands. What could be more startlingly different a treatment of the female body from that use as spectacle we are all so familiar with, or its medical uses in Hollywood melodrama. In that sequence by Mészáros a woman's body carries no symbology beyond its mutely eloquent humanness.

*Adoption* is full of striking faces, like that of the young Anna, fiercely beautiful, or Kata's middle-aged face, the affecting, worn, alive sadness of it inseparably part of its beauty. (There is an interesting age leap from the young girls of *The Girl* and *Riddance*, to the mature beauty of Kata—Mészáros herself was 44 when *Adoption* was released. The two age levels in that film and other later Mészáros work provide, it seems to me, a device for working with a more mature heroine, while focussing as strongly as ever on the wounded young spirit.)

In *Adoption* Mészáros also repeatedly pans past rows of faces, most poignantly in the girls' home, where the girls all look up alertly toward the stranger, and toward the camera and us. We watch with an awareness of a woman behind the camera looking at women, and we women in the audience looking at these shared looks. Sometimes the panning seems to go on too long, even pointlessly, as in the wedding sequence at the end of *Adoption*, showing us many people we don't recognize, faces not distinctive enough to warrant repeated circling—only to have the camera movement justified the second time around the table as it starts to reveal stresses, all silently (and eloquently) done. The camera pans over Anna's friends from the home crying or looking unhappy, without specific causes stated or needed—and finally, fluidly, picks up a fight between Anna and her groom, indicating that all will not end happily with this marriage.

That scene is entirely wordless, like many of Mészáros' strongest moments, as in another sequence in *Adoption* when a girl, unimportant to the film before or after that moment, reads Kata a letter she has written to her parents who have abandoned her. The reticence, and at the same time the intensity of what passes between the two, in simple strong black and white two shots, is extraordinary, the emotion propelling Kata to intercede in behalf of Anna.

It is a repeated motif in Mészáros' work that men and women are at cross-purposes, continually reaching for one another and continually missing. This is so in *Adoption* not only for the young girl but for the older woman, who brings her yearning for a child to her married lover, only to meet his recoil, her own consequent bereft feelings evident though unstated. Joska is ultimately more interested in his own comfortable arrangement with his two women, secretly maintained, than he is with Kata's happiness. Yet he is obviously troubled, resorts to the unprecedented step of taking her home with him to clarify to her his own domestic situation, drinks as a reaction to her sadness, withdraws from her but finally seeks her out passionately in renewal of their relationship—all of which shows Mészáros' sympathetic recognition of his point of view. (These sequences are again remarkably thick with reverberations between people though little or nothing is actually said.) But it is a severely limited relationship, and whether Kata's acceptance of those limits is a statement of her own independence and her liking of privacy, or a masochistic fitting to the man's needs, is a question that Mészáros leaves open. Young Anna gets angry for her when Joska does not show up for an appointment, saying she should drop him, that it's not right that she should live for his convenience, almost as Joska's wife accepts his rule and his constriction on her life. After Kata unsuccessfully attempts to persuade Joska, she repeatedly expresses the wish that he will not be cross with her, in the form of a mental letter that she keeps composing, so great is her worry of losing him. Men and women often blunder around at odds in Mészáros' films, the mesh between their needs or understandings poor, much separation and misunderstanding between them.

As a consequence, women often turn instead to other women for closeness. When Joska does not show up as he promised, and Kata is tearful, she and Anna go off together to a restaurant, delighted with one another, leaning in subtly provocative, somewhat erotic intimacy toward one another over a table, with the men around seen by the camera as staring gargoyles. Mészáros keeps the sequence in closeup, as the women only see each other. She does not give us an establishing shot until late, with a young man approaching Anna to ask her to dance, and an older man approaching Kata, both refused by the women, who clearly prefer each other. Their table is finally seen in long shot as a kind of oasis—an island on an island—surrounded by men. The vision is used again, even more effectively, in *The Two of Them*, with Mari and Juli talking about intimate things—the violence and sexuality of Juli's marriage—in a cafe surrounded by men at tables, who begin to push their tables and chairs in toward the women, closing in around them, a very disturbing image of violation, but really only an exaggeration of commonplace male public intrusions on women. (These intrusions were alluded to from the beginning in *The Girl*. So too from the start does Mészáros frame Zsonyi's search for parents, and for a man, with a friendship between girls. In that first feature the two friends talk, backs to the camera, at the film's beginning; one looks with special intensity at the other from her bunk bed late in the film; and the relationship constitutes a stronger thread through the narrative than is obvious, because Zsonyi's friend in this early film is an undefined, hence weak character.)

But there is no mistaking that at the very heart of *Adoption* (and *The Two of Them* as well) are the laughter, talk, shared pain, and especially the looks exchanged by the two women. Those intent looks begin from the time Anna first sees Kata with Joska, strangers at a nearby table, to when she enters Kata's house with a group of girls, and later as the relationship between the two deepens, as they exchange their life secrets, lying head next to head together in a bed, looking with full depth and understanding at one another. Woman viewed by woman, viewed again by the intent director, and at yet another remove by the woman spectator, fully endows woman as subject in Mészáros, as in von Trotta and elsewhere.

The question of where this kind of attraction and sympathy becomes actual lesbian love again is raised by a number of scenes in Mészáros' films, particularly in *Adoption* and in *The Two of Them*—but the films move past those highly charged moments without commenting on them, not dealing with the issue at all. However, it seems too ingenuous—given the erotic charge of the intimacy, often highlighted by the camera's keen awareness of bodies at such times—simply to say, as von Trotta did when I asked her about similar sequences in her films, that what is involved is just closeness, as between a mother and a daughter. Mészáros, remarking on the difficulty of making a film about lesbians in Hungary (Karoly Makk's *Another Way* is an entirely uncharacteristic exception, though to Western eyes not a very successful one) has a script for a film with a lesbian love story, sure to be fascinating if she is ever able to make it.

But whatever the strong pull between women, the men in Mészáros' films are at once sympathetic and impossible figures. In *Adoption*, they are necessary to both women, though not finally satisfactory. The pain and desperation of those necessary relationships is far more powerfully communicated still in Mészáros' next two films. In *Nine Months* the difficulties between Juli and Janos include something very like a rape; and the alcoholic Janos of *The Two of Them* is entirely hopeless, however full of charm, sadness, enchantment. Lies, Zsuzsi says, about adult accommodations and attempts to smooth life out. *Diary for My Children* moves away from the whole issue in its focus on pre-adult love, and love for father. But never do man and woman live happily ever after in Mészáros, one reason for the jarring quality of her endings. As already noted, this is true even in her first film, *The Girl*, which seems to end with true love after the painful struggle to find mother and father is somewhat resolved. The lyrics of the wonderful song in that final sequence of *The Girl* (the film's Hungarian title means "The Sun Has Gone") have to do with the sun's departure for the night, imagining another one equally bright, and a new sun emerging, all related to loneliness and new love—but though the man's attraction to Zsonyi and their embrace are lingeringly extended—the conclusion is unsettling.

In *Adoption* not only is young Anna's wedding no resolution to the film, or to Anna's painful life, but neither is Kata's adoption of a baby with which the film ends. There is too much suffering in Mészáros' world for that to be possible—often taking the form of insomnia (like Kata's in *Adoption*), drinking (as in *The Heiress*, or Janos' in *Diary for My Children*, and of course Janos' in *The Two of Them*). There is a tormented substructure to Mészáros' characters that often is not expressed in words, hardly in gestures, but that one strongly senses. Because Mészáros will never impose a lying resolution on these heavy human struggles, the endings of her films are as jarring as the lives she depicts. Kata, having spent the whole of *Adoption* struggling with the issue of wanting a child, tries—when refused by Joska—to mother through her relation with the girls at the home, especially with Anna. But when she actually has her newly adopted infant in her arms, she holds it awkwardly, and the camera cuts away to a final long-shot sequence of Kata looking small as she hurries, white bundle in arms, toward an approaching bus, her anxious harried breathing loud on the soundtrack, freeze frame before ever reaching it—a final sense of unremitting struggle, burden, difficulty.

This is even more true of *Nine Months*. Juli's work in the factory lifting heavy ceramic bricks while she prepares for her exams, is strongly metaphorical of her heavily burdened life, as the job she ends up with is metaphorical as an affirmation of her life and her future. Still, Juli's solitary path is difficult, with as much bleakness as promise. One feels she pays, in isolation and struggle, a very high price for going her own way. Mészáros gives her a most problematic ending again, though the director clearly endorses this heroine who refuses to be ashamed of having an illegitimate child with the man she loves but cannot marry. She has the strength to study for exams while working in a large iron foundry, to ensure that she will have a work life that enables her to be independent. She has the determination to persist despite the attempts of Janos, the foundry foreman who falls in love with her, to deflect her, by seduction and then by force.

And she bears Janos' baby painfully alone because marriage to him would mean giving up too much of herself.

In *Nine Months* the new house that Janos has spent five years building and preparing for his wife-to-be, long before he has met Juli, is a fine metaphor for the ready-made quality of conventional/traditional life visions, the plan made apart from the particularities of the people, waiting for the live woman to step into the otherwise finished box of a life. Such a house would clearly be a cage and a burial for Juli, but the film also catches how Janos, in his passionate pursuit of her, can be at once an ordinary decent man and also terrible, resenting Juli's son, her drive, her independence— jealous of other people and interests in her life, wanting full control and all her attention. To Janos' mother, Juli is simply a whore, and both mother and son are seen as at one with their world, with Juli entirely outside it. *Nine Months* leaves us not only with a memorable image of a woman who stays true to her own vision of life, but delicately conveys how convention binds people and makes them enraged and bewildered when confronted by anything that subverts the values they unthinkingly live by.

This is particularly strongly shown in one scene when Janos, in his opposition to Juli's continuing her schooling, angrily rapes her—attempting to make her compliant by imposing his physical power over her. Immediately afterward, however, she slowly undresses him, gently shares food with him, teaches him about mutual love. That these two scenes flow from one another involves a level of surprise, human unpredictability, daring, that makes Mészáros' work stay powerfully in one's memory. Mészáros constructs a world where no real villains or heroes exist, just confused people failing to come together, to understand one another's needs.

Juli herself is no superwoman. That she is so small and waif-like in her feistiness makes her act of bucking the enormity of conventional expectation all the more touching, since her vulnerability is even conveyed by her appearance. And sturdily game and tough though she seems in undertaking such a physically difficult job, that vulnerability is further borne out by her dreams of bricks falling on her. It is most touchingly exposed directly before the final childbirth scene, when she stands alone in the apartment that comes with her new job and for once permits the full anguish that she carries to show. Despite her powerful desire for autonomy, she has need for father figures, both Pista and Janos being much older than she is. Less a rebel than determined to be true to her own integrity, she is one of a line of Mészáros heroines distressed to be put in the position of having to lie (like Zsonyi in *The Girl*, and the heroine of *Riddance*, who has to pretend to be a student rather than the factory girl she is). Yet in *Nine Months* Juli is perhaps unnecessarily abrasive in insisting against Janos' wishes on informing his family that she has an illegitimate child. Though she is motivated by a commitment to honesty, the action is perhaps a destructive and self-destructive one in the context, exposing Janos to ridicule and causing him to brutally rage at her. While *Nine Months* is clearly a feminist film, there is no idealization here, and no simple ideology, but the incalcitrant contradictory stuff of life and art, to which Mészáros always remains true. So although Juli is steadfast to the end, and although the film concludes with live birth and experimental irrigation project, the film's ending is no simple affirmation of Juli's independence and her new life. Freedom, and bravely going beyond the confines of her world, brings Juli a great deal of pain and isolation.

Mészáros' next film, *The Two of Them* (again, also known as *Women*) focuses on a friendship between two women of different classes, and on their respective marriages, bringing a still greater complexity to Mészáros' exploration of marriage. The principal heroine of this film, an older woman, Mari, played by the elegantly handsome Marina Vlady, manager of a factory hostel for women, takes in a younger woman, again named Juli and played by the same Lili Monori of *Nine Months*, who is seeking sanctuary with her little daughter from her heavily alcoholic husband Janos, played again by Jan Nowicki, the Janos in *Nine Months*. (Mészáros denies any continuity in these characters despite some links.) Juli's marriage, with its violence and chaos, is an obvious mess; and the orderly, calm, strong and motherly Mari tries to help. She breaks the rules and allows the child into the hostel—an issue, though peripheral, that is a feminist one. Mari uses her authority with humility and humanity, in contrast to her subordinate, Mrs. Berek, also called Magda, a nasty enforcer of rules who foreshadows the communist aunt, Magda, in *Diary*.

The film is shot largely from Mari's point of view and above all, it concerns her awakening, through a crisis precipitated by the death of her old mother at the beginning of the film, a reminder of mortality, her own sense of aging, an urgency about defining—and living—her life. In an intimate scene between Mari and Juli's alcoholic husband Janos, in which they share their life stories and their pain, Mari speaks of feeling that after long years of marriage and having grown children, she is as empty as her house is; feeling as if she never really made love to anyone, indeed never lived at all, and now it's all gone. Janos, who is also very tender with his own daughter and wife, hears Mari sensitively and encouragingly responds that she was a spectator before but now is starting to live, and mustn't clean, cook, limit her life to that. As in *Nine Months*, the themes are directly feminist, though Mészáros denies she is a feminist. (In an interview with me her explanation was that Jan Nowicki is her closest friend, knows her better than any woman, and has been more nurturing to her than anyone. And it *is* true that the men in Mészáros' films, especially those played by Jan Nowicki, often are given a special centrality as advice givers and supporters).

At the same time, again, Mészáros' men characters are mostly hopeless. Janos himself in *The Two of Them* is utterly degraded by the alcoholism cure. His promises to reform are utterly unreliable. He is finally seen bitterly cursing out both women, calling Juli a whore for not being there, and cursing Mari because she *is* there. These are not men to pin one's hopes on, though the women do. For all the bitterness of Mari's own marriage, she waits for Ferenc to come to the hostel party and in her despair when he does not, drinks herself almost into unconsciousness.

In that state she must be tended by Juli and Janos, but for the most part it is Mari who plays a maternal role, engaged in coolly authoritative care-taking both in general work situations, and in relation to Juli. She conveys an almost radiant calm, but in her genteel reserve she represses the kind of emotions that Juli acts out outrageously. Juli appears willing to do anything, even kiss the Party Secretary on the lips, show her bare behind to the uptight informer Mrs. Berek, be passionately sexual toward Janos, get into the shower with her clothes on just to be funny. Juli tends to wear pants through the film, and has short boyish hair, as Mari, with Marina Vlady's grace and beauty, elegantly wears skirts and sweaters and, when she releases it, long hair—codes that both von Trotta and Mészáros use to signify a woman character's distance from traditional or conventional femininity. Juli's de-fiance, wildness, recklessness, passion, refusal to be polite, all draw Mari to her. Mari like a mother intercedes and covers for her, protects her, as Juli repeatedly says no to things. Of course Juli's look of toughness and defiance masks vulnerability, and in one affecting scene, Juli, having gone back briefly to clean Janos' messed up flat while he's away, cries as she sweeps the floor. Juli has a frank, free expressiveness that Mari lacks, and the strong woman needs the more apparently needy one, the mother moth-ered by the child again, with that interesting fluidity of the currents of interaction earlier true of the alternate mothering/daughtering between Kata and Anna in *Adoption*.

So too in *The Two of Them*, despite the desperation of Juli's marriage, it gradually becomes clear that Mari's is in even deeper trouble. Her husband, with his interesting intellectual good looks, is even more outrageously per-emptory to Mari than Janos was toward Juli in *Nine Months*, reproaching her for not staying home to take care of him and her grown children (she is obliged to sleep at the hostel), mocking her sense of accomplishment, asserting the far greater importance of his own work. However destructively impulsive the other couple is, Mari sees in them a tenderness and sexual passion that she cannot find with her own husband, whose heading for Mongolia is a fitting geographical equivalent for his psychic remoteness—most dramatically seen as he turns away from her sexually without even noticing she is left out of it. His indifference to her subjects her to a sexual humiliation so quiet and stunning, as to be one of the moments for which one most prizes this director. There is also an effective crosscutting between this sequence and a parallel lovemaking between Juli and Janos, passionate and tender but equally doomed. The camera lingers on the unhappiness of each woman's face during the lovemaking, not interested in the bodies, but in the woman, looking. What the women are looking at through most of the film is the hopelessness of their lives with their men.

Again, through the inadequacy of those lives, the women in *The Two of Them* become enmeshed with one another. They laugh together, support and commiserate with one another, become the deepest of friends. They casually undress in one another's presence, and one is struck how here and in other Mészáros films, like *Adoption*, the camera just quietly observes the woman's naked body as part of a wholeness, rarely divorcing body from face and self—though Mészáros is a sensual director for whom the physicality of life is important, and she does sexual scenes excitingly—even shockingly, as early as the glimpsed parental bedroom scene in *The Girl*—if reticently by American standards.

Through the impact of Juli and Janos, Mari changes, experiencing herself anew sensually, for one thing. A man, nicely left unidentified, expresses interest in her, and the shower sequence that follows conveys her renewed sense of body. When Mari tells Ferenc, "You never loved me," during a brutal fight, it is a cry of discovery as much as of distress, no doubt coming from a new assertiveness and capacity to look at the reality of their lives. But though the trajectory of *The Two of Them* has Mari seeming to be fashioning a new life of independence, the film's conclusion again will give us no certitude or comfort. Our final image is of all three women, two adults and one girl-child, talking with deepest concern about the beloved man, Janos, though the film concludes with a sense of total impasse between men and women.

The startling moment at the film's very end makes closure impossible. When Mari tries to reassure Juli that Janos is alright, Zsuzsi, mute, barely noticed witness to these adult lives all through the film, watches with disbelief the evasions of the adults around her, and cries out that it's all lies. It's a moment that takes one completely by surprise, easily seen as gratuitous, yet on reflection one of the best things in the film, that Mészáros had the courage to let happen. Given this accusation, against the dark cold wintry bleak setting of the closing shot, there can once more be no great hopes for the working out of things. But there is a ferocious insistence on truth, which goes to the heart of Mészáros. It is not accompanied, however, by a sense of cynicism, nihilism, even despair, and Mészáros never seems superior to her characters. On the contrary, she brings a compassionate understanding, without softness, and a keen eye, to the attempts of her women characters to find their way.

Themes of parenting, and the yearning for parenting, take particularly heart-rending form in Mészáros' *Diary for My Children*, and Mészáros' concern with work also takes the interesting form there of a young girl's rite of passage as she moves toward her future as a filmmaker. While *Diary for*

*My Children* undertakes the impressively ambitious and moving project of telling the story of Mészáros' generation in Hungary, along with the large political tragedy she wished to record for the young, Mészáros also tells a poignant personal story—the public and the personal hauntingly intertwined—of a young girl orphaned by Stalinism, a girl who loves movies, of a difficult female adolescence. We watch young Juli primping in front of mirrors, her first love, her intellectual and paternal mentors, but most affecting of all, her memories of her parents and of her loss of them in early childhood[9]—material Mészáros never dealt with directly before. (Oddly, though, that material *does* appear in *The Girl*, through the apparently fraudulent man who comes to tell Zsonyi the story of her parents' fate. She mocks that story as untrue, while on the soundtrack a harshly grating railway whistle jars us. The disturbing sound in effect gives the lie to the lightness of tone and to the denial—an interesting instance of Mészáros' sounding the depths of anguish while at the same time maintaining a distancing composure.)

The first of a planned trilogy, and much more political than Mészáros' earlier films, *Diary for My Children* takes fourteen-year-old Juli back to her native Hungary in 1947, from Russia where she has been living, through to 1953, harsh Stalinist years in Hungary. As we watch the growing oppressiveness of the handsome, highly intelligent Magda, the aunt with whom Juli lives, it is clear that we are also watching the darkening of a time. Magda, at first editor of the Party newspaper, takes a new, more powerful and more sinister position as governor of a prison, and in her boots and military uniform grows increasingly harsh and inhuman. Juli's "grandfather" Deszo (who is Magda's brother), and also Janos, the most sympathetic figures in the film, both older men loved by young Juli, and both themselves associated with Communism from their youth, speak to Juli with respect for Magda. Janos remembers the young girl full of brains and spirit he loved and almost married along ago. Deszo tells Juli about the strength that permitted Magda to survive all sorts of hardships and to fight on. But theirs is a respect mixed with fear, even revulsion.

At the same time, the film avoids any reduction of the Communist leadership to a single monolithic type, ranging from careerist bureaucratic hacks; to once idealistic intellectuals now rigidified into inhumanity over years of struggle, like Magda; to wistfully disillusioned and still humane figures like Janos and Deszo. The trilogy's time span is from 1948 to 1956, the second Communist regime in Hungary, an eight year reign of terror under the absolute rule of the Moscow-trained leader Matyas Rakosi, during which Communists were as fiercely punished as non-Communists, and the Hungarian wartime Communist leader Rajk was among the executed (alluded to in one of the political speeches beautifully interwoven throughout the film). The 1956 uprising, which was Hungary's response to Khrushchev's denunciation of Stalin, brought into power the current relatively benign long-time regime of Janos Kadar, which has allowed such a rich flowering of Hungarian films as *Diary* is part of.

But *Diary* ends in the early 1950s, and not only concludes with the enormously appealing Janos put in prison, but has the young Juli living in a kind of prison with Magda, and continually at war with her. When Juli comes to the actual prison that Magda supervises, the guard who unlocks and locks the doors salutes her, in stunning Newspeak, with "Freedom's Greeting." It is interesting that even at her most political, Mészáros envisages the struggle in terms of a relationship between two women, in terms of the family—and the representative of the State as a bad mother, one who yearns for a daughter.

Juli's conflict with Magda arises not only over Magda's wanting to adopt Juli and to erase the fact of Juli's parents, but also because Magda is, in her essence, at war with artists like Juli's father. When I interviewed her, Mészáros—speaking of the murder of her own father, the sculptor Laszlo Mészáros, in the Stalin death camps in Russia in 1938—kept returning to people saying that he was not political, but a person who wouldn't toe anyone's line, who said what he felt. Her own work is clearly drawn to just the kind of independent individuated spirits who were most quickly ground up in the Stalinist murder machinery. She argues that *Diary for My Children* is no more political than earlier films like *Nine Months* were, in their own way, and says further that "instinctively I loathe and hate politics. I consider a priori all [political] systems a fundemental lie and a struggle for power." Those most loved in Mészáros' films are the deviant ones, like Lili Minori's Julis in *Nine Months* and *The Two of Them*—those who are, like Janos here, people who are different, who have special reserves of their own, however hard they may work for the collective good—maybe drinking too much in order to be able to live with what they must.

Jan Nowicki is most affecting in his double role here as the bearded Janos and also as Juli's clean-shaven sculptor father, returned to life in the girl's memory by flashbacks. We are long accustomed to male directors loving their actresses with the camera, and it is lovely to see a woman director do likewise. Janos, a large figure who has suffered for his socialist ideals, and who continues to work tirelessly at his plant as an act of service, though a long way from his early idealistic commitment, has a particularly powerful scene recalling his various hairbreadth escapes from death when all around him died, including his wife and child. He says he has to live, in place of the others; for them he can't give up. There is a fearful weight, on him and on the film, of historical tragedy, of living with political extremes, as we here live with psychological extremes. But the experience of being thrown into the whirlwinds of history, of public cataclysms—that is not familiar to us. It is, however, the ground of this work. The dead, for instance, are a constant presence in Juli's room, as photos of mother and daughter look out at us all the time, and similarly in Janos' house. The man and girl are brought together by their losses.

But though Juli loves Janos, and though she too bears the severest wounds from history, she also has the cockiness—the shallow arrogance—of youth, that enables her to reproach him for his caution—cowardice, in her eyes— he, who has managed to survive in a world that is one continuous minefield. While in contrast to such strongly women-oriented Mészáros films as *Nine Months* and *The Two of Them*, this film invests the men with all the wisdom and humanity, has as its most painful theme the yearning for a father, and has its two women characters relate as combatants only—still, *Diary* at the same time gives us again a remarkably independent, strong-willed heroine, a kind of female rebellious adolescent rarely seen on screen because likely only to come out of the actual experience of the director. Juli is duplicitous from the start, despite an innocently blank freckled face—stealing movie passes, lifting a phone to stop the ringing, some very sharp-edged responses to Magda, abrasive moments of truth, that indicate poise and self-posses- sion, a strength of will, equal to Magda's own. She reminds one of the headstrong young girl Juliane in Margaretha von Trotta's *Marianne and Juliane*. *Diary* has a mood of bleakness, of sadness, less evident in other Mészáros films because they are so concerned with the empowering strug- gles of women who—whatever the ambiguities of their fates—grow in the course of each film. But this film at the same time contributes a notably strong figure to the growing ranks of important explorations of adolescent girls moving toward womanhood.

Juli, like Juliane, is rebellious, and her rebelliousness largely takes the form of continual moviegoing. The film works skillfully with images of movies, from footage of 1940s fashion shows, to political rallies, to a final grotesque socialist-realist vision of art as uplifting. This last clip, near *Diary's* conclusion, has a serious composer reprimanded for not cheering up the workers, and replaced by a mass of undifferentiated smiling faces singing what appears to be a hymn to socialism. This film insert makes a devastating contrast with the final sequence that follows it, of Juli and Janos' son finally getting to visit Janos in prison, he hazy and sad-faced between layers of wire barrier, this vivid man who could never be merged in a faceless mass of uplift. Juli says to him, in the last words of the film, "Janos, you've gone grey."

Though the film works very well with politics, in a black and white full of quietly radiant images, its richest moments are personal. From the early sequences of the girl's return to Hungary, and her remembrance of her mother holding her hand, to the final, glowing, slow-motion memory image of her father raising her above his head, just as Janos (in present time) is removed to prison, the film gives us—through the idealized vision of the child's eyes—a series of moving flashbacks. There are images of Juli's parents embracing in a lake counterposed to bleak, chill, snowy landscapes of the present; the little girl Juli awkwardly waiting for her mother through a childbirth and joining in her mother's screams; or looking through a window (in both her present self and her little girl self at once) as her father works the stone; watching him cover a clay bust with a wet cloth to keep it moist as the soldiers take him away; or, most plaintive of all, Juli's voice crying "Father" through the vast white stoniness of a quarry that seems of a limitless depth and vacancy. To have had such an early childhood experience, and to survive it and create beyond that painfulness, needs a valiant and strong spirit and clearly Mészáros has one. She has made a rending work of art out of this tragedy.

On one level the film is a portrait of the artist as a young girl, a growing but still underpopulated genre, given the small number of women filmmakers able to make "art" feature films. The second part of the trilogy, *Diary for My Loves*, concerns Juli's education as a filmmaker, though it disappointingly fails to truly take us into that work life. In the third part of the *Diary* trilogy Juli will be a fully grown woman making her own films. Juli's hunger for the screen in *Diary for My Children* is an affecting foreshadowing of that, as well as it is a hunger for the information about the world that films can provide—the mysteriously destructive world Juli has experienced without being able to understand. There are also memorable moments of the young girl practicing for womanhood by miming a gesture of Greta Garbo's in her constant film-watching, or vulgarly putting on make-up in imitation of a cheap magazine cover girl. Mészáros gives Juli a gentle, awkward boyfriend who tells her he loves her and with whom she can fully share her painful story. Juli's eyes govern the film, her eyes on the outer world and her eyes on the world she carries within, memory scenes witnessed both by the bland-faced little girl and by the young adolescent looking back, the older Juli as present on the scene of the past in memory as the little Juli was in actuality. Her eyes take everything in, though the emotional impact of what they see is often conveyed indirectly, through characters in a film she is watching, or by memories that show us where her mind is.

A girl with her own special mix of vulnerability, stubborn willfulness, and courage, she moves through the usual adolescent turbulences at the same time as she swims willy-nilly in waters of history so deep and dark they would take anybody a full lifetime to sort out, to undo the damage. But the human spirit, and the female spirit, does not drown in Márta Mészáros' work. In film after film, as her women have looked at one another in ways new to us, she has continued to look at the truth of those women's experiences. Amid all the struggles and uncertainties of Mészáros' film world, she takes her stand on that truth, and like little Zsuzsi, cries "Lies" to anything less, and that is enough to give her work great impact and, periodically, to take our breath away.

## LARISA SHEPITKO

Seeing the films of Russian director Larisa Shepitko for the first time is a painful kind of discovery, because the more you admire her work, the greater the sense of loss—her talent and enormous potential destroyed when she was killed in a car accident, along with four members of her shooting team, in 1979 at age 40. Still, she did succeed in making at least four full-length films (and possibly a banned film never distributed) in the brief time she turned out to have. And the growth she shows from her first film *Heat*, a diploma film made when she was only 22, to her last and most applauded film *The Ascent* a decade and a half later, is in itself dazzling and also a measure of the loss that her death represents.

Although surprisingly little has been written in the United States about Shepitko either before her death or in the years since, her work did receive international recognition toward the end of her life, especially with *The Ascent*, described in the *International Film Guide* as having "won every prize in sight at the 1977 Berlin Film Festival,"[10] especially the prestigious Golden Bear. When Shepitko returned to Berlin in 1978 as a jury member, a retrospective of her four films was given in her honor. Yet she is unknown to most of us, even though Ronald Holloway described her in *Variety* at the time of her death as "one of the finest directors working in the Soviet cinema today"[11]; Claire Kitson remarks in BFI/National Film Theatre notes that Larisa Shepitko "looked set to become one of the world's most influential directors"[12]; and Jeanne Vronskaya thought "Shepitko had shown an original talent and inimitable mastery."[13] In her earlier book on young Soviet filmmakers, Vronskaya places Shepitko under the heading of "Controversial Directors," right after the entry on Shepitko's husband, director Elem Klimov, who himself made a twenty minute documentary, *Larisa*, in memory of Shepitko after her death, excerpting the most striking sequences from her films, and conveying the broad outlines of her life.

Shepitko was born in the Ukraine in 1939, and entered the Moscow Film School (VGIK) as a pupil of the great Alexander Dovzhenko. Though she had only 18 months to work with him before his death in 1956, his influence is strongly evident in her work, especially in her powerful feeling for the natural world. Klimov, when I interviewed him recently about his wife, after speaking of her beauty and "some kind of magic around her," repeated several times how she made "her own fate. Nobody helped her. She came from a primitive family of Ukrainians, a provincial family, no father, so nobody helped her. She came to Moscow on her own initiative, at sixteen, and entered the Institute of Cinematography." She graduated from the VGIK in 1963 with a prize-winning diploma film, *Heat*, that established from the start her concern with physical as well as moral adversity, conditions that test the human spirit to the limits of endurance.

Klimov's short on her allows us to listen to Shepitko herself speak, particularly memorably about her mentor Dovzhenko, as a humanist who worked according to his conscience, no insincerity, compromise, hackwork. Every day, she says, wants you not to speak out but in art such guile is severely punished; you cannot be dishonest about your work without the work showing it. Actually, Klimov's own career is striking for integrity and the courage to make critiques and take risks, political as well as artistic. *Welcome* (1964), his diploma work, was about a Young Pioneer (Communist Youth) summer camp, whose director has put up Forbidden signs everywhere, everything is restricted, and "escape is impossible."[14] Although the young hero does figure out how to escape, his family is so filled with shame, done with comic hilarity, that he decides to go back, but to lead an underground existence. Because of this clear-speaking allegory, the film was not passed for general release while Khrushchev was alive, but Klimov came to be admired widely, his reputation further enhanced by *The Adventures of a Dentist* (1967), and the much discussed *Agony* (released here as *Rasputin*), kept out of distribution for years by the censors. Klimov also completed the project Shepitko was just embarking on when she died, *Farewell to Matyora*; and Klimov's last film *Go and See*, about the sufferings of Byelorussia under the Nazi occupation, recently took top honors in the Moscow International Film Festival. Finally, as part of a cultural thaw under Gorbachev's encouragement, the Union of Cinematographers in May 1986, after sweeping the old guard out of leadership positions, elected Klimov as its head, with one of his first actions "to set up a commission to review films that had been rejected by the State Committee for Cinematographers."[15]

Shepitko's work too shows a level of engagement of the deepest parts of the self, and an unmistakable integrity in conveying that vision. Her sense of how an artist's involvement has to be total reflects an unsparing demand on the self, a view of the holiness of art, and specifically film art, that reminds one of an older world and is moving in its level of commitment. Also of particular interest in the short, *Larisa*, is Shepitko speaking of how her being a woman affects every frame she makes—an inevitable question because women directors are as unusual in Russia as anywhere else.[16] In Klimov's view, "Larisa was the only genuinely interesting woman director. With a lot of masculine strength in her hands." When I asked him why he thought the only woman heroine in Shepitko's work, Nazda in *Wings*, is strongly male looking, he responded, "Perhaps Larisa herself sensed there was some kind of danger of turning a bit too masculine in herself."[17] Shepitko herself expectedly speaks quite differently in the short, saying that women's attempts to imitate man's cinema are a failure, and senseless. She continues: "Women can tell the world amazing things," that no man can tell, of the human psyche and of nature. But at the same time she carefully distinguishes between being ladylike and being a woman.

There is certainly nothing ladylike about her work, about her attraction from the very first film to extreme physical states, to intense heat or intense cold, to severe vast sweeps of land (and in *Wings*, her second film, of sky). *Heat* concerns one of the farm communities being created in the mid–1950s in the Central Asian region of the USSR by official national policy, and was shot on the barren Kirghizian steppes where the heat was so gruelling that the film stock literally melted. Shepitko got ill with jaundice early in the shooting, but carried the film forward to its conclusion anyway, even directing from a stretcher when necessary, such was her determination. There is nothing ladylike either about her fascination with powerful machinery in *Heat*, which she can invest with a nightmare fearfulness, as with the thresher-plow relentlessly driven by an angry older man intent on proving something to the young boy who has just joined this band of workers in a frontier location. Also frightening in the same film is the way Shepitko works with the massive force of huge trucks, which play wild games with one another when the boy decides to go away, the man having succeeded in making his life miserable. Young as the director was at this time, she had a remarkable capacity for empathy with older people. Appealing, clever, and quick though the young boy/man is, the dogged, mean, worn and powerful older worker has the director's deepest sympathy. Shepitko gave an interview in Cuba in 1975, as part of the Russian delegation at an antifascist film festival, to a woman journalist who had never seen her films or even heard of her, and just interviewed her out of feminist solidarity. Looking back at her first film *Heat* at that time, Shepitko says it was a marvel of a virtuoso debut work for a twenty-two year old director to have made, but speaks of it as subverted by the fact that her feelings did not go in the same direction as the film's noble intention did. Jeanne Vronskaya, calling it a "cruel film about hard work and human conflicts," notes that it is "without the usual propagandist highflown phrases of the official press and newsreels."[18]

Shepitko's next film *Wings* (1966) is a full and powerful expression of the director, so much so that it created controversy and got little domestic exposure. It is the story of a woman not at one with her time, but of the older more heroic time of World War II, a much decorated war fighter pilot who shot down many German aircraft, but who—though she is respected by the local people—is out of sync with her own daughter and with the young in the vocational school where she is principal. Vronskaya comments: "Such a film naturally aroused a violent controversy in the Press: 'We have no conflicts between parents and children,' 'To show a war veteran in this way is to jeer at the war heroes,' and so on."[19] To a Westerner however, the expression of this theme is quite mild, even oblique, no doubt deliberately so. *Wings* at first looks as though it will turn for its central theme once more to generational tension, in which our sympathy goes not to the troubled and defiant young students in the film but to the older woman.

Klimov intriguingly told me of this character, "Larisa used to say, 'this character is my mother with whom I am still living together.' And she was right." A middle-aged authority figure, seemingly severe, worn out and saddened by a difficult life, she is another heroine it is quite impossible to imagine a male director building a film around, and it is not surprising that the actress, Maya Bulgakova, had had only small roles before this film and "was not likely to have a breakthrough" after it.[20]

The character, Nazda, or Nadezhda Petrovna, is in fact the only female central character in Shepitko's films. Shepitko in general gives women rather stereotypical roles in her other films, but this is an affecting portrait of a very capable woman, a flier, a national heroine, and her growing feelings of malaise toward the more mundane daily life of a school official, as well as toward the changing values of the larger society and its new, individualistic morals. Responsible, deferred to by all kinds of people, a figure of importance, she gives a strong sense of authority and also of humaneness, and of liveliness. She lacks delicacy, however, as in the gusto with which she butchers a gift cake she tries to cut. She conveys no conventional womanliness, giving up on cooking to eat in restaurants because she won't spend her Sundays peeling potatoes; or wearing man-tailored suit jackets and hair so mannish in styling that her gender periodically is ambiguous. Yet to Shepitko and to us she is without question an attractive woman. Shepitko has no trouble seeing her as a love object, though to a dry-as-dust, ancient-bone museum collector. Nazda sees herself too as a museum exhibit (and she is one, literally, for her flying feats during the war). In a lovely mixture of tones that Shepitko does well, Nazda at a moment of most lonely vulnerability can joke at her own expense about being the only stuffed hen in a museum.

All in all, she is given great personal appeal in the film, both before and after we realize that something is deeply amiss in her life. She doesn't get on well with her adopted daughter, whose love affair outside of marriage she frowns upon, and her loneliness becomes increasingly palpable, as well as her sense that her work, which is captivating for us to watch in various situations, finally has no real meaning for her. Throughout, her present is punctuated with marvellous interludes of sky images, of turning through vast expanses of sky and cloud formations. Only gradually do we realize what these interludes mean. On one level, they historically evoke the memory of another time when, as Nazda tells her daughter, she was part of a collective world governed by duty, where one couldn't pick and choose, a world that she affirms. But also for Shepitko the sky interludes punctuate the mundane with the call of something grander, they are a thrilling opening out—even when we don't know what the visuals relate to. Correspondingly, the bankruptcy of the woman's life becomes clearer to us, disguised earlier by her competence and energy and feisty zest for life. Her loneliness for instance is presented to us in a fine scene during which she goes to a bar to eat (where earlier she was told a woman couldn't come unescorted during evening hours). She talks warmly with the woman who runs the place, and then the two women begin to sing and dance together, waltzing among the empty tables and chairs. It is one of those moments that certain women filmmakers can create that are worth whole movies by others.

There are such moments in each of Shepitko's films, and a remarkable number of them. One of the loveliest in *Wings* is a flashback near the film's end when we meet Nazda's wartime love and fellow pilot Mitya (who reappears as the hero of Shepitko's next film *You and I*) and then watch a sequence in the air when Mitya's plane gradually descends, trailing smoke, and then crashes, as Nazda flies around him in her plane, like a partner bird, anguished but helpless. But the most powerful parts of Shepitko's films are her endings. *Wings* ends with Nazda wandering around the airfield, exchanging an intense momentary look with a passing young girl pilot, perhaps the girl she once was; mounting a plane, with middle-aged difficulty; and later becoming the center of playful celebration of the younger generation of fliers, as they push her along in the little planes. Then, in the midst of all the jollity, and as she sees the hangar before her and they all merrily call out "The Last Lap," she looks directly into the camera at us, an amazing moment, her eyes filled with tears, and gently shakes her head from side to side. She taxis the plane off into the fields and, wonderously, simply takes off. It is an astonishing ending, a poem, not an undermining of complexity, but rather, a transcending of it.

Still, for all its exhilaration—everything it means to watch a woman, especially such a woman, truly take wing—Shepitko's work is disturbing and with each passing film it becomes more disturbing, rather than affirming. Or if there is affirmation, it is of a strange deathward sort—the eeriness with which her work points with increasing urgency, and seeming acceptance, to the death that befell her accidentally.

Of her next film *You and I* (1971), which she wrote in collaboration with a fellow graduate of VGIK, Derek Elley noted that "the starting point for the film was the mental watershed reached by many people in their early thirties"[21] and he went on to quote, apparently from Shepitko herself, "The film is really about us—that is why it is called *You and I*." The film is built around a breakdown, of a sensitive looking, appealing doctor named Pyotr, played by Leonid Dyachkov, who suddenly abandons his post and his wife and takes off for the wastes of deepest Siberia, in quest of himself. Pyotr's story is told to us in complexly rearranged time chunks, counterpointed with a kind of liaison between his worried, chic wife Katya (played by the lovely Bella Akmadulina, a famous poetess and a former wife of Yevgeni Yevtushenko) and Pyotr's old friend Sasha, both intelligent, urbane sophisticates. Both men have compromised their earlier ideals and potential as neurosurgeons, doing research on dogs,[22] but there is also a deeper more personal sense of something gone very wrong, of life at an impasse. Derek Elley too writes, "After the Press controversy stirred up by her last work, *You and I* is both a brave and challenging film to emerge from the Soviet Union," and concludes his review: "*You and I* is in every way as fascinating and innovative as Tarkovski's *Solaris*, and signifies a major film talent in the Soviet Union." When I remarked to Klimov on the courage of Shepitko's following *Wings* with a film like *You and I*, and asked whether she fully weighed the risk, he said, "You know this is the path that she had chosen for herself and this is my path too. I know beforehand, well before, that I'm going to face a lot of trouble, and she knew that too. But I'm still doing that."

The approach of *You and I* is existential, not psychological. Pyotr presents himself to his friend Sasha at the jazzy start of the film toying with a gun; he then wanders off on an aimless lost journey. There is a profound sense of estrangement from others, and of everything gone haywire, despite some joyfully luminous moments—like a woman stranger offering Pyotr a motherly apple or he playing, suit and all, with a water hose with workers. His experience is paralleled by a harrowing episode in which his old friend Sasha impetuously volunteers to ride an Arabian steed at a circus to which he has taken Pyotr's wife. Totally out of control and in grave danger in the midst of circus merriment, Sasha's ride is in its desperation a metaphor for the psychic state the film chronicles.

But the most terrible metaphors are carried by two young girls in the film. *You and I* opens with a wonderful funny-sad sequence of images of caged dogs with bandages wrapped around their heads and other parts, related, we discover at the film's ending, to Pyotr's old medical research days when things were well with him. In his later work with patients, two young girl sufferers are vivid. One patient he is taken to by plane, to a remote loggers' camp, which allows Shepitko fine footage of a bridge being constructed over a powerful rushing river, footage that looks like it was dangerous and took courage to obtain. The earthy, witty banter with which the newcomers are greeted does not prepare us—and it is again Shepitko's skill to mix tones with this complexity—for the bloody sight of a young girl who has tried to kill herself and insists that she doesn't want to live.

More disturbing is an encounter in another infirmary, where again Shepitko catches us off guard by having the hero in a hurry to leave for a holiday and having to deal hurriedly with a number of waiting patients, including one who swallowed a spoon. In the midst of this, a luminous young girl's face appears, head shrouded with bandage-like hood, a sweet, gentle, patient face, whose skull x-rays tell Pyotr she is doomed. She stands and waits and looks at him and at us, a painful presence, as she touches a bit of snow to her forehead. The dread she communicates has to do with the length of the takes of the closeups of her face, and the tension of the accompanying sound track. (Shepitko in all her films relies on sound very heavily, and uses it skillfully, to convey troubling and also sanctified moments.) It also has to do with her silent waiting, her unspoken but obviously enormous need for help, when there is no help. It has to do also with the gentle passivity with which she stands—a moral reproach to the hero, who might have saved her had he been more seriously committed to his earlier ideals. But she also evokes some looming, inescapable horror on a larger more existentially suggestive level. As women in Shepitko's earlier films are often cooks and mollifiers, the two here are the wounded, the underside of the wandering Pyotr's plight, or the victims of his moral failure. In the final sequences of the film, Pyotr, participating with a friend in a hunt, collapses and puts a bit of snow to his forehead, echoing the sick girl. Shepitko concludes by filling the screen with the swaddled face of the same anonymous girl, looking at us in intense closeup that is held and held. It is a moment that speaks on a disturbing visceral level, without anger, rather an acceptance—or at least an endurance—of pain and death. This figure leads directly to the saintly soldier in *The Ascent*, and though it derives from traditions of Christian endurance in Russian culture, it is hard—given Pyotr's profoundly troubled condition—not to speculate that the film itself may have also issued from some personal crisis. Certainly, though its hero is male, it expresses itself in a female language that to a woman spectator is searing.

At the same time there is absolutely nothing feminist in this director's films. With the large exception of *Wings*, she avoids the female psyche for the most part, and when she does deal with it, often does so as stereotypically as any male director. The dramas are mostly male dramas; the pain and the crises do not appear to be gender-based as Shepitko conceived them, or at least presented them; and whatever the power, control, aggression and boldness that went into becoming a great woman director in a decade, Shepitko's own vision turns more and more, it would seem, toward a saintly yielding up of oneself, as with the saintly wounded soldier reconciled to death in her last film.

*You and I*, Shepitko's one film in color, and radiant color at that, is also her first film that shows a heavy influence of Western filmmaking styles, perhaps one reason it was much praised at the Venice Film Festival but got little exposure in the Soviet Union. With *The Ascent*, the film that brought her most strongly to Western attention, Shepitko goes back to ur-Russian materials, World War II sufferings, a genre that has had strong appeal for Soviet filmmakers during various periods, tapping as it does into powerful emotions, enormous communal tribulations, heroic efforts, national solidarity.[23] Indeed, Shepitko's very last film, *Farewell to Matyora*, which she had just begun shooting when she died, involved a similar kind of choice—of an island community having to deal with the state's decision to create a hydroelectric plant on their island, thus flooding it and destroying their world forever. Despite outbursts of resistance and anger, they must accept the policy. What principally gets expressed is grief and an enormous sense of loss, so great that a number of the women, especially the central, weathered old grandmother figure, choose to stay on, and essentially to die, rather than leave. For the others, at least as Klimov made the film, there is a rejoicing in the blessedness of the natural world, and its indestructability—symbolized by an enormous tree, that endures despite all that officialdom can do to destroy it. There is also powerful anguish over the need to separate from all one has known and loved, to say farewell to it all. People burn down their own homes as they evacuate. With a subject matter that reminds one of all the passionate anguished concern of women over the destruction of the earth, in its feeling for a bleak and primitive but lovely natural world, and for elders, in its elegiac material, this film would have been a fascinating development of earlier concerns of Shepitko's. As it ended up, it is a testament by her husband, himself saying his own grieving farewell.

Shepitko's last completed film, *The Ascent*, chronicles the ordeals of two members of a partisan unit in White Russia during a harsh winter in 1942, with the Russian title of the film an allusion to the Passion, the Way of the Cross, and the Resurrection. The film focusses on circumstances of the most severe sufferings, from the first image unabated to the final one, images in uncompromising black and white more beautiful frame by frame than anything in Shepitko's earlier work. As the cold north was the setting of Pyotr's trials in *You and I*, here Shepitko creates images of snowy-woods terrain that simply stun. Among these are repeated frames of white blankness marked by the barest kind of patterning—which, along with their aesthetic exquisiteness, carry suggestions in their vacancy of a strong metaphysical questioning, even despair.

Shepitko considers not only individual suffering but how that impinges on others. The film begins with the partisan group, of adults and children, under attack—her focus here as later on people in groups tending to one another, sharing pitiful handfuls of seed, the only nourishment. Two men go on a dangerous mission to get help for the others, and the stronger, more active one—Rybkov—watches over the man with him, from simply telling him it is easier to walk in his footsteps through the deep snow, to rolling with him through snow toward cover after he is wounded. There is tenderness, loyalty, and shared hardship of the most severe sort. At the same time the very attempt to save the wounded partisan destroys other innocents: a mother is torn away from her helpless babies for harboring men she actually wanted no part of. Every face is strong and striking, every image equally so, and the cumulative pain great as we follow the two men, the young mother, and two other captives through a process of questioning, torture, imprisonment, and finally hanging. One of the others is a young Jewish girl with enormous eyes who tells of how she hid in a bush and was afraid to move from it even as the leaves fell off and seasons changed.

The five who are to die are unromanticized and fragile, but the compositions that convey them increasingly have the stark classic grandeur of crucifixion scenes. The wounded saintly soldier, Sotnikov, grows larger and more idealized as the film proceeds, his beautiful dark eyes increasingly suggesting another world. This evokes more and more dismay in his mate who, in a shift from his heroic behavior earlier in the film, becomes the spokesman for life at any cost, or at the least a fierce struggle to go on living. What is ultimately most disturbing about the film is not its unrelenting engagement with terrible suffering, but its assent to that suffering as ennobling (no doubt part of a strong traditional sense in Russian culture of suffering as redemptive)—and its coming out on the side of death, not on the side of struggling for life.

The prime representative in the film for choosing life at any price is a collaborator with the German Occupation forces, a figure of interesting intelligence, once an educated pillar of the community, now an alienated, disturbing figure, who in a religious framework would be of the devil. In his dark isolation he is starkly contrasted to the little group who have one another, as well as the sympathy, even tears, of all the onlookers of the town. Shepitko is interested in that kind of painful aloneness, which in fact later befalls the more active of the two soldiers, Rybkov, when he is spared while the other four are hanged, for his agreement to join the Nazi police. Sotnikov, the saintly figure, on the other hand, just before his death has a long intense silent final communion with a boy who watches him, intent and tearful, like his younger self, or like his replacement. The soldier who survives by joining the enemy has periodically throughout the film imagined himself running away but each time imagined himself killed in the process of trying to escape. The conclusion of *The Ascent* leaves him solitary amidst the enemy, weeping for himself in total anguish, alone in a courtyard near an open gate that leads into the countryside, a gate which he cannot go through.

Shepitko constructed this, her last film, around male figures of formidable, historic suffering. It was suffering she herself participated in, in very early childhood, through the war and the hard postwar years. According to Klimov, when Shepitko and her family were evacuated during World War II, her mother was wounded, and hospitalized, in a "very difficult hospital, for people whose wounds did not heal." Larisa, all of four years old, had to "support" her family by doing errands in the hospital, a place which must have presented a most traumatic experience of war suffering to the young child.

Perhaps after what was perceived as too free a critique of an older war heroism, at odds with contemporary Russian values, in *Wings*, and after the estrangement and breakdown of *You and I*, Shepitko may have felt it necessary to move on in *The Ascent* to the firmer ground of Russian patriotism and war sacrifice, with intense though unidentified Christianity intermixed. One still wonders about possible other, more personal sources of the pain in her films. One wonders too about what seems her intuition of her own untimely death, uncannily evident not only in the films themselves, but, according to Klimov, in a last interview she gave a month before her death.[24] "Only a person who somehow foresaw she was not going to live long could give such an interview." Klimov said that as she was leaving on the final trip to find a location, she said farewell to everyone but himself. "To me she said we will never meet again. When I read her interview after her death, well, I felt my hair move."

There is no question that Larisa Shepitko was a brilliant director, who might easily have gone on—would surely have gone on, at least if the Soviet cultural context permitted—to tell us on film, as a woman, in a woman's voice, amazing things that no one has ever told us before. There is cause to grieve that she couldn't go through the door that these films opened to her and, so tantalizingly, to us.

## VĚRA CHYTILOVÁ

Věra Chytilová was not only the only woman director associated with the important Czechoslovak New Wave,[25] but one of its most boldly creative forces. Peter Hames, in a recent book on that cinema, maintains that when Chytilová's films, largely unavailable now, can be viewed again, "she will be seen as one of the most radically innovative filmmakers of the sixties."[26] The great time for Czech cinema was a pathetically short handful of years, 1963 to 1968, with its full flowering occurring in the brief spring of 1968, after Dubcek came to power in January 1968, and its brutal destruction with the armed intervention of the Warsaw Pact troops in August of 1968. Its beginning was in fact ushered in—as Antonin Liehm describes it—by a special showing of Stefan Uher's *Sunshine in a Net*, and the simultaneous release, after endless delays, of Věra Chytilová's first films, *The Ceiling* (1961) and *A Bag of Fleas* (1962). These Chytilová films were soon to be followed by her first feature, *Something Different* (1963), which Liehm calls "one of the best films made in Czechoslovakia in the sixties." But already in 1967, before the great burst of uncensored freedom in the famous Czech Spring, crises were developing. A troubled critic at the time notes that "the strong stylization and extreme metaphorical character of [the] latest films [of Chytilová and Nemec] quite clearly break all the 'rules of the game' adopted by Czechoslovak filmmakers to date"[27]; and that the present crisis "manifested itself by the severe official censure of two films— Nemec's *The Feast and the Guests* [a.k.a *Report on the Party and the Guests*] and Chytilová's *Daisies*."[28] *Daisies* attracted great international interest at the time; Amos Vogel for instance called it "visually and structurally perhaps the most sensational film of the Czech film renaissance,"[29] and Claire Clouzot's *Film Quarterly* review of *Daisies* in 1968 proclaimed: "This woman, at 39 the 'dean' of the new Czech cineastes, has surprised everybody, including her compatriots, by making the most uncompromising and mature work ever to come out of the Barrandov studios."[30] In short, Chytilová was a major eminence of the Czech New Wave, her first films ushering it in, her most exciting film a major issue of its demise.

Chytilová came to film at a comparatively late age and after many detours. She set out to study medicine and "dropped out. . . . She was strangely beautiful and she even worked as a model,"[31] and then as a script girl in a film studio, where she decided that film was to be her future life. The studio gave her no help, refused to recommend her for admission to the Film Academy, refused her a scholarship.

But Věra Chytilová is, and apparently always was, incredibly obstinate. She took the tests without a recommendation, she was accepted, and she battled her way through. She finished school at an age when others were already teaching. . . . The studio never forgave her for achieving her goal against their will. They were never very fond of her. But she didn't ask for love. Just that they let her do her job.[32]

Joseph Skvorecky, in a recent article on "What Was Saved From the Wreckage" of the Czech New Wave, confirms Hames' statement that Chytilová "has personal enemies within the industry," and elaborates in explanation: "She is a woman; moreover an exceptionally talented one."[33] That women directors seem, like Chytilová, disproportionately persons of unusual strength, originality, force of will, and often integrity is no accident. One thinks of an early figure like Esther Shub (see Jay Leyda's article on her in Eren's *Sexual Strategies*)—her passion, perfectionism, the fastidious care she gave to the historic film footage she used for her collages, in startling contrast with the sloppiness and irresponsibility shown by male directors who used her material, pirating *her* work without making any effort to preserve or replace it. The uncompromising totality of Shub's commitment, or Larisa Shepitko's,[34] surely has to do with the kinds of obstacles each of those women, or someone like Chytilová, had to overcome before she could make films at all, a struggle that would only be taken on by a woman of unusual force.

And of course the barriers faced by Chytilová as a woman were many times multiplied by the political situation occurring as she was trying to do her work. Some suggestion of the cost comes through in Liehm's interview with her in the fall of 1967:

I'm catching it from all sides, but I still have trouble believing it. I am exhausted from all the commotion with *Daisies.* . . . So I haven't been able to follow through and see whether it might not be better if I didn't work at all. And not just me. A lot of things look like nothing, like ordinary obstacles, all sorts of nonsense. But they're not. When you look back, you suddenly see all the energy they robbed you of, all the time, and how little got done in the long run. Not much at all. And what for? . . . One wages a constant, eternal struggle with external conditions for the opportunity to work. . . . Maybe we're all washed up, but we just don't know it yet."[35]

After three early films, then three full features, and then the Russian invasion of Czechoslovakia in Fall 1968 and the crackdown that followed,

Chytilová was not allowed to make films at all for seven years. Though most of the prominent Czech male directors fled, she stayed on, as did Ester Krumbachová—the very highly regarded screenwriter and art designer with whom Chytilová often worked. Krumbachová tells Liehm about some French cultural officials in 1966, very enthusiastic about her work, who urged her at that time to leave at once. "I tried to explain to them, my roots are here, and they go very deep; and the roots of my work are here, too."[36] One can assume Chytilová stayed for similar reasons. After the seven years of enforced silence she began directing again in the later 1970s, with more unevenness of quality, lighter work done in a more conventional narrative style, but still interesting, and still feminist, in a series of films about womanizers.

As has been the case with so many women directors, Chytilová was married to a film person—Jaroslav Kucera—a top-flight cameraman, and the two worked as a team on *Daisies* (1966) and on Chytilová's next film, *The Fruit of Paradise* (1969). Chytilová's close collaboration with Ester Krumbachová—also on *Daisies* and *The Fruit of Paradise*—has continued even into Chytilová's recent *The Very Late Afternoon of a Faun* (1983). Krumbachová, a very influential figure in Czech cinema though not as a director, did in fact direct one film of her own, *The Murder of Mr. Devil* (1970), "at the moment when it was all coming to an end."[37] Liehm describes the film as a "sarcastic tract on the myth of maleness . . . practically the only really Brechtian film made in Czechoslovakia during the period."[38] The quality of the film is hard to determine, since it has hardly been seen at all. Hames reports "some disappointment . . . among those who saw her as the brains behind Chytilová and Nemec,"[39] but Freddy Buache in *Positif* regarded the film as a "penetrating analysis of the possessive relationship between a bourgeois couple, with Krumbachová taking the side of the woman."[40] He also remaks on "her dialogue, sparkling with intelligence [which] passes from corrosive attack to phlegmatic burlesque with an extraordinary verve," and praises the "inventive qualities of the known scriptwriter . . . found again with this new director who, if she can work, has not finished astonishing, enchanting, and provoking us."[41]

As for those who found Krumbachová's film a rehash of *Daisies*, though it is impossible to comment without being able to view the film, it is possible that the similarities simply reflect how closely attuned the two women are to one another in concerns and attitudes, and that their combined work comes from a central place in each one. In Liehm's interview with Krumbachová, (the only other woman, along with Chytilová, in a book of 32 male interviews), he asks her whether she believes "there is such a thing as a feminine approach to reality, to creativity." She answers,

The feminine temperament is, of course, quite different from the masculine. . . . We are still living as guests in a man's world. Naturally, this also implies a certain advantage for women, since we can laugh at the world made by men. . . . It's hard to define the woman's outlook precisely, but I think there's no question but that women are more spontaneous. They don't filter everything through reason. And yet they have brains . . . men and women take different things seriously. It would be good if all these traits could be more mixed up.[42]

In Liehm's interview with Chytilová, she describes the film she was then writing with Krumbachová, *Fruit of Paradise* as about "the unequal struggle between a man and a woman."[43] Her thoughts during the interview, as pointed out earlier, are all on work, the enormous difficulties even at that time of just getting the work done. "The most important thing is getting beyond yourself, trying not to work on something familiar, but rather trying to penetrate further. You don't really begin working creatively until you are at a point where you don't know, where you are finding out. Each step forward involves an immense amount of strenuous effort."[44] Even were one ignorant of the films themselves, hers is the language of a boldly original figure.

It is grim to consider what the clampdown must have been like for such a fiercely independent and resistant person; humor and irony are life-and-death survival instruments in such cultural circumstances. Perhaps the light assaults in Chytilová's recent work on male folly and sexism are also some small way of venting the grief caused by the repressive forces of the (male) state.[45] Though no doubt marvellous women's talents, maybe even genius, are wasted daily everywhere, and remain unexpressed here too, the vividness in her case of a fine talent halted in its prime—not destroyed, but severely muzzled—is painful to contemplate.

From early on, Chytilová's work has been involved with women, from her graduation film at FAMU, *The Ceiling* (1961), a strongly feminist short that reflects her own wayward career by positing a medical student who becomes a model, as Chytilová herself did. The "boredom of the model's life is repeatedly emphasized and seen from a feminist standpoint."[46] With obvious relevance to *Daisies*, some scenes show the "ritual application of make-up," and the conversations of fellow models, "superficial and materialistic."[47] Several modeling sessions "are linked in a stylized and elliptical manner as the backs of two male heads move from one episode to the next as though watching play in a nonexistent tennis match. The fact that these images of women for women are the creation of men is emphasized. . . . Even [the woman's] subjective thoughts are spoken by a man," all of which sounds quite remarkable in a 1961 film. Even more pertinent to *Daisies* is Hames' criticism of *The Ceiling* in terms of Chytilová's undermining the social criticism she is obviously making, and the critique of consumerism, by "a sense of alienation that the film conveys, not merely from work in a male-dominated industry but from society as a whole."[48] Chytilová's second medium-length film, *Bag of Fleas* (1962), "a hilarious description of working girls in a dorm,"[49] and the full feature, *Something Different*, which parallels the lives of two women, a housewife and a gymnast—for all their inventiveness could not, according to Clouzot, "prepare us for the shock of *Daisies*."[50]

*Daisies* (1966), happily available in the United States, is a film that resists summary around an overall unified idea, a total statement.[51] It works rather through a series of sequences, each one making its statement, individual lines and images blossoming beyond themselves. *Daisies* generates interpretations on many levels: a political and social level—having to do with the nuclear threat and the earth generally, and also with the specific Eastern European tragic context; an existential level; the level of aesthetic experimentation, a formal freeing inseparable from the rest; and, of greatest interest here, a feminist and/or female level.

Chytilová builds *Daisies* around two girls, takeoffs on all the cuties with sugar daddies down through film history, their brainless simperings and cavortings, and showgirl/gold-digger comradery. Yet Chytilová also invests Marie I and Marie II with charm and playfulness as they dance around an apple tree, walk down a staircase arms linked, in perfect unison, or bounce around watching a cabaret act, usually to wittily matched music. Chytilová often places their near-naked bodies on display, to please and divert, though with a deliberate Brechtian detachment that allows for little eroticism. She uses their Bardot-style cuteness while mocking it and playing with it (as the girls themselves also self-consciously use it)—their lightness a leavening for the dark vision of the film, which despite its exciting exuberance and inventiveness is filled with anger, nihilism, helplessness, despair.

Ending with the promise of greater disaster still, glorious feast reduced to chaos, pillage, and finally a nuclear bomb exploding, it is easiest to read the film, as do the critics who have commented on it most fully, as about silly, unscrupulous, materialistic girls who are uncaring, who have no objections to anything, and so create the destruction of the world. But the film contains much more suggestive resonances and ambiguities than that.

For one thing, notes of existential pain and alienation, as well as political alienation, are sounded throughout. The pair of girls begin by saying (Chytilová in effect immediately laying down the film's premises): "Doesn't get us anywhere. . . . Nothing gets us anywhere," intercut with some old newsreel footage of a building front falling down. But the girls' funny manner of speech and their silliness work against solemn moralism, portentousness, and so add greatly to the effectiveness. The various philosophic concerns the film voices, and its apparent moral import, come instead out of an atmosphere of play and high spirits. At the same time the opening stylization of the girls, like puppets or robots, along with the machine imagery— suggests (in addition to many other reminders of Chaplin) another version of our modern times.

"Nobody understands anything," they say, and again, "Everything is spoiled for us in this world." They refer several times to someone who said "What will become of us?" They state, "You're not registered, no proof you exist." They peep through a hole, see grass, and say, "Something but what?"—as if nothing at all can be taken for granted, as if the most simple things have other levels. This text, reminding one of Kafka or Ionesco or Beckett, has the resonance not only of the poetic or metaphysical—humans adrift in a meaningless universe—but of the special tragedy of Eastern Europe, but without taking a tragic, or even somber, tone, expressed instead through a sardonic carnival atmosphere.

That the film offers us no alternative women makes it tempting to generalize from the two Maries to all women, and to all men/women relationships. Hence the film seems to be saying not only that romance is irrelevant and absurd to such shallow using girls; it appears to view romance as ridiculous, and the whole human scene as idiocy, despite the call for defiance and commitment of the ending. Hence the girls operate like ciphers who expose the outside void of things and relationships, less culpable themselves than pointing to all the varieties of malaise.

Chytilová does lovely things with such familiar minutiae of female surfaces as the mess of objects that fall out of the girls' handbags, the search for a handbag conveyed only by restless movements in a room, the exaggerated putting on of make-up and continual primping in front of lavatory mirrors. Food too is of course a dominant unifying motif in the film's loosely episodic structure, having a special place in women's lives—eating disorders like anorexia and bulimia being women's illnesses. Female self-adornment is another governing motif, the trying on of bizarre items of clothes; at one point the blonde Marie is wrapped in a wire gate like a net stole, and the other Marie has dried, curled grasses piled on her head like a hat. The banquet orgy of destruction ends up as a fashion show.

Along with the continual inventive play on female self-adornment, the film brilliantly spoofs, and thus makes us highly conscious of, female masks and roles assumed in courting situations—especially in the sequence of three dinners the girls have in restaurants with three different men. Clouzot, viewing the two girls largely in terms of "devouring, gorging themselves," sees the film as "a series of fluctuations between gorging and de-gorging, a come and go between deluxe restaurants and ladies' rooms. Our entire civilization could not be mocked more brutally."[52] Nor male/female relations. During the first of the dinner engagements, the blonde Marie—comically without the slightest discomfort—commits the taboo intrusion of sitting down at the couple's table. She then proceeds to make incredible (and funny) demands for food, ordering with great specificity and determination. The darker Marie, who draws the men, plays at being demure, polite, flirtatious, behaving as women on a dinner date are expected to behave, though this is signalled to us as entirely a performance—while the blonde (Tina to the other's Gina in the first tableau) in her unapologetic ferocity and rapacity would seem the other face of the same Eve. The whole very funny sequence conveys a strong feeling of the Absurd. Also the girl's savage hunger and aggressiveness are full of hostility, for all the zany humor. The girls cannot be simply dismissed as silly things—functioning as they do as detached instruments for drawing attention to various realities—hence engaging neither our identification with them nor, nasty though some of their behavior is, our criticism.

Their interchangeable and also constantly changing names through the film confirm that they are meant to sum up various experiences, all different and all the same, and that the two represent multitudes. At the same time it feels too heavily programmatic to say that the film suggests that all relations between men and women are using ones, the men out for sex, the women in their turn out for getting as much as they can from the men. That the various men call the girls by these different names suggests that the men do not know who they really are. The men are even more clearly rendered interchangeable by the women's treatment of them; the two women in league together, getting rid of each man on a train, with funny variations. The fierce blonde's hostile questioning of each dinner partner as to what his wife's age is, or about his kids, draws attention to what the man is in this for, and so allows no sympathy for those victimized men at all, only remorseless mockery.

Even more audaciously debunking is how Chytilová renders love absurd, in the person of a lyrical young man who proclaims his grand emotions to the blonde girl. Sardonic irreverence permeates a "love" scene between the two, the Marie here called "Julie" by her suitor, the camera panning over rows of butterflies in cases, encased butterflies over breasts and pubis of the wooed girl, obvious emblems of sexuality as well as beautiful images (though prevented by the film's humorous nihilistic shrug from feeling arty). As her farcical suitor reaches for those butterflies of the girl's, her face registers horror, she says "I don't know what it's all about" and butterfly cases start slipping off the wall, he trying to hold them back. Later those love words come over the phone, disembodied, ridiculous and meaningless, the more so as we watch the girls not only ignore the phone but proceed with great deliberation and very long scissors to slice pickles and bananas. The lover at the other end of the line, oblivious to everything, continues to proclaim his feelings, which have no appropriateness whatsoever to the woman who is their object.

This scathingly scornful vision of the romantic, given the film's very high level of anger, easily gets pushed over into actual violence. The continual play with those huge castration scissors is both startling and funny, though partly also just creating a Marx brothers kind of anarchic mess. Destructiveness crosses gender lines with a mutilation and cannibalizing of one girl by the other—the two cutting each other's heads off, becoming parts of the wallpaper, lost in the environment, identities breaking down before our eyes, even the inturned violence of an attempted suicide. The desire to destroy is highly aestheticized but strikingly insistent. Let's do something big, one says, and they set fire to paper strips hanging from the ceiling of their room. After some outrageous act, one of the mannequin girls turns to the other and asks "No objection?" and the other answers, "No objection." Chytilová would seem to have made this film to assert her own profound objections, though even in her closing words she expresses those objections indirectly and ironically—perhaps the only way possible even in 1966—in dedicating the film to all those whose indignation is not limited to a smashed up salad. The smashed up salad on *her* mind is the world and its larger violence, both the world of the nuclear holocaust suggested by the final bomb image of the film, and her more particular Eastern European world. In this context, despite Chytilová's own pronouncements at the time of the film's release, it is hard to feel that all her indignation is aimed at the two girls, whatever their messiness, boredom, consumerism. It's all very well to say, " 'The smashed-up salad' is what the 'Daisies' produce; if they were governments, they would manufacture the bomb of Hiroshima!"[53] but the film's joyful high spirits and fierce rebelliousness set off wilder resonances.

The violence is expressed most fully in the final banquet orgy, culmination of all the food imagery. The food elevator that the girls go up in takes them first past a raw meat section, and then immediately after, past a full orchestra playing, like the range of our very lives. The intense whisper on the sound track through the whole scene of the assault on the beautifully laden banquet table contributes to the anarchic urgency. The girls fall to like rapists, breaking glasses, eating in an increasingly frenzied way, squeezing, tearing, finally throwing cream cakes at one another, rebellion as much as orgy (a Prague Orgy indeed). The reversal that follows, introduced in Brechtian style as a possible alternative ending, makes its own powerful statement. The two whisper that they must be good, be tidy, clean it all up, put it back as it was (of course impossible, not only the food but the broken plates). With great energy they in effect set about being good obedient citizens, proclaiming still in whispers how everything will be wonderful because they are diligent and clean. At this point Chytilová's scorn seems clearly revolutionary, at the thought that being a good citizen could possibly get you anywhere in a situation that is ruinous. Wrapped in bizarre clown-like costumes made of newspapers, hence clothed in official voices on political events, the two dutiful girls lie out like corpses to accept their final destruction. Obviously the mindless destructions and petty subversions of their earlier behavior are infinitely preferable to this accommodation, the film in effect offering only these two alternatives.

Those final moments—with Chytilová's dedication presented through letters typed to sound like gunshots, against a rapid panning over war ruins—conclude the film on a very powerful note of angry defiance, which works dramatically though it is uncertain whether it can be justified in terms of an understanding of the film as a whole. The film seems more nihilistic and generally destructive than the ending suggests, conveying a general sense of the worthlessness and futility of everything. The girls' having no objection may speak to general attitudes Chytilová regards as leading to destruction, but their simultaneous anarchy and destructiveness certainly could not be ascribed to a general population. Ambiguous too is whether the girls' disorder is a paradigm for the final nuclear destruction; or part of a revolutionary refusal to comply with the order of things. The film seems to represent itself in its conclusion as such a refusal, both for its formal rejection of realism, and its content.

There is no question but that *Daisies* leaves us with loose ends, out of the same improvisatory freedom that gives it its excitement and suggestiveness. Further, *Daisies* sometimes runs a risk, not unusual in Eastern European cinema, of crossing the delicate line between controlled (necessary) ambiguity and intellectual confusion. Moving back and forth from the zany to the disturbing, its techniques also link it to avant garde filmmaking. *Daisies* is the unusual product of three creative forces in collaborative high spirits and a time that permitted it: with Krumbachová's remarkable decor and dialogue, a brilliant sound track, and superb visual effects by Kucera, involving the continual use of cuts and jumpcuts to emphasize the discontinuity of the narrative, unusual effects with color filters, and other color and texture devices for the same end and many other ends, full discussion of which would in itself require a lengthy essay. And finally the film also remains a stunning expression of a remarkable woman director's sensibility—to which gender is a key aspect.

The way the film works with gender is perhaps the most fascinating thing about it—even in the female types on which it chooses to construct a paradigm of the largest destruction. On one level, while the film sees women as assertive and aggressive, their getting what they want translates only into greed, selfishness, destructiveness, something monstrous—with the only visible alternatives the older motherly matrons in the ladies' rooms who live on nostalgia and sentimentality. But with "No Entry for Women," as one boldly printed sign reads, and various pans of many locks on doors and No Entry signs, the film alludes to the fate of aspiring women, as well as more general grim Eastern European realities (before and, as it turned out, after the film) that have an obvious pertinence to its fierce anger.

It is also as if Chytilová were saying that even the most robotlike, bimbolike, commonplace-as-daisies kind of women, who in real life would never consciously parody the world, have within them a rage against the order of things, a central part of which is the male/female order—impulses here allowed free play. And as women, and women artists too, have often been constrained to deal with the personal, with love and male/female relations,

Chytilová too chooses to work through these (unlike the other important male Czech satires of the same time, such as Forman's *Firemen's Ball* or Nemec's *Report on the Party*) but with what a difference! She works with and through the fabric of female worlds, and the anger of gender relations, to rebellion against all patterns of proscribed behavior in a society that is not free. The remarkable achievement here is that the sociopolitical, existential, and metaphysical are all embedded in the female and male (which also has its own important reality in the film). The personal is yet again political, with a special savage edge peculiar to the Eastern European tragedy, all of it brilliantly interwoven through a woman's vision of the world, allowed full expression for only a moment in Czech history.

The last film Chytilová made "freely"—*The Fruit of Paradise*—was made with a dark cloud visibly hanging over her, as her comments to Liehm indicate. So it is not surprising to find Hames noting that compared with *Daisies*, this film "does not have the same passionate attack," and rather delights in "formal and visual beauty in its own right."[54] Built around the Adam and Eve story, focussing on a relationship between a wife (Eva) and her lover (Robert), a man who murders women and intends to murder her but whom she instead murders, the film continues the dark vision of man–woman relations in *Daisies*. Motifs of trees, like those of apples, recur like melodies through Chytilová's films, and this film closes with the beautiful trees of the beginning now "stunted and lifeless."[55] Hames notes that the film's "resolutely experimental nature has the appearance of a last fling,"[56] and doubtless his sense that the film evades an audience's understanding is accurate and the obscurity deliberate. Most painful is Hames' sense that the film's "verbal message clearly lies in Josef's [the husband's] comment that he does not understand anything, Robert's [the lover's] view that everything is a dream, and Eva's [the heroine's] wish to give up the search for truth. To search for truth . . . is to court death."[57] The full poignancy of this content, coming from the uncompromising and questing Chytilová, does not escape Hames, who drily comments: "It is, of course, a fulfillment of the biblical prophecy . . . but in view of Chytilová's earlier insistence on 'truth,' it could also be interpreted as a personal testament."[58]

As for *The Apple Game*, Chytilová's first film made after an officially imposed seven year silence—one cannot hold Chytilová responsible for the sad disappointment of that film, though it is a tedious, crude, and technically sloppy piece of work. Director Jiri Menzel (*Closely Watched Trains*) is cast in the role of the hero, a gynecologist womanizer, who is out to make each new nurse, who is having a heavy affair with his doctor partner's wife, and who lives with his overbearing Mom. The tone is sitcom—bedroom romps and goings-on in the labor room—without serious feminist content, and the technical sloppiness ranges from terrible lighting to a meaninglessly jumpy camera.

The exception is the wonderfully inspired, audacious play with childbirth throughout the film. From the opening, old Chytilová images of ripe apples being shaken off trees crosscut with babies' heads repeatedly making their amazing, bloody appearance at the entrance of life; a little rolling stand filled with two layers of infants stacked like so many sardines; the endless procession of huge bellies and poking stethoscopes into them to listen; and the mothers' cries and moans. The irreverent meat market quality of this presentation certainly demystifies the holy birth process (which Mészáros used about the same time powerfully at the end of *Nine Months*)—and certainly communicates the humdrum in-and-out-endless process of a childbirth clinic, perhaps also conveying a directorial mood of total life disgust. There's a free-floating mocking contempt in *Daisies* too, but the brilliance of the total effort there gives it a great life force and charm. But it seems unfair to even judge an effort made after a brutal government ban, and after how much pressure over her previous work, and the crushing impact of all that on the creative spirit. This is especially so when even to have gotten the film made, just getting back to filmmaking, Josef Skvorecky says, was a "triumph of the director's cunning and intrigue,"[59] though he also notes it is a Pyrrhic victory, given the restraints imposed.

Happily, however, in *The Very Late Afternoon of a Faun* (1983) Chytilová evokes again the theme of outrageous male treatment of women, and creates something with depth and power even within the much narrowed parameters that she is compelled to work within. *Faun* is entirely concerned with a middle-aged womanizer, and the series of women he moves through, all the while a dizzily moving camera—often jerking and lurching—shows green in a hundred ways turning to sere, the autumnal falling of leaves punctuating the film throughout. The repetition is not excessive, but instead builds a sense of loss, the poignance of time passing and mortality (a note already struck in *Daisies*). The remarkable thing about the film is again its complex mixture of levels: that it at once conveys the emptiness of such a life of conquests, of a procession of interchangeable women, and yet keeps the man human, even strongly sympathetic, with its sense of his aging and his acute repeated awareness that he hasn't done anything yet, and soon death takes it all away. Further, for all the ridiculous vanity of his pink shirts, white suits, light shoes, romantic flower in lapel—a bulky though attractive man who looks like an intellectual, with more than a little white in his beard—he has a winning bravado and charm that makes it clear why women are attracted to him. Beyond this, he has an appealing lust for life, a capacity for joy, even if expressed through woman-chasing. So though the film seems to agree with the final judgment of the girl who loves him, that he's a nil, a zero, an undeveloped person, and though it presents his pursuit of women as tedious and meaningless (and finally he experiences it that way himself), there is no small amount of compassionate good will toward him in this portrait, shot almost entirely from the man's point of view. Further, the alternatives the film offers are very unappealing. The hero's good friend is long married and acts his age, but is full of lecherous extramarital yearnings and voyeurism, is afraid of his wife, and in the end walks out on her for a mistress and new baby. So there is no model for male "maturity" around, and Chytilová strikes out in all directions.

The same complexity marks the most interesting of the hero's encounters, with a hippy-style girl, beautiful though the hero is also repelled by her odd clothes and dirty nails, as he elsewhere opts for the conventional. The girl speaks for a younger generation's fears of water pollution, of war, concerns that barely touch him. At the same time she gives off something nihilistically wild, with sinister possibilities of destructiveness as she waves lit matches around. She is like the still living spirit of *Daisies* in Chytilová, with a sadder, older part as well, embodied in the hero, full of pain about how little has been achieved. Interestingly, the Don Juan protagonist by this final section of the film, in contrast to the girl, looks gentle, old-fashioned, courtly—and in the girl's eyes, very old (though the film keeps distant from the various girls' points of view).

There is another woman in the film, the hero's boss, a woman who he went to school with and who is therefore exactly his age and a powerful woman of authority. He sees *her* as old, and unthinkable therefore in a romantic way. This theme has not been much touched on in women directors' work, and it is a sign of Chytilová's complexity that when she does deal with it, she makes the older woman not only strong but bitter and vindictive, no simple picture. At the same time there is an unmistakably sardonic mood in the film's conclusion when the hero is left to this boss, his own peer, who approaches in dark glasses like death itself. It is the final joke of the film, and indeed she *is* like death because she represents for him an acceptance of his age and his mortality, which all the rest of his life is a refusal of.

As the film is continually punctuated with falling yellow leaves, a camera poking into green places and showing them, with great beauty and energy, in decline—so too the camera goes repeatedly back to the roofs of Prague, panning with love over beautiful minarets and towers. Chytilová testifies that Prague is still there, and that she is still there, and still making films, and that in itself is immense. Someone seeing this film who had never seen her earlier work would—whatever the diminutions, the necessary diminutions, evident in this one—know that this was a director of size and originality. She survives and keeps working, and it is affecting to find in 1983 yet another film by these two women, as valiant an act in its own way as the bravely venturing innovation of the earlier films when that was possible. Indeed, a humanity and compassion is now evident, absent from the ferocity of the early work, perhaps reflecting the passing of time and its erosions, perhaps reflecting suffering and the reconciliation necessary for survival. There is at once an unwaveringly pure feminist scorn in this film, and a compassion for aging human flesh and spirit, anguished over what is unrealized—a multiple tone that is not jarring but rather a most touching vision.

Chytilová's most recent film to reach us at the time of this writing, *Wolf Hole* a.k.a *Wolf Chalet* (1986), has her trying her hand at a horror/sci-fi genre film. And whether or not one feels the film effectively develops its narrative situation, with its company of young people trapped in a mountain retreat, and their growing desperation, its metaphors again speak powerfully to spectators attuned to Eastern European realities and history. On the one hand the buoyant young people happily and innocently walk into a snare, told they are privileged to enter it. On the other hand, the older man who presents himself as leader of the group, who indeed looks like an intellectual, continually lies and deceives, as they increasingly become aware. He tries to turn them against one another, to get them to turn one of their number in; and the tension and hostility mount within the group, completely cut off from all communication in this barren place of snow and mountain. Chytilová continually cuts from the interactions of the characters to pans of snowy woods or icy expanses. More specifically, she crosscuts frequently from human situations to images of ice visibly thickening—the coldness and isolation intensifying moment by moment as the film proceeds. The young people are literally locked into this situation, with no escape route. A familiar Chytilová motif, food, marks the deterioration; hunger grows, nourishment becomes more impossible. Even more strikingly reminiscent of an earlier Chytilová is a pair of twins who speak in the cadences of the two Marias in *Daisies*, though here the two girls are unkempt, dressed in horrible colors, wearing thick glasses, one of them even deaf with a hearing aid. Chytilová's feminism is not apparent in this film. The evil force is an older man, and the heroic figure a defiant, highly intelligent looking boy. The girls likely to show strength fizzle out strangely.

The young finally make their way out, not by sacrificing one of their number, but by each sacrificing his warm cover for the good of the others, a touching image of communal caring in the midst of calamity. But despite the beatific, religiously suggestive music that accompanies this image at the film's conclusion, as someone cries out "saved," Chytilová's characteristically skittish camera makes its own sardonic final comment. The camera weaves and bobs toward the cluster of distant lights that the young people are making their escape to, presumably the community from which they originally came. But the camera's panning around only shows that small cluster of lights to be surrounded by more, apparently endless, bleak dark icy expanse.

When I interviewed Maria Luisa Bemberg and Chytilová's name came up, Bemberg recalled seeing Chytilová's *Something Different* in Argentina, decades earlier, and what the film meant to her: "You know that when I left the cinema my strides were like a giant. I felt so invigorated and so encouraged. It was a wonderful film. . . . I remember the effect it had on me when I walked out of the cinema and I realized that's what I want to do with my films, I want to make women walk with big strong strides." No one could call *Wolf Hole* an important film in itself, but coming from Chytilová, her latest letter to the world, it carries a special sadness.


## AGNIESZKA HOLLAND

Agnieszka Holland, born in Warsaw in 1948 and graduated in 1971 from the Prague Film School, is a director with a gift for interpersonal subtlety, especially of the painful sort. Apart from her own directing, she has collaborated on screenplays with Zanussi and with Andrzej Wajda, most notably on Wajda's searing *Without Anaesthesia* (1977). That film's powerful emphasis on the personal, the subtle intimacy with which it observes the destruction of a man, and his marriage, points to Holland's input, as well as revealing Wajda's usual greatness.[60] Holland's own outspokenness made it difficult for her to make films in Poland, and she speaks of Wajda's having protected her[61] ("Without Wajda I would not exist"), especially because of her earlier political activities in Prague. Now she, like so many other Eastern European directors, has moved on to the perils of directing outside of her native country. Although women are important to her films, feminism is not. When I asked her about women in film school and film work, she said, "I was always with men," but feels that for Eastern Europeans "in a film milieu, our enemy is censorship. And because censorship affected everyone, you were natural allies. So this has had a kind of integrating effect that crossed gender, a male/female solidarity."

*Provincial Actors* (1979), Holland's third film, made in Poland, is built around a double story: of a company of provincial actors putting on a classic Polish play called *Liberation*; and of the dissolution of a marriage, the husband an actor who plays the hero of the play. The use of a play (a great and revered national classic) within the film, though hardly new to this film, keeps before us eloquent formulations of the yearning for freedom, the scornful rejection of tyranny, the sense of darkness falling. Also effective is the idea of the bland smoothie of a director, straight from Warsaw and intimidating to everyone in the provincial company, who keeps cutting out the most telling and meaningful passages of the play, to the hero Chris' increasing anguish. One beautiful long shot shows Chris, a man with a delicate, sensitive face, whose sleep is disturbed by his days with this director, going out at 2 in the morning into a dark deserted park, rolling around on the grass, gesturing wildly, and speaking the play's words of freedom. Even though the theatre director, and another man who supports him and seems the head of the company, are stick figures, and there is little attempt to get inside them, Holland gets the chilling quality of an art, and a life, censored at every turn, the process muffled with rationalizations and justifying lies.

But the film is most interesting for the complex intimacy with which it deals with the troubled couple's marriage. Much of the film is shot in closeup, often very tight closeup, and though occasionally we are less than fully oriented to the context, Holland intimately enmeshes us in the fabric of her people's lives. The trouble between the couple is clearly connected to the larger desperation, the national plight that has half the film's characters heavy into drink. However, the unhappy marriage situation is viewed on a number of levels, among them the wife Anka's seemingly having had some high promise in her years at school and then having settled into the compromise of being a puppeteer for children. Anka's wild and strange emotions, at first appearing inappropriate, gradually become clearer. Holland beautifully captures the marital bitterness, though motivations are unclear, of two people who care for one another, who are interesting in themselves, but who are totally at loggerheads. She catches the cruelty with which they each know how to hurt the other, as she tells him he can't act or that as an actor all he can do is speak someone else's words, or his returning her words about taking brave risks by pointing out that all she's done is puppeteering. Holland finally shows the helplessness with which each of the pair is locked into his/her own despair, not sleeping together, hardly talking. The rage and misery of the outer and the personal world are inseparable.

Other little tragedies are interwoven, particularly a proxy figure of a victimized old man who becomes a correlative for Chris' final sense of despair and futility. As the film proceeds, Chris himself seems gradually to be having a breakdown, as does his wife. Though he ends up arguing that all ideals come to nothing, during the actual performance of the play he defiantly speaks the lines that the director had cut during rehearsal. The ultimate pain however is that such an act doesn't matter, will change nothing, that no one else noticed anyway. After his wife has left him and he seeks her out again, the two of them end up looking utterly miserable, clinging together in darkness, he becoming luminous only in reciting the great playwright's words about summer harvest, while she seems to sink further into darkness. The film closes in a very depressed mood, somehow excessive for what we are given, though what we are given is grim enough.

Holland works in other telling ways with the theatre world, which is presumably communist, although the director in the film is elitist and contemptuous of workers. He insists that the actors must trust him, though as a result of his cuts they can no longer follow the meaning of the play. A corrupt theatre critic whose good opinion is assured, demands to be supplied with girls and with a car to go a short distance, in the most spoiled capitalistic way. The one prop man who loves the theatre, and longs to enter it because of how it can be used to tell people important things, is wrongly accused of drunkenness and negligence. Holland presents a world where even on small, daily, seemingly unimportant levels injustice is rampant, and every questing spirit is quietly and casually squashed.

While the ideals and sympathy are largely bestowed here on the man, Chris, his wife is piercingly intelligent, and was thrown out of theatre school for the wrong mental attitude, though this is not further defined for us. She seems excessively upset much of the time, but her fuming fault-finding is clearly shown to be a displacement of her feeling that she is not heard by Chris, that he is only involved in himself—her "nagging" an index to much deeper misery. Her anger is finally such that she puts a razor to Chris' neck while he is apparently sleeping, a horrifying image though not a little sensational.

Holland creates intriguingly subtle moods and interactions all through. Her feeling for intimacy and at the same time for the largest human issues is Eastern European and also bears out von Trotta's notion of women's films as not separating the large and small issues, nor feelings from ideas. The film is not without problems, ellipses that may confuse, a little too much underlining. Its heavy debt to Czech films like *The Firemen's Ball* is apparent in little homely touches in the characterizations within the provincial acting company. But the strong things are very strong.

*A Woman Alone* (1981),[62] the last film Holland made in Poland, appears to have come out of a mood of great fatigue, disgust, even revulsion. The Poland of the film is an utterly dismal place peopled with cripples, endless queues that look like prison camp lines, poverty, terror behind every door, a sense of everyone at the end of his/her tether, and extraordinary meannesses—a place of grotesques. Holland speaks of the film in terms of the large percentage of Poles actually below the poverty line, and presents herself as speaking in outrage for those no one else will speak for, though the film would seem to come out of a darker place than that. But its heroine Irene is a touching figure, with a worn face that can light up in the rare happy moment. She staunchly struggles each day to survive, in a very confined domestic space that is one of several ways the film points ahead to *Angry Harvest*. Holland gives both films an excessively, though not inevitably, dark and sensational ending. (Holland says she pillaged this film for the later one, thinking no print of *Woman Alone* would ever leave Poland, the film itself never having been shown there.)

The heroine's livelihood as a mail-carrier betokens her doggedness, but her sturdiness is not sturdy enough for the load she carries, the special hardships of a woman alone, with a mean landlord, a savage school parents group, a nasty-spirited dying aunt, and her son's father, who beat her. The great redeeming factor, in a life piled high with disasters, is Irene's son—and Holland deals beautifully with Irene's tenderness toward him, her delight in his boyish aliveness and curiosity. But the film's ending has him waiting in a foster home for a mother who will never come for him. The final bleak disaster snuffs her life out altogether, at the hands of her lover who is both crippled and comically oafish (pitiable too). Along with Irene's other experiences of being beaten by men, even this delicate person turns out to be brutal enough first to strike her and finally to destroy her. Because both characters are life's castoffs, on the economic bottom, and the film is engrossed in very basic emotions, *Woman Alone* allows little play for Holland's complex intellectuality, which is certainly not true of *Angry Harvest*. But despite the basicness of the couple in *Woman Alone*, the yearning for flight that it records is powerful, as is the sense of a hopeless world killing the strong woman at its center.

*Angry Harvest*, technically a highly polished film, is about a Jewish woman on the run during WWII (beautifully played by Elisabeth Trissenaar) taken into hiding by a repressed, very Christian German farmer (brilliantly played by Armin Muller-Stahl) and the complex love affair that develops between the two. The woman is filled with the trauma of what she has experienced, as well as the terror of being caught. The film has a particularly effective and painful introduction, largely aural, of a mother urging her young daughter to jump from a train (on a journey clearly destined for a death camp), and to leave her doll behind, and the child's responses. Holland rightly leaves the connection between this sequence and the heroine indirect, understood by surmise and then by later allusions to a lost child—who perhaps jumped to her death, at her mother's urging in order to save her. To any woman who has experienced being a mother, especially in a politically precarious situation (as Holland herself has), no anguish could be more terrible.

Other opening sequences are equally powerful, especially of Rosa appearing out of the woods, in a fur coat, gnawing on some food like a ravenous animal, or almost unable to drink the hot milk the farmer gives her. The extremities of her preceding ordeal, conveyed indirectly, are related in words only once in the film—Rosa explaining her detachment in terms of losing father, mother, sister, child, and husband. She is alive only because she is asleep, she says, and if she awakens she will die, because she does not have the strength to feel. Holland dramatizes this mood of tragic suffering powerfully but also with a fine reticence. She is equally effective with moments of joyful respite, as when Rosa, living in basement darkness and secrecy, runs outside for a few moments, beside herself with joy; or later, when she hears music and dances and gets Leon Wolney, the farmer, reluctantly to dance too.

The film seems to give us woman-as-victim again, the cultural factors—Eastern European and Jewish—combining with gender-derived powerlessness. But though Rosa is entirely in the man's power, and increasingly obviously so, and though she finally is destroyed, she is viewed in the film as a very strong character, put through excruciating trials. The film also evades easy sexual stereotyping by having the farmer Wolney be an unusually nurturing man, who tended his ill brother and who tenderly nurses the devastated woman long before he becomes sexually engaged with her. He is also interestingly problematic in other ways in gender and class definitions, a complex character. Looked down upon as a nobody because he is poor, he has worked relentlessly to become rich. His avoidance of women and discomfort with them, and his tormented sexuality—guilty masturbation—make the relationship more equal, since it saves him as well as Rosa. Both the class and sexual factors also mark him as himself familiar with victimization and powerlessness. During a visit he pays to an old gentlewoman and her daughter, fallen on hard times, we see his flunky deference, as we do when this same daughter enters his life again later in the film—a person he never dared speak to as a young farmhand. So too Rubin, a desperate Jew who comes to Wolney trying to use his property to save himself and his daughter, once looked down on Wolney and his father, a groom of horses. While Rubin is seen very sympathetically in all the dignity of his desperation, Holland also gives us the moral and psychological complexity of Wolney's response as coming from one who was himself heavily victimized—though not grossly crippled like the male characters of *Woman Alone* or *Provincial Actors*.

The film shows a similar complexity in its treatment of the Polish attitude toward the Jews in their midst and the horror of their fate. It extends compassion to some Poles, who fear helping Jews lest their houses be burned. Others however are out only to make deals and profits, driven by greed, with no moral reservations; so, it is a carefully balanced portrait. Though the farmer seems truly to want no part of the gain, there is booty even he cannot resist. Having himself wanted to be a priest, questions of good and bad and of his own moral standing are very important to Wolney, and through him, to Holland, in the morally complex world she creates. Wolney is distressed that while others suffer, he enlarges his property, only to have the priest in effect condone and endorse his behavior. Wolney must also face the irony of being called a good man by Rosa just when he is hiding from her his discovery that her husband is still alive. Or the final irony that Rubin's daughter, to whom he gives the money he chose not to give Rubin, at the film's end calls him a good man though we know he is responsible for the deaths of both Rubin and Rosa.

But the film does not quite accuse him. Even in the case of Rosa's death the nature of his responsibility is not fully clear, as Holland loads the circumstances and prevents easy judgments. Rosa's safety in staying where she is *is* in question, while at the same time her removal does clear Wolney's way for a rich wife. Further, we can understand why that means so much to him, as well as knowing the stresses that have now developed between Rosa and Wolney. Still, his not heeding Rosa's pleas, as he did not heed the cries of Rubin when he too was in utterly desperate circumstances, is unforgivable. In the final exchange between them, Rosa pleading to stay,

Wolney insisting on her leaving, he stands high on the ladder above her, looking down, his boots prominent in the frame. His lusting after a maid between that scene and his discovery of Rosa's suicide is further accusation.

Even Wolney's deceiving Rosa into believing that her husband is dead, though he knows the husband is alive and hiding nearby, is presented as morally ambiguous. Wolney wants to tell Rosa the truth about her husband, but cannot bear to end their relationship at the start, and so refrains. As the relationship continues it darkens into Wolney's subtly torturing Rosa, playing on her fears in order to control her better—as she indeed senses—and mocking her for her "Jewish ghosts." With Wolney's behavior growing more overbearing, Rosa's vulnerability is more evident to us. In one sequence she rocks a memory of a child in her arms, telling her all the cautions and reassurances mothers do. The film then cuts to the train window of the film's painful opening, followed by Leon's yelling at Rosa for smoking and keeping a light on, and her feeling that he deliberately torments her— a sequence that layers victimization upon victimization, until Leon is finally reduced in his drunkenness to acts of brutal domination and humiliation of her. Still, the film also convinces us that his apologies and his love are sincere, no small feat.

Holland's treatment of people here as always is complex, comprehending the drives that place the pair at tragic cross purposes. Further, even though she is working outside of Poland, Holland is able to make the terms of this tragedy as much social and political as personal. There are also arguments about Jewishness, the farmer instructing Rosa in the true faith, Rosa stubbornly insisting that Christianity rests on Jewishness; and that compared with one crucified Jesus, WWII created hundreds of thousands of similar martyrs. Holland herself has a complicated relationship to Jewishness. She is half Jewish, though brought up without knowing this, her father having entirely suppressed his own Jewishness[63]—whether for survival, out of communist ideological commitment, or for other reasons is not clear.

The film also includes a resistance struggle, which poses yet another morally ambiguous situation. The fate of a priest's sister (another female victim), infatuated with the farmer and innocently destroyed by taking his place, raises questions about whether Wolney acted to protect himself or only, as seems the case, to protect his Jewish fugitive. The film's canvas, with all this moral complexity, is also aesthetically effective, especially for the sense of confinement. Themes of female enclosure are of course all too familiar, but the suffering at the core of Holland's vision would seem to be primarily that of a Polish exile, and hence to cross gender lines. There are a few weak directorial decisions, like following the farmer's horrified discovery of Rosa's suicide immediately with the coming of her husband to find her. (Holland has difficulties with endings.) But what works most wonderfully are the two-person intensities, marvellously rendered twists and turns of a relationship which is also, as almost always in Eastern European cinema, tragically embedded in history.

Holland has a large talent and intelligence. She is currently at work in Paris, where she now lives, on projects that seem likely to allow her to engage both. Since *Angry Harvest*, set in WWII Germany, received an Oscar nomination, she should be able easily to maintain her career outside Poland now, if she chooses to. While anyone familiar with the situations of Eastern European emigre directors knows that such translations are not easy, there is reason to be very hopeful for Holland's career. She is very young still, and it will be exciting to see how her work develops.

## NOTES

1. Some recent Soviet women directors and films that we do not get the opportunity to see: Lana Gogoberidze, *Interviews on Personal Problems* (1979); Iskra Babich, *Men!* (1981); Marina Babak, *Marshal Zhukov—Pages from a Biography* (1984); and Irina Poplavaskaya, *Vasily and Vasilisa* (1982).

2. See Annette Insdorf, *Indelible Shadows: Film and the Holocaust* (New York: Vintage Books, 1983), 129–33, for a fuller discussion of the film.

3. J. Hoberman, "New Kid on the Bloc," *American Film* (November 1983), 54.

4. Ibid.

5. From Hungarofilm, quoted in Harriet Halpern Martineau, "The Films of Márta Mészaros, or the Importance of Being Banal,"*Film Quarterly* (Fall 1980); 25; this is a good introduction that called early attention to Mészáros' work.

6. From a Hungarofilm Bulletin.

7. Interview included in the New Yorker Films press packet.

8. See the solitary reference to Mészáros in Ann Kaplan's *Women and Film*, 112.

9. It should also be said that being orphaned by violence is not an unusual experience among Eastern European filmmakers, many of whom lost fathers or parents (though usually to the Nazis and usually because they were Jews) in their early years. The work of Istvan Szabo of Hungary, for instance, from *The Father* to *Colonel Redl*, is haunted by removed fathers.

10. Ronald Holloway, *International Film Guide*, edited by Peter Cowie (New York: A. S. Barnes & Co., 1984); 341.

11. Holloway, "Obituary," *Variety* (July 25, 1979); 4.

12. Claire Kitson, NFT/BFI programme (June 1985), 10.

13. Jeanne Vronskaya, *International Film Guide* (1980), 333.

14. Jeanne Vronskaya, *Young Soviet Film Makers* (London: George Allen and Unwin, Ltd., 1972), 36.

15. *New York Times* (June 30, 1986).

16. This is true despite a tradition of female filmmaking from Esther Shub and Olga Preobrazhinskaya in the 1920s, through Vera Stroyeva and Julia Solntseva, to such current directors as Dinara Asanova, who also recently died prematurely.

17. Klimov continued about Nazda: "It is important that one's former trade, occupation, profession, leaves some kind of imprint on one's appearance. And that's what happened with this woman. During the wartime she was not only a pilot, she

was a commander. In the postwar life, in peacetime, she also continued to be a commanding woman. Larisa emphasized her masculine features from the very beginning."

18. Vronskaya, *Young Soviet Film Makers*, 38.

19. Ibid., 39.

20. Ibid.

21. Derek Elley, *International Film Guide*, 355.

22. Klimov renders the film entirely in these terms, in my view reducing the power of it and making it something smaller and moralistic—perhaps reflecting a pressure in Soviet film to make anguish social and not privatistic, personal, existential.

23. According to "Soviet Cinema of the Great Patriotic War," an unpublished paper by Louis Menashe, "so powerful is the collective memory of the war," so deeply integrated into the national psyche were the sufferings, that it remained a central trauma even of those born later. In her anthology of women's recollections of the conflict, *War Does Not Have A Woman's Face*, Svetlana Alexeyevich notes that almost every Russian lost family members.

24. Klimov is in process of publishing this interview and other material about Shepitko in a book.

25. With the partial exception of her friend and collaborator Ester Krumbachova, who made one film.

26. Peter Hames, *The Czechoslovak New Wave* (Berkeley: University of California Press, 1985), 206.

27. Jan Zalman, "Question Marks on the New Czechoslovak Cinema," *Film Quarterly* (Winter 1967), 20.

28. Ibid.

29. Amos Vogel, *Film as a Subversive Art* (New York: Random House, 1974), 141.

30. Claire Clouzot, "Daisies," *Film Quarterly* (Spring 1968); 35.

31. Antonin Liehm, *Closely Watched Films* (White Plains, NY: International Arts and Sciences Press, 1974), 241.

32. Ibid., 242.

33. Joseph Skvorecky, "What Was Saved From the Wreckage," *Sight and Sound* (Autumn 1986), 278–81.

34. Also see descriptions of Leni Riefenstahl at work, ordering "ramps, towers, and bridges built for her camera positions.... She would tell them what to shoot and how and why.... 'She would rush around from one cameraman to the other like a maniac.' " And at the end of a sixteen-hour day on *Olympia*, "she would get the whole gang together around a big table. We were all falling asleep. She had been with us all day long. But that woman was full of energy. She would assign you to your position.... go into minute detail." Henry Jaworsky, interviewed by Gordon Hitchens, Kirk Bond, and John Hanhardt, *Film Culture* 56–57 (Spring 1973), 122.

35. Liehm, *Trains*, 243.

36. Ibid.

37. Liehm, Mira and Antonin, *The Most Important Art: Soviet and Eastern European Film After 1945* (Berkeley: University of California Press, 1977), 287.

38. Ibid.

39. Hames, *The Czechoslovak New Wave*, 260.

40. Freddy Buache, *Positif* 121 (Nov. 1970), 51.

41. Ibid.

42. Liehm, *Trains*, 281.

43. Ibid., 245.

44. Ibid., 243.

45. Cf. Makaveyev in *W.R.: Mysteries of the Organism*, equating Stalin with a large, erect penis.

46. Hames, 207.

47. Ibid.

48. For this film and others also unavailable, I am indebted to descriptions by Liehm and Hames. Hames in particular is very painstaking in providing detailed descriptions for this very reason, and though these are hardly satisfying substitutes for the films themselves, under the circumstances at least they give us some sense of the work.

49. Clouzot, "Review of *Daisies*," 35.

50. Ibid.

51. See Hames' similar response: "While *Daisies* is full of references lost to a non-Czech audience, there is every reason to share Skvorecky's doubt that the meaning of the film can be restricted to a parable on the destructive force of nihilism and aimless provocation. . . . Again, the moralistic idea from which it develops is but the starting point for a highly allusive and diverse superstructure" (p. 212).

52. Ibid.

53. Ibid.

54. Hames, 223.

55. Ibid., 226.

56. Ibid., 227.

57. Ibid., 226.

58. Ibid.

59. Skvorecky, "Saved from the Wreckage," 280.

60. One of Wajda's most powerful movies, the film works particularly strongly with the hero's rejecting wife and with her relation to an ambitious, competitive, insecure, much younger lover. Wajda presents a very painful political situation indirectly, through these personal conflicts—for instance, presenting a divorce proceeding as though it were a purge trial—all of which bears the mark of Holland.

61. Although Holland has also been regarded as the model for the Krystyna Janda character in both *Man of Marble* and *Man of Iron*, she herself says she was not.

62. The film was shown in the New Directors/New Films 1987 series with the title *The Woman Alone*, but according to Joanna Ney of the Lincoln Center Film Society, the title should read *A Woman Alone*.

63. Holland, thirteen when her father died, told me that he never spoke to her about Jewishness, never told her how his parents and entire family died (he himself survived the war by being sent by the Party to the Soviet Union), never even told her his parents' names.

# Notes on Third World Women Directors

While the numbers of Third World or Asian or Latin women directors are, as one might expect, fewer than in the West, what is surprising is that they are very much there, in China and India, even in Japan, the Philippines[1] and the West Indies—and that they are good. The following chapter is intended only to give a very introductory sense of the diversity of women's film projects, in cultures with widely varying levels of cinematic sophistication, and very different levels of treatment of women. These are sometimes inversely related—Japan, for instance, having perhaps the most highly developed film culture, and yet probably the most psychologically oppressive of worlds for women. Yet the Japanese woman director Sachiko Hidari chooses as subject the plight not of women but of a railroad worker who cannot comprehend new technologies, and the impact of his frustration and the family's economic struggle on its members and their interactions. Sometimes these directors choose not to make women their subjects—the West Indian filmmaker Euzhan Palcy in *Sugarcane Alley*, for instance, focuses on a boy's education, and the oppression of a black people. Often other social problems in these cultures seem more pressing than those of women, or there is a pre-feminist kind of vision. Maria Luisa Bemberg speaks of women directors as influenced by men to feel that politics is male politics, that anything concerning women is lesser, unimportant.

Still, for the most part here again the concerns do "articulate gender." The central characters are almost all women, often women on the margins of society, in the Indian films tragically so, in a recent Chinese film valiantly. Again, no formulas can or should be imposed on these varied experiences. I attempt to indicate briefly the nature of the film experience, especially since these are not all generally available films, and to indicate those issues—

from the historical injustice to Indian girl widows, to imagery of pregnancy or of a girl private eye pursuing a girl killer/victim—that reverberate as women's themes while also serving as genre-structuring devices. Whatever their limits, these films are quite moving, and often reveal truths about the daily world of the respective culture that more august figures of the same national cinema may not.

Most strikingly, these films do not feel parochial in the least to a Western woman spectator but entirely recognizable. Even at their most exotic, as with the nun-like renunciations imposed on child widows in India, they strike deeply resonant chords, speaking with remarkable strength to our own experiences across the differences of cultures. While, given the limits of space imposed on this study, it was not possible even to venture into issues of women's circumstances in each culture, much less the circumstances for women directors in each culture's film industry, it seems important to convey something, even if necessarily brief and sketchy, of the interesting things happening with women's filmmaking in those parts of the world, and to see that activity as part of a story that goes beyond American and European women's situations.

## *SUGARCANE ALLEY* AND OTHER BLACK WOMEN'S CINEMA

Euzhan Palcy's *Sugarcane Alley* (1983), an artful, gentle, and humane film about a poor black boy's education and coming of age, is also about colonialism and the victimization of a people—and more concerned with the general plight than with women's roles or visions. (This is also true of Sara Maldorer's *Sambizanga*, from Angola.[2]) Set in Martinique in 1931, the world Palcy presents is clearly one for which the director feels love and pain, of a poor, terribly overworked people full of spirit, communal concern, and often beauty. We experience this world through the eyes of an eleven-year-old boy, Jose Hassam, particularly in his relation to two old people, Mr. M, a storyteller, who delights him with riddles, folk poetry, folk medicine, and wisdom, and his grandmother, Ma Tine, who raises the boy because her daughter is dead. Ma Tine is beautifully observed and celebrated, though entirely without sentimentality, in her weariness from trying days in the cane fields, in her relaxing by rocking and singing and taking pleasure in her pipe, in her stern disciplining and her fiercely proud self-respect. Her insistence on refined manners, dreams of education and of a life different from working in the cane fields, is clearly what spurs Jose on. It is her ferocity of will, her proclaiming herself a fighter, that enables them both to carry forth this dream against seemingly hopeless odds, with no money and her old-woman declining strength.

The boy's brilliance rewards her tenacity. We see his classroom performance twice—the first a kind of celebration of life, the second conveying the bitterness of the lives of those he has left behind in his village—a double mood that is really the statement of the film as well, always framed by the gentle, lovely presence of the boy as speaker. He is not without mischief but loving and loyal to those dear to him, in his bright-eyed alertness and capacity for delight. There are affecting sequences of the boy's reactions to Mr. M's playful rituals, and the old man's fierce teachings of the history of black servitude, his yearnings for return to Africa, his anguished sense of being part of a misplaced people in a cursed land, abducted there by whites.

The secondary figures show energy, wit, and communal concern. One strong visual sequence, with a dignified, dirge-like quality, shows the community looking for Mr. M. with torches, all converging when Jose comes upon the old man's body. The other children are nicely conveyed through small acts of mischief. Jose's one good friend, rich and seemingly white, is the film's means of addressing the racial dilemma more directly. The boy's father, a white overseer who contemptuously forbids him to play with black children, even though his mother is dark-skinned, stings the boy into the one overtly angry political action of the film. The rich whites in the film are grossly caricatured, while blacks express a range of responses and values, above all a solidarity.

This debut film, made from a book about this boy, reveals Palcy to be an original, skillful, and affecting director. Shown at MOMA's New Directors/New Films Festival of 1984, Vincent Canby called it a "film debut that could be as important as any in the festival's 13 years of existence."[3] Doubtless *400 Blows* and other great French films were an influence on Palcy, who went to university and graduate school in Paris. Her work is tender but never soft, given the fierce things contained in her vision and the wish to serve as witness for a people. Where she turns next will be of the greatest interest.

Other black women's cinema—discussed here because of the strong international nature of the themes—has been less successful at this point in time. The struggle of black women for a cinematic voice is a particularly poignant, special case of the more general women's struggle, with all the added complications introduced by race, accompanying poverty, and, in the American situation, what the threat of Hollywood's inauthenticity means to a black woman director trying to be true to her own particular history. Also in the case of American and British black feminists, the important conflict between honesty to their own vision, and a sense of disloyalty to their men—in the past seen as needing their support differently from men in the dominant culture—is an issue finally being bravely confronted.

Particularly strong in its treatment of this material is *The Passion of Remembrance* (1986) written and directed by Maureen Blackwood and Isaac Julien, an intensely feminist and political English film focusing on a black

West Indian family living in England. The film moves back and forth from several stories of young people, to a running dialogue—actually argument—about black political activism, with exciting newsreel-style footage of various demonstrations, a film the Greater London Council and Channel 4 deserve credit for funding.

At the moment there appears to be no black American woman director on anything like Palcy's level, or on Blackwood's level, and no commercial black women directors at all. Perhaps the success of Spike Lee's *She's Gotta Have It* and Robert Townsend's *Hollywood Shuffle* may change that, drawing more black directors, male and female, into American feature filmmaking. A small body of independent films has emanated from students at UCLA in the early 1970s (also helped by the training offered through the PBS television magazine program Black Journal, from 1968 to 1971). Julie Dash and Alile Sharon Larkin, of this group, have directed feature films with intriguing shaping ideas and moments, though not yet fully professional skills. Larkin's *A Different Image* (1982), despite its technical inadequacies, works interestingly with a black woman's construction of her self-image as pieced together from images of African women as well as the women in her own U.S. family; and with her attempt to be a friend with a man, in a culture where maleness demands making women sexually and not seeing or even trying to see who they are. Julie Dash's *Illusions* (1982) ambitiously takes on classic Hollywood, working with footage from old newsreels, with old Hollywood sound studios and the movie business, to present the idea of a woman making her way into power who looks white but is really black, and who intends to put back into film history the black contribution to the American saga that the movies have left out.

## ASIAN WOMEN DIRECTORS: TWO PRC WOMEN DIRECTORS

Films by Asian women directors turn out to be more abundant than one would have anticipated. The Chinese situation is particularly interesting. Since the emergence of Wang Ping as a director in 1952, a small number of women directors have worked over the years in China but important changes have again taken place very recently. Indeed, in a paper on "China's New 'Women's Cinema,' " Chris Berry speaks of a symposium organized in May 1986 by the editors of the bi-monthly "Contemporary Cinema" in recognition of the "sudden growth in numbers and in prominence of Chinese women directors."[4] More and more women filmmakers are also coming to our attention from the People's Republic of China. According to one of them, Zhang Nuanxin, "There are maybe twenty or thirty women directors working in China out of maybe 300 overall. At the Beijing Film Institute, maybe one-fifth of the directing students are women, and that seems to be holding at a constant."[5] But sounding a less sanguine note,

Zhang Nuanxin then adds, "I have more opportunities because I'm able to work with my husband."

Chris Berry notes that not only are there over thirty full-fledged women directors making features in the Chinese film industry (an industry that now produces 125 features a year) but many of these have been major prize winners: "Out of 15 Ministry of Culture Outstanding Film Awards for 1985, fully 7 were won by films directed by women, a figure disproportionate to their numerical representation in the industry."[6] Among the women directors becoming known in the West are Shi Xiaohua (*Bubbling Spring*), a former apprentice to the famous Chinese director Xie Jin (who made it a point to train women in filmmaking), Ling Zi (*The Savage Land*), Zhang Nuanxin, quoted above (*The Seagull* and *Sacrificed Youth*), and Lu Xiaoya, who directed *The Girl in Red* (1984). *The Girl in Red* won China's Best Picture Award in 1985 as well as the Best Actress Award for its fifteen-year-old heroine, Zou Yitian. Its director, Lu Xiaoya, was born in 1941 in Hunan province, acted in her first film at age 9, went to acting school for two years and then went to the Beijing Film Academy to study film direction for two years. Before making *The Girl in Red*, she co-directed three films with her husband, Cong Lianwen, one of which, *In and Out of Court* (1980), was considered daring in China for its story about a coverup in high places.

*The Girl in Red* (*Hogyi shanou*) is a charming film that opens with a wonderful little girl running along a road asking an endless series of questions. The heroine of the film, the sixteen year old that the little girl grows up to be, named An-ran and nicknamed Ran Ran, gets into repeated trouble because she refuses blind obedience to authority, openly challenging and correcting a teacher who makes a mistake in class. She is different. Laughing at the mannequins in shop windows all dressed in standardized blue uniforms, she herself wears a unique bright red tunic. In many ways she also seems surprisingly like a girl from anywhere, a universal adolescent: dancing around her room to pop music; or, when her mother questions her closely about a bike outing with boys, irately replying that she won't be questioned about all her actions and crying out how she despises her mother. Later, she complains to her older sister that no one understands her.

But where the film gets unfamiliar, and a little chillingly reminiscent of, say, the Hungarian film *Angi Vera*, is when the class has a kind of self-criticism session with the teacher asking the students to say how they feel about each student in turn and to vote on their being "model students." An-ran comes in for criticism for being different, and for the red tunic, symbol of her energy and uniqueness. The degree to which the girl is stung by the censure and immediately takes to wearing something like what everyone wears, the film's intense concern with relationships and feelings— An-ran's for her classmates, toward her good friend, within her family— is something it shares with films by women from very different cultures.

An-ran's unusualness can perhaps be partly accounted for by her father's being a painter, and through the film he is seen taking great pleasure in her spiritedness and sensitivity. Among other interesting images of the family is the girl's mother's angry outburst at having to continue to do the menial things and be at the command of everyone, and how she is sick of it.

Despite some awkward timing and some naive cinematic devices, there are very winning scenes, as with the children, all little girls, saying various skip-rope rhyming poems. The film generally is charming and well done, and the interesting, bold girl at its center raises in her person a challenge to the whole country's working in unison. We see students' hands go up as a result of the pressure of the others who have raised their hands, an unpleasant consensus by intimidation and uncomfortableness—a surprising note in a film from a Communist country. When the girl gets a model student award only as a favor to her sister, she tries to refuse it—knowing that she does deserve it but not from the teachers' notion of a model student. She insists she can see with her own eyes, and the camera confirms the statement with a closeup of the eyes of this seeing heroine, the film ending as it began, with a mother and a little daughter walking away from the camera.

### Zhang Nuanxin: *Sacrificed Youth*

When Asian CineVision showed two recent Chinese films, both concerned with the time of the Cultural Revolution, in an Asian Film Series at N.Y.U. in the winter of 1986, one of the two—and the favorite—was directed by a woman, Zhang Nuanxin's *Sacrificed Youth* (1985). Both *Sacrificed Youth* and *The Girl in Red* indicate the new high level of technical proficiency in Chinese cinema, and its profound departure from the ex-aggerated melodrama of earlier traditional Chinese cinema. After a ten year hiatus in filmmaking during the Cultural Revolution, Chinese cinema is taking a new direction, one most appealing to Western audiences. And women directors have a major role in this exciting process.

*Sacrificed Youth* (China, 1985), the second film of Zhang Nuanxin, who graduated from the Directing department of Beijing Film Academy in 1962, and stayed on to teach there, deals with the decade from 1966 to 1976 of the "Great Cultural Revolution," a time of enormous social turmoil, death, and suppression, giving rise to a whole genre of literature called "scar literature"—and of films based on these books called "scar cinema." *Sacrificed Youth* begins with the arrival of a seventeen-year-old girl, sent from the city to live in a village of the Dai people, a minority people in southern China. (The northern Mongolian people that director Nuanxin comes from are also a minority people.) The film examines the gradual process of the girl's adjustment in her appearance, as she learns to make herself more attractive in the villagers' eyes by getting rid of her austere city look of braids and pants for the long skirts and upswept hair the Dai women wear.

She adjusts in her work, too, learning to do hard physical work, cutting down slender trees—and even learning enough doctoring from a medical handbook to save a dying child. Because this is a Chinese film, work has an importance and centrality in this treatment of a young girl's coming of age.[7] The family is a prime value, the surrogate family the girl lives with becoming much like her own family—particularly the old ninety-year-old mother, to whom the heroine shows most loving and deferential feelings—as the family also treats her like a daughter, the uncle looking for her at length after she leaves, the whole village worrying about her when she gets lost after work.

The film works with the difference between the Han majority people and the Dai, with their freeness, the young women swimming naked and singing flirting and courting songs to the young men, people saying and showing what they feel. The heroine becomes friends with a Han boy, also from the city and terribly unhappy to be where he is, and the two speak of their difference in the world in which they find themselves. The film is not political, in fact moves away from the harshness of the general events of the time to a faraway place of gentleness and beauty, though the film's end is abruptly bleak. A sudden mudslide buries both the Dai community and the Han boy who so yearned to leave, one more metaphor for sacrificed youth.

The emphasis on physical appearance—the girls queuing up and having to pay for one brief full length look at themselves in a long mirror—seems very Western, though it also relates to the Dai/Han difference the film revolves around. The girl experiences a range of emotions, even a surprisingly strong sense of sexual attraction, though while flirting, she holds men off in ways reminiscent of the United States of the 1940s and 1950s. The girls talk a great deal among themselves about adornment, and the heroine feels jealousy of the most beautiful one. But the film seems finally to be concerned with homelessness, displacement—more perhaps a function of the director's being Mongolian than of her being a woman. Only girls do the tree-cutting work. The film also draws attention to the fact that only girls do water carrying in that community, and that before the heroine arrives, the uncle did it, but would have been devastated had anyone seen him. The film offers an intriguing glimpse into a very different world, a world highly differentiated by gender, but also marked by extraordinary gains for women directors in a very young and very rapidly developing Chinese film industry.

Both of these films are clearly part of the same climate for changed ideas and more openness, emanating largely from the graduates of the Beijing Film academy, closed for twelve years by the "Cultural Revolution" and reopened in 1978. Tony Rayns speaks of these "fifth-generation" filmmakers as a uniquely positioned group, who "came to the academy with very particular experiences behind them," of formal education curtailed, "forced to spend years labouring in rural backwaters,"[8] an experience recorded in *Sacrificed Youth*. This group, as well as "revitalised 'fourth generation' directors," has brought us a new Chinese cinema, fragile and endangered but fascinating, in which women directors have played an important part.[9]

## A HONG KONG WOMAN DIRECTOR: ANN HUI'S *SECRETS*

Ann Hui is one of the most productive of Chinese directors now, born in Northeast China in 1947, educated in Hong Kong, for two years at the London Film School. Her TV work on the plight of the Vietnamese refugees arriving in Hong Kong in great numbers went into the making of *Boat People*, Hui's fourth feature film, found to be crudely melodramatic and disturbingly violent by some, but as exhibiting an enormously forceful talent by others. Hui herself argues that the violence was mild compared to the realities of refugee sufferings. Costing $3.5 million to make, with the help of a Chinese co-production, the film was a big box office success in Hong Kong.[10]

Ann Hui's first theatrical film, *Secrets* (1979), a noir murder mystery made well before *Boat People*, reveals a professionalism from the first, and a commercial talent, as well as suggestive material relating to women. The camera is slick and quickly-paced, with fancy overhead shots, geared for a highly commercial genre, dark sex/violence sensational mystery. The film begins intriguingly like a female takeoff of *The Godfather*, with a blind Chinese grandmother. It gives us a horrible killing, it toys with ghosts and other superstitions, and it ends up a lurid and perfectly modern story about a love triangle: a discarded pregnant girl's jealousy of the other woman, and the subsequent murders of both lover and other woman. A woman friend works all this out, taking the old genre detective role; thus both the detective/pursuer and the killer/pursued in the film are women. The final horror, of a crazy boy's seemingly deranged mother wielding an ax, turns out to be the performing of a caesarian, issuing in the birth of a big, fully live baby, held up at the film's conclusion. The woman-dominated quality of the work (*Secrets* not surprisingly had women not only directing but as screenwriter, producer, and in other major roles in the production), combined with genre elements, made for an intriguing launching of Ann Hui's commercial career.

## A JAPANESE WOMAN DIRECTOR: SACHIKO HIDARI

Sachiko Hidari, the director of *The Far Road* (1977), born in 1930, had a long career as an actress, often in films directed by her former husband, director Susumu Hani. Hidari is not alone as a Japanese woman director—Kinuyo Tanaka before her, for instance, also came to directing from acting—but it is noteworthy that Joan Mellen, a strong feminist who put together a book of interviews of Japanese directors in 1975, included twelve interviews with men directors, and none with women directors. She does however include an interview with Hidari as an actress, and also interviews with a woman set designer and a woman film distributor/promoter.

While Hidari in the interview with Mellen talks repeatedly about the plight of women in Japan, she speaks of the false sense people have that the Japanese are rich, when someone serving a company for five years, with a university degree, only earns $150 a month. "Do you think a family can live on that salary? Someone has to kill all his personal desires and manage the household. Japanese women have done this year after year,"[11] an emphasis evident in the film Hidari directed a short time after the Mellen interview. *The Far Road* is radical in vision, compassionate toward plain people's lives, working with railway workers, the poor at the bottom of the labor barrel. Hidari is interested in union struggle, and how hard management made it in the past for those active in the union, and what happens to a man who can do valuable service but is instead passed over, bewildered, exposed to great stress and feelings of defeat by a technological advancement he can't deal with. It is an heroic theme, and though this is not a great film, it conveys to a remarkable extent the human pain involved. At the same time the camera gives a grounded attention to the growing daily stuff of life; it brings a sensitive attention to little children, and in one fine scene catches a glowing intimacy between a mother and her now grown son, achieved less by technical skill than through powerfully true feelings, as is the case with the film as a whole.

## TWO INDIAN WOMEN DIRECTORS: APARNA SEN AND PREMA KARANTH

Though India is one of the great film-producing countries in the world, topping worldwide feature film production, and though it is also one of the very few democratic countries to have been led by a woman, it has had only a very few women directors. Again these have emerged largely in the last few years, in the 1980s, and they have been confined to serious art films (though a few earlier Indian women directors made commercially and traditionally oriented films). The new recent importance of feminist groups in India may soon make even more visible changes.[12]

*36 Chowringhee Lane* and *Phaniyamma* are both first films by their respective directors, relatively young women who strikingly have chosen painful stories of outsider older women to tell, women living unconventional unmarried childless lives. These are heroines who even by non-Hollywood standards would be seen as unattractive as women. In India too a film like *36 Chowringhee Lane* is extremely hard to get financial backing for (in this case produced by Sheshi Kapoor, husband of the star, the late Jennifer Kendall). While the heroines of the two films are regarded as very sad because of elements lacking in their lives that render them solitary, each film asserts that an elderly woman, "spinsterish," set outside the family and apart from the usual draw of love and passion with a man, can still be of great interest for herself, with her own beauty, dignity, and admirable values.[13] Women looking at women, the directors view each woman with great compassion and, in the case of *Phaniyamma*, with a strong element of feminist feeling as well.

*36 Chowringhee Lane* (1981) is the first film directed by Aparna Sen, a leading Bengali actress who appeared in many Satyajit Ray films over twenty years, and who was raised on film, as daughter of a well-known film critic. Her film is about an elderly Anglo-Indian schoolteacher, Violent Stoneham, living a lonely life and facing imminent old age without close ties, who takes a young couple into her apartment. The schoolteacher, beautifully played by Jennifer Kendall Kapoor, is Anglo-Indian, a group that "always occupied a kind of no-man's land between the Indians to whom they felt superior, and the British whose customs, clothes and language they imitated but who never really accepted them as social equals."[14] Shortly before Independence, thousands of Anglo-Indian families, alarmed as to what lay in store for them, left India permanently to settle elsewhere, usually in Britain. The few who remained "clung to their old ways and found it difficult to adapt to the realities of a modern, independent India."[15] Aparna Sen modelled her central character on many teachers at the convent school she attended as a girl.

Her film can be seen as quite daring in an Indian context, for taking on the plight of an Anglo-Indian as its central subject; for its sexuality in an Indian cinema where characters don't even kiss, although the film in this respect will look reticent to Western eyes and although Indian cinema is also becoming a little more permissive; for the extra-marital status of that sexuality; and for the callousness the film ascribes to the attractive, upper-class, highly educated young Indian couple.

Miss Stoneham is an appealing heroine from the start for her sweetness and for her stoical suffering, even to her painful mounting of the steps to her flat. Her only living relative, Eddie, a brother in a nursing home, is senile and dying, and the gargoyles of old people she sees when she visits him are a forewarning of her own end. She teaches Shakespeare to young girl students who are utterly uninterested, and a nice touch is Sen's having her be a worse teacher than her young replacement, who can truly engage the students in the plays. The young couple to whom Miss Stoneham grants the use of her apartment while she is away at work—apparently for the man's writing but actually for lovemaking—develop a charmingly playful relationship with the older woman, and give her a feeling of comradery, even friendship. She is only undeceived after the two marry, set up a trendy affluent home with the chic young set, and entirely turn away from her.

Despite some melodramatic pathos, the film is memorable for a convincing and underplayed portrait of lonely and sweet old age by Kendall, perfect in her awkward, weary gait. And it is not only her sadness but her charm, grace, openness to delight, and a generous engagement with other people, that makes one care about the character. In the fullness of its empathy, it extends something of a daughter's pain, guilt, perhaps love, to its central older woman heroine—in a way reminiscent of Shepitko's treatment of the heroine of *Wings*. The film also gives us some incidental glimpses of Calcutta, quiet pans of homeless people sleeping in the streets or railway stations—as indeed we finally recognize that proper Miss Stoneham herself is one of the homeless. The film's box office success in Calcutta may make it easier for more women directors to follow.

Aparna Sen's most recent film, *Parama* (1985), not yet shown in the United States, concerns the "self-awakening of an upper middle-class middle-aged housewife."[16] The film raises questions about "the institution of marriage. . . . women without a choice, husbands who are uncaring, wives who sustain others emotionally but are often in need of emotional nourishment themselves. . . . issues [that] do not concern the typical Indian screen woman." Sen is credited with breaking away from stale treatments of women and having the courage to create "fresh and distinctive images"[17] of Indian women.

Prema Karanth, another of the very few women who direct in India, points out to a questioner that for a woman to survive in such a male-dominated field, she must "have tremendous self-confidence and strength of character. Weaken a little and you're done for,"[18] a sentiment not unfamiliar in Europe and the United States. The interviewer felt that Karanth, "like her character, Phani, is a woman of extraordinary strength and purpose. Orphaned as a baby, she grew up with her grandparents in a small village in Karnataka."[19] Passionately interested in theatre, she trained as a director, and has acted in film herself. She has also been married to a well-known filmmaker, B. V. Karanth, for the past twenty-five years, the two having started out as drama students together.

Prema Karanth's *Phaniyamma* is taken from a book by a woman biographer, M. K. Indira, who as a child saw the central figure, an actual person, at her house, and heard Phani's story as Phani told it to Indira's mother. *Phaniyamma* again has its flaws but is a strong film. Beginning with the image of a light in darkness, a woman is called out of her sleep to aid an agonizingly long childbirth—rendered not physically but through closeups of the faces of the woman in labor, the midwife, and Phani, who delivers the baby and saves the mother. Gradually we understand that Phani, a nun-like figure in white garb, shaven head draped in the same white, is herself barred from the processes of birth and lovemaking—with flashbacks explaining how she came to her present situation as a woman outside such human engagements.

Taken from school as a little girl to learn women's functions of prayers and housework, she is married at age ten but is to continue to live with her parents to puberty. However, the boy husband dies of a snakebite; and since she is now his "widow," the men in the community decide she must live an austere life, jewelry stripped off, head shaved, always in white. The shining bangles particularly beloved by the little girl are shattered, as her life is. We see her in her exquisite young beauty turned into a strange looking thing. Still, as her life develops, she is clearly loved by the people whose lives she moves through, who run to her with their troubles. By her own strength she turns an intolerable sentence bestowed on the most innocent of children into something fine.

The shape of that life is at the center of the film and makes it powerful. The image of Phani stripped of everything others seek, unwillingly but not old enough to even think to fight for herself, the sadness with which she as an older woman looks back to that younger self, the burdened way she moves as her white shrouded form and shorn head make her sexually ambiguous and outside of everything—there is a grief about this image, that seems to sum up all the ways women have been buried, have been turned into selfless helpers in their various kinds of captivities in different cultures, have tended to others and done without for themselves. Phani is the woman who is not allowed to ask for a life, who is forced not to want. Something archetypal in the image makes it rending, beyond Phani's pathos as an individual character. And the film is not only concerned with woman as a victim again. In its quiet, unpolemic, unsensational, and very disturbing way, the film is made, one feels, not for the sake of pathos but for protest.

From the opening childbirth the film focuses on experiences shared by women, as in Phani's support of a girl of another generation facing the same sentence and refusing it, though pitted against her whole family. Phani continually surprises people toward the end of her life by opposing traditional ways that are cruel and senseless, while everyone else mindlessly follows them. Her experience allows her independent judgments that those who live normal lives seem incapable of. These contemplations get larger, until she is saying to herself that no one has the brains to change the system. She has the courage to voice her views aloud too, unacceptable though they are to most people—although otherwise she is seen abjectly bending over to serve the man whose house she lives in and his visitor, and then sitting apart from them, like a servant, in a humiliatingly servile posture.

On the other hand, the younger more modern girl, who *does* protest her widowhood—going on to marry and presumably have another life, rather than to be seen as simply an extension of her husband, to essentially die when he dies, a walking living death—is too polemically conceived, as a modern and progressive figure of contrast. Yet the film is courageous in an Indian context where such practices are very much in existence still, and is clearly feminist in the way it establishes the alternatives now possible.

Societies where clitorectomies are common, as in Africa, or where it is not unusual for brides to be burned to death by the groom's family—as through parts of India—for not having brought enough dowry or for not being fertile, may be profoundly different from and alien to our own. Yet these films by women directors from those worlds, in which women— even if not subjected to mutilating or murderous practices—are so much more submerged and powerless than they are in our society, still speak to us eloquently, not of something exotic outside our experience, but re- markably of our experience. Apart from the sheer fact that a range of compelling films is being made by women in these societies, this more than anything else is the unexpected revelation these films carry.

## LATIN WOMEN DIRECTORS

These days melodrama—in the form of operatic, often gothic films re- lating to love, scandalous or illicit[20]—comes to us largely from Latin feature directors, the most well known of these Argentinian Maria Luisa Bemberg (*Camila*). The heroines of these lushly filmed stories often find themselves through illicit love at odds with patriarchal authority, either within the family or in other social institutions, like the church. Camila rebels against both, surrounded by hateful male authority figures (the nastiest of them her father) who function to lock up women's passion and sexuality, as they locked up Camila's grandmother, who threw the world away for love. The whole male power structure closes in on Camila for her action, which involves not only a woman's rebellion but also a woman's intensely ro- mantic sexual passion, an emotion that appears currently to hold little in- terest for European or American women directors, perhaps because the traditional definition of woman in terms of love is itself seen as captivity by many Western women directors. In choosing the forbidden love of her confessor priest, Camila however is placed in the active position. Her choices shape the destiny of the pair, with an inversion again in the untouchable purity of the man as pursued love object. (Venezualan Fina Torres' *Oriane* is another example.[21])

While Bemberg plays the lush melodrama more or less straight, Chilean Valeria Sarmiento in *Our Marriage* (shown in the 1985 New Directors/New Films series at the Museum of Modern Art) gives us a bizarre, overblown Oedipal drama about a girl whose adopted father becomes her husband. Striking visually and a send-up of soap opera, the film's sardonic tone gives it a strange under-the-surface explosive power that doubtless derives from anger, to judge from Sarmiento's more direct documentary *A Man When He is a Man* (1983), a strong feminist inquiry into the relations between men and women in Costa Rica. In that documentary men tell the camera how they come on to women in a constant, interchangeable, irresponsible pursuit of sex, culminating with two low-keyed interviews with men who killed their wives. Bits of pop songs and film clips all through the film celebrate love in the most extreme and exaggerated terms.

*Camila*, which was nominated for an Academy Award here and was an unprecedented hit in Argentina, is Bemberg's third film—her two earlier ones both feminist treatments of women's themes, *Momentos* (1981) about a woman's loneliness and adultery, and *Nobody's Wife* (1982) (*Senora de Nadie*) about a housewife who decides to abandon her home and begin a new life. *Camila*'s superheated romanticism and eroticism turn up in Bemberg's next film, *Miss Mary* (1986), in more subsidiary, reticent style, in the attraction between an older English governess (Julie Christie), come to work in an aristocratic Argentinian family, and the young son of the family, a delicate and tender youth. Bemberg's attempts in this film to link the family's dramas to the larger political world of the late 1930s and 1940s— and her individual characterizations and the portrait of upper-class life— could be subtler or more persuasive. What is effective and stays with one most is the extent to which the film cares about the women characters, from the malaise of the neglected mother, her authoritarian husband womanizing elsewhere, leaving her to play sad songs on the piano, to the two daughters of privilege, whose futures are blighted, historical figures caught in women's traps. The younger daughter is discovered making love and forced to marry the man. The older sister, observing this and struggling with feelings and thoughts that place her in opposition to her society, is defined as neurotic, placed in psychiatric care, and told to calm herself by typing out the names in a telephone book, a chilling paradigm of the busy work meant to keep women out of trouble.

The director's attraction to the young boy of the family, his beauty and his sensitive, uncertain, shy vulnerability—is yet another addition to the cinematic lexicon created by this new body of films by women. The boy here reminds one of the soft, gentle burning beauty of the young Jesuit priest/lover in *Camila*, a view of the erotic that one couldn't imagine getting from a male director. It contributes to *Miss Mary*'s truth that the boy and the governess both subscribe to the conservative values of the ruling class; they maintain and support the values of the family, as indeed such people would have been likely to do. But the lonely governess' character needs more distinctiveness than Julie Christie or Bemberg are somehow able to give her.

Bemberg's next film project concerns a historical figure, a uniquely gifted nun who chose an unmarried life in order to be able to realize her gifts, and who does do remarkable things only finally to be broken back into the shape of female martyrdom. With this project Bemberg will address what is a new area for her, a heroically strong woman. She also provides another angle on what history has done to women, Bemberg herself seeking to create consciousness where there was little before. Asked why it took her so long to start making films, the 62-year-old director speaks of her own growth of consciousness: "I had to unlearn everything I was taught in order to be strong and be a filmmaker. It's a common problem we women have.

I was married and had four children and felt my priorities had to be with them, so I kept postponing my inner voices. My first step toward realizing them was in getting a divorce. After that, little by little I felt free."[22]

Brazilian director Susana Amaral shares something of that history, having made her first film *The Hour of the Star* (1985) at the age of 52 after raising nine children, going to film school in Sao Paulo, and then graduating from NYU Film School. Her film, which she calls an anti-melodrama,[23] works not with upper-class lush romanticism but sad ordinary mediocrity and the unpleasantness of poverty. Her focus is a nineteen-year-old girl who is incompetent, ignorant, yearning, and yet human, life at a minimal level, "the unreflective, primitive woman in all women."[24] Macabea, the film's heroine, wipes her nose on her clothes, smells bad, takes sensual pleasure in the maleness and the odors of the men's bodies around her in the subway, and is associated with a red flower as suggestive, sexually and otherwise, as those Georgia O'Keefe painted. Again the film offers a woman's vision of a woman known from inside—and outside. The camera rests on sad drab garments hanging on a wall, or the little white barrette in Macabea's unwashed hair.

The man Macabea gets involved with, an orphan as she is, is also as ignorant as she but her deference to him, her tentativeness—to him and to everyone else—contrasts sharply with his macho swagger and vanity. Their encounters largely consist of her asking him a barrage of questions, drawn from pathetic stupid information she hears on a night radio talk show. Although he knows no more than she, he answers wrongly with airs of authority, or puts her down, or gets irritated with her for asking[25]—though because we see he also is a wounded, barely socialized being, we do not fault him. He laughs at the absurdity of her dreams of stardom, though he harbors equally pathetic, grotesque, and impossible dreams of becoming famous, a congressman. Odd couple though they are, from a very distant provincial world, they sound classic chords.

But more resonant still are several images of Macabea looking at herself in a marred mirror. She makes clumsy gestures at primping, but what she is really doing is confirming her existence—the irreducible self that we take into the world: the female selfhood, pared down to its plainest, facing its own image, thoughtfully examining itself.

## NOTES

1. Philippine women directors include Lupita Aquino-Kashiwahara, sister of the slain Philippine opposition leader, and media coordinator for Cory Aquino's presidential campaign; and 31-year-old Marilou Diaz-Abaya, who studied in Los Angeles, then at the London Film School, and made several films before *Moral* (1982), an "outspoken" film about private lives almost in the way of American soap opera. The film is structured around the lives of four young women friends, their struggles

for careers and their problems with their men—a combination of sociological documentary of current Philippine life and unedited gossip, at once crudely blunt and entertainingly energetic, with an interesting range of portraits of women's situations.

2. *Sambizanga* is far more directly and rawly about Angolan colonialism, made by a woman director, Sarah Maldoror, in 1972. Maldoror was born in France of Guadaloupe parents, studied film in Moscow under Donskoi, and was Gillo Pontecorvo's assistant for *The Battle of Algiers*. She collaborated on the screenplay of *Sambizanga* with her husband, Mario de Andrade, a leader of the Angolan resistance, about an Angolan uprising in 1961 in a country where 5 million blacks are governed by half a million whites. The film concerns a construction worker, imprisoned for secret resistance activity (unknown even to his wife), and ultimately beaten to death in jail. The film follows his wife's long journey by foot, infant on her back, to locate him, only to find him dead.

3. Vincent Canby, review of *Sugarcane Alley, New York Times* (April 22, 1984).

4. Chris Berry, "China's New 'Women's Cinema,' " paper delivered at the Society for Cinema Studies, June 1987.

5. This information comes from an interview with the director included in a book about Chinese directors by George Semsel, for Praeger, forthcoming.

6. Ibid.

7. A very different view comes out of an earlier Hong Kong. *The Arch* (1969), by woman director Shu Shuen, an older, more traditionally-oriented film, has as its subject a woman who, though she is rewarded for her difficult, hard-working, caring life by an arch constructed in her honor, at the same time is viewed as having lived an empty and increasingly desperate and unstrung life because there is no man in it.

8. Tony Rayns, "The Fifth Generation," *Monthly Film Bulletin* (the British Film Institute) 53, no. 633 (Oct. 1986).

9. However, lest one think all new Chinese films are enormously sympathetic to women and the equality of women, it is worth noting that a brave film like *The Black Cannon Incident* (1985), a political satire focussed on a male hero and, largely, his relations with other men, still obliquely suggests subtle patterns of denigration of women.

10. See Karen Jaehne, "*Boat People*: An Interview with Anne Hui,"*Cineaste* 13, no. 2 (1984), 18.

11. Joan Mellon, *Voices from the Japanese Cinema* (New York: Liveright, 1975), 202.

12. This is the view of Kavary Dutta, an Indian-American filmmaker, who also thinks that change is more likely to come through the Pune Film Institute than through the Indian film industry itself. Thanks in this section too to Udayan Gupta for his help.

13. Kavary Dutta speculates that the two directors were drawn to such outsiders because to be a woman director in India at this time is in itself to be an extraordinary oddity.

14. Rani Burra, ed., *Indian Cinema 1980–1985* (Bombay: Directorate of Film Festivals, 1985), 91.

15. Ibid., 93.

16. Burra, *Indian Cinema*, 95.

17. Ibid.

18. Ibid., 84.

19. Ibid., 83.

20. See Ana Lopez, "The Melodrama in Latin America," *Wide Angle* 7, no. 3, 4–13, for a discussion of the importance of melodrama for Latin American popular entertainment—and as a tool, particularly by politically-conscious directors, for accessibility to large audiences.

21. *Oriane*, also a melodrama, has a heroine held captive by a patriarchal, jealous father who actually kills her lover. Despite some hokey mystery, the film works, not uninterestingly, with time layers, three generations of women, and girls' sexual initiation.

22. J. Hoberman, "True Confessions," *Village Voice* (March 26, 1985), 52.

23. See Ruby Rich, "After the Revolutions: The Second Coming of Latin American Cinema," *Village Voice* (February 10, 1987), 26.

24. Mollie Haskell, *Vogue* (January 1987); 32. Haskell finds in the film "cinematic poetry."

25. A fortune teller advises Macabea to love women since men are too brutal for her, advice Macabea does not take seriously, caught as she is in the impossible love dream that the film shows as taking her to her destruction. However, the one other important woman in the film, Macabea's officemate Gloria, sacrifices Macabea to her own dream of a relationship with a man.

# Selected Bibliography

Abel, Elizabeth, ed. *Writing and Sexual Difference*. Chicago: The University of Chicago Press, 1982.

*Before Hollywood: Turn of the Century Film from American Archives*, edited by Jay Leyda and Charles Musser. New York: American Federation of the Arts, 1986.

"A Blow for Independents," *New York Times* (Jan. 27, 1985):17.

Buache, Freddy. *Positif* 121 (Nov. 1970): 51.

Burra Rani, ed. *Indian Cinema 1980–1985*. Bombay: Directorate of Film Festivals, 1985.

Burton, Julianne. *Cinema and Social Change in Latin America: Conversations with Filmmakers*. Austin: University of Texas Press, 1986.

Chodorow, Nancy. *The Reproduction of Mothering*. Berkeley: University of California Press, 1978.

Clouzot, Claire. "Review of *Daisies*." *Film Quarterly* (Spring 1968):35–7.

Confino, Barbara. "An Interview with Agnes Varda." *Saturday Review* 55 (Aug. 12, 1972):35.

Corliss, Richard. "Calling their own shots: Women directors are starting to make it in Hollywood." *Time* (March 24, 1986): 82–83.

De Courtivon, Isabelle, and Elaine Marks, eds. *New French Feminisms*. Amherst: University of Massachusetts Press, 1980.

DeLauretis, Teresa. *Alice Doesn't: Feminism, Semiotics, Cinema*. Bloomington: Indiana University Press, 1984.

————. *Feminist Studies/Critical Studies*. Bloomington: Indiana University Press, 1986.

————. "Review of *The Night Porter*." *Film Quarterly* 30 (Winter 1976/77):76–77.

Doane, Mary Ann. "Woman's Stake in Representation: Filming the Female Body." *October* 17 (1981):23–36.

Dozoretz, Wendy. "The Mother's Lost Voice in *Hard, Fast and Beautiful*." *Wide Angle* 6, no. 3:50–57.

Ecker, Gisela, ed. *Feminist Aesthetics*. Boston: Beacon Press, 1986.

Ellsworth, Elizabeth. "Illicit Pleasures: Feminist Spectators and *Personal Best*." *Wide Angle*, 8 no. 2, 46–56.

Erens, Patricia, ed. *Sexual Strategems: The World of Women in Film*. New York: Horizon, 1979.

Fehervary, Helen, Claudia Lensson, and Judith Mayne. "From Hitler to Hepburn: A Discussion of Women's Film Production and Reception," *New German Critique* 24–25 (Fall/Winter 1981–82):184.

Fernley, Allison, and Paula Maloof. "Yentl." *Film Quarterly* (Spring 1985):38–45.

Flitterman, Sandy. "Theorizing 'the Feminine': Woman as the Figure of Desire in *The Seashell and the Clergyman*." *Wide Angle* 6, no. 3:32–39.

French, Brandon. *On the Verge of Revolt: Women in American Films of the Fifties*. New York: Ungar, 1978.

Gentile, Mary C. *Film Feminisms: Theory and Practice*. Westport, CT: Greenwood Press, 1985.

Gledhill, Christine, and E. Ann Kaplan. "Dialogue on *Stella Dallas* and Feminist Film." *Cinema Journal* 25, no. 4 (1986):44–53.

Hames, Peter. *The Czechoslovak New Wave*. Berkeley: University of California Press, 1985.

Hansen, Miriam. "Pleasure, Ambivalence, Identification: Valentino and Female Spectatorship." *Cinema Journal* 25, no. 4 (1986):6–32.

Harvey, Stephen, "A Passion for Her Work." (Bemberg) *Village Voice* (March 26, 1985):52.

Haskell, Molly. *From Reverence to Rape: The Treatment of Women in the Movies*. New York: Holt, Rinehart, Winston, 1974.

Heck-Rabi, Louise. *Women Filmmakers: A Critical Reception*. Metuchen, NJ, and London: Scarecrow Press, 1984.

Herman, Jeff. "Just Like At Home." *Film Quarterly* (Fall 1980):56–59.

Hoberman, J. "New Kid on the Bloc." *American Film* (November 1983):53,87.

Houston, Beverle. "Missing in Action: Notes on Dorothy Arzner." *Wide Angle* 6, no. 3:24–31.

Insdorf, Annette. *Indelible Shadows: Film and the Holocaust*. New York: Vintage Books, 1983.

Jaehne, Karen. "*Boat People*: An Interview with Ann Hui." *Cineaste* 132 (1984):16–19.

Johnston, Claire, ed. *The Work of Dorothy Arzner: Towards a Feminist Cinema*. London: British Film Institute, 1975.

Johnston, Claire. "Women's Cinema as Counter Cinema," in Bill Nichols, ed., *Movies and Methods: An Anthology*. Berkeley: University of California Press, 1976.

Kael, Pauline. *When the Lights Go Down*. New York: Holt, Rinehart Winston, 1980.

Kaplan, E. Ann. *Women and Film: Both Sides of the Camera*. New York: Methuen, 1983.

Kaplan, E. Ann, ed. *Women in Film Noir*. London: British Film Institute, 1980.

Kay, Karen, and Gerald Peary, eds. *Women and the Cinema*. New York: Dutton, 1977.

Koszarski, Richard. *Hollywood Directors 1914–1940*. New York: Oxford University Press, 1976.

Koszarski, Richard. "The years have not been kind to Lois Weber." *Village Voice* (Nov. 10, 1975): 40.

Kuhn, Annette. *Women's Pictures: Feminism and Cinema.* London, Boston; Routledge & Kegan Paul, 1982.

Levitin, Jacquelin. "Mother of the New Wave: An Interview with Varda." *Women & Film* 1, nos. 5/6 (1974):63–66, 103.

Liehm, Antonin J. *Closely Watched Films: The Czechoslovak Experience.* White Plains, NY: International Arts and Sciences Press, 1974.

Liehm, Mira and Antonin. *The Most Important Art: Soviet and Eastern European Film After 1945.* Berkeley: University of California Press, 1977.

Lopez, Ana. "The Melodrama of Latin America: Film, *Telenovelas* and the Currency of a Popular Form." *Wide Angle* 7, no. 3:4–13.

Lupino, Ida. "Me, Mother Directress." *Action* 2, no. 3 (June 1967):15.

Markham, James. "Behind 'Men' Stands a Woman With a Sense of Humor." *New York Times* (July 27, 1986):19, 25.

Martineau, Barbara Halpern. "The Films of Márta Mészáros, or, The Importance of Being Banal." *Film Quarterly* (Fall 1980):21–27.

Mellen, Joan. *Voices from the Japanese Cinema.* New York: Liveright, 1975.

Mellencamp, Patricia, Linda Williams, and Mary Ann Doane, eds. *Re-Visions: Feminist Essays in Film Analysis.* Los Angeles: American Film Institute, 1983.

Modleski, Tania. *Loving with a Vengeance.* New York: Methuen, 1982.

———. "Time and Desire in the Woman's Film." *Cinema Journal* 23, no. 3 (Spring 1984):19–30.

Neale, Steve. "Art Cinema as Institution." *Screen* 22, no. 1 (1981):11–39.

Nichols, Bill. *Movies and Methods: An Anthology.* Berkeley: University of California Press, 1976.

Norden, Martin F. "Women in the Early Film Industry." *Wide Angle* 6, no. 3, 68–75.

Ostriker, Alicia Suskin. *Stealing the Language: The Emergence of Women's Poetry in America.* Boston: Beacon Press, 1986.

Pally, Marcia. "Object of the Game." *Film Comment* (June 1985):68.

———. "Come Hither—But Slowly: Dessert with Diane Kurys." *Village Voice* (Jan. 31, 1984): 52,62.

Parker, Francine. "Discovering Ida Lupino." *Action* 2 (1967):19.

Petrie, Graham. *Hungarian Cinema Today.* Hungary: Corvina Kiado, 1978.

Quart, Barbara. "A Conversation with Agnes Varda." *Film Quarterly* 40, no. 2 (Winter 1986):3–10.

———. "Bette Gordon's *Variety*." *Ms.* (May 1985):51, 53.

———. "*Diary for My Children*." *Film Quarterly* 38 (spring 1985):46–49.

———. "*Entre Nous* and *A Question of Silence*." *Cineaste* 13, no. 3 (Summer 1984):45–47.

———. "Friendship in Some Recent American Films." *Film Criticism* 6, no. 2 (Winter 1982):51–57.

———. "*Sheer Madness*." *Cineaste* 13, no. 4(Fall 1984):48–49.

———. "*Vagabond*." *Ms.* (July 1986):17.

Rayns, Tony. "The Fifth Generation." *Monthly Film Bulletin* (British Film Institute) 53, no. 633 (Oct. 1986).

Rich, B. Ruby. "Desert Heat." *Village Voice* (April 8, 1986):71.

————. "Good Girls, Bad Girls." *Village Voice* (April 15, 1986):89.

Rickey, Carrie. "Where the Girls Are." *American Film* (Jan.-Feb. 1984):49–53, 68.

Rosen, Marjorie. *Popcorn Venus.* New York: Coward, McCann & Geoghegan, 1973.

Roud, Richard. "*Cleo de 5à 7.*" *Sight and Sound* 31 (Summer 1962): 145–46.

Ryall, Tom. "Art House, Smart House." *The Movie* 90 (1981):8.

Scheib, Ronnie. "Ida Lupino: Auteuress." *Film Comment* 16 (January 1980):54–64.

Showalter, Elaine, ed. *The New Feminist Criticism: Essays on Women, Literature, Theory.* New York: Pantheon Books, 1985.

Sklar, Robert. *Movie-Made America: A Cultural History of the Movies.* New York: Vintage, 1975.

Skvorecky, Joseph. *All the Bright Young Men and Women.* Toronto: Peter Martin Associates, 1971.

Skvorecky, Joseph. "What Was Saved from the Wreckage." *Sight and Sound* (Autumn 1986):278–81.

Slide, Anthony. *Early Women Directors.* New York: A. S. Barnes, 1977.

————. "Restoring The Blot." *American Film* 1 (Oct. 1975):72.

Slide, Anthony, ed. *The Memoirs of Alice Guy-Blache.* Metuchen, NJ, and London: Scarecrow Press, 1986.

Smith, Sharon. *Women Who Make Movies.* New York: Hopkinson and Blake, 1975.

Spoto, Donald. *The Dark Side of Genius: The Life of Alfred Hitchcock.* New York: Ballantine Books, 1983.

Suter, Jacquelyn. "Feminine Discourse in *Christopher Strong.*" *Camera Obscura* (Summer 1979): 135–50.

Vogel, Amos. *Film as a Subversive Art.* New York: Random House, 1974.

Vronskaya, Jeanne. *Young Soviet Film Makers.* London: George Allen and Unwin, 1972.

Walker, Janet. "Psychoanalysis and Feminist Film Theory: the Problem of Sexual Difference and Identity." *Wide Angle* 6, no. 3:16–23.

Williams, Linda. "Something Else Besides a Mother: Stella Dallas and the Maternal Melodrama." *Cinema Journal* 24, no. 1 (Fall 1984):2–27.

Winfrey, Carey. "Claudia Weill: It's Her Turn Now." *New York Times* 1, 15.

Zalman, Jan. "Question Marks on the New Czechoslovak Cinema." *Film Quarterly* (Winter 1967): 18–27.

# Index

acting and screenplay-writing as route to directing, 95

*Adam's Rib*, 7

*Adoption*, 98, 194, 195, 197–200, 203, 204

*All That Heaven Allows*, 28

*All the Way Home*, 194

Amaral, Susana, 9, 255

*Angry Harvest*, 233, 234–37; woman as victim in, 234

*Another Way*, 79, 199

*Apple Game, The*, 227; and childbirth, 228

Arthur, Karen, 4

Arzner, Dorothy, 1, 2, 22, 23, 24, 25, 26, 32, 35 n.32, 43, 47; heroines, 23, 24, 25; male-coded clothes, 25; non-talking direction, 23; ties between women, 25; work, 23, 25; and Zoe Akins, 25

*Ascent, The*, 209, 215, 216–17

Bellon, Yannick, 154

Bemburg, Maria Luisa, 4, 5, 241, 253

Bergman, Ingmar, 93, 106–7, 109

Berry, Chris, 244–45

*Between the Lines*, 53

*Bigamist, The*, 27–28

*Birds, The*, 73

*Black and White*, 153

black women directors, 244

Blackwood, Maureen, 243–44

*Blot, The*, 20

*Boat People, The*, 248

Borden, Lizzie, 11, 14 n.20

Box, Muriel, 26, 95

*Camila*, 5, 9, 253–54

Canby, Vincent, 66, 80

*Chilly Scenes of Winter*, 51, 54

"China's New 'Women's Cinema,' " 244

Chinese women directors, 244–45

Chodorow, Nancy: *Reproduction of Mothering*, 5, 78, 84, 105, 106

Chopra, Joyce, 3, 4, 9, 72–73; adolescent girl, 69, 70, 73; daughter/mother conflicts, 71; family, 73; initiation, 72, 74; sexual behavior of young girls, 70, 73

Christa Klages, forerunner of Marianne, 99

*Christopher Strong*, 7, 24, 76

*Chytilová's impact on Bemberg*, 230

*Chytilová, Věra, 191, 218–31*

*Citron, Michelle, 11, 12*

*Cixous, Helene, 7*
*Clarke, Shirley, 142*
*Cleo From 5 to 7*, 29, 136–39; compared with *Vagabond*, 138–39
*Cocktail Molotov*, 145, 148–49
comedies of sex disguise, 76
*Conformist, The*, 31
contempt for women in Wertmuller and May, 30
Coolidge, Martha, 14 n.21, 74, 76, 77
Cornwell, Regina, 20
counter-cinema, 11–12
*Coup de Grace*, 96
*Craig's Wife*, 24
Cultural Revolution (China), 246
Czechoslovak New Wave, 218

*Daisies*, 136, 218, 219–20, 221–27, 228; and aesthetic experimentation, 222; the avant garde, 226; as a collaboration, 226; female self-adornment in, 223; female masks, 223; feminist elements, 222; food imagery, 223, 225; gender, 226; male/female relations, 223; nihilism, 226; scorn of the romantic, 224; sexuality, 224; violence, 225
*Dance, Girl, Dance*, 25
Dash, Julie: *Illusions*, 244
*Daughter Rite*, 12, 69
de Lauretis, Teresa, 8, 12
Deitch, Doris, 78–79, 81
Delorme, Charlotte, 95, 96
Deren, Maya, 95
*Desert Hearts*, 66, 78–82
*Desperately Seeking Susan*, 62–63, 64, 65, 66, 70, 74
*Diary for My Children*, 4, 70, 193, 194, 200, 204–8
*Diary for My Loves*, 194, 208
*Documenteur*, 5, 143
Dörrie, Doris, 5, 76; and authoritarian fathers, 128, 129; female masochism, 128–29; female road movies, 129; feminism, 134; filial anguish, 134; German male authority, 130, 133; girl's coming of age in, 128; male bonding, 134; violence in, 129
Dulac, Germaine, 6, 17–18, 20–21

early women directors, 17–22, 32, 33, 34 n.11
Eastern European state film industry: political restrictions, 192; supportive to women directors, 192
Eastern European themes in Chytilová, 222, 226, 230
*Entre Nous*, 6, 48, 79, 145, 147, 148, 149–50
European art film, 10

*Farewell to Matyora*, 210, 215
*Fast Times at Ridgemont High*, 75
female Billy Liar, 82
female bonding as a central theme, 6
feminism, 8–9, 37, 39, 76, 84, 85, 243–44, 249; corrupted, 90; in *Girlfriends* and *Hester Street*, 57, 58; in Mészáros, 308; in von Trotta, 93–94, 95, 96, 99, 102, 121, 123, 126; von Trotta's feminist cinema, 94
Fonda, Jane, 85
*Frauen und Film*, 95
*Fruit of Paradise, The*, 220, 221, 227
*Future of Emily, The*, 135

German material in Dörrie, 134–35; in von Trotta, 113–14, 118, 119, 120
*Germany Pale Mother*, 135
*Girl in Red, The*, 7, 245–46
*Girl, The*, 193, 195–96, 197, 199, 200, 201, 205
*Girlfriends*, 7, 8, 10, 44, 51, 54, 66, 78
Gledhill, Christine, 11, 15 n.27
Gorris, Marleen, 13, 155
Gottlieb, Lisa, 75
Guy-Blache, Alice, 18, 19

*Hard, Fast, and Beautiful*, 25, 27
Haskell, Molly, 12, 125–26, 127
Hawn, Goldie, 3, 82, 86; authoritarian fathers, 88; Barbie doll, 88; iron buttercup roles, 89; JAP, 87; other woman, 88; patriotism, 90; pop feminism, 90
*Heartbreak Kid*, 39, 40, 41, 42, 43
*Heat*, 209–10, 211
Heckerling, Amy, 3, 5, 75

Heiress, The, 194, 200
Hester Street, 10, 51
Hoberman, J., 192
Holland, Agnieszka, 231; complicated relationship to Jewishness, 236, 239 n.4; moral and psychological complexity, 235; relation to feminism, 231
Hour of the Star, The, 5, 9, 255
Hui, Ann, 248

In the Belly of the Whale, 74, 75, 128–29, 130–34
independent films and women directors, 10–11
initiation, male: 400 Blows, Sound of Trumpets, Closely Watched Trains, 145
initiation, female, 4, 55, 72, 74, 81, 82, 116, 128–29, 152, 208, 232, 245
Ishtar, 39, 40, 48
It's My Turn, 58–59
I've Heard the Mermaids Singing, 81, 82

Jacubowska, Wanda, 192
Jeanne Dielman, 5, 8
Jewishness and women directors, 51, 57; Jewish woman, 42, 43; Jewish material in von Trotta, 109, 116, 119
Johnny Dangerously, 75
Johnston, Claire, 27, 140
Joyce at 34, 9, 54, 68
Just One of the Guys, 75, 76

Kael, Pauline, 24, 36 n.59, 84
Karanth, Prema, 25
Kauffmann, Stanley, 97, 119, 159 n.5, 160 n.25
Klimov, Elem, 191, 210
Krumbachová, Ester, 220, 221
Kurys, Diane, 4, 78, 95, 145; autobiographical allusions, 149; and fathers, 148; and female dress, 147–48; and feminism, 147; and Jewish content, 150; lesbian love, 149; marriage, 150; sexuality, 151; women's bondings and friendship, 147, 149, 150; young woman's coming of age, 152

Lange, Jessica, 85
Larisa, 209
Larkin, Alile Sharon: A Different Image, 244
Last Stop, The, 192
Le Bonheur, 136, 139–41, 143
Les Creatures, 141–42
lesbian identity vs. female-centered identity, 78
lesbian love, 80, 81, 82, 84, 100; affirmation of, 82; erotically charged look between women, 147
Lessing, Doris, 150
Lianna, 78, 79
Liehm, Antonin, 219, 221
Lindblom, Gunnel, 4, 155
Lost Honor of Katarina Blum, The, 94, 96
Lupino, Ida, 22, 23, 26, 27, 28, 32, 95; experimentation with out-of-the-way film subjects, 26; male characters, 28; male wisdom and authority in Lupino's work, 26; marriage, 28, 36 n.56; as producer, 26, 28; women, "womanly" vs. business skills, 28

Mädchen in Uniform, 29
Making Mr. Right, 66, 68
Maldorer, Sara, 242
male buddy films, 44, 45
male gaze, the, 6
Man In Love, A, 151–53
Man When He is a Man, 253
Marianne and Juliane, 4, 7, 10, 94, 95–97, 101, 103, 105, 108, 111–12, 113–20, 124, 127, 130
marriage as closure device, 85
May, Elaine, 2, 9, 76, 95
—budget, 48
—cinema world of betrayal, 40; darkness, 40; hostility, 45; humiliation, 46; mistrust, 44; sibling ties, 44
—derogatory images of women, 40, 49; clumsy, 41; incompetent, 40, 41; insecure, 41, 42, 46; intellectual, 41; masochistic, 41, 46; needy for love, 42

—ethnicity, 41
—film noir, 44
—genre, 39, 43, 46, 47
—male point of view, 45, 46
—psychological orientation, 46
—showbusiness background, 39, 48–49
—WASP, 43
Mayne, Judith, 11
Mellen, Joan, 248–49
*Men*, 128, 129, 133–34
merging personalities in von Trotta, 104–5, 106, 117–18
Mészáros, Márta, 4, 6, 8, 78, 95, 149, 150, 191; and age, 197, the body, 197, 204; childbirth, 195; deviance, 314; and documentary filmmaking, 193, 197; and endings, 200; and erotic intimacy, 198; feminism, 202; friends, 204; heroines, 195; Hungary, 205, 207; lesbians, 192; little girl, 194; marriage, 203; men, 193, 202–3; movies, 205, 207; orphaning, 193; politics, 206; portrait of the artist as a young girl, 208; realism, 195; rebelliousness, 196, 207; sexual humiliation, 203; Stalinism, 205; traditional female domestic roles, 195; women in, 202; work in, 196–97
*Mikey and Nicky*, 9, 39, 40, 43, 44, 46, 47, 153
*Miss Mary*, 254
mother, the, 27, 69, 71, 74, 115, 124, 130
mother/daughter bonding, 107, 110
Mulvey, Laura, 11, 98
*My Brilliant Career*, 85
Narrative cinema, 12
*Never Fear*, 26, 27
*New German Cinema* (Timothy Corrigan), 93
*New Leaf*, 39, 40–42
Nicols, Mike, 39, 40, 47, 48
*Night and Fog*, 114, 117
*Night Porter, The*, 31
*Night Wears Garters, The*, 5, 75, 154
*Nine Months*, 194, 197, 199, 200–2, 203, 206, 207
*Not Wanted*, 26

Naunxin, Zhang, 244–45; *Sacrificed Youth*, 246

Oates, Joyce Carol, 69, 72
*Old Acquaintance*, 57
*Old Enough*, 66
older women, 4, 5, 156; older women friends, 155
*One of the Guys*, 75
*One Sings, The Other Doesn't*, 8, 98, 143
*Our Marriage*, 253
Ouspenskaya, Maria, 25, 39
*Outrage*, 26

Palcy, Euzhan, 241
*Passion of Remembrance*, 243–44
patriarchal ideology, 11, 25, 28, 113, 124
*Peppermint Soda*, 4, 8, 145–48, 151
*Phaniyamma*, 249–50
*Private Benjamin*, 83, 85, 86–87, 88
*Protocol*, 83, 86, 88
*Provincial Actors*, 231–33, 235

*Question of Silence, A*, 5, 8, 13, 66, 155, 157–59; female oppression in, 157

Rainer, Yvonne, 11, 15 n.29
*Re-Visions*, 11–12
*Real Genius*, 76, 77
"real woman" in *Yentl*, 85
realism, 11, 93, 195
*Redupers*, 7, 135
Reifenstahl, Leni, 50
*Return of The Secaucus Seven, The*, 53
Rich, Adrienne, 78
Rich, B. Ruby, 72–73, 79, 80
Rickey, Carrie, 60
*Riddance*, 196, 197
*Rosa Luxemburg*, 96, 97, 103, 105, 108, 109, 113, 114, 118–19, 126–27
Rosen, Marjorie, 17
*Rosie the Rivetter*, 87
Rozema, Patricia, 81

*Sacrificed Youth*, 246–47; young girl's coming of age, 247

*Sambizanga*, 242, 256 n.2

Sander, Helke, 7, 95, 135

Sanders-Brahms, Helma, 7, 95, 135

*Sarah and Son*, 24

Sarmiento, Valeria, 253

Schlondorff, Volker, 94–96, 127

*Seashell and the Clergyman, The*, 21

*Second Awakening of Christa Klages, The*, 95–96, 97–98, 99–102, 109, 111, 113, 115

*Seduction of Mimi, The*, 9, 29–30

Seidelman, Susan, 5, 10, 50, 153; and Barish, Leora, 65; budget, 65; codes of dress, 64; commercialism, 65, 66; friendship between two women, 65; humor, 61; men, 67; reverse-gender Pygmalion, 67; romance, 64; sex, 64; suburbanites, 63, 64

Sen, Aparna, 5, 250, 251

Serreau, Coline, 153

*Seven Beauties*, 29, 31, 32

sexual inversion, 75

sexuality, 5; sexuality between women, 80–81

*Sheer Madness*, 5, 84, 94, 96, 97, 101–3, 105, 107, 108, 109, 112, 114, 115, 118, 119, 120–26, 130

Shepitko, Larisa, 9, 95, 191, 219; childhood wartime sufferings, 217; and Dovzhenko, 209; Christianity in, 217; conventional use of women in 212; extreme physical states in her films, 211; not a feminist, 215; suffering in, 216; unusual heroine in, 211–12

Showalter, Elaine, 7–8

Shub, Esther, 192, 219

Silver, Joan Micklin, as a feminist director, 53, 54

Singer, I. B., 83

*Sisters*, 96–97, 102–13, 114, 115, 118, 120, 126

Slide, Anthony, 18–19, 20

*Smiling Madame Beudet, The*, 6, 20

*Smithereens*, 7, 8, 10, 60–65; and *Desperately Seeking Susan*, 63, 134; and Doris Dörrie, 132, 134; *Smithereens'*

Lower East Side milieu, 61; treatment of marriage, 61

*Smooth Talk*, 4, 9, 10, 68–70, 72, 73–74, 129; feminist ending, 74

solidarity, 158

solidarity of women at Auschwitz, 192

*Something Different*, 218, 222, 230

*Sotto, Sotto*, 30

*Soul of the Artist, The*, 21

space and women, 79

*Sparrows Can't Sing*, 136

*Straight Through the Heart*, 128–29, 132–33

Streisand, Barbra, 82–83

*Sugarcane Alley*, 241

*Summer Paradise*, 4, 6, 155–57

*Swept Away*, 9, 29, 31

*Swing Shift*, 86, 87–88

*36 Chowringhee Lane*, 249–51; and old age, 250–51

*3 Men and a Cradle*, 75, 153

Toye, Wendy, 153

Trintignant, Nadine, 154

*Two of Them, The*, 194, 196, 197, 199, 200, 202–4, 206, 207

Universal Pictures, 18, 20

*Unmarried Woman, An*, 55, 85

*Vagabond*, 61, 136, 138–39, 143–44

Varda, Agnes, 8, 95, 136; domesticity in, 136, 140, 141–42; family, 139–140, 142; feminism, 145; freedom, 144; loneliness, 143; pregnancy, 141–42; sexual yearning, 143; sexy, conventional blonde heroines, 136

*Very Late Afternoon of a Faun, The*, 220, 228–30; mortality in, 228

Vogel, Amos, 218

von Trotta, Margarethe, 4, 78, 93–128, 149; her childhood, 96; activist heroine, 95; closure and von Trotta's endings, 94; erotic bonds between women, 124; genre elements in, 95, 96, 101, 111; the home, 109, 122; imprisonment and freedom themes, 103, 104, 116, 117, 120, 126, 127; intellectual political heroine, 97; look

between two women, 97–98; male
characters, 100, 111, 112, 123, 124;
male need to dominate, 123; rebellious young-girl intellectual heroine,
115, 116; use of female voiceover,
101, 103; women bonds, 100, 112,
122; work, 108, 109, 111

Wanda, 29
Weber, Lois, 19–20
Weill, Claudia, 8; and Bergstein,
Eleanor, 58–59

Wertmuller, Lina, 9, 29, 42; contempt,
40; male identifications, 29, 30; opportunism, 29
Wildcats, 86, 89
Wings, 24, 210, 211–13, 217, 251
Without Anaesthesia, 231
Woman Alone, A, 233–34, 235
woman and early cinema, 33 n.2
woman as subject, 6, 21
woman-oriented films, 8, 9

# About the Author

BARBARA KOENIG QUART is Associate Professor of English at the College of Staten Island, City University of New York. She has written frequently on film and literature, often relating to women, for *Ms. The Nation, Film Quarterly, Cineaste, Massachusetts Review*, and other publications.